P9-CMA-925

The Talmud
of the
Land of Israel

Chicago Studies in the History of Judaism
Edited by William Scott Green and Calvin Goldscheider

The University of Chicago Press
Chicago and London

The Talmud
of the
Land of Israel

*A Preliminary
Translation and
Explanation*

Volume 1   Berakhot

Translated by   Tzvee Zahavy

ST. PHILIP'S COLLEGE LIBRARY

The Talmud of the Land of Israel
A Preliminary Translation and Explanation
Jacob Neusner, General Editor

The University of Chicago Press gratefully acknowledges the support of the Philip and Florence G. Dworsky Center for Jewish Studies, University of Minnesota, in publication of this volume.

Tzvee Zahavy is professor of Classical and Near Eastern Studies and director of the Center for Jewish Studies at the University of Minnesota, Minneapolis, where he received the Distinguished Teaching Award of the College of Liberal Arts in 1985. He is also author of *The Traditions of Eleazar Ben Azariah* and *The Mishnaic Law of Blessings and Prayer*.

The University of Chicago Press, Chicago 60637
The University of Chicago Press, Ltd., London
© 1989 by The University of Chicago
All rights reserved. Published 1989
Printed in the United States of America

98 97 96 95 94 93 92 91 90 89   5 4 3 2 1

Library of Congress Cataloging in Publication Data

Talmud Yerushalmi. Berakhot. English.
    Berakhot / translated by Tzvee Zahavy.
        p.   cm. — (Chicago studies in the history of Judaism) (The Talmud of the land of Israel ; vol. 1)
    Bibliography: p.
    Includes index.
        1. Talmud Yerushalmi. Berakhot—Commentaries.   I. Zahavy, Tzvee.   II. Title.   III. Series.   IV. Series: Talmud Yerushalmi. English. 1982 ; vol. 1.
    BM498.5.E5   1982 vol. 1
    [BM506.B6]
    296.1'2407 s—dc19   89-5112
    [296.1'24]   CIP
    ISBN 0-226-57658-2 (alk. paper)

⊗ The paper used in this publication meets the minimum requirements of the American National Standard for Information Sciences—Permanence of Paper for Printed Library Materials, ANSI Z39.48-1984.

To my master and teacher

Rabbi Dr. Joseph B. Soloveitchik

mentor, sage counselor,
and beacon of rationality
for the Jewish people
in the age of modernity

Contents

Preface

This book makes available the first English translation in the
past one hundred years of Berakhot, the opening tractate of the
Talmud of the Land of Israel (Yerushalmi, Palestinian Talmud),
composed in the Land of Israel at the beginning of the fifth cen-
tury C.E.

I call this translation preliminary because the state of scholarship on Yerushalmi texts is still at an early stage. The lack of
lexicographic, philological, and text-critical tools for these texts
necessitates that I qualify and label provisional any effort at systematic work of history, history of religion, or translation based
on the texts of Yerushalmi. Fortunately, this translation is somewhat less preliminary than that of other tractates in this series,
because modern scholars, such as A. M. Luncz (*Talmud Hierosolymitanum* [Jerusalem, 1907]) and L. Ginzberg (*A Commentary
on the Palestinian Talmud* [1941; reprint New York, 1971]), have
produced some published critical textual and analytical scholarship on Berakhot.

I based my translation on the texts of the standard printed
editions and not on either a manuscript or critical edition. Nevertheless, I used and found helpful the critical apparatus of A. M.
Luncz in *Talmud Hierosolymitanum* (Jerusalem, 1907). I also
compared the standard printed text directly with the *editio princeps* of Daniel Bomberg (Venice, 1523), and with the Leiden
manuscript, *The Palestinian Talmud Leiden MS. Cod. Scal. 3: A
Facsimile of the Original Manuscript* (reprint Jerusalem: Kedem
Publishers, 1970). I checked the text further against *Palestinian
Talmud Codex Vatican 133* (reprint Jerusalem: Makor, 1971),

and *Yerushalmi Fragments from the Geniza. I.*, edited by L. Ginzberg (New York, 1909; reprint Jerusalem, 1969).

Other works also served as assets in my task. Schwab's now century-old translation of the tractate first into French and then into English, *Le Talmud de Jerusalem* (reprint Paris, 1960); *The Talmud of Jerusalem*, first edition 1886 (reprint New York, 1969), formed an important basis for my efforts despite the errors and imperfections of that early rendition. I also made use of Charles Horowitz's German translation, *Der Jerusalemer Talmud in deutscher Ubersetzung, Band I Berakhoth* (Tubingen, 1975).

Among the numerous manuscript variants and traditions discovered in my comparisons of the versions, I have found very few places in the tractate where a divergent reading changes the meaning of a passage. I included these few instances in my translated text, indicating the source of the variant (R = Vatican [Rome], L = Leiden, V = Venice).

In piecing together my interpretation, I consulted many secondary works and commentaries, including the following: *Sde Yehoshua*, commentary and edition of Y. Benvenisti (Constantinople, 1662; reprint Jerusalem, 1972); the commentary of Z. Frankel (reprint 1971); of S. Ginzberg (1941); of S. Goren, *HaYerushalmi HaMeforash* (Jerusalem, 1961); of Y. Tamar, *Ale Tamar* (Givataim, 1979), as well as the standard commentaries found in the printed editions of the tractate, such as *Pene Moshe* and *Sefer Haredim*.

These commentaries were most valuable for explaining the meaning and background of the legal materials in the text, for explicating the larger context of specific laws and discussions, and for providing rich cross-references to other parallel or related units in Yerushalmi or elsewhere in rabbinic literature. Throughout the translation I have used Moses Margolies's commentary *Pene Moshe* more frequently than any other secondary source to help explain the meaning of technical, elliptical, or complex discussions. An unattributed explanation in my translation usually rests on the insights of *Pene Moshe*. Where I rely on the viewpoint of another commentator, who disagrees with or goes beyond *Pene Moshe* in his interpretation, I so specify in the translation.

I have added my own brief commentary to my translation of Yerushalmi Berakhot. At the end of each section of Talmud, before turning to the next Mishnah selection, I review and summarize the redactional flow of the material just covered and specify the relationship of the preceding Talmudic units of discourse to the concerns of the relevant Mishnah passage. I hope this effort helps bring into focus more sharply the redactional agendum of the editors of the tractate.

Though I strove to convey the original form and meaning of the text through the translation, and though I based the translation on the major classical commentaries, the framers of the Talmud never conceived nor intended that their books be perused casually in translation. I emphasize strongly that, to fully appreciate the linguistic forms and to comprehend the many nuances of meaning of this complex and elusive text, one must study it in its original along with the numerous creative and comprehensive standard commentaries.

A complete bibliography of manuscripts, editions, commentaries, and scholarly works may be found in Baruch Bokser's "Annotated Bibliographical Guide to the Study of the Palestinian Talmud," in *Principat (ANRW II. 19.2)*, edited by Wolfgang Hesse (Berlin and New York, 1979).

Recent scholarship establishes the basic underpinnings of the present translation. My own most relevant work includes:

The Mishnaic Law of Blessings and Prayers: Tractate Berakhot. Brown Judaic Studies 88. Atlanta, 1987.

Studies in Early Jewish Prayer. Studies in Judaism. Lanham, MD: University Press of America, forthcoming. Especially see the chapters, "The Editorial Structure of the Talmud of the Land of Israel Tractate Berakhot," and "The Synagogue in Mishnah, Tosefta and Yerushalmi."

"A New Approach to Early Jewish Prayer." In *History of Judaism: The Next Ten Years*. Edited by B. Bokser. Brown Judaic Studies 21. Chico, CA: Scholars Press, 1980.

"Sources for the Seasonal Ritual in the Third through Fifth Centuries." In *Proceedings of the Ninth World Congress of Jewish Studies*. Jerusalem, 1986.

"Kavvanah for Prayer in the Mishnah and the Talmud." Chapter 3 of *New Perspectives on Ancient Judaism*. Edited by J. Neusner. Lanham, MD: University Press of America, 1987.

"Tosefta Tractate Berakhot." In *The Tosefta Translated from the Hebrew. First Division. Zera'im*. Edited by J. Neusner. New York, 1986.

The three volumes most pertinent to this project by Jacob Neusner are:

The Talmud of the Land of Israel. Volume 35. *Introduction: Tax-onomy.* Chicago: University of Chicago Press, 1983.

Judaism in Society: The Evidence of the Yerushalmi. Toward the Natural History of a Religion. Chicago: University of Chicago Press, 1983.

The Talmud of Babylonia. An American Translation. I: Tractate Berakhot. Brown Judaic Studies 78. Chico, CA: Scholars Press, 1984.

The theory of the present translation follows that of the series as a whole. I strive to adhere closely to the text so that the reader has a sense of the structure and balance of the original. Yet at the same time I try to convey the flow of the legal arguments and debates, the dramatic unfolding of events in stories, and the sensitivities to words and language in the exegetical texts. My aim is to facilitate a smooth conversation between readers and the text so that, without consulting the original Hebrew and Aramaic version, they can appreciate the substantive meaning and recognize some major aspects of the style of the Talmudic text.

With this goal in mind, this English translation is molded in many ways by the complex literary style of the document itself. Some characteristics of the Talmud in particular required that I employ distinctive techniques in my translation to allow me to be literal in my rendering of the text, to avoid having to paraphrase throughout, and yet to maintain a high level of intelligibility for the English reader.

Several distinctive aspects of my translation contribute to making it more of a colloquy. The text is stylized, as I have indicated above, and sometimes terse to an extreme in its style of expression. Accordingly, I interpolate a fair amount of explanatory language into my translation to make it more comprehensible. This additional explication helps me unpack the laconic linguistic style of the document.

By adding explanation within the translation I also expand upon the progression of ideas, clarify the arguments of the Talmud, define unfamiliar materials, and generally elucidate the meaning of the text. When adding my own language within the translation, to make it clear where the words of the Talmud end and where my explanations begin, I set off my additional interpolations with brackets, rather than allowing them to stand as indistinguishable parts of a paraphrased rendition of the text.

I break the text into smaller units and mark these according to the style of translation as a whole in this series. The original text has little if any punctuation or division to demarcate where one sentence or thought ends and another beings. In addition, the Talmud abounds in discussions about legal points and debates with internal cross-references and citations. To help the reader navigate through the text and its pathways, to know where one thought pauses or stops and another begins, I demarcate by capital letters each discrete unit of discourse. With Roman numerals I mark each larger editorial section.

Within the text, to easily demarcate frequent citations from Scripture, Mishnah, and Tosefta, and thus make these components of the composite Talmudic text more readily visible, I set these passages off from the remainder of the text as follows: I put quotations from Scripture in quotation marks; passages from the Mishnah in oblique type (an italic-like type); and citations from Tosefta in boldface. All other discussion provided by the Talmud for the Mishnah-pericope at issue is in regular type.

These external and internal attributes of my translation enhance its readability and increase accessibility to the text for the reader of English who seeks to join into conversation with this rich corpus of Talmudic thought.

I thank the Graduate School of the University of Minnesota for research grants-in-aid and the American Council of Learned Societies for a fellowship in support of the project.

My wife, Bernice, encouraged me throughout this project. She carefully read and offered criticism to early drafts of this translation. My children, Yitzhak and Barak, inspired my work as I studied parts of this and other tractates with them every day. I thank also my students at the University of Minnesota, several who served as research assistants, who contributed in many small but significant ways to the translation.

My colleague Lawrence Schiffman, professor of Hebrew and Judaic Studies at New York University, served as a critical reader of this volume. His comments saved me from inaccuracies and greatly enhanced the precision of this translation. I thank him for his kindness in taking the time and effort to so thoroughly study this tractate and review this book. I bear responsibility for any shortcomings which may remain in this translation.

I recognize my great debt to my Talmud teachers at Yeshiva University's Rabbi Isaac Elchanan Theological Seminary. I had the honor of studying the Babylonian Talmud as an undergraduate with Rabbi Gershom Yankelewitz and Rabbi Aharon Lichtenstein and the privilege of receiving postgraduate instruction for four years in both the Talmud and Shulkhan Arukh from HaRav Joseph B. Soloveitchik.

Above all I acknowledge the influence on this translation of the work of my teacher, Jacob Neusner, professor of Judaic Studies at Brown University. He has shown us all how to render the wisdom of our sages into our own language through his own lucid and systematic work in his translations of tractates of the Mishnah, the Tosefta, the Talmud of the Land of Israel, the Babylonian Talmud, the Midrash, and in his ongoing work on the remaining documents of rabbinic literature. I am grateful for what he has given me to work with. I know that without the benefit of Neusner's paradigmatic work, my translation of Yerushalmi Berakhot could not have succeeded in whatever small measure it has.

Tzvee Zahavy
Minneapolis, Minnesota

Introduction to Berakhot

Tractate Berakhot of the Talmud of the Land of Israel (Yerushalmi) is organized around tractate Berakhot in Mishnah. More than three-quarters of the Talmud's materials in the tractate engage in citation and explanation of Mishnah, or legal speculation and reflection primary to Mishnah, or harmonization of two or more passages of Mishnah, or of a Mishnah passage with a rule from Tosefta. Accordingly, to introduce the tractate before us we must first focus our attention on the agendum of Mishnah Berakhot.

M. Berakhot appears at first to be a somewhat disjointed tractate comprising disparate units on a variety of loosely related topics. M.'s laws deal with the recitation of the *Shema'*, the recitation of the Prayer of Eighteen Blessings, the requirement to recite short blessings before one eats foods, the collective recitation of blessings after the meal, other rules for the dinner, and blessings to be said on other occasions.

One common concern lends coherence to the laws and rules of the tractate. That basic unifying principle is the idea that a person must recite one or more formulaic blessings in each instance of religious ritual mentioned in the tractate. Hence the title: "Berakhot," "Blessings."

Accordingly, M. rules that before and after the recitation of the biblical verses that comprise the *Shema'*, one recites blessings. For daily prayers, one recites liturgies of eighteen blessings. At meals, one recites blessings before and after eating any foods. In times of danger, or when one obtains new clothes, or when one hears good news, or when one comes into a town from a trip abroad, or in a number of other instances, one recites blessings.

Let us summarize the laws of the compilation in order. The tractate Berakhot in Mishnah begins with the rules for the recitation of the *Shema'* and unfolds in seven major divisions as follows:

A. *Rules for the recitation of the* Shema' *and its blessings* (1:1–5)

1:1   Dispute regarding the time for the recitation of the *Shema'* at night.
1:2   Dispute regarding the recitation of the *Shema'* in the morning.
1:3   Houses' dispute over the exegesis of Deut. 6:7. Scriptural basis for reciting evening and morning.
1:4   The rabbinic blessings which frame the *Shema'*. General rules regarding forms of blessings.
1:5   Scriptural basis for reciting the last verse of the *Shema'* at night.

B. *Concentration during the recitation. Social status and the recitation of the* Shema' (2:1–3:6)

2:1–2   Intention needed for reciting. Distractions from reciting. The basis for the order of the paragraphs.
2:3   One who erred in reciting.
2:4   Special rule for craftsmen. May recite atop a tree. It is no distraction for them.
2:5–7   Bridegroom exempt from the *Shema'*. He is distracted. Gamaliel's practice and two more units about Gamaliel.
2:8   Bridegroom has the option to recite.
3:1–2   Those involved in a funeral are exempt from the *Shema'*.
3:3   Women, slaves, and minors are exempt from the *Shema'*. Their other obligations.
3:4   One for whom the rabbis declared uncleanness (because of a bodily discharge) may not recite the rabbinic blessings before and after the *Shema'* and before the meal.
3:5   Related rules: prayer-obligation of one who remembered he was unclean. Reciting the *Shema'* while unclothed. Prayer near human wastes.
3:6   Others who are unclean from a discharge must dip in a pool before they can recite the *Shema'*.

C. *Rules for the recitation of the Prayer of Eighteen Blessings* (4:1–5:5)

To sum up, A and B cover the nature of the obligation to recite the *Shema‘* morning and evening (1:1–5); intention which is needed for reciting the *Shema‘* and the kinds of distractions which disrupt the recitation of the *Shema‘* (2:1–3:2). This material ends with rules for individuals who are not obliged to recite the *Shema‘* or its blessings (3:3–6). C turns to the second daily liturgy, the Prayer, and deals with: the times (4:1) and forms of the Prayer (4:3–4), one's orientation during Prayer (4:5–6), the additional Prayer (4:7). Interpolations into this Mishnaic unit deal with the short special Prayer for the study hall and for places of danger (4:2, 4:4). It turns then to the frame of mind one needs for the Prayer (5:1) and to other regulations. D covers food blessings (6:1–7), E addresses the blessings after the meal (6:8, 7:1–5) and F deals with dinner regulations (8:1–8). G concludes with rules for special blessings. The Mishnah tractate's loose substantive conceptual internal coherence is given its unity through the perspective of the editor who brought together a variety of subjects which share in common one practice: the recitation of the rabbinic blessing formula in each of these instances of daily activity. I spell this out at length in my study, *The Mishnaic Law of Blessings and Prayers: Tractate Berakhot* (Atlanta, 1987).

I Yerushalmi Berakhot
Chapter One

1:1

[A] *From what time do [people] recite the Shema' in the evening?*

[B] *From [after sunset, that is,] the hour that the priests enter [the Temple court] to eat their heave-offering,*

[C] *"[They may recite the Shema' at any time thereafter up to three hours into the night, that is,] until the end of the first watch [in the Temple],"*

[D] *the words of R. Eliezer.*

[E] *And sages say, "[They may recite the Shema'] until midnight."*

[F] *Rabban Gamaliel says, "Until the break of day."*

[G] *Once [Gamaliel's] sons came from the banquet hall.*

[H] *And they said to him, "We have not [yet] recited the Shema'."*

[I] *He said to them, "If the day has not yet broken, you are obligated to recite [the Shema']."*

[J] *And it is not only [in] this [case that the sages] said [that one may perform a religious obligation until daybreak]. But regarding all cases in which the sages said [that one must carry out his obligation] "until midnight," [if a person should perform] the religious obligation by daybreak [it is acceptable].*

[K] *[For example, one may acceptably perform the obligation to] offer the fats and entrails [of sacrifices in the Temple and to eat the paschal sacrifices] until the break of day.*

[L] *[Another example:] All [sacrifices] which must be eaten within*

one day [i.e., before midnight of the day they are offered], their
obligation [may legitimately be carried out and they may be
eaten] until the break of day.

[M] *If so why did [sages] say [that these actions should be performed*
only] until midnight?

[N] *In order to keep man far from sin.*

[I.A] It was taught [in the Mishnah], *[People may recite the* Shema‘
after sunset, that is,] from the hour that the priests enter [the
Temple court] to eat their heave-offering.

[B] R. Hiyya taught, "**[They may recite the** *Shema‘***] from the**
hour that people are accustomed to enter [their houses] to eat
their bread on Sabbath eve," [the words of R. Meir. (**Regard-**
ing the recitation of the *Shema‘***, when does night begin?) An**
indication for (when night begins is) the emergence of the
stars] [Tosefta Ber. 1:1].

[C] And it was taught regarding these rules [in A and B]: These
opinions [in M. and T.] are nearly identical. [That is, they refer
to the same time of day.]

[D] But observe [by way of objection that M.'s rule appears to conflict with T.'s law]: *From the hour that the priests enter [the*
Temple court] to eat their heave-offering [is right after the end
of] the day [i.e., before the time that people enter their houses
to eat the meal on the Sabbath].

[E] But [T. rules that one may recite the *Shema‘* from] **the hour that**
people enter [their houses] to eat their bread on Sabbath eves
[which] is after [the emergence of the] stars, that is already an
hour or two into the night!

[F] And yet you say, "These opinions are nearly identical!"

[G] Said R. Yose, "[This apparent contradiction between M. and T.]
may be resolved [by explaining that Tosefta's ruling refers to a
special case wherein people return home early, i.e., those residents of] small villages who leave [their weekday work and return
home] while it is still day, who prepare [and eat their Sabbath
meals] while it is still early. [P.M. Under these circumstances the
rulings of M. and T. do not disagree. They refer to nearly identical times of day. According to both rules, one may recite the
Shema‘ right after sunset.]"

[II.A] It was taught: One who recites [the *Shema'] before the time [that the priests enter the Temple court at sunset to eat their heave-offering, cf. M. 1:1B] does not [thereby] fulfill his obligation [to recite the Shema']."*

[B] If so why do they recite [the *Shema'*] in the synagogue [where they say the service while it is still day]?

[C] Said R. Yose, "They do not recite it in the synagogue in order to fulfill the obligation [to recite the *Shema'*]. Rather [they recite the *Shema'* in the synagogue] so that they will rise to [recite] the Prayer [of Eighteen Blessings] after speaking the words of Torah [that comprise the passages of the *Shema'*]."

[III.A] R. Zeira in the name of R. Jeremiah, "If one had a doubt whether or not he had recited the grace after his meal, he must recite the grace,

[B] "for it is written, 'And you shall eat and be full, and you shall bless [the Lord your God for the good land he has given you]'" [Deut. 8:10]. [Since the obligation to recite the grace after meals is derived from a verse in Scripture, if one had any doubt whether he had recited it, he must say the grace forthwith. The principle behind this reasoning is: one must be especially scrupulous in any case of doubt concerning the performance of an obligation based directly on a verse in Scripture.]

[C] "But if one was in doubt whether he had recited the Prayer [of Eighteen Blessings], he need not recite it [for it is a rabbinic obligation, not derived directly from a verse in Scripture. And the corresponding principle is that one need not be as scrupulous regarding such an obligation]."

[D] But this rule [that one need not recite the Prayer in a case of doubt] does not accord with the view of R. Yohanan. For said R. Yohanan, "But oh, that a person might [have the opportunity to] pray all day long." [That is to say, nothing is lost by repeating the Prayer.]

[E] Why [does Yohanan say that one may pray all day long]? Because prayer never loses its value [cf. Y. to M. 4:4, unit **III**].

[F] [In light of this distinction, Y. poses a question.] If one was in doubt whether he had recited [the *Shema'*, what is the ruling? Must he recite it or not]?

[G] Let us deduce the answer from the rule [stated above at **II.**A]: "One who recites the *Shema'* before the time [that the priests enter the Temple court at sunset to eat their heave-offering] has not fulfilled his obligation [to recite the *Shema'*]."

[H] Is it not [reasonable to draw the following conclusion:] [The phrase] "before the time [that the priests enter]" [may be understood to refer to and include] a case in which one was in doubt [whether he had fulfilled his obligation to recite the *Shema'*. How so? For instance, the phrase may refer to a case of one who recites the *Shema'* at the moment of sunset and is not sure whether at that time it is day or night].

[I] Yet [in such a case] the rule is, "He must recite [the *Shema'* again because by reciting it too early he may not have fulfilled his obligation to recite it at night]." It then follows that [we may state a general rule on the basis of this reasoning]: "If one was in doubt whether he had recited [the *Shema'*], he must recite it."

[**IV.**A] [With respect to the obligation to recite the *Shema'*, when does night begin?] *We may find an indication concerning this [in the verse]: "Until the stars come out . . ." [Neh. 4:21]. Even though there is no proof [in Scripture that night begins when the stars come out], there is an allusion [in the verse]. "So we labored at the work and half of them held the spears from the break of dawn until the stars came out [Neh. 4:21]." [T. 1:1E–F].*

[B] And it is written, "[Let every man and his servant pass the night within Jerusalem,] that they may be a guard for us by night and may labor by day" [Neh. 4:22]. [They labored until night, i.e., when the stars came out. These verses thus imply that it is night when the stars come out.]

[C] How many stars must come out so that it is deemed night?

[D] R. Pinhas in the name of R. Abba bar Pappa, "[If one sees] one star, it is certainly day. [If one sees] two [stars], there is doubt [whether it is] night. [If one sees] three [stars], it is certainly night."

[E] "[If one sees] two [stars], there is doubt." [Why is there any doubt?] For it is written, "Until the stars came out!" [Neh. 4:21]. The minimum number of stars [plural] is two. [After two stars come out, it should be deemed night.]

[F] [There is doubt because] we do not count the first star of the evening [for when it appears, it is deemed still to be day. Hence

when two stars appear, it still may be day. We therefore must
wait for three stars to appear before we deem it to be night].

[G]   [It was taught, in support of Pinhas's teaching at D:] On the
Sabbath eve, if one saw a single star and then unintentionally
performed labor which is forbidden on the Sabbath, he is free
[from any liability because it is still day]. [If one saw] two [stars
and unintentionally performed an act forbidden on the Sabbath,]
he must bring a suspensive guilt offering [i.e., a sacrifice offered
in a case of doubtful transgression, because we do not know
whether he transgressed the Sabbath]. [If one saw] three [stars
and performed an action which is forbidden on the Sabbath], he
must bring a sin offering [because we are sure that night has
fallen and that he has transgressed a Sabbath prohibition].

[H]   [Analogously,] at the end of the Sabbath, if one saw a single star
and then [unintentionally] performed labor which is forbidden
on the Sabbath, he must bring a sin offering [for it is surely still
the Sabbath day]. [If one saw] two [stars and he unintentionally
performed a forbidden act], he must bring a suspensive guilt
offering [for we do not know if it was day or night and, accordingly, whether he transgressed a Sabbath prohibition]. [If one
saw] three [stars and unintentionally performed some act which
would be forbidden on the Sabbath], he is free [from any liability for it surely is night and the Sabbath has ended. This
discussion supports Pinhas's premise that we determine the
onset of nightfall by counting the number of stars which one can
see].

[I]   R. Yose b. R. Bun speculated, "If we say '[If one saw] two [stars],
there is a doubt,' [then consider the following case in which a
person certainly would be liable for transgressing a Sabbath prohibition even if he performed a forbidden act during the time
that only two stars were visible—that period of doubt—at either
the beginning of the Sabbath on Friday night or at the end of the
Sabbath on Saturday night:] One saw two stars on the Sabbath
eve [just at the time of nightfall] and witnesses warned him [that
labor is forbidden on the Sabbath] and [nonetheless at that time]
he performed forbidden labor. Then he saw two stars at the termination of the Sabbath, and they warned him, and [nonetheless
again] he performed forbidden labor.

[J]   "Any way you look at it [he should be guilty of transgressing a
Sabbath prohibition, because he was duly warned and then he

deliberately performed a forbidden labor on the Sabbath according to the following reasoning:]

[K]   "For if [we determine that] the first [two stars he saw at the beginning of the Sabbath were deemed to be seen] in the day, then [we conclude that] the last [two stars which he saw at the end of the Sabbath also were deemed to be seen] in the day. And [therefore] he should be liable [for transgressing a Sabbath prohibition] by virtue of [performing a forbidden act during the Sabbath day while] the last [stars which he saw just prior to the end of the Sabbath were visible].

[L]   "And if [we determine that] the last stars [which he saw at the end of the Sabbath were deemed to have been seen] at night, then [we conclude that] the first [stars, which he saw at the beginning of the Sabbath were deemed to have been seen] at night, and he should be liable [for transgressing a Sabbath prohibition] by virtue of [performing a forbidden act while] the first [stars were visible, after the Sabbath had already commenced]." [Hence, as described, one would be guilty of transgressing a Sabbath prohibition by virtue of a forbidden act which he performed at the time that two stars were visible. It can then be said that depending on the circumstances in the eyes of the law this time period is either day or night, not an interim of doubtful status.]

[M]   [Alternatively another case could be constructed in which a person certainly would be guilty of transgressing a prohibition of the Sabbath eve if when he performed a forbidden act only two stars were visible at the beginning of the Sabbath on Friday or at the end of the Sabbath on Saturday night:] [The law is that the act of harvesting produce equivalent to the measure of a fig's bulk on the Sabbath constitutes a forbidden act.] "If one saw two stars on Sabbath eve and harvested [the equivalent of a measure of] half-a-fig, [and] on Sabbath morning he harvested [the equivalent of a measure of] half-a-fig, [and] if one saw two stars at the end of the Sabbath and harvested [the equivalent of a measure of] half-a-fig,

[N]   "in any event [he should be liable for transgressing a Sabbath prohibition according to the following reasoning:] if [we deem that the two] first stars [on Friday were seen by] day, then also the last [i.e., those two stars he sees at nightfall on Saturday] were [deemed to be] seen by the day, and [the measure harvested in] the morning should combine with that harvested near the end of the Sabbath, and he should be liable [for completing the performance of a forbidden act on the Sabbath at the time he sees the] last stars [on Saturday night].

[O] "And if [when he sees] the last stars [on Saturday] it is [deemed to be] night, then also [when he sees] the first stars [on Friday] it is [deemed to be] night, and the [measure harvested in] the morning should combine with that [harvested] after the onset of the Sabbath on Friday evening and he should be liable [for the completed act of violating a Sabbath prohibition which he began at the time he saw the] first stars [on Friday night]."

[V.A] The [stars] about which we speak are those that do not customarily shine by day. As to those that do customarily shine by day, we take no account [of them].

[B] Said R. Yose b. R. Bun, "[When one sees three stars, it is night,] provided that three others are seen besides the first star [i.e., four stars in all. We are sure that when he sees the first star it is still day. Thus we do not take it into account]."

[C] R. Jacob of the south in the name of R. Judah b. Pazzi, "[If one sees] a single star it is certainly still day. [If one sees] two [stars] it is night."

[D] And does he not allow for a case in which there is doubt? [Does his definition not admit the possibility of defining a time period as twilight?]

[E] He allows for doubt in discerning one star from another [i.e., in deciding which stars one may count to determine whether it is night].

[VI.A] It was taught [as an alternative definition of twilight:] As long as the eastern horizon is red, it is [still deemed to be] day. Once [the horizon] darkens, then [we deem it to be] twilight. Once [the horizon] blackens, so that the skies above and [near the earth] below are equally [dark], then [we deem it to be] night.

[B] [Another alternative:] Rabbi says, "When the moon is full, [the period of time between when] the orb of the sun begins to set and the orb of the moon begins to rise is twilight."

[C] [Hanina disputes the preceding:] Said R. Hanina, "[The period of time between when] the orb of the sun sets fully, and the orb of the moon begins to rise [is twilight]."

[D] [The following implies that there is a period of time, twilight, between when the sun sets and when the moon rises, in reference to and support of B and C:] Samuel taught thus, "The moon does not shine at the time that the sun sets [i.e., it rises later]. And [the moon] does not set at the time that the sun shines [in the morning. It sets earlier]."

[E]   [The twilight period may be explained in another way based on the law of *Tebul Yom*, i.e., the requirement that an unclean priest who immerses to purify himself must wait for sunset before he can eat heave-offering.] R. Samuel bar R. Hiyya bar Judah in the name of R. Hanina, "[Consider a case where] the orb of the sun begins to set. A man [who is an unclean priest] standing on top of Mount Carmel [sets out to] run down to immerse in the Mediterranean [to purify himself at the end of the day] and [when he] comes up to eat of heave-offering [he may do so because it is night]. The presumption is that he dipped while it was still day [as required in Scripture, cf. Lev. 22:6, and when he returns to the top it is night, and he may legitimately eat heave-offering. Twilight is the intervening period of time during which he ascends the mountain]."

[F]   This [rule at E] applies to one who goes [up the mountain from the sea] the short way, but not concerning one who went [the long way] on the main road. [Such period of time in which one climbed the mountain the long way would not be an accurate representation of the length of the interval of twilight.]

[G]   [Further traditions regarding twilight:] What is [the duration of] "twilight"? Said R. Tanhuma, "[One may define it] as [the time it takes for] a drop of blood, which was placed on the cutting edge of a sword, to split in half. That [short time-span] is [the duration of] twilight."

[H]   What is [the duration of] "twilight"? "[The time from] when the sun sets until [the time it would take a person to] walk a half a mile," the words of R. Nehemiah.

[I]   R. Yose says, "Twilight is like the blink of an eye." And the sages could not determine [the length of this last interval].

[J]   R. Yose and R. Aha were sitting [and discussing the apparent dispute between Nehemiah and the elder Yose concerning the duration of twilight.] Said R. Yose to R. Aha, "Is it not reasonable to assume that the end of R. Nehemiah's interval, [of the period of twilight, i.e., from when the sun sets until one could] walk half a mile, would be [considered to be the exact moment of] R. Yose's interval of the blink of an eye?" [Hence, according to Yose's view, Nehemiah's interval of "twilight" is entirely part of the day.] He said to him, "I agree."

[K] R. Hezekiah did not agree. [He argued that Nehemiah's opinion does not preclude Yose's view.] Rather he said that [we may harmonize the two views as follows: Yose's rule tells us that] we [may] have a doubt concerning each moment of R. Nehemiah's [interval of the time it takes to walk] half a mile [whether that moment is twilight. Thus, according to Yose, Nehemiah's entire interval of "twilight" is a period of doubt. In Hezekiah's view the opinions of Yose and Nehemiah are not mutually exclusive].

[L] Said R. Mana "[By way of objection to Hezekiah's preceding conclusion,] I posed the [following] question before R. Hezekiah." It was taught there: *If [a person suffering from seminal discharges] saw one [emission] by day and one by twilight, or one at twilight and one on the morrow [what is the law? Do we say that he saw both emissions on the same day or do we conclude that he saw emissions on two successive days?] If he knows that part of his observed [emission] belongs to this day and part to the morrow—he is certainly unclean and certainly must bring a sacrifice. [The law is that one who sees emissions on successive days is deemed unclean.] But if he has a doubt that part of his observed [emission] belongs to this day and part to the morrow—[we deem him to be] certainly unclean. [The principle is that in a case of doubt with regard to uncleanness we decide in favor of the more stringent alternative.] But [in this case] there remains a doubt whether he must bring a sacrifice* [M. Zab. 1 : 6].

[M] [And Mana explained, based on this law in the Mishnah,] "R. Hiyya bar Joseph inquired before R. Yohanan, 'Who was it that taught that one observation [of an emission at twilight] may be divided into two? R. Yose.'" [Cf. T. Zabim 1 : 4. It is according to his view that twilight is as the blink of an eye. You count the one emission at twilight as if it was two emissions on two consecutive days. And if one observes emissions on consecutive days, he must bring a sacrifice.]

[N] [Accordingly, Mana] said to [Hezekiah,] "Your opinion [that Yose's ruling concerning twilight may refer to several moments over an extended time] is problematic. For you said that [according to Yose] there is a doubt concerning each moment of R. Nehemiah's [interval of twilight, i.e., the time it takes to walk] half a mile. [If each moment of that interval is twilight, then we cannot say that a seminal emission which occurs at twilight belongs partly to one day and partly to the next and thus may be counted as two emissions. Rather we must conclude that such an emission which occurs at twilight remains a case of doubt and cannot be divided between two separate days. There is doubt about the time of the entire emission. Did it occur during one day or the next? This leaves Hezekiah with a problem. How does he explain the statement above that according to Yose we may divide between two days one observation of an emission seen at twilight?]

[O]   [Hezekiah responded to Mana, "The objection you raised is not only] a problem [according to my interpretation of Yose's ruling. Any interpretation of Yose's ruling poses problems.] For when Elijah [the prophet] comes [to clarify all doubts of the law] and says this [moment] is twilight [at that time, Yose's opinion above, that one observation of an emission may be divided into two, will be rendered illogical. For Elijah will determine the exact time of the instant of twilight. Then it will not be logical to say that one can divide into two an emission that occurs at twilight, as Yose claims, because after Elijah determines the instant of twilight, then an emission that occurs at twilight will last only for that one brief instant, as long as the blink of an eye. We must conclude then that it is Yose's view that is problematical, not Hezekiah's interpretation of it. And if Yose's view can be explained as at all tenable, then Hezekiah's interpretation of Yose's view in conjunction with Nehemiah's will be as plausible as any other interpretation]."

[VII.A]   Who disputed [the views stated above, in unit IV, that if one observes two or three stars, we deem it to be night]? R. Hanina the associate of the rabbis [disputed this view].

[B]   [By way of objection to this definition of the beginning of night Hanina] asked, "[This ruling is not logical, because] if you say, 'In the evening if three stars were observed, even if the sun is yet [visible] in the middle of the firmament, it is night, would you [likewise] say that in the morning the same [is true and if the sun were visible and three stars were out still it is night']? [But of course not. Everyone agrees that the day begins with the break of dawn. Hence the notion that the appearance of stars determines the beginning of the night is not tenable.]"

[C]   Said R. Abba, "[The rise and set of the sun and not the appearance of stars defines the beginning and end of the night.] It is

written, 'The sun had risen on the earth when Lot came to Zoar'
[Gen. 19:23]; and it is written, 'When the sun is down he shall
be clean' [Lev. 22:7]. [These verses indicate that] we link our
definition of the sun's rise to its setting [and that these events
determine the beginning and end of the day]. Just as its setting
[and the beginning of the night] occurs when [the sun] is concealed from all creatures so its rising [and the start of the day]
occurs when [the sun] is revealed to all creatures." [The observation of stars does not determine when night or day begins.]

[D]   [Another teaching indicates that neither the appearance of stars
nor the rise and set of the sun determine the beginning of day or
night:] Said R. Ba, "It is written, 'As soon as the morning was
light' [Gen. 44:3]. The Torah called 'light' morning [and does
not refer to visible stars or to sunrise as determining factors]."

[E]   [The discussion moves on to define the factors that determine
the beginning of the day.] Taught R. Ishmael, "[Scripture uses
the phrase,] 'Morning by morning' [Exod. 16:21]. [The Torah
used this expression to teach that the period of time from the
first glow of the light of dawn before sunrise] is an extension of
[the day in] the morning." [The verse indicates that there is a
time called the morning, i.e., from the first glow of light, before
the time usually referred to as the morning, i.e., the rise of
the sun.]

[F]   Said R. Yose b. R. Bun [by way of objection to the preceding],
"If you assign [the time period when the sun is in] the firmament to the [time we call] night both in the evening [after
sunset] and morning [before sunrise], we must conclude that
[the duration of the] day and night are never equal. [Night is
always longer than day.] But [to the contrary] it was taught, 'On
the first of the season of Nissan and on the first of the season of
Tishre [i.e., the equinoxes] the [duration of the] day and night
are equal.'"

[G]   Said R. Huna, "Let us deduce [a basis for this ruling in E about
the extension of the day in the morning from analogy to] common custom. [In anticipation of a royal entourage, people may
commonly say,] 'The king's officers have gone forth.' Even
though they have not yet [actually] gone forth, they [tend to]
say, 'They have gone forth.' [Likewise even before the sun has
come out, while it is thought to be concealed in firmament,
people tend to say, 'The day has begun.' But in fact it begins at
sunrise.]"

[H]   "But [to continue this analogy, concerning] the hosts of heaven [like those of the king], they do not say, 'They have gone back,' until the time they [actually] have gone back. [Likewise people do not say that the day ends until the sun disappears into the darkness of the firmament.]"

[VIII.A]   One who stands and prays must keep his feet even.

[B]   Two Amoraim [disputed the interpretation of A]: R. Levi and R. Simon. One said, "[He must keep his feet even] like the angels." And one said, "Like the priests."

[C]   The one who said, "Like the priests," [referred to this saying:] "And you shall not go up by steps to my altar" [Exod. 20:26]. [We interpret this verse to mean] that they used to walk heel to toe, and toe to heel. [Similarly one's feet should be positioned in this manner during prayer.]

[D]   And the one who said, "Like the angels," [referred to the verse,] "Their legs were straight" [Ezek. 1:7] [i.e., next to one another, toe to toe and heel to heel. Likewise one's feet should be together in this fashion during prayer].

[E]   [Another teaching about this last verse, Ezek. 1:7:] R. Hanina bar Andrey in the name of R. Samuel bar Soter, "The angels do not have knee joints [in their legs. That is what the word 'straight' in this verse implies.]"

[F]   And what is the reason [they have no need for joints? Another verse explains,] "I approached one of them who stood there" [Dan. 7:16]—[the angels] stood [all the time].

[IX.A]   [The reference to the priests in the preceding unit leads to a discussion of the verses which members of the congregation must recite while the priests stand before the congregation to bless them.] Said R. Huna, "One who sees the priests in the synagogue [reciting the priestly blessing during the morning service must do as follows].

[B]   "Upon hearing the first blessing [which the priests recite, Num. 6:24,] he must say, 'Bless the Lord, O you his angels' [Ps. 103:20].

[C]   "For the second [Num. 6:25, he must say], 'Bless the Lord, all his hosts' [Ps. 103:21].

[D]   "For the third [Num. 6:26,] 'Bless the Lord, all his works' [Ps. 103:22].

[E]   "Upon hearing the [priestly blessing during the] additional service: for the first blessing one must say, 'A Song of Ascents.
Come Bless the Lord, all you servants of the Lord, who stand by
night in the house of the Lord' [Ps. 134 : 1].

[F]   "For the second [one must say], 'Lift up your hands to the holy
place' [Ps. 134 : 2].

[G]   "And for the third, 'May the Lord bless you from Zion' [Ps.
134 : 3].

[H]   "If there were four [services recited on one day, such as on public fast days or on the Day of Atonement], then for the third
[service in the afternoon] one repeats [the verses] of the first [the
Morning Service], and for the fourth [in the Ne'ilah he repeats
the verses] of the second [the Additional Service]."

[X.A]   [This unit expands upon the discussion of the terms used to refer to the period of time preceding sunrise.] Said R. Hinnena
[vars.: Hasna, Haninah], "From the [time in the morning sometimes called the] 'hind of the dawn' [a poetic expression
comparing the pattern of the first rays of light to the antlers of a
deer,] until the [sky in the] east is lit [entirely] one [has enough
time to] walk four miles. ['Mile' refers to 2000 paces, about 1470
meters, which is somewhat less than the modern English mile of
about 1609 meters.] From [the time] the east is lit until sunrise,
[one has enough time to walk another] four miles."

[B]   And whence [do we know] that from [the time] the east is lit
until sunrise [one has enough time to walk] four miles? As it is
written, "When morning dawned, the angels urged Lot saying,
'Arise, take your wife and your two daughters who are here, lest
you be consumed in the punishment of the city'" [Gen. 19 : 15].
And it is written, "The sun had risen on the earth when Lot
came to Zoar" [Gen. 19 : 23]. [Between the first light and the rise
of the sun Lot walked from Sodom to Zoar.]

[C]   But is the distance from Sodom to Zoar four miles? It is more!

[D]   Said R. Zeira, "The angel shortened the way for them." [Though
it was more, he made it as if it were four miles.]

[E]   And whence [do we know] that from the first rays of dawn ['hind
of dawn'] to [the time] the eastern sky is lit [completely, one can
walk] four miles? [Scripture says,] "wkmw [lit: and like]—When
morning dawned" [Gen. 19 : 15]. And kmw is a comparative
term. [It implies that the two intervals, from when the eastern

sky is lit until dawn, and from when the first rays of light appear until the eastern sky is lit, are of equal duration.]

[F]   Said R. Yose b. R. Bun, "[Concerning] this term 'the [time of the appearance of the] hind of dawn,' he who says it refers to [time of the appearance of] a [morning] star, [presumably Venus,] is in error. For at times [this star] appears earlier, and at times, later."

[G]   What is then [the definition of this term]? It refers to [the appearance of] two rays of light which originate in the eastern sky and illuminate [the heaven]. [The word qrn means both 'ray' and 'antler.']

[H]   And once R. Hiyya the great and R. Simeon ben Halafta were walking in the valley Arbel at daybreak. And they saw the first rays of dawn ["hind of dawn"] as the daylight broke forth [into the sky].

[I]   Said R. Hiyya the great to R. Simeon ben Halafta b. Rabbi, "[Like the break of day] so is the redemption of Israel. It begins little by little and, as it proceeds, it grows greater and greater."

[J]   What is his basis [for this comparison of daybreak and redemption]? [Scripture says,] "When I sit in darkness the Lord will be a light to me" [Mic. 7:8, i.e., he will redeem me].

[K]   [By way of illustration of this last teaching:] So it was at the outset [the redemption of Israel in the time of Esther, for example, proceeded slowly as it says,] "And Mordecai was sitting at the king's gate" [Esther 2:21].

[L]   And thereafter [it grew greater as the passage indicates], "So Haman took the robes and the horse [and he arrayed Mordecai]" [Esther 6:11].

[M]   And thereafter, "Then Mordecai went out from the presence of the king in royal robes" [Esther 8:15].

[N]   And thereafter, "The Jews had [the] light [of redemption] and gladness and joy and honor" [Esther 8:16]. [The redemption proceeds slowly at first and then quickly shines forth like light, a term used in the last verse.]

[XI.A]   And R. Hiyya's [var.: Haninah's, cf. X.A] [teaching that one can walk four miles in the time between the appearance of the first rays of light in the morning and the time that the eastern sky is lit entirely, and that one can walk another four miles from the time that the sky is lit and the rise of the sun] is in accord with [the view] of R. Judah. For it was taught in the name of R. Judah, "[To traverse the distance of that area of the heavens called] 'the darkness of the firmament' is a journey of fifty years." [That is, it would take a person fifty years to walk across this part of the heavens.]

[B]   [We calculate that] an average man can walk forty miles a day. [We now know that from the start of the sun's passage through the firmament in the morning] until the sun passes out of [the darkness into] the firmament is a journey of [the distance a person can walk in] fifty years [and, according to Haninah, the sun traverses that distance in the time] a man can walk four miles.

[C]   Consequently we may conclude that the [distance the sun travels through the] darkness of the firmament is one-tenth [of the total distance it travels] in a day [i.e., a day equals the time it takes an average man to walk forty miles and the sun passes through the darkness of the firmament in the time that it takes an average person to walk four miles, one-tenth of that time. We may calculate then that in one day the sun travels the equivalent of ten times the distance it crosses as it moves through the darkness of the firmament. Accordingly, in one day the sun travels the distance that a man can cover in a five hundred years' journey. The formula for this calculation is expressed by a ratio. The time to traverse darkness: is to the time to traverse entire firmament:: as the distance to traverse darkness: is to the distance to traverse entire firmament.]

[D]   And just as the [width of the] darkness of the firmament is [equivalent to the distance one may travel in] a fifty-year journey, so too the [width of other spheres of the heaven such as the] darkness of the earth and the darkness of *tehom* [interior of the earth] are [equivalent to the distance one may travel in] a fifty-year journey.

[E]   And what is the basis [for this conclusion about these other heavenly distances? Scripture says,] "It is he who sits above the circle of the earth [*hwg h'rṣ*]" [Isa. 40:22]. And it is written, "And he walks on the circle of heaven [*hwg šmym*]" [Job 22:14]. And it is written, "When he drew a circle on the face of the deep [*hwg 'l pny thwm*]" [Prov. 8:27]. [The use of the same words] *hwg, hwg* [teaches through] *gezerah šawah* [a process of

deduction based on the use of common words, that the widths of
the darkness of the firmament, of the earth, and of the *tehom* are
the same length, i.e., the distance one can cover in a journey of
fifty years].

[XII.A]   It was taught [another teaching about the cosmological bodies]:
The Tree of Life [was as wide as] the distance one can walk [in a
journey of] five hundred years.

[B]   Said R. Judah b. R. Ilai, "[This measure does] not [include] the
[width of the] branches which spread out from the foliage, but
[it includes only the width of] its trunk."

[C]   And the source of every stream of the waters of creation flows
from beneath [the Tree of Life]. And what is the basis [in Scripture for this statement]? "He is like a tree planted by streams
of water" [Ps. 1:3]. [The Tree of Life is the source of all the
world's streams.]

[D]   It was taught [another teaching concerning cosmological dis-
tances]: The Tree of Life is one-sixtieth [of the area] of the
garden. The garden is one-sixtieth of Eden. [This calculation is
based on the verse which says,] "A river flowed out of Eden to
water the garden" [Gen. 2:10]. [The calculation is based on the
following principles: the rule of thumb is that] the effluence of a
koor irrigates a *tirqab* [and a *koor* = 30 *seah* = 180 *qab*. So the
effluence of a *koor* waters three *qab*, or one-sixtieth its measure.
Eden's effluence waters the garden which was accordingly one-
sixtieth its area.]

[E]   The effluence of Ethiopia irrigates Egypt [i.e., the Nile which
flows out of Ethiopia can irrigate Egypt, one-sixtieth the area
of Ethiopia]. Then we conclude that to walk across Egypt is a
forty-days' journey and to walk across Ethiopia is more than a
seven years' journey [or sixty times the area, actually—2,400
days, or 78 days less than seven lunar years.]

[F]   And [in another related tradition] the rabbis say, "[The number
of years it takes to traverse the width of the firmament is equivalent to] the [sum of the] years of the lives of the patriarchs."
[This is alluded to in the verse,] "That your days and the days of
your children may be multiplied in the land which the Lord
swore to your fathers to give them [and they lived] as long as the
heavens are above the earth" [Deut. 11:21]. [This verse implies
that there is a connection between the distances of areas in the
heavens and the days of the lives of the forefathers. The sum

total of both is the same. The width of the firmament is the distance one may travel in a journey of five hundred years. And the lives of the patriarchs add up to five hundred years: Abraham, 173 years, Isaac 180, and Jacob, 147.]

[G]   And just as [the distance] between the earth and the firmament [is equivalent to the distance one may travel in] a journey of five hundred years, so [the distance] between one firmament and the next firmament [is equivalent to the distance one may travel in] a journey of five hundred years, and the [width of the] darkness of the firmament is [itself equal to the distance a person may travel in] a five hundred years' journey. [This disputes Judah's view at **XI.**A that the width is a fifty-year journey.]

[H]   And what could the source be for the statement, "The [width of the] darkness of the firmament is [equal to the distance a person can travel in a journey of] five hundred years?"

[I]   Said R. Bun, "[The source is the verse which says,] 'Let there be a firmament in the midst of the waters' [Gen. 1:6]. [This implies] let the [width of the] firmament in the middle [be equal in width to the distance on either side of it, that is the distance one can traverse in a five hundred years' journey]."

[J]   [There are other interpretations of this verse:] Rab said, "The heavens were wet on the first day [of creation] and on the second they dried up."

[K]   Rab said, "Let there be a firmament' [means] let the firmament be strong, let the firmament be dry, let the firmament be hardened, let the firmament be stretched out."

[L]   Said R. Judah b. Pazzi, "['Let there be a firmament' means God] would let the firmament be hammered out like metal [is processed]. As it was said, 'And gold leaf was hammered out [*wyrq'w*]'" [Exod. 39:3].

[M]   [Another alternative to Judah's view in **XI.**A above,] it was taught in the name of R. Joshua, "The darkness of the firmament is as [wide as] two fingers."

[N]   The words of R. Haninah are in dispute [with Joshua's view]. For said R. Aha in the name of R. Haninah, "[A verse in Scripture says,] 'Can you, like him, spread out [*trqy'*] the skies, hard as a cast mirror?' [Job 37:18]. *Spread out* teaches that they were formed like a tray [*ts*, Greek: tasis] [thinner than two fingers].

[O]   "One might infer that [the skies] are not firm [because they are so thin]. [Scripture] teaches that [the firmament] is 'hard.' One might infer that [the skies] may weaken [i.e., deteriorate]. [Scripture] teaches that [the firmament] is 'as a cast mirror.' At all times it appears [as if it were just] cast [i.e., as if brand new]."

[P]   R. Yohanan and R. Simeon b. Laqish [made the following observations in reference to this verse, "Hard as a cast mirror"]. R. Yohanan said, "It is expected that when one spreads his tent after a while it weakens [and sags]. But here [concerning the heavens it is written, 'Who stretches out the heavens like a curtain,] and spreads them like a tent to dwell in' [Isa. 40:22]. And it is written, they are '*hard*'" [Job 37:18]. [They do not sag and weaken!]

[Q]   R. Simeon b. Laqish said, "It is expected that when one pours vessels [into a mold] after a while they corrode. But here [we are told they are] 'As a cast mirror,' [which implies] at all times they appear as [new as they did] at the time of their casting!"

[R]   R. Azariah said concerning this [teaching] of R. Simeon b. Laqish, "[Scripture says,] 'Thus the heavens and the earth were finished, and all the host of them. And on the seventh day God finished his work. . . . So God blessed the seventh day' [Gen. 2:1–2]. What is written thereafter? 'These are the generations of the heavens [and the earth when they were created]' [Gen. 2:4]. And what has the former [subject] to do with the latter? [They are juxtaposed to teach that] days come and go, weeks come and go, months come and go, years come and go, but it is written, 'These are the generations of the heavens and the earth when they were created.' [The verse implies that the heavens remain in the same condition as] 'In the day the Lord God made the earth and the heavens'" [ibid.]!

[XIII.A]   **Rabbi says, "There are four watches [*ashmorot*] in the day and four watches in the night."**

[B]   **The *'onah* is one twenty-fourth of an hour. The *'et* is one twenty-fourth of an *'onah*. The *rega'* is one twenty-fourth of an *'et* [T. 1:1H–J].**

[C]   How much is a *rega'*? R. Berekhiah in the name of R. Helbo said, "As long as it takes to say [the word] *'rega'.'*"

[D]   And the rabbis say, "The *rega‘* is [a momentary interval like] the blink of an eye."

[E]   Taught Samuel, "The *rega‘* is one-56,848th of an hour [i.e., about one-fifteenth of a second]."

[F]   **R. Nathan says, "There are three watches in the night."**

[G]   **"As it says, 'At the beginning of the middle watch'"** [Judg. 7 : 19] [T.1 : 1].

[H]   R. Zeriqan and R. Ammi in the name of R. Simeon b. Laqish [suggested] the basis [in Scripture] of Rabbi's [teaching]. [One verse says concerning King David,] "At midnight I rise to praise thee, because of thy righteous ordinances" [Ps. 119 : 62]. And [another verse] says, "My eyes are awake before the watches of the night" [*ashmorot*] [Ps. 119 : 148]. [This implies that there are two watches left in the night after he awakens at midnight.]

[I]   R. Hezekiah said that R. Zerekin and R. Ba [explained T. as follows]: One suggested the [scriptural] basis for Rabbi's [teaching] and the other suggested [the scriptural] basis for R. Nathan's.

[J]   The one who stated the basis for Rabbi's view [explained that] "midnight" [Ps. 119 : 62] is his basis in Scripture. And the other who stated the basis for R. Nathan's opinion [explained,] "At the beginning of the middle watch" [Judg. 7 : 19] in his Scriptural basis.

[K]   How does R. Nathan interpret [the verses in Scripture which serve as] the basis for Rabbi's [teaching in H above]? "Midnight"—[means] sometimes [he awakens at] "midnight" and sometimes, "My eyes are awake before the watches of the night," [he awakens before two watches of the night, before midnight].

[L]   How so? When David dined at the royal dinner, he would rise at "midnight." And when he dined at his own [private] dinner, he would rise [at the time about which it says,] "My eyes awake before the watches of the night."

[M]   In either case, at dawn one would not find David asleep. As David said, "Awake, my glory! Awake, O harp and lyre! I will awake before dawn" [Ps. 57 : 8].

[N]   [One should interpret the verse as follows:] In glory I awaken to recite my words. My glory is as naught until I recite my words [of praise for you].

[O]   "I will awake the dawn" [means] I will awaken before the dawn.
The dawn will not awaken me.

[P]   But his [evil] impulse tried to seduce him [to sin]. And it would
say to him, "David. It is the custom of kings that the dawn
awakens them. And you say, 'I will awake the dawn.' It is the
custom of kings that they sleep until the third hour [of the day].
And you say, 'At midnight I rise,'" And [David] used to say [in
reply], "[I rise early,] 'Because of thy righteous ordinances'"
[Ps. 119:62].

[Q]   And what would David do? R. Pinhas in the name of R. Eleazar
b. R. Menahem, "He used to take a harp and lyre and set them
at his bedside. And he would rise at midnight and play them so
that the associates of Torah should hear. And what would the
associates of Torah say? 'If King David involves himself with
Torah, how much moreso should we.'" [S adds: We find that all
of Israel was engaged in Torah study on account of David.]

[R]   Said R. Levi, "A lyre was suspended at David's window. And
the north wind would blow at night, set it swinging around, and
it would play by itself [and wake him]. Similarly [Scripture says
concerning Elisha], 'And when the minstrel [lit.: the instru-
ment] played [*kngn hmngn*]' [2 Kings 3:15]. It does not say,
'When he played on the instrument [*kngn bmngn*]' but rather
when the instrument played [*kngn hmngn*]. The lyre would play
by itself."

[S]   [We return to the previous discussion of the text from T., cited
above at G.] How does Rabbi interpret [the verses that serve as]
the basis for R. Nathan's [i.e., teaching,] "At the beginning of
the middle watch" [Judg. 7:19]?

[T]   Said R. Huna, "[It means] the end of the second and the beginning of the third watch—that is the division of the night." [Var.:
the beginning of the second and the end of the third—these
(watches) divide the night.]

[U]   Said R. Mana "Very well! But does it say, 'The middle ones
[plural]?' No it says, 'The middle one [singular].' [The verse in
Judges does refer to a single middle watch. For] the first is not
taken into account, because up to [the end of the first watch]
people remain awake [and there is no need for guards to be set
around the camp. So there may be four watches which divide
the night, but guards are out only in the latter three watches.]"

[**XIV.**A]   *And sages say, "[They may recite the evening* Shema'*] until midnight."* [M. 1:1E.] R. Yosa in the name of R. Yohanan, "The law follows the sages."

[B]   R. Yosa [V has Yona] directed his students [*hbryyh*], "If you wish to be involved in [the study of] the Torah [all night], then [remember to] recite the *Shema'* before midnight and be involved [thereafter with the study of Torah]."

[C]   From his words we may deduce that, "The law follows the sages." And from his words we may deduce, "He recited additional [prayers] after 'True and upright' [cf. M. 2:2G]." [He did not go right to sleep after reciting the evening *Shema'*.]

[D]   It was taught, "One who recited the *Shema'* in the synagogue] in the morning fulfilled his obligation. [One who recited the *Shema'* in the synagogue] in the evening [i.e., at the time of the public evening service] did not fulfill his obligation." [He must recite again at home because he recited before nightfall.]

[E]   What is the difference between one who recites [in the synagogue] in the morning and one who recites in the evening? [Why did they not establish the practice of reciting the evening *Shema'* later so that people would not have to repeat the recitation at home later?]

[F]   [We may infer from the following that a person has an additional reason to recite the *Shema'* at home at night.] R. Huna in the name of R. Joseph, "On what basis must one recite the *Shema'* in his house in the evening?"

[G]   "So that he may chase away the demons." [Reciting in the synagogue does not serve to keep demons away from one's house when one is asleep.]

[H]   We may infer [from the words of R. Huna] that one may not recite more [prayers] after 'True and upright.' [Contrary to the second inference based on Yosa's dictum in C above.]

[I]   We may [in turn] deduce this from the words of R. Samuel bar Nahmani. [The story is told that] when R. Samuel bar Nahmani would go down to [celebrate the] intercalation [of the year], he would be received [as a guest] by R. Jacob Gerosa. And R. Zeira would hide in the closet to hear how he [Samuel] would recite the *Shema'*. [Zeira saw the following:] And he [Samuel] would recite over and over until he fell asleep. [This shows that Samuel bar Nahmani recited nothing else afterward.]

[J]   And on what basis [is one obligated to recite the *Shema'* at bedtime]? R. Aha and R. Tahlifta his son-in-law in the name of R. Samuel bar Nahman, "[It is based on the verse], 'Be angry but sin not; commune with your own hearts on your beds and be silent. Selah' [Ps. 4:4]. [This also implies that the *Shema'*, whose recitation requires intention, "directing one's heart," be recited at bedtime, and that nothing be said thereafter.]"

[K]   This [teaching of R. Samuel bar Nahmani from which we deduce that one may not recite any prayers after reciting 'True and upright,' the paragraph of liturgy which follows the *Shema'*] disputes [the following tradition concerning R. Joshua b. Levi]. For R. Joshua b. Levi used to recite psalms after [reciting the *Shema'* at bedtime].

[L]   And lo, it was taught [in H above], "One may not recite more [prayers] after [reciting the paragraph of liturgy which follows the *Shema'* which begins with the words] 'True and upright.'"

[M]   [Joshua b. Levi] resolved this [apparent contradiction by explaining that L refers to a different case, the recitation of the paragraph of liturgy which begins with the words] 'True and upright' [recited after the recitation of the *Shema'*] in the morning. [This implies that one may not recite more prayers after the morning *Shema'* before one recites the Prayer of Eighteen.]

[N]   Accordingly, said R. Zeira in the name of R. Abba bar Jeremiah, "These are three [cases in which one must] juxtapose [without interruption two consecutive actions]:
        [1] One must juxtapose [the ritual of] laying of hands [on an animal sacrifice] with [the act of] slaughtering [the sacrifice];
        [2] One must juxtapose [the ritual of] washing one's hands with the recitation of the blessing [before eating bread];
        [3] One must juxtapose [the recitation of] the 'Redemption' [i.e., benediction of the liturgy which follows the *Shema'* in the morning] with [the recitation of the] Prayer [of Eighteen Blessings]."

[O]   One must juxtapose [the ritual of] laying of hands [on an animal sacrifice] with [the act of] slaughtering [the sacrifice, as it is written,] "He shall lay his hand . . . then he shall kill" [Lev. 1:4–5].

[P]   One must juxtapose [the ritual of] washing one's hands with the recitation of the blessing [before eating bread, as it is written,] "Lift up your hands to the holy place, [i.e., this suggests the act of washing one's hands,] and bless the Lord!" [Ps. 134:2].

[Q]   One must juxtapose [the recitation of] the "Redemption" [i.e., the liturgical benediction which follows the *Shema'* in the morning] with [the recitation of the] Prayer [of Eighteen, as it is written,] "Let the words of my mouth [and the meditation of my heart be acceptable in thy sight, O Lord, my rock and my redeemer]" [Ps. 19:14]. [This is an allusion to the redemption liturgy.] And what is written thereafter? "The Lord answers you in the day of trouble" [Ps. 20:1]. [A reference to the requests in the Prayer of Eighteen.]

[R]   Said R. Yose b. R. Bun, "Any time one juxtaposes [the ritual of] laying of hands [on an animal sacrifice] with [the act of] slaughtering [the sacrifice], no impropriety will occur in [the ensuing offering of] that sacrifice [to invalidate it].

[S]   "And any time one juxtaposes [the ritual of] washing one's hands with the recitation of the blessing [before eating bread], Satan will not intervene to disrupt that meal.

[T]   "And any time one juxtaposes [the recitation of] the 'Redemption' [the liturgy which follows the *Shema'* in the morning] with [the recitation of the] Prayer [of Eighteen], Satan will not intervene to disrupt [one's activities during] that day."

[U]   Said R. Zeira, "I juxtaposed my [recitation of] the 'Redemption' to [my recitation of] the Prayer and [nevertheless I got into trouble]. I was conscripted through the angaria [service tax] to haul a myrtle tree to the palace."

[V]   They said to him, "Master, is this a big deal? [It is to your benefit, not trouble.] Some people would pay good money [for a chance] to visit the palace."

[W]   Said R. Ammi, "To whom may one who does not juxtapose [his recitation of the] Prayer [of Eighteen] to [his recitation of the] 'Redemption' be compared? To a beloved friend of the king who came and knocked on the king's door [and then departed]. The king went out to find out what he wanted and he found that he [the beloved] had gone away. And so he [the king] went away [and the beloved lost his opportunity to address his request to the king].'' [Accordingly, one should not interrupt between his recitation of these two prayers and lose the chance to address one's requests to God.]

[**XV.**A]   *Rabban Gamaliel says, "Until the break of day"* [M. 1 : 1F].

[B]   Rabban Gamaliel's [ruling] agrees with [that of] R. Simeon. For it was taught in the name of R. Simeon: **Sometimes one recites the *Shemaʿ* [twice in one night,] once before the dawn and once after the dawn, and we find that he fulfills his obligation for the [recitations of the *Shemaʿ*] of the day and of the night** [Tos. 1 : 1G–H].

[C]   Lo, [the opinion of] Rabban Gamaliel agrees with [the view of] R. Simeon regarding the evening [recitation of the *Shemaʿ*. Both masters rule that one may recite it until dawn].

[D]   Is this also the case [that the masters agree as to the rule] for the morning [recitation of the *Shemaʿ*, that Gamaliel would agree one may recite it right after dawn]?

[E]   Or shall it be [that we say that he agrees with] this [alternative view]: Said R. Zeira, "The brother of R. Hiyya bar Ashia and R. Abba bar Hannah taught, 'One who recites [the *Shemaʿ*] with the men of the watch [in the Temple] did not fulfill his obligation. For they used to rise up early [and recite it before sunrise, i.e., too early]."

[**XVI.**A]   *Once [Gamaliel's] sons came from the banquet hall. And they said to him, "We have not yet recited the* Shemaʿ.*" He said to them, "If the day has not yet broken, you are obligated to recite [the* Shemaʿ*]"* [M. 1 : 1G–I].

[B]   And Rabban Gamaliel disputed the [view of the] sages [who said one may recite *until midnight* [M. 1 : 1E]]. And did he [then go ahead to defy their ruling and] act in accord with his own view?

[C]   And, lo, [in another instance] R. Meir disputed the [view of the] sages and he did not act in accord with his own view. [He accepted sages' ruling as authoritative.]

[D]   And, lo, [in yet another case] R. Aqiba disputed the [view of the] sages and he did not act in accord with his own view. [S adds: "And, lo, R. Simeon . . ." Cf. O–U below.]

[E]   And where do we find that R. Meir disputed the sages and [nevertheless he] did not act in accord with his own view?

[F]   For it was taught: **They may prepare [and administer] a wine potion for a sick person on the Sabbath. Under what circumstances? When it was [already] mixed [with wine and oil] on the eve of the Sabbath. But if it was not mixed by the eve of the Sabbath [but on the Sabbath proper] it is forbidden [for a person to then go and to mix it on the Sabbath because one may not initially prepare medicine to administer it on the Sabbath].**

[G]   It was taught [in the continuation of this passage]: **Said R. Simeon b. Eleazar, "R. Meir used to permit them to mix wine and oil [as a potion] for a sick person on the Sabbath. And one time R. Meir fell ill, and we wanted to prepare it [i.e., a potion] for him, but he did not let us do so. And we said to him, 'Master, will you nullify [by your actions] your own opinion during your lifetime?' And he said to us, 'Even though I do rule leniently for others, I rule stringently for myself because my colleagues disagree with me'"** [T. Shabbat 12:12].

[H]   And where do we find that R. Aqiba disputed the sages and did not act in accord with his own view?

[I]   In this which was taught in the Mishnah: *[A house that contains:] The backbone and the skull from two corpses, or a quarter-log from two corpses, or a quarter qab of bones from two corpses, or limbs [taken] from two corpses, or a limb [taken] from two living men—R. Aqiba declares unclean [by virtue of the corpse uncleanness that is transmitted in an enclosed area] and sages declare clean [because the corpse material in the house is not of sufficient quantity to transmit uncleanness in an enclosed area]* [M. Ohalot 2:6].

[J]   It was taught, **M'sh: They brought buckets of bones from Kefar Tabya and they left them in the open air [i.e., not in a closed container] at the synagogue in Lod.**

[K]   **Theodorus the physician came in, with all the physicians with him [to examine the remains].**

[L]   **Theodorus said, "There is not present a backbone from a single corpse, nor a skull from a single corpse."**

[M]   **They said, "Since some of us here declare [a house that contains such material] unclean and some of us here declare [such a house] clean, let us arise for a vote."**

[N]   **They began from R. Aqiba, and he declared [such a house] clean. They said to him, "Since you, who [in the past] declared [a house that contains such matter to be] unclean, [and now you] have declared [it] clean, let such cases [now surely] be clean"** [Tos. Ahilot 4:2].

[O]   And where do we find that R. Simeon [b. Yohai] disputed the sages and did not act in accord with his own view?

[P]   In this which was taught in the Mishnah: *R. Simeon [b. Yohai] says, "All aftergrowths [i.e., crops which grow wild] are permitted [to be harvested and eaten in the Seventh year], except for the aftergrowths of cabbage, for there is no other like it among the greens of the field. [It grows so wildly that they fear people may plant and eat it in the Seventh year.]"*

[Q]   *And sages say, "All aftergrowths are forbidden [to be harvested for consumption]"* [M. Shebi'ith 9:1].

[R]   R. Simeon b. Yohai acted in this manner in the Seventh year. He saw a person gathering aftergrowths of the Seventh year.

[S]   He said to him, "Is it not forbidden? Are these not aftergrowths?"

[T]   He said to him, "Are you [Simeon b. Yohai] not the one who permits?"

[U]   He [Simeon] said to him, "Do my colleagues not dispute me and recite this verse about me: 'And a serpent will bite him who breaks through a wall'?" [Qoh. 10:8]. And so it was [that he acted in accord with the ruling of the sages].

[V]   And [in spite of the fact that these other rabbis submitted to the views of the sages who ruled against them, nevertheless, as our Mishnah indicates,] Rabban Gamaliel disputed the sages and acted according to his own view!

[W]   We may explain this case is different because [one might explain that in practice he accepted the view of sages and still] he permitted [his sons to recite the *Shema'*] in order to study [the biblical passages and not to fulfill the obligation of recitation].

[X]   [But this is not a satisfactory explanation.] For, if so, even after the break of day [they should be permitted to recite for the purpose of study. And Gamaliel specifically tells them that they may recite only if the day has not yet broken].

[Y]   But you may say that [this instance differs from the preceding cases]. Elsewhere [in the cases of Meir, Aqiba, and Simeon] they [actually] could follow the view of the sages [in practice, and thus did not act in accord with their own views].

[Z]   Here [in the case of Gamaliel's ruling concerning his son's recitation of the *Shema'*,] midnight already passed, and they could not follow the view of the sages. He said to them [i.e., Gamaliel said to his sons, in this case], "Act according to my view."

[XVII.A]   *And it is not only [in] this [case that the sages] said [that one may perform a religious obligation until daybreak]. But regarding all cases in which the sages said [that one must carry out his obligation] "until midnight," [if a person should perform] the religious obligation by daybreak [it is acceptable].*

[B]   *[For example, one may acceptably perform the obligation to] offer of the fats and entrails [of sacrifices in the Temple and to eat the Paschal sacrifices] until the break of day [M. 1:1J–K].*

[C]   [In some versions of M.] we have the phrase, "And the eating of Paschal sacrifices." Other versions omit the phrase.

[D]   Which authority stands behind the version which includes [the phrase], "And the eating of Paschal sacrifices?" The sages.

[E]   And which authority stands behind the version which omits, "And the eating of Paschal sacrifices?" R. Eliezer. [S and V have "b. Azariah."]

[F]   And what [source serves] as R. Eliezer's basis? One verse says, "[They shall eat the flesh that] night" [Exod. 12:8], and another verse says, "[For I will pass through the land of Egypt that] night" [Exod. 12:12]. Just as the latter [period referred to in the second verse ends at] midnight, so the former [period in the first verse ends at] midnight. [So, according to Eliezer, one may not eat the Paschal sacrifice after midnight and Mishnah should omit any reference to it here].

[G]   Said R. Huna, "[The phrase,] 'The eating of Paschal sacrifices' should not appear here even according to the [view of] sages. For it was taught, *The Paschal sacrifice after midnight renders the hands unclean* [i.e., it is no longer fit for consumption]" [M. Pes. 10:9].

[XVIII.A]   *[M. continues with another example:] All [sacrifices] which must be eaten within one day [i.e., before midnight of the day*

*they are offered,] their obligation [may legitimately be carried
out and they may be eaten] until the break of day* [M. 1:1L].

[B]   *All which must be eaten within one day*—[this refers to offerings classified as] the lesser holy things.

[C]   And [what is the explanation of,] *If so why did [sages] say [that
these actions should be performed only] until midnight?* [M.
1:1M]?

[D]   If you say, *Until the break of day,* one might [erroneously] think
the day did not yet break, and he might eat [late] and become
liable [to be punished].

[E]   But if you say to him, *Eat until midnight,* even if he eats [late],
after midnight, he will not become liable for transgressing the
law. [This is what sages meant in saying, *In order to keep man
far from sin*] [M. 1:1M].

Unit **I** compares two tannaitic texts which deal with the time
for reciting the *Shema*ʿ and shows how they appear to contradict one another. Then the Talmud resolves the contradiction
through a harmonization, to show that rules in M. and T. do not
conflict with one another.

Unit **II** points out a logical inconsistency between M.'s law
regarding the practice for reciting the *Shema*ʿ and common synagogue practice. The post facto resolution introduces an important conceptual link between Torah and prayer by suggesting
that the study of Torah is a desirable preparation for the recitation of prayers. Unit **III** compares the recitation of the grace
after meals, the prayer, and the *Shema*ʿ with regard to whether
one who was not sure he had previously recited must then do so.

In unit **IV** after citing a relevant Tosefta passage, the Talmud
enters into a lengthy discussion which begins by exploring the
premise that the appearance of stars in the sky determines the
legal start of the night. Y. cites Pinhas's statement [D] regarding
the number of stars one needs to see, a secondary issue, and an
analysis of its implications. The citation of Yose b. Bun's observation [I], leads to the tertiary stage of the *sugya* with its
typically talmudic abstract hypothetical cases, used to investigate
the ramifications of Pinhas's lemma.

Unit **V** continues with further rulings regarding the link
between the observation of stars in the sky and the legal deter-

mination of the beginning of the night. A makes a general point.
B appears to be a comment on Pinhas's lemma at **IV.D.** C gives
us an alternative to Pinhas's rule. In Jacob's view, twilight is not
defined by the appearance of a second star but rather by the
uncertainty over whether a given star may be counted to legally
define the onset of the night.

Unit **VI.A**, B, and E present alternative definitions of the twilight period. At G, the Talmud turns to an independent issue,
the duration of the twilight period giving the views of three authorities—Tanhuma, Nehemiah, and Yose. At J–K the younger
Yose and Hezekiah examine the difference between the views
of Nehemiah and the elder Yose. At L–N Mana objects to Hezekiah's conclusion. Hezekiah responds at O.

As an alternative to the positions presented in unit **IV,Y**. proposes in **VII** different criteria for defining night based on the
movement of the sun, not on the appearance of the stars [A–D].
E–H take up the related question of when we deem it to be the
time that the sun comes out.

The long, involved, and difficult, mainly independent materials in **IV–XII** continue in units **VIII** and **XI** with materials
regarding practices for prayer and for the priests. **VIII** is unrelated to the preceding. Its interest is the proper posture for
prayer.

Unit **IX** continues with further rulings regarding the recitation of the prayers, dealing with the proper congregational responses to the verses of the Priestly Blessing in the synagogue.
X–XII give additional interesting independent materials on cosmological subjects.

The lengthy digression in **X** concerns the duration of the two
periods before sunrise—from the first rays of light until the
break of day across the sky and from daybreak until sunrise.
Appropriate verses prove the points of the unit, and a homily
regarding the redemption of Israel closes the section.

Unit **XI** digresses further from the main themes of the chapter. Its interest in the length of heavenly realms is only distantly
related to the question of when a person may recite the morning
Shema'.

Unit **XII.A–B** refers to the width of the Tree of Life, the
subject also of C and D, with a related tangential tradition at
E. F returns to the subject of **XI.A**, the width of the firmament.
F–I provides an alternative to Judah's teaching in **XI.A** regarding the width of the darkness of the firmament. J–L goes off

on a tangent regarding the verse cited in I. M–R adds another alternative to Judah's view and discusses it appending further exegetical teachings about the nature of the firmament.

Unit **XIII.**A–J cites a Tosefta passage relevant to our Mishnah and explains it, with interpolations and additions in the discussion. At L–R the unit turns to traditions related to the verses cited concerning King David. S–U comes back to finish the discussion of T.

XIV.A takes us back to M.'s statement regarding the latest time for the recitation of the evening *Shema'*. B–E discusses several aspects of the evening *Shema'*. F–G introduces the concept that the *Shema'* be recited at home at bedtime and gives a justification for that practice. H–J discusses another aspect of the practice, leading us to the give and take of K–M. The related independent unit at N–W includes as one of its three cases the practice of juxtaposing the recitations of the *Shema'* and of the Prayer of Eighteen.

At unit **XV**, the Talmud cites M. and a corresponding passage from T. to analyze the views of the two authorities therein and to see if they concur. In the end Y. does not resolve the issue of whether Gamaliel's view regarding recitation in the morning agrees with Simeon's.

The tightly constructed unit at **XVI** draws on relevant illustrations from several tractates to show that some of Gamaliel's actions, such as those described in our Mishnah, were not consistent with the practices of other rabbis. In the end the unit suggests an explanation to defend Gamaliel and resolve the apparent inconsistency.

Unit **XVII** examines two variant readings in Mishnah and seeks to identify the authority behind each. Unit **XVIII** looks at a line of M. and explains that through its language it subsumes under it a law for the time limit for eating ordinary sacrifices.

1:2

[A]   *From what time do they recite the* Shema' *in the morning?*

[B]   *From [the time that] one can distinguish between blue and white.*

[C]   *R. Eliezer said, "Between blue and green."*

[D]   *[And one completes the recitation] before sunrise.*

[E]   *R. Joshua says, "[One may recite] until the third hour."*

[F]   *"For it is the practice of royalty to rise at the third hour."*

[G]   *One who recites after this time has not lost [the purpose of the action. For though he does not fulfill the obligation of reciting the* Shema', *he is] like one who recites [passages] from the Torah.*

[I.A] Interpret the Mishnah [B] in this way: Between the blue [fringes on the corner of a garment] and the white [ones] on it.

[B]   And what [verse] serves as the basis for the rabbis' view?

[C]   "[And it shall be to you a fringe] to look upon" [Num. 15:39]. [At the time one recites this in the *Shema'*, one should be able to discern the blue in the fringe from the white] next to it.

[D]   And what serves as the basis for R. Eliezer's view?

[E]   "To look upon" [refers to the cord of blue in Num. 15:38. At the time one recites the *Shema'* there must be enough daylight] so that one may distinguish it [i.e., the blue in the fringe] from other colored material [close to it in hue, i.e., green].

[F]   It was taught in the name of R. Meir, " 'To look upon it' [using the feminine pronoun] is not what is written here [in the verse.] Rather, 'To look upon it' [using the masculine pronoun]. This suggests to us that it is as if anyone who fulfills the commandment of [wearing] fringes stands in the divine presence, [of Him, i.e., God]."

[G]   [One may associate the blue fringe with the presence of God in another way.] [S omits: It tells us that] *the blue* [color of the fringe, Num. 15:38] is like that [color] of the sea. And the sea resembles the grasses. And the grasses resemble the firmament. And the firmament resembles the throne of glory. And the throne resembles the sapphire. As it is written, "Then I looked, and behold, on the firmament that was over the heads of the cherubim there appeared above them something like a sapphire, in form resembling a throne" [Ezek. 10:1, an association with the divine presence].

[H]   **Others say [you may understand the verse], " 'To look upon [him,' i.e., another person. Before one recites the *Shema'* it should be daylight enough] so that one may be four cubits from his fellow and recognize him" [T. 1:2B].**

[I]   R. Hisda said concerning that [statement] of "others," "To what [kind of 'fellow' do they refer]? If it is [a case of one who sees] a familiar person, then even from further [than four cubits away] he will recognize him. And if it is [a case of] an unfamiliar person, then even closer [than four cubits] he will not recognize him.

[J]   "Rather we hold that it is a case of one [who sees a 'fellow'] who is familiar, but not so familiar, such as a person who comes occasionally to him for lodging."

[K]   There is a Tanna who taught, "[He may not recite the *Shema'* in the morning until it is light enough so that he can distinguish] between a wolf and a dog, or between a donkey and a wild ass."

[L]   And there is a Tanna who taught, "[One may recite the *Shema'* when it is light enough] so that one may be four cubits from his fellow and recognize him."

[M]   He [R. Hisda] would say that he who says, "[One may recite when it is light enough to distinguish] between a wolf and a dog, between a donkey and a wild ass," [holds the same view] as the one who said, *"Between blue and green"* [M. 2:1C, Eliezer].

[N]   And he who said, **"[One may recite when it is light enough] so that one may be four cubits from his fellow and recognize him"** [T. 1:2B], [holds the same view] as the one who says, *"[One may recite when it is light enough to distinguish] between blue and white"* [M. 2:1B]. [This is an earlier time.]

[II.A]   [Concerning the requirement to recite the *Shema'* in the morning:] **But they said, "Its obligation is [best fulfilled] at sunrise so that one may adjoin [the blessing following the *Shema'* called] 'Redemption' to the Prayer [of Eighteen Blessings] and it turns out that [thereby] he recites the Prayer in the daytime"** [T. 1:2C].

[B]   Said R. Zeira, "And I explained that the basis [of this rule is in this verse], 'May they fear Thee [i.e., by reciting the *Shema'*] while the sun endures'" [Ps. 72:5, i.e., at sunrise].

[C]   Said Mar Uqba, "The pious used to rise early to recite [the *Shema'*] so that they might adjoin to it [the recitation of] their prayers at sunrise."

[D]   It was taught [T. 1:2D–H]: **Said R. Judah, "Once I was walking on the road behind R. Eleazar b. Azariah and behind R. Aqiba.**

[E]   "And they were preoccupied with [fulfilling] commandments.

[F]   "And the time came [at sunrise] for the recitation of the *Shemaʿ* [and they did not recite].

[G]   "And I thought that they perhaps had neglected to recite the *Shemaʿ* [that morning because they were preoccupied with other religious obligations].

[H]   "And I recited and studied and afterward they began.

[I]   "And the sun [had risen earlier and] was already visible across the mountaintops."

[**III.A**]   [And one completes the recitation of the *Shemaʿ*] *before sunrise* [M. 1:2D]. [When is sunrise?] R. Zebadiah b. R. Jacob bar Zabdi in the name of R. Jonah, "When the sun begins to shine across the mountaintops [that is sunrise]."

[B]   *R. Joshua says, "[They may recite the* Shemaʿ*] until the third hour"* [M. 1:2E].

[C]   R. Idi and R. Hamnuna and R. Ada bar Aha in the name of Rab, "The law follows R. Joshua [only] in the case of one who forgets [to recite earlier at sunrise]."

[D]   R. Huna said, "Two Amoraim [disputed the interpretation of Joshua's lemma]. One said [that Joshua's ruling applies only] to the case of one who forgets [to recite at sunrise]."

[E]   His associate responded to him, "And is there a law [that applies only] to one who forgets?

[F]   "The law is the law. [It must apply to everyone in all cases.]

[G]   "And why then did they say that it applies [only] to one who forgets?

[H]   "So that a person should be zealous to recite it in its proper time."

[**IV.A**]   [Y. contrasts the obligation to recite the *Shemaʿ* with the obligation to recite the Prayer of Eighteen Blessings.] There it was taught [M. Shabbat 1:2]: *They interrupt [activities such as a bath, meal, or a trial] for the recitation of the* Shemaʿ *but they do not interrupt [these activities] for the [recitation of the] Prayer.*

[B]   Said R. Aha, "[The reasoning behind this rule is based on this distinction.] The recitation of the *Shemaʿ* [is an obligation which] derives from the Torah. But the [obligation to recite the] Prayer does not derive from the Torah." [And the principle is that only a practice based on the Torah takes precedence over other obligations.]

[C]   Said R. Ba, "[The reasoning behind the rule in M. Shabbat is based on another distinction.] The recitation of the *Shema'* [is an obligation] whose time is fixed. But the Prayer [is one] whose time is not fixed." [And the principle is that a practice which may only be carried out at a fixed time takes precedence over another practice which need not be carried out at a fixed time.]

[D]   Said R. Yose, "[The rule above is based on another distinction.] The recitation of the *Shema'* [is an obligation which] does not require intention [for the entire ritual]. The Prayer [is one] which does require intention." [A person involved in other activities cannot have the requisite intention to recite the Prayer and so does not stop to do so.]

[E]   Said R. Mana, "[Concerning the issue of intention for the recitation of the *Shema'*] I raised this objection to R. Yose, 'But even if you say that the recitation of the *Shema'* does not require intention [for the entire recitation, for at least] the first three verses [you surely] require intention.' [How then does this distinction help us explain why one can interrupt those activities mentioned in M. Shabbat to recite the *Shema'*? Because he is preoccupied he will not be able to muster the proper intention. He therefore should not interrupt even to recite the *Shema'*.]"

[F]   [He replied,] "Because, [unlike the Prayer of Eighteen Blessings, the *Shema'*] is short, so one can [muster the proper] intention [for these three initial verses even if one interrupts other activities to do so]."

[V.A]   R. Yohanan in the name of R. Simeon b. Yohai, "Those [professional scholars] like us who are engaged [constantly] in the study of Torah, do not interrupt it even for the recitation of the *Shema'*."

[B]   R. Yohanan said on his own, "Those [people] like us who are not engaged [constantly] in the study of Torah [must] interrupt [our activities, including our study,] even for the [recitation of the] Prayer [which requires intense concentration]."

[C]   Each man's opinion [in A–B] is consistent [in principle] with his ruling elsewhere.

[D]   R. Yohanan [in B is consistent] with his opinion [elsewhere]:
For, said R. Yohanan, "But oh, that a person might [have the
opportunity to] pray all the day long. Why? For prayer never
loses its value. [He places great emphasis on prayer, cf. above
M. 1:1 **III.D**]."

[E]   R. Simeon b. Yohai [in A is consistent] with his opinion [else-
where]: For R. Simeon b. Yohai said, "If I had been at Mount
Sinai at the time the Torah was given to Israel, I would have
asked God to give man two mouths, one to talk of the Torah and
one to use for all his other needs [including prayer among them
so that a person would not have to interrupt his study when
reciting prayers]."

[F]   [On second thought], he reconsidered and said, "But the world
can barely continue to exist because of the slander [spoken by
each person out of] one [mouth]. It would be worse if there were
two [mouths for each person to speak with]."

[G]   Said R. Yose before R. Jeremiah, "R. Yohanan [in B] follows the
view of R. Hanina b. Aqabya. For it was taught, **Those [scribes]
who are writing [Torah] scrolls [i.e., they are like those who
study Torah], phylacteries, and mezzuzot interrupt [their writ-
ing] for the recitation of the *Shema'* but do not interrupt for
the [recitation of the] Prayer**" [T. 2:6A].

[H]   **R. Hanina b. Aqabya says, "Just as they [the scribes] interrupt for the recitation of the *Shema'*, so too they interrupt for
the [recitation of the] Prayer [T. 2:6C], and for the [ritual of
putting on] tefillin, and for [performing] all the other commandments of the Torah [in their proper time]."** [This agrees
with Yohanan's rule in B.]

[I]   But [going back to the rule of A,] does not R. Simeon bar
Yohai admit that they interrupt [even the study of the Torah]
to make a sukkah or a lulab in its proper time? [Why then did
he say in A that one does not interrupt study to fulfill other
commandments?]

[J]   And [furthermore] does not R. Simeon bar Yohai hold [that] one
who learns in order to practice [acts properly]. But one who
learns without concern for practice does not [act properly].

[K]   For it would have been better for a person who learns without
concern for practice not to have been born.

[L]   And said R. Yohanan, "It would have been better for a person who learns without concern for practice if his placenta smothered him [at birth] and he never entered the world."

[M]   [Now to return to the analysis of A:] The basis of R. Simeon bar Yohai's [teaching is derived not from the preceding principle but from a different argument. He would say the study of Torah and the recitation of the *Shema'* are equal in importance]. They are both acts of study. And one does not desist from one act of study for another act of study.

[N]   But, lo, it was taught [in apparent contradiction of this argument,] *One who recites after this time has not lost [the purpose of the action. For though he does not fulfill the obligation of reciting the* Shema', *he is] like one who recites [passages] from the Torah* [M. 1:2G].

[O]   [This implies that the recitation of the *Shema'*] in its proper time is a more desirable act than [the study of] words of Torah. [They are not equivalent.]

[P]   That is so [for most people but not for Simeon. For] said R. Yudan, "Because R. Simeon b. Yohai constantly studied words of Torah, therefore [for him the recitation of the *Shema'*] was not more desirable than [the study of] words of Torah."

[Q]   Said R. Abba Mari, "[In addition to this last argument we may defend R. Simeon's position at A in another way.] Did we not learn [one who recited *Shema'* after the proper time is] like, *One who recites from the Torah* [M. 1:2G]. Lo, [we may infer from this that the recitation of the *Shema'*] in its proper time is like [a higher form of study, i.e., equivalent to] the [study of] Mishnah." [Simeon studied Mishnah. Hence he did not have to interrupt his study for an equivalent action, the recitation of the *Shema'* in its proper time.]

[R]   [Accordingly,] R. Simeon bar Yohai is consistent with his own view [as follows:]

[S]   R. Simeon b. Yohai said, "Engaging in the study of Scripture is not such a big deal." [It is less significant than the study of Mishnah.]

[T]   And the rabbis considered [study of] Scripture equal to [study of] Mishnah. [As a rule they interrupted their study to recite the *Shema'* at its proper time.]

Unit **I** discusses B of M. It cites a biblical phrase as support of
the rule and continues the unit with a discussion of the meaning
of the phrase and the import of the blue fringe [A–G]. H–J
takes up and examines T.'s related rule. K–N introduces related
alternative traditions and harmonizes them with the corresponding rules of M.

Unit **II** speaks to the ramifications of Mishnah's rule, adding
the appropriate passage from Tosefta.

Unit **III** comments on two lines of the Mishnah. Unit **IV** cites
a passage from M. Shabbat to explore the difference between the
obligations to recite the *Shema'* and the Prayer. In the discussion
Y. invokes several important principles: (1) obligations which
derive from a verse in the Torah carry greater import than rabbinic obligations with no direct basis in the Torah, (2)
obligations whose time is fixed take precedence over other obligations, (3) one must establish a proper context to perform
rituals which require special intention.

The main interests of unit **V** are the statements of Simeon bar
Yohai and Yohanan cited at A–B. Priority in the performance
of religious obligations is the issue. Which is more important,
study or prayer? C–F shows that the two Amoraim are consistent with their own views elsewhere. G–H cites a passage from
T. and tries to harmonize it with Yohanan's rule. I–Q examines
the logic of Simeon's opinion and suggests justifications for the
law consistent with his opinion elsewhere (R–T).

1:3

[A]   *The House of Shammai says, "In the evening everyone should
      recline and recite, and in the morning they should stand.*

[B]   *"As it says, 'When you lie down and when you rise'"* [Deut. 6:7].

[C]   *And the House of Hillel says, "Everyone recites according to his
      own manner."*

[D]   *"As it says, 'And when you walk by the way'"* [ibid].

[E]   *If so why does [the verse] say, "When you lie down and when
      you rise up?"*

[F]   *[It means recite the Shema'] at the hour that people lie down [at
      night] and at the hour that people rise up [in the morning].*

[I.A]   The House of Hillel [M. 1:3F] derives its [rules] from two Scriptural passages [as M. 1:3D–E explains]. What [rules] do the House of Shammai derive from the passage, "When you sit in your house, and when you walk by the way" [Deut. 6:7]?

[B]   [They derive the following, as we see in T.] **"When you sit in your house" excludes those who are [out] engaged in fulfilling commandments [from the obligation to recite the *Shema'*]. And "When you walk by the way" excludes the bridegroom [because he is involved in the obligations of marriage] [T. 1:3B].**

[II.A]   And it was taught: **M'sh: R. Eleazar b. Azariah and R. Ishmael were staying in one place.**

[B]   **And R. Eleazar b. Azariah was reclining and R. Ishmael was sitting upright.**

[C]   **When the time came for the recitation of the [morning] *Shema'*, R. Eleazar b. Azariah sat up and R. Ishmael reclined.**

[D]   **Said R. Eleazar b. Azariah to R. Ishmael, "I will say [it is analogous to] an individual from the marketplace [who was asked], 'Why do you grow your beard long?' And he said, 'It is a protest against the destroyers [who cut their beards. But there is no other reason for it].'"**

[E]   **"I who was reclining, sat up [to recite in the proper posture]. And you, who was upright reclined [for no good reason just as a protest to my action]."**

[F]   **He [Ishmael] said to him, "[Eleazar,] you sat up in accordance with the words of the House of Shammai [who said to recite while upright]. And I reclined in accordance with the words of the House of Hillel [who said one may recite in any position]."**

[G]   **[An alternate explanation: "[I reclined] so that the students should not observe me [standing] and establish the law in accordance with the words of the House of Shammai." [T. 1:4. See Eleazar, pp. 16–20, for a discussion of the several versions of this story.]**

[III.A]   *Said R. Tarfon, "I was coming by the road and I reclined to recite the* Shema' *in accordance with the words of the House of Shammai. And I placed myself in danger of [attack by] ban-dits."*

[B]   *They said to him, "Fittingly, you have only yourself to blame
[for what might have befallen you]. For you violated the words
of the House of Hillel."* [Continuation of M. 1 : 4.]

[C]   The associates in the name of R. Yohanan, "The words of the
scribes [i.e., rabbinic teachings] are relative [in importance] to
the words of Torah and dear like the words of Torah." [As it
says,] "And your palate [i.e., the words of the scribes are] like
the best wine [i.e., the words of the Torah]" [Song of Sol. 7 : 9].

[D]   Simeon bar Abba [Wawa] in the name of R. Yohanan, "The
words of the scribes are relative [in importance] to the words of
Torah and more dear than the words of Torah." [As it says,]
"For your love [i.e., words of the scribes,] is better than wine
[i.e., words of Torah]" [Song of Sol. 1 : 2].

[E]   R. Ba [Abba] bar Kohen in the name of R. Judah ben Pazzi,
"I will prove to you that the words of the scribes are more dear
than the words of the Torah. For lo, if R. Tarfon [in the story
in M.] did not recite [the *Shema'* at all], at most he would have
been liable for neglecting to fulfill a positive commandment [of
the Torah for which there is no punishment].

[F]   "But because he violated the words of the House of Hillel,
[words of the scribes,] he was liable to be put to death [at the
hands of bandits], in accord with [the principle,] 'And a serpent
will bite him who breaks through a wall [i.e., one who violates
a rabbinic regulation]'" [Qoh. 10 : 8].

[G]   R. Ishmael taught, "The words of the Torah contain some prohibitions, permissions, leniencies, and stringencies. But the
words of the scribes are all stringencies."

[H]   I will prove to you that this is true. For it was taught in the
Mishnah, *One who says, 'There are no [such obligations to
wear] tefillin,' in order to transgress the words of Torah, he is
free [from any punishment]. [But if he says,] 'There are five
compartments [in the tefillin],' in order to add to the words of
the scribes, he is liable [to punishment]* [M. Sanhedrin 11 : 3].

[I]   R. Haninah the son of R. Ada in the name of R. Tanhum b. R.
Hiyya, "The words of the elders are more stringent than the
words of the prophets." As it is written, "[I tell them,] 'Do not

preach'—thus they preach. [I tell them,] 'One should not preach of such things,' [and they say,] 'Disgrace will not overtake us'" [Mic. 2:6]. And it is written, "[If a man should go about and utter empty words and lies, saying,] 'I will preach to you of wine and strong drink,'" [he would be the preacher for this people] [Mic. 2:11]. [That is, if the people do not wish to hear words of the prophet, God says do not preach it to them. But you must preach to them the words of the elders whether they want to hear them or not.]

[J] To what may the [relation between] prophet and elder be compared? [This parable explains:] A king sent his two agents to a province. Concerning one he wrote, "If he does not display to you my seal and my stamp do not give him credence." And concerning the other he wrote, "Even if he does not display to you my seal, lend him credence without seal or stamp."

[K] Accordingly concerning the prophet it is written, "[If a prophet arises among you . . .] and gives you a sign or a wonder" [Deut. 13:1] [then you should give him credence].

[L] However here [concerning the elders] it is written, "That [you shall heed the priests and the judge] according to the instructions which they give you" [Deut. 17:11] [you must give them credence even though they do not display any sign or wonder].

[IV.A] [Regarding Mishnah's story of Tarfon's vulnerability to danger, which resulted from his adherence to the Shammaite view:] This [principle that one who follows the Shammaite view endangers himself] applies only after the Heavenly voice [Bat Qol or echo] went forth [to decree that the law follows the view of the House of Hillel]. But before the Heavenly voice went forth, anyone who wished to adopt for himself a stringency [in the law] and act according to the stringent rulings of both the Houses of Shammai and Hillel—[they permitted him to do so but] concerning him it was said, "The fool walks in darkness" [Qoh. 2:14].

[B] [And one who wished to adopt for himself] the leniencies of both [Houses] was called "wicked."

[C] Rather [one could follow] the leniencies of one [House] and stringencies of that House or the leniencies of the second and the stringencies of that House.

[D] All this applied [to the period] before the Heavenly voice went forth. But once the Heavenly voice went forth, thereafter the law always followed the words of the House of Hillel. And whosoever violated the words of the House of Hillel was liable to [be put to] death.

[E]   It was taught: A Heavenly voice went forth and proclaimed, "Both [Houses speak] the living words of God. But the law follows the words of the House of Hillel."

[F]   In what place did the Heavenly voice go forth? R. Bibi said in the name of R. Yohanan, "In Yavneh the Heavenly voice went forth."

Unit **I** cites the Shammaite rules in T. Unit **II** gives the next T. text without comment. Unit **III** is an independent unit that compares the authority of rabbinic traditions to that of Scriptural traditions. E–F uses M.'s story about Tarfon to prove that rabbinic teachings are more important. G–L further develops this theme. Unit **IV** explains that Tarfon's actions in the story in M. preceded the announcement of the Heavenly echo that the law follows the House of Hillel. After that time, one was not permitted to follow the view of the House of Shammai.

1:4

[A]   *In the morning one recites two blessings before [the Shema'] and one after it.*

[B]   *And in the evening two before it and two after it.*

[C]   *Whether a long or a short [blessing, the rule is the same].*

[D]   *Where they said to lengthen [the formula of a blessing by both beginning and ending with the formula "Blessed art Thou"], one is not permitted to shorten it [by omitting it].*

[E]   *[Where they said] to shorten [by only beginning with "Blessed art Thou"], one is not permitted to lengthen it [by also closing with "Blessed art Thou"].*

[F]   *[Where they said] to seal [to conclude a blessing with the formula "Blessed art Thou" at the end], one is not permitted not to seal.*

[G]   *[Where they said] not to seal, one is not permitted to seal [by adding to it].*

[I.A]   R. Simon in the name of R. Samuel bar Nahman, "[They recite these blessings before and after the *Shema'*] based on [the verse], "But you shall meditate on it day and night" [Josh. 1:8]. [That implies] that the meditations [i.e., the number of blessings] of the day and the night should be equal. [The additional blessing after the *Shema'* in the evening substitutes for the third scriptural paragraph, Num. 15:37–41, which is not recited at night. If one counts the blessings before and after together with the scriptural paragraphs, the number of sections in the day and night recitations come out equal (P.M.).]

[B]   R. Yose bar Abin in the name of R. Joshua b. Levi, "[These seven blessings, two before and one after in the morning, and two before and two after in the evening, are recited] based on [the verse,] 'Seven times a day I praise thee for thy righteous ordinances'" [Ps. 119:164].

[C]   R. Nahman in the name of R. Mana, "All who fulfill [the obligations of the verse,] 'Seven times a day I praise thee,' [by reciting the *Shema'*, morning and evening with its blessings,] it is as if they had fulfilled [as well the verse,] 'But you shall meditate on it day and night.' [That is, it is as if they had studied Torah all day and night.]"

[II.A]   Why do they recite these two passages [Deut. 6:4–9 and Deut. 11:13–21] each day? R. Levi and R. Simon [disputed this question].

[B]   R. Simon said, "Because in them we find mention of lying down and rising up [in Deut. 6:7 and Deut. 11:19. These are allusions to the beginning and end of each day when the *Shema'* is recited]."

[C]   R. Levi said, "Because the Ten Commandments are embodied in the [paragraphs of the *Shema'* as follows:]

[D]   [1] "I am the Lord your God" [Exod. 20:2] [is implied by the phrase], "Hear, O Israel the Lord our God" [Deut. 6:4].

[E]   [2] "You shall have no other Gods before me" [Exod. 20:3] [is implied by the phrase], "One Lord" [Deut. 6:4].

[F]   [3] "You shall not take the name of the Lord your God in vain" [Exod. 20:7] [is implied by the phrase], "And you shall love the Lord your God" [Deut. 6:5]. [How so?] One who loves the king does not swear falsely in his name.

[G]   [4] "Remember the Sabbath day, to keep it holy" [Exod. 20:8]
       [is implied by the phrase], "So that you shall remember [and do
       all my commandments]" [Num. 15:40].

[H]   [Rabbi teaches that the Sabbath is equivalent in importance to
       all the commandments as follows:] Rabbi says, "[The phrase,
       'All my commandments,' refers to the commandment [to keep]
       the Sabbath, which is equivalent in weight to all the other com-
       mandments of the Torah. As it is written, "And you did make
       known to them thy holy Sabbath and command them command-
       ments and statutes and laws by Moses thy servant" [Neh. 9:14].
       This informs you that it [the Sabbath] is equal in weight to all of
       the commandments of the Torah."

[I]   [5] "Honor your father and your mother [that your days in the
       land may be long]" [Exod. 20:12] [is implied by the phrase],
       "That your days and the days of your children may be multi-
       plied" [Deut. 11:21]. [The reference to a long life is an allusion
       to the reward for honoring one's parents.]

[J]   [6] "You shall not murder" [Exod. 20:13] [is implied by the
       phrase], "And you [shall] perish quickly" [Deut. 11:17]. [This
       implies that] whoever murders, will be killed.

[K]   [7] "You shall not commit adultery" [Exod. 20:14] [is implied
       by the phrase], "[And remember. . .] not to follow after your
       own heart and your own eyes" [Num. 15:39].

[L]   [This accords with the following teaching:] Said R. Levi, "The
       heart and the eyes are the two procurers of sin. As it is written,
       'My son, give me your heart, and let your eyes observe my ways'
       [Prov. 23:26. In the verses that follow, Prov. 23:27–35, the
       harlot is a metaphor for sin.]

[M]   Said the Holy One, Blessed be He, "If you give me your heart
       and your eyes then I shall know that you are mine."

[N]   [8] "You shall not steal" [Exod. 20:15] [is implied by the
       phrase], "That you may gather in your grain [and your wine and
       oil]" [Deut. 11:14]. [Your grain implies that you may gather
       only yours] and not the grain of your fellow.

[O]   [9] "You shall not bear false witness against your neighbor"
       [Exod. 20:16] [is implied by the phrase] "I am the Lord your
       God" [Num. 15:41]. [This is followed in the liturgy of the

blessings of the *Shema'* by the word "true." Just as God is true, so should a person tell the truth.]

[P]   And [in further support of this teaching] it is written, "But the Lord is the true God" [Jer. 10:10].

[Q]   What is [another interpretation of the word, 'True']? Said R. Abun, "That means he is the living God and King of the Universe." [The word *'mt*, true, is an acronym for the Hebrew *'lwhm mlk tmyd*, God the everlasting king (P.M.).]

[R]   Said R. Levi, "Said the Holy One blessed be He, 'If you bore false witness against your friend, I deem it as if you had borne witness against me, that I did not create the heavens and the earth.'"

[S]   [10] "You shall not covet your neighbor's house" [Exod. 20:17] [is implied by the phrase], "And you shall write them on the doorposts of your house" [Deut. 6:9]. [Write them on] "your house" and not on those of your friend's house [Do not covet your neighbor's house].

[III.A]   It was taught in the Mishnah [Tamid 5:1]: *The officer said to them, "Recite a single blessing." And they recited a blessing.*

[B]   What blessing did they recite? R. Matna said in the name of Samuel, "It was the blessing over the Torah." [Because they next recited passages from the Torah concerning the Ten Commandments.]

[C]   *And they recited the Ten Commandments, [the passage,] "Hear, O Israel . . ." [Deut. 6:4–9], [the passage,] "And if you will obey my commandments" [Deut. 11:13–21], [the passage,] "The Lord said to Moses" [Num. 15:37–41]* [M. Tamid 5:1].

[D]   R. Ammi in the name of Resh Laqish, "This implies that [if one omits reciting] the blessings [before and after the *Shema'*, it] does not invalidate [his recitation. From this M. we deduce that the blessings are dispensable because in M.'s example they did not recite them]."

[E]   Said R. Ba [Abba], "From this [Mishnah] you would not deduce at all [that the blessings are dispensable]. For the Ten Commandments are the essence of the *Shema'* [as Levi explained above in unit **II**]. [And once one has recited them, he has fulfilled his obligation to recite the *Shemaʿ* and need not recite it again with its blessings (P.M.).]

[F]   [F–J discusses the practice of not reciting the verses of the Ten Commandments and the story of Balaam.] R. Matna and R. Samuel bar Nahman said, "By rights they should recite the verses of the Ten Commandments every day. And why do they not do so? On account of the claims of the heretics. So that people should not have any cause to say that only these [Ten Commandments] were given to Moses on Mount Sinai."

[G]   R. Samuel bar Nahman [said] in the name of R. Judah bar Zebuda, "By rights they should recite the passages [which recount the story of] Balak and Balaam [Num. 22–24] every day. And why do they not recite them? In order not to trouble the congregation [with too much daily recitation]."

[H]   [And on what basis could they justify the recitation of the story of Balak and Balaam?] R. Huna said, "Because that passage contains a reference to lying down and rising up. [Like the *Shemaʿ* it should be recited twice daily. For it says, 'Behold a people! As a lioness it rises up and as a lion lifts itself; it does not lie down till it devours the prey'" (Num. 23:24).]

[I]   R. Yose be R. Bun said, "[They could have justified the recitation of the story of Balaam] because that passage contains a reference to the exodus from Egypt, ['God brings them out of Egypt' (Num. 23:22),] and to kingship ['And the shout of a king is among them'" (Num. 23:21)].

[J]   Said R. Eliezer, "[They could have justified the recitation of the story of Balaam] because the story is referred to in the Torah [Num. 22–24], in the Prophets, ['My people remember what Balak king of Moab devised and what Balaam the son of Beor answered him' (Mic. 6:5)], and in the Writings ['No Ammonite or Moabite should ever enter the assembly of God; for they did not meet the children of Israel with bread and water but hired Balaam against them to curse them' (Neh. 13:1–2)]."

[K]   [K–L repeats A–B.] *The officer said to them, "Recite a single blessing." And they recited a blessing* [M. Tamid 5:1].

[L]   What blessing did they recite? Said R. Matna in the name of Samuel, "The blessing over the [study of] Torah."

[M]   But did they not recite [the blessing which concludes,] "Who creates the luminaries?" R. Samuel the brother of R. Berekhiah, "[They began reciting early and] the luminaries had not yet appeared. How then could they say, 'Who creates the luminaries'?"

[N]   *[M. Tamid 5:1 continues: They recited three blessings for the people: (1) "True and upright"; (2) and [a blessing for the] Temple service; (3) and the Priestly Blessing.] And on the Sabbath they added one blessing for the departing priestly watch.*

[O]   What is this blessing? Said R. Helbo, "This is it: 'May he who dwells in this Temple set in your midst fraternity, and love, and peace and friendship.'"

[IV.A]   Samuel said, "One who awoke early [in order to begin] to study [Torah] before reciting the *Shema'*, must [first] recite the blessings [for study of Torah]."

[B]   [But if he began to study] after reciting the *Shema'*, he need not recite the blessings [for the study of Torah, because the [*Ahavah Rabbah*] blessing he recites before the *Shema'* serves in their stead.]

[C]   Said R. Ba, "[This rule only applies] if he studies right away [after he recites the *Shema'*]."

[D]   R. Huna said, "This is my view of matters: [If one studies] Midrash, he must recite the blessings [for Torah study]. [If one studies laws] *halakhot*, he need not recite the blessings."

[E]   R. Simon in the name of R. Joshua b. Levi, "For [the study of] either Midrash or *halakhot*, he must recite the blessings."

[F]   Said R. Hiyya bar Ashi, "We were accustomed to sit before Rab. And he required us to recite the blessings for both [the study of] Midrash and for *halakhot*."

[V.A]   It was taught: One who recited [the *Shema'*] with the members of the watch [*ma'amad*] did not fulfill his obligation because they used to delay [and recite too late]. [These were the members of the Israelite delegations who came to the Temple to watch over their offerings.]

[B]   R. Zeira in the name of R. Ammi, "In the days of R. Yohanan we used to go out [to gather for prayer] on the public fast day and recite the *Shema'* after the third hour and he did not intervene [to prohibit us from so doing]."

[C]   R. Yose and R. Aha went out [to pray] on a public fast day. The congregation went ahead and recited the *Shema'* after the third hour. R. Aha wanted to stop them.

[D]   Said to him R. Yose, "They have already recited it on time! They are only reciting it [now again] so that they can rise to recite the Prayer from amidst words of Torah."

[E]   He said to him, "[Nevertheless I object to this] on account of the simple folk, lest they conclude that they now are reciting it on time [when it really is already after the third hour and too late to recite]."

[VI.A]   **These are the blessings [whose formulae] they may lengthen: those for the New Year, the Day of Atonement, and the blessings for a public fast.**

[B]   **From a man's blessings one can tell whether he is a boor or a disciple of the sages.**

[C]   **These are the blessings [whose formulae] they may shorten: [those recited over] the [performance of individual] Commandments, over the produce, the blessing of the invitation [to bless after the meal], and the last meal-blessing after the meal [T. 1:6].**

[D]   Lo, may one then lengthen all other blessings?

[E]   Said Hezekiah, "That which was taught, 'He who lengthens [his blessings] is blameworthy, and he who shortens [his blessings] is praiseworthy,' implies that this is not a valid generalization [and one must be discouraged from lengthening the texts of blessings.]"

[F]   It was taught: On a public fast day one must lengthen [the blessing which concludes] "Redeemer of Israel" [the seventh of the Prayer of Eighteen].

[G]   [The implication of this teaching is] that he may not lengthen those six [other blessings for a public fast day] which he adds [to the Prayer of Eighteen, contrary to T.'s ruling in A that one may lengthen the blessings added on a public fast day.]

[H]   Said R. Yosah, "[No you may not deduce this. But the teaching serves to teach us] that you should not infer that since it [the blessing 'Redeemer of Israel'] is one of the eighteen, one should not lengthen it. And because that [might be your conclusion], it

had to say [specifically], 'On a public fast day, one must lengthen
[the blessing which concludes] redeemer of Israel.'"

[VII.A]   **These are the blessings for which they bow [when they recite
them]: For the first [paragraph of the Prayer of Eighteen at
the] beginning and end [of the paragraph, for the eighteenth
blessing,] "We give thanks," [at the] beginning and end.**

[B]   **One who bows for each and every blessing [of the Prayer of
Eighteen,] they instruct him not to bow [so that he should not
appear arrogant]** [T. 1:8].

[C]   R. Yitzhak bar Nahman in the name of R. Joshua b. Levi, "The
high priest bows [upon reciting] the conclusion of each and
every blessing. The king [bows upon reciting] the beginning of
each and every blessing, and at the conclusion of each and every
blessing." [This shows their piety and humility.]

[D]   R. Simon in the name of R. Joshua b. Levi, "Once the king
kneels, he does not rise until he completes all his prayers." [This
rule disputes C.]

[E]   What is the basis [for this teaching? It is the verse,] "Now as
Solomon finished offering all this prayer and supplication to the
Lord, he arose from before the altar of the Lord, where he had
knelt [with hands outstretched towards heaven]" [1 Kings 8:54].

[F]   What is "kneeling"? And what is "genuflection" [from the word
brykh, which also implies bending the knee]? [Are they different
actions?]

[G]   [The following shows that they are distinct actions.] R. Hiyya
the great demonstrated "genuflection" before Rabbi, and became lame, but was cured.

[H]   R. Levi bar Sisi demonstrated "kneeling" before Rabbi, and became lame, but was not cured.

[I]   [Return now to discuss 1 Kings 8:54, Solomon's prayer, cited
above at E:] "With hands outstretched to heaven." Said R. Abo,
"[That means] he would stand still like these spots [without
moving]."

[J]   Said R. Eleazar bar Abyna, "[He showed his hands to indicate
that he had not personally gained from the construction of the
Temple (P.M.). He wanted to show that,] 'These hands did not
benefit from the building of the Temple.'"

[K]   Taught R. Halafta b. Saul, "All bow with the cantor [when he recites the blessing of] thanksgiving."

[L]   R. Zeira said, "[The obligation is to bow along with the leader], specifically [at the time he recites] the words, 'We give thanks.'" [As he recited,] R. Zeira sought to follow [the leader] closely so that he could bow at the beginning and end [of the blessing, "We give thanks," along with the leader].

[VIII.A]   When R. Yasa came here [to Israel], he saw them bowing and whispering [during the recitation of the Blessing of Thanksgiving in the Prayer of Eighteen].

[B]   He said to us, "What are they whispering?"

[C]   [They said to him,] "Did you not hear what R. Helbo [and] R. Simeon [said] in the name of R. Yohanan in the name of R. Jeremiah, R. Haninah in the name of R. Misha, R. Hiyya in the name of R. Simai, and some say that the associates said in the name of R. Simai? [While the leader recited the blessing, the congregation said in an undertone,] 'Master of all creatures, God of all praises, rock of ages, eternal, creator, resurrector, who brought us life and sustained us, and gave us the merit, and helped us, and brought us near, to give thanks to Thy name. Blessed art Thou, O Lord, God of praises.'"

[D]   R. Ba bar Zabda in the name of Rab, "[The congregation says this prayer in an undertone:] We give thanks to Thee. For we must praise Thy name. 'My lips will shout for joy when I sing praises to Thee; my soul also, which Thou hast rescued' [Ps. 71: 23]. Blessed art Thou, O Lord, God of praises."

[E]   R. Samuel bar Mina in the name of R. Aha said [the congregation recited the following in an undertone], "Thanksgiving and praise to Thy name. Greatness is Thine. Power is Thine. Glory is Thine. May it be Thy will, Lord, our God, and God of our fathers that You support us when we fall and straighten us when we bow over, for Thou support the fallen and straighten those who are bowed over, and are full of mercy, and there is none beside Thee. Blessed art Thou, O Lord, God of praises."

[F]   Bar Qappara said [they recited the following], "We kneel to Thee, we bow over to Thee, we prostrate ourselves to Thee, we genuflect to Thee. For to Thee every knee must bend, every tongue must swear. 'Thine, O Lord is the greatness, and the

power, and the glory, and the victory, and the majesty; for all
that is in the heavens and in the earth is Thine; Thine is the
kingdom, O Lord, and Thou art exalted as head above all. Both
riches and honor come from Thee, and Thou rulest over all. In
Thy hand are power and might; and in Thy hand it is to make
great and to give strength to all. And now we thank Thee, our
God, and praise Thy glorious name'" [1 Chron. 29:11–13].

[G]   "With all our heart, and with all our soul we prostrate ourselves.
All my bones shall say, 'O Lord, who is like Thee, Thou who
deliverest the weak from him who is too strong for him, the
weak and needy from him who despoils him?' [Ps. 35:10].
Blessed art Thou, O Lord, God of praises."

[H]   Said R. Yudan, "The rabbis are accustomed to say all of these
[prayers in C–G in an undertone while the leader recites, 'We
give thanks.']"

[I]   And some say, "[They said only] one or the other of these
[prayers]."

[IX.A]   It was taught: [One may bow during prayer] as long as he does
not bow too much.

[B]   Said R. Jeremiah, "[One may bow during prayer] provided he
does not position himself like a turtle [that is, bow his body
down while holding the head up]. Rather [one must bow every
bone in his body as the verse implies,] 'All my bones shall say,
O Lord, who is like Thee'" [Ps. 35:10]. [The verse also suggests that one must bow before reciting the name of God.]

[C]   A tradition of Hanan bar Ba disputes this [latter teaching]. For
Hanan bar Ba said to his associates, "Let me tell you about
something good which I saw Rab do. [He bowed in a certain
way during his prayer,] and I described this in front of Samuel,
and he got up and kissed me on the mouth."

[D]   [And this is what Rab did. When he said,] "Blessed art Thou,"
he bowed. When he mentioned the name [of God, "O Lord,"]
he straightened up. [Rab straightened before reciting the name
of God.]

[E]   Samuel said, "I will tell you that the basis for this [Rab's action
is the verse,] 'The Lord lifts up those who are bowed down'"
[Ps. 146:8]. [Accordingly, when one who is bowed down recites
the name of the Lord, he should straighten up.]

[F]   Said R. Ammi, "This does not stand to reason [because another verse says,] 'He bowed in awe of my name'" [Mal. 2:5].

[G]   Said R. Abin, "If it was written in the verse, 'At my name [bšmy] he bowed,' very well, [i.e., that would contradict Rab's practice.] But is it not written, 'He bowed in awe of my name?' [That could mean] previously, before he mentioned the name, that he was already bowing down." [It could then be said that when he mentioned God's name, he straightened up. That is not a contradiction of Rab's custom.]

[H]   R. Samuel bar Nathan in the name of R. Hama bar Haninah, "Once a [leader of the service] bowed too much and Rabbi removed him [from leading the service]."

[I]   R. Ammi said, "R. Yohanan used to remove [a leader who bowed too much]." Said to him R. Hiyya bar Ba, "He [Yohanan] would not remove him. Rather he reprimanded him [to stop bowing so much]."

[X.A] **These are the blessings which begin with [the formula] "Blessed [art Thou . . .]." All the blessings begin with 'Blessed,' [except the blessings which adjoin the recitation of the *Shema'* and any blessing which adjoins another blessing. They need not begin these with [the formula] 'Blessed' [T. 1:9]].**

[B]   And if a blessing adjoined another as in the case of the recitation of the *Shema'* or the Prayer, they do not have to begin these with 'Blessed.'

[C]   R. Jeremiah objected, "What about the 'Redemption' [i.e., the blessing recited after the Hallel in the Passover Seder liturgy? Is it not a blessing that adjoins another? Yet it begins with 'Blessed']."

[D]   This case is different. [It is not a good example of a blessing which adjoins another. How so?] As R. Yohanan said, "If one heard the Hallel recited in the synagogue, he fulfills his obligation." [One must omit it from the Seder liturgy at home. In such a case the Redemption blessing will not adjoin another blessing. Hence, it must begin with 'Blessed,' and Jeremiah's objection is of no consequence. T.'s rule still holds true.]

[E]   R. Eliezer b. R. Yosah objected before R. Yosah, "What about the conclusion [of the Redemption blessing]?" [It ends with a formulaic sentence beginning with 'Blessed.' Why does it follow this form, beginning and ending with 'Blessed'?]

[F]   He said to him, "This blessing is really two blessings. One for the future [redemption]. One for the past [redemption]."

[G]   They raised another objection, "What about the Prayer of Division?" [The blessing of the Prayer of Division recited on Saturday night adjoins the blessing for the light, yet it begins with 'Blessed.']

[H]   This case is different. [There may be some cases where it is not an instance of a blessing that adjoins another. Thus the Prayer of Division blessing must begin with blessed.] As R. Ba bar Zabda said, "Rabbi used to split up [his recitation of the blessings of the Prayer of Division service] and afterward repeat them together over a cup of wine." [Because in some instances they may be recited separately, each needs to have a complete opening formula of its own.]

[I]   R. Hiyya, the great, used to gather them together [and say all the blessings of the Prayer of Division service at once].

[J]   They raised another objection [to B based on the rule for the blessing following the meal], "What about [the invitation to recite the blessings after the meal,] 'Let us recite the blessings.' [Does it not adjoin the first blessing of the meal? Why then does that first meal blessing begin with the formula 'Blessed'?]"

[K]   This case is different. If [only] two people sat and ate, they do not say, "Let us recite the blessings." [They do not extend an invitation to recite the blessings unless three or more eat together. Hence the first blessing must contain a full opening formula in case they say it without the preceding invitation.]

[L]   What about [the conclusion of the first blessing after the meal], "He who sustains all?" [Why does it conclude with a full formula?]

[M]   That is a valid question. [There is no adequate explanation for its formulary construction.]

[N]   What about [the fourth blessing of the meal,] "He who is good and does good"? [Why does it open with the formula 'Blessed'?]

[O]   This case is different. For said R. Huna, "When the martyrs of Betar [the last fortress to fall in the Bar Kokhba war] were interred, the [blessing] 'Who is good and does good' was estab-

lished [as part of the blessings of the meal." Since it was formulated apart from the original meal-liturgy, it has a complete
formulary structure and begins with 'Blessed.' It retained that
form when it was added to the original blessings for the meal].

[P]   [How does this blessing relate to the martyrs of the Bar Kokhba
war?] [When we recite,] "He who is good," [we give thanks]
that the bodies did not decompose. [When we say,] "He who
does good," [we give thanks] that they were able to inter them.

[Q]   What about the [Friday evening] Prayer of Sanctification? [On
Sabbath and festivals the Prayer of Sanctification adjoins the
blessing for the wine. Why does it open with 'Blessed'?]

[R]   This case is different. For if he was sitting and drinking while
it was yet day, [and night fell] and the Sabbath began, he [re-
cites the Prayer of Sanctification but] does not say [the blessing
over the wine,] "Who creates the fruits of the vine" [before the
Prayer of Sanctification liturgy. Thus it must have a full formulary structure of its own because in some cases it does not adjoin
another blessing.]

[S]   What about its conclusion? [Why does the Prayer of Sanctification also end with the formula 'Blessed'?]

[T]   Said R. Mana, "The form of blessings is this way [as Yudan
next explains, blessings follow either a long or a short pattern.]"

[U]   Said R. Yudan, "[One who recites blessings of the] short formula begins them with 'Blessed,' but does not conclude them
with 'Blessed.' [At the end of the paragraph he does not once
again recite a short-blessing formula.]

[V]   "[One who recites blessings of the] long formula begins them
with 'Blessed' and concludes them with 'Blessed.'" [At the end
of the paragraph he recites another short-blessing formula. For
Mana and Yudan the relative position or context of a blessing
does not determine its composition.]

[XI.A]   [A rule regarding the recitation of blessings:] [The efficacious-
ness of] a blessing is determined by [the correct recitation of the
blessing at] its conclusion. [That is if one erred and at first recited
the wrong formula for the blessing but concluded with the correct
formula for the blessing, that constitutes valid recitation.]

[B]   [Another rule which seems to contradict the previous is,] They
do not split up the recitation of a blessing. [One does not say

parts of a blessing separately; for it to be effective, one must say the entire blessing correctly.]

[C]   R. Yitzhak b. R. Eleazar objected before R. Yosah, "Since you say, 'It is based on its conclusion,' [how can you also say,] 'One does not split up the recitation of a blessing'?" [B appears to contradict A. If one recites the wrong concluding or starting formula, it is as if he has split up the blessing.]

[D]   He said, "Take a look at this kid. He thought, What does ['a blessing] is based on its conclusion' mean? [It means] that if one was standing reciting the morning prayer and he forgot and mentioned the [formula of the] evening prayer and then returned and ended [his recitation properly] with the [conclusion] for the morning liturgy, he then fulfilled his obligation."

[E]   [But this is not the correct interpretation of this statement. Rather it means that the conclusion of the liturgy of all long blessings makes reference to its main theme. For example, the first blessing of the Prayer of Eighteen ["Shield of Abraham"] refers to the preceding theme of the liturgy, God as "protector" (P.M.)] [Accordingly,] said R. Aha, "All blessings resemble [in content], their conclusions [i.e., the formulary close of the liturgy]."

[F]   And those who say, "Shout and sing for joy, O inhabitant of Zion" [Isa. 12:6] [in the third blessing of the meal [S.H., Schwab]], this is [not a case of] a split-up blessing.

Unit I supplies brief statements about M.'s rules regarding the blessings before and after the *Shema'*. Unit II A–B gives a straightforward explanation of the obligation to recite the *Shema'* twice a day. C–S adds a lengthy homily connecting the Ten Commandments with the Recitation of the *Shema'*.

Unit III cites a passage from M. Tamid and analyzes it in A–E. F–J explains why the Ten Commandments and the Story of Balaam are not part of the daily liturgy. One might assume that these were once part of the regular cycle of prayers, but were removed. K–O continues the discussion of the passage from M. Tamid.

Unit IV asks whether the blessings of the *Shema'* may replace other blessings. The unit gives further rules regarding the obligation to recite blessings before Torah study. Unit V provides various traditions regarding the recitation of the *Shema'* at a late hour. Unit **VI** cites T. and discusses the issue of long and short prayers. Unit **VII** cites the next passage from T. and brings together various traditions regarding the practice to bow during the recitation of the Prayer.

Unit **VIII** deals with prayers that are said in an undertone during the leader's recitation of the "Thanksgiving" blessing in the Prayer of Eighteen. Unit **IX** takes up various traditions regarding customs for bowing during the recitation of one's prayers. Unit **X** examines the important issue of the formulary patterns of various blessings. That unit establishes a basic dichotomy between the long and short formulae. Unit **XI** deals appropriately with the closing formula of blessings and inquires about the ramifications of splitting up one's recitation of blessings.

1:5

[A]   *They mention the exodus from Egypt at night.*

[B]   *Said R. Eleazar b. Azariah to them, "I am like a seventy year old and was not worthy [of understanding why] the exodus from Egypt [in the third paragraph of the* Shema'] *is said [in the recitation] at night until Ben Zoma expounded it."*

[C]   *As it says, "So that all the days of your life you may remember the day when you came out of the land of Egypt"* [Deut. 16:3].

[D]   *"The days of your life" [implies only] the days. "All the days of your life" [includes] the nights.*

[E]   *And sages say, " 'The days of your life' [includes only your life in] this world. 'All the days of your life' also encompasses the messianic age."*

[I.A]   [Why does it say concerning Eleazar b. Azariah, *I am like a seventy year old?* It teaches us that] even though he achieved greatness, he lived a long life. [He became the patriarch after the deposition of Gamaliel. See Eleazar, pp. 146–59.]

[B]   But this means that [normally, achieving] greatness shortens one's life. [Nevertheless, Eleazar lived a long life.]

[II.A]   They say there [in Babylonia], "He should not begin [to recite] 'And God said' [the third paragraph of the *Shema'*, Num. 15:

37–41, at night.] But if he began, he may finish [reciting the passage]."

[B]   And our rabbis here [in the Land of Israel] say, "He may begin [to recite] but he may not finish [reciting the passage. He must omit the last verse which mentions the exodus.]"

[C]   Our Mishnah contradicts the [view of] the rabbis here [in the Land of Israel]. [For we learned in the Mishnah,] *They mention the exodus from Egypt at night* [M. 1:5A].

[D]   [To resolve this contradiction] R. Ba [said in the name of] R. Judah in the name of Rab, "[They may mention the exodus at night not by saying the verse in Num. 15:41, but by reciting the following:] 'We give thanks to Thee for Thou brought us forth from Egypt and freed us from the house of bondage to give thanks to Thy name."

[E]   [A statement in the] Mishnah [Ber. 2:2] disputes [the view of] those rabbis [in Babylonia]. [For the Mishnah says,] *"And God said"* [Num. 15:37–41] *is customarily [recited] only by day.* [That implies that] the entire passage "And God said" may be recited only by day. [And the rabbis said in A that if one began at night to recite, one might recite this passage.]

[F]   R. Ba bar Aha went there [to Babylonia]. He saw them beginning and finishing [the recitation of this passage, Num. 15:37–41]. [And he was surprised that they recited at all. For he had not heard] that there they say [in a baraita,] "He should not begin to recite the paragraph, 'And God said.' But if he began, he may finish."

[III.A]   But our rabbis here [in the Land of Israel] say, "He may begin, but he may not finish. [He may not recite the last verse, Num. 15:41.]"

[B]   The question was posed to R. Ahya b. R. Zeira, "What was your father's custom? Did he practice according to [the views of] these rabbis [of the Land of Israel] or according to those rabbis [of Babylonia]? [Zeira had moved from Babylonia to Israel.]

[C]   R. Hezekiah said [Zeira practiced,] "According to [the custom of] these rabbis [of the Land of Israel, i.e., not to recite]."

[D]   R. Yosah said, "[Zeira practiced] according to [the custom of] those rabbis [of Babylonia]."

[E]   Said R. Haninah, "R. Yosah's view makes more sense. For R. Zeira was strict and we [in Babylonia] are strict, and we always acted alike."

[IV.A]   We learned, **One who recites the _Shema'_ in the morning must mention the exodus from Egypt in [the blessing which follows the _Shema'_ and begins with the words] "True and upright."**

[B]   **Rabbi says, "One must mention [God's] kingship in [that paragraph]."**

[C]   **Others say, "One must mention the [miracles of the] splitting of the sea and the smiting of the first-born" [T. 2:1].**

[D]   R. Joshua b. Levi says, "One must mention all of these and he must say [in addition], 'The rock of Israel and its redeemer.'"

[V.A]   R. Simon in the name of R. Joshua b. Levi said, "If one did not mention the Torah in [the blessing of] the Land, [the first blessing of the Grace after the meal,] they make him repeat it. On what basis? [Scripture says,] '[So he led forth his people with joy . . .] and he gave them the lands of the nations.' Why [did he give them the lands]? In order that 'they should keep his statutes and observe his Torah'" [Ps. 105:43–45].

[B]   R. Ba b. R. Aha in the name of Rabbi, "If one did not mention the covenant [of circumcision] in the blessing of the Land, or if one did not mention in the blessing concerning the rebuilding of Jerusalem [the third blessing of the Grace] the Kingdom of the House of David, they make him repeat [the recitation]."

[VI.A]   Bar Qappara said, "One who calls Abraham 'Abram' violates a positive commandment."

[B]   R. Levi said, "[He violates both] a positive and a negative commandment."

[C]   "And you shall not be called by your name Abram" [Gen. 17:5] [is the source of] the negative commandment.

[D]   "And your name shall be Abraham" [ibid.] [is the source of] the positive commandment.

[E]   They raised an objection: Lo, the Men of the Great Assembly called him Abram [as we see in the verse,] "Thou art the Lord who chose Abram" [Neh. 9:7].

[F]   This case is different. Because [it merely implies that earlier] while he was [still called] Abram, you chose him [not that later he called him Abram].

[G]   And similarly, one who calls Sarah "Sarai" violates a positive commandment [but not a negative commandment because] only [Abraham] was commanded not to call her [Sarai].

[H]   And similarly, does one who calls Israel "Jacob" violate a positive commandment?

[I]   No. This case is different. The [new name] was added. The first name was not taken away from him.

[J]   And why was the name of Abraham changed and the name of Jacob changed, but the name of Isaac was not changed?

[K]   [Because] these others were given their names by their parents. And Isaac was given his name by God. As it says, "And you shall call his name Isaac" [Gen. 17:19].

[VII.A]   Four persons were named before they were born. And these are they: Isaac, Ishmael, Josiah, and Solomon.

[B]   [Regarding] Isaac [Scripture says,] "And you shall call his name Isaac" [ibid.].

[C]   [Regarding] Ishmael [Scripture says,] "And you shall call his name Ishmael" [Gen. 16:11].

[D]   [Regarding] Josiah [Scripture says,] "Behold a son is to be born to the House of David. Josiah is his name" [1 Kings 13:2].

[E]   [Regarding] Solomon [Scripture says,] "Solomon shall be his name" [1 Chron. 22:9].

[F]   This is the case with regard to the righteous people [God may give some of them names before they are born]. But regarding the wicked people [Scripture says,] "The wicked are strangers from the womb" [Ps. 58:4]. [They are not given names before they are born.]

[VIII.A]   Ben Zoma says, "Israel is destined not to mention the exodus from Egypt in the future age."

[B]   What is the basis for this statement? "And thus the days are coming says the Lord, you shall no longer say, 'God lives, who took us out of the Land of Egypt;' but 'God lives, who took us out and who brought the seed of the House of Israel from the Land in the North" [Jer. 23:7-8].

[C]   This does not mean that the exodus from Egypt will be removed [and no longer mentioned]. Rather [mention of the redemption from] Egypt will be added to the [mention of] the redemption from the Kingdom [of the North]. The [mention of the redemption from the] Kingdom [of the North] will be primary and [the mention of the redemption from] Egypt will be secondary.

[D]   And so it says, "Your name shall no longer be called Jacob. Israel shall be your name."

[E]   They said, "That does not mean that the name of Jacob will be removed. Rather Jacob will be added to Israel. Israel will be the primary name and Jacob will be secondary."

[F]   And so it says, "Do not mention the first [redemption]"—this refers to [the redemption from] Egypt. "And pay no heed to the early [redemption]"—this refers to [the redemption from] the Kingdom of the North, "Lo, I am making a new [redemption]"—this refers to [the redemption to come in the time of] Gog.

[G]   They gave a parable. To what case is this matter similar? To the case of a person who was walking by the way and he met up with a wolf and was saved from it. He began to tell the story of [his salvation from] the wolf.

[H]   Afterward he met up with a lion and was saved from it. He forgot the story of [his salvation from] the wolf and began to tell the story of [his salvation from] the lion.

[I]   Afterward he met up with a serpent and was saved from it. He forgot both the previous incidents and began to tell the story of [his salvation from] the serpent.

[J]   Just so was the case with Israel. Their [salvation from] the later troubles caused them to forget [to mention the story of their salvation from] the earlier troubles.

Unit **I** explains the phrase in the Mishnah regarding Eleazar b. Azariah's age. Unit **II** examines traditions about the difference in practice between Israel and Babylonia concerning the recitation of the *Shema'* at night. Continuing on a related subject, unit **III** discusses rules relating to the recitation of the third paragraph of the *Shema'*.

Unit **IV** cites T. 2:1 and adds a brief comment. Unit **V** takes up the issue of the phrases which must be included in the blessings of the Grace after meals. Units **VI–VIII** conclude the chapter with an interpolated and reorganized citation of T. 1:10–13, mainly unrelated to the earlier concerns of the chapter.

2 Yerushalmi Berakhot Chapter Two

2:1

[A] *One who was reciting from the Torah [at Deut. 6:4] and the time came for the recitation of the Shema',*

[B] *If he had intention [to do so], he fulfilled his obligation [to recite the Shema'].*

[C] *And if he did not [have intention to do so], he did not fulfill his obligation.*

[D] *"At the breaks [between the paragraphs of the Shema'] one may extend a greeting [to his fellow] out of respect, and respond [to a greeting extended to him].*

[E] *"And in the middle [of reciting a paragraph] one may extend a greeting out of fear and respond," the words of R. Meir.*

[F] *R. Judah says, "In the middle [of a paragraph] one may extend a greeting out of fear and respond out of respect.*

[G] *"At the breaks [between the paragraphs] one may extend a greeting out of respect and respond to the greeting of any man."*

[I.A] Said R. Ba, "That is to say [we deduce from M.'s rule at 2:1 A] that [if one omits the recitation of the] blessings, it does not invalidate [his recitation. Ba derives this from M.'s case: a person was reciting from the Torah and presumably did not recite the rabbinic liturgical formulae before and after the *Shema'*. Still, the Mishnah says that if he had the proper intention, he fulfilled his obligation.]"

[B] Said R. Yosa, "If you say [contrary to R. Ba] that one must recite the blessings [to fulfill his obligation, then our M. may be explained as follows:] once he has recited the blessings he must have the proper intention [while reciting] all of the scriptural passages." [That is, according to Yosa one may still infer from this ruling in M. that blessings are a necessary part of the effective performance of the ritual.]

[C]   They asked [concerning R. Ba's inference]: [We know that] one may not interrupt [between the paragraphs of the *Shema'*] even though it is not taught explicitly in our Mishnah. [That is, while reading from the Torah when one comes to Deut. 6:4 and finishes reciting the first paragraph of the *Shema'*, he then must go directly and recite Deut. 11:13–21 to complete the second paragraph.] Here [too, we may argue that] while it is not taught explicitly in our M., we know that [to fulfill his obligation] one must recite the blessings. [We may deduce no conclusion from M.]

[D]   [Now, if we follow Yosa in B to his logical conclusion,] that means that one must have proper intention for all the passages [of the *Shema'* including the blessings, for it is a single act of recitation and hence requires intention throughout].

[E]   Let us learn [that this is not the case] from the following: R. Ahi said in the name of R. Judah, **"If one had intention [to fulfill his obligation] during his recitation of the first paragraph, even though he did not have intention during his recitation of the second paragraph, he fulfilled his obligation"** [Tos. 2:2]. [From T. we may deduce that even though the blessings and Scriptures together comprise one unit and must all be recited, one must have intention only for the first paragraph of Scripture but need not have special intention during the recitation of the blessings. C's objection then remains valid and we may conclude that Ba's deduction is wrong. But we must not extend Yosa's ruling too far either.]

[F]   What is the difference between the first and second Scriptural paragraphs?

[G]   Said R. Haninah, "All that we find written in the latter is already written in the former." If so why not read only one?

[H]   Said R. Ila, "The first is addressed to the individual [in the second person singular]. The second is addressed to the congregation [in the second person plural]. The first is [primarily to teach us regarding the] study [of the laws]. The second is [mainly to teach us regarding the] practice [of the laws]."

[I]   Bar Qappara said, "One needs to have intention while reciting only the first three verses." And it was taught in support of this [in the fourth verse, Deut. 6:7], "And you shall teach them." Up to here you must have [special] intention [to fulfill the commandment to recite]. From here on you may recite [without special intention to fulfill the commandment as one does when reciting something he is studying.]

[II.A]   R. Huna, R. Uri, R. Joseph, R. Judah in the name of Samuel, "One must accept upon himself the yoke of the Kingdom of Heaven [i.e., recite the first verse of the *Shema'* in Deut. 6:4] while standing."

[B]   What [does this mean]? If one was sitting, must he stand up? No. [It means] if one was walking he must stand still.

[C]   It was taught: One must stretch out his pronunciation of the word, "One" [i.e., *'eḥad*, the last word in Deut. 6:4].

[D]   R. Nahman b. R. Jacob said, "[One must stretch out his pronunciation of] only the [last letter,] *dalet* [of the word, *''eḥad'*]."

[E]   Symmachus bar Joseph says, "Whoever stretches out the pronunciation of [the word] *'eḥad*, his days and years are stretched out for him, and his years are filled with goodness."

[F]   R. Jeremiah used to stretch out his pronunciation too long [of the word, "One"]. Said to him R. Zeira, "You need not [stretch it out] that much. But only enough time for you [to have to contemplate upon the thought,] to enthrone Him in the heavens and the earth and the four corners of the world."

[G]   Rab asked R. Hiyya the great, "[Why is it that] I never saw Rabbi accept upon himself the yoke of the kingdom of heaven [i.e., recite the *Shema'*]?"

[H]   He [Hiyya] said to him, "When you saw him put his hand over his eyes [at that moment] he was accepting upon himself the yoke of the kingdom of heaven [and reciting the first verse of the *Shema'*]."

[I]   He [Rab] said to him, "Was he not obliged to make mention of the Exodus from Egypt [by reciting the third paragraph of the *Shema'*, something which Rab apparently never saw him do]?"

[J]   He [Hiyya] said to him, "It is impossible that [Rabbi] did not utter a word [concerning the Exodus at all during the day. Rather, at another time each day he spoke of the Exodus during his teaching and he did thereby fulfill his obligation]."

[K]   R. Tabyomi asked R. Hezekiah, "Does this [i.e., Rabbi's practice] not imply that [to fulfill your obligation] you need to have intention for [the recitation of] only the first verse. [Rabbi covered his eyes for an instant, enough time to recite one verse]?" [This contradicts Bar Qappara in unit **I** where he says that one must have intention while reciting the first three verses.]

[L]   He said to him, "He had enough time to recite [the first three verses] until, 'And you shall teach.'" [Accordingly, Rabbi's actions do not contradict Bar Qappara's teaching].

[**III.**A]   R. Mana said in the name of R. Judah who said in the name of R. Yose the Galilean, "If one interrupted [his recitation] long enough for him to recite it [the *Shema'*] entirely, he did not fulfill his obligation."

[B]   R. Ba, R. Jeremiah, in the name of Rab, "The law follows R. Mana who said in the name of R. Judah who said in the name of R. Yose the Galilean."

[C]   R. Yohanan in the name of R. Simeon b. Yehozadaq, "Also concerning the [recitation of] Hallel and the recitation of the Megillah it is so [i.e., the law follows Mana. One who interrupts his recitation long enough to recite it all does not fulfill his obligation]."

[D]   Abba bar R. Huna and R. Hisda were sitting [together reviewing the preceding law]. They said, "So too concerning the soundings [of the shofar on New Year's day. An interruption whose duration equals the time it would take to complete the sounding of the entire sequence of blasts invalidates the ritual]."

[E]   They went off to the house of Rab. There they heard [the teaching of] R. Huna [Leiden has Hunah] in the name of Rab [MS R omits: Huna], "Even if one heard them [i.e., nine shofar blasts] over a span of nine hours, he fulfilled his obligation."

[F]   Said R. Zeira, "While I was there [in Babylonia], I was in doubt [concerning this law]. When I came here [to the Land of Israel], I heard [the teaching of] R. Yosa in the name of R. Yohanan, 'Even if one heard them over a span of an entire day, he fulfilled

his obligation as long as he heard them in the proper
sequence.'"

[G]   R. Yose asked, "[If two persons heard the same shofar-blast,]
and one needed to hear the first blast [of the New Year sequence
to fulfill his obligation for he had heard nothing yet] and the
other needed to hear the last blast [to fulfill his obligation for he
had heard the entire sequence of blasts elsewhere, except for the
last]—can this one blast serve to fulfill the obligation of both
these persons?" [Yose's question is not answered in the text. But
MH suggests it could serve both, and SH insists on a stringent
decision as it is a case of doubt in a law based directly on a verse
in the Torah.]

[H]   R. Abun bar Hiyya asked, "[How do we figure the time span of
an interruption that invalidates the recitation of the *Shema'*, A
above? The time it takes to recite both] the Scriptural verses and
the blessings? Or the verses without the blessings? Or the blessings without the verses?"

[I]   [And he asked further: "What if one began reciting,] then interrupted for a third of the time it takes to recite the whole, then
continued reciting a bit, then interrupted for another interval of
a third of the time [it would take to recite the whole, and so on.
Do the intervals of interruptions combine together to invalidate
the recitation?]

[J]   [And he asked further:] "Do we measure the time span [of the
interruption that invalidates the] recitation differently for each
individual? Or do we measure according to the average time it
takes all persons to recite?"

[K]   Said R. Matnya, "It makes [no] sense to go according to the
time it takes each individual to recite." [MS R and the parallel
version in Y. Meg. 2 : 2 add the word "no" insisting that an average interval be applied to all cases.]

[L]   R. Abahu asked R. Yohanan, "While I was reciting the *Shema'*,
if I passed by filthy alleyways and interrupted my recitation,
have I fulfilled my obligation?" [According to T. 2 : 17, one is
forbidden to recite near filthy alleyways.]

[M]   He [Yohanan] said to him, "Abahu my son. If you interrupted
for an interval [that itself was as long as the time it would take]
to complete the entire recitation, you did not fulfill your
obligation."

[N]   R. Eleazar went to visit R. Simeon bar Abba [who was ill]. He said to him, "While I was weak I dozed off while I recited the *Shema'*. Did I fulfill my obligation?" He said to him, "Yes."

[O]   R. Jeremiah asked before R. Zeira, "Was it because R. Eleazar knew that R. Simeon bar Abba was particularly scrupulous in fulfilling commandments that he so ruled in this case? Or was it because he was ill that he so ruled? [If so, the leniency should apply only to a sick person.]"

[P]   He said to him, "[The law for this case of a sick person who dozed off while reciting the *Shema'*] is an explicit dispute.

[Q]   "R. Eleazar said, 'He fulfilled his obligation.'

[R]   "R. Yohanan said, 'He did not fulfill his obligation.'"

[S]   They dispute [this rule in the case of one who dozed off during the] recitation of the *Shema'* because it is made up of separate paragraphs [from three different places in the Torah]. But concerning the recitation of the Hallel and of the Megillah, even R. Eleazar would be forced to admit [that interruptions for a nap invalidate the ritual because these are made up of contiguous passages from Scripture in the book of Psalms and the scroll of Esther, respectively.]

[IV.A]   It was taught: [One who wishes to interrupt his recitation of the *Shema'*] to greet his teacher or [to greet] one who is greater than he in Torah-learning—he is permitted to do this. From this rule we deduce that a person must greet one who is greater than he in Torah learning.

[B]   And also from this [next discussion we deduce that same practice.] For it was taught: If one tore [his garment as a sign of mourning for a relative who appeared to have died] and he [the relative] was revived and then died, if this happens right away [after he first tore his garment], he need not tear [his garment again]. If it happens over some time, he must tear [his garment again].

[C]   How long is "right away"? The time it takes to utter [a greeting]. How much time is that? R. Simon in the name of R. Joshua b. Levi, "The time it takes a man to greet his associate."

[D]   Abba bar bar Hannah in the name of R. Yohanan, "The time it takes a student to greet his teacher and say to him, 'May peace be upon you, my teacher.'" [From this we learn that a student must greet his teacher.]

[E]   R. Yohanan was leaning on R. Jacob bar Idi [as they were walking]. R. Eleazar saw them and hid from them.

[F]   He [Yohanan] said, "This Babylonian [Eleazar] did two [improper] things to me. First, he did not greet me [even though I am his teacher]. Second, he did not attribute a teaching to me [see b. Yebamot 96b]."

[G]   He [Jacob bar Idi] said to him, "That is the way they act towards each other [in Babylonia out of respect]. The lower among them [in status] does not greet the greater [among them in status so as not to bother him to respond]. For they uphold the verse, 'The young men saw me and withdrew'" [Job 29:8].

[H]   While they were walking, he [Jacob bar Idi] showed him [Yohanan] a certain study hall.

[I]   He said to him, "That is where R. Meir used to sit and expound. He [Meir] recited teachings in the name of R. Ishmael but he did not recite teachings in the name of R. Aqiba."

[J]   He [Yohanan] said to him, "Everyone knows that R. Meir was a student of R. Aqiba. [He did not have to attribute any teaching to him. All of his anonymous teachings came from Aqiba.]"

[K]   He [Jacob] said to him [Yohanan], "[Likewise] everyone knows that R. Eleazar is a student of R. Yohanan [and he need not directly attribute traditions to him]." [In this way Jacob justified Eleazar's act of reciting one of Yohanan's teachings without attributing it to him.]

[L]   He [Jacob] said to him [later], "May we pass before a procession of an idol?"

[M]   He [Yohanan] said to him, "Do you wish to give it honor [by going out of your way to avoid it, thereby imputing some importance to it]? Rather pass before it and close your eyes [and ignore it]."

[N]   He [Jacob] said to him, "R. Eleazar acted well. By not passing before you [he treated you with reverence]."

[O]   He [Yohanan] said to him, "Jacob bar Idi, you certainly know how to appease someone."

[V.A]   Now [contrary to **IV**.G above] R. Yohanan required that [his students] attribute his teachings to him [whenever they repeated them]. Accordingly, even King David [implied that a person who repeats his words attribute them to him]. He asked [God] for mercy, "Let me dwell in thy tent for ever!" [Ps. 61:4]. [How should one interpret this verse?] R. Pinhas, R. Jeremiah in the name of R. Yohanan, "Did it ever cross David's mind that he would live forever? Rather so said David, 'Let me merit that my words be spoken in my name in the synagogues and in the study halls.'"

[B]   And what benefit is there [in attributing a teaching to another sage]?

[C]   Levi bar Nezira said, "When one recites a tradition in the name of its original author [who has passed away], the author's lips move in unison with him in the grave [reciting the tradition. On account of the attribution the author merits a moment of life after death in the world to come]."

[D]   What is the Scriptural basis for this teaching? "[And your kisses are like the best wine that goes down smoothly] gliding over the lips of sleepers" [Song of Sol. 7:9]. [After death one's lips move] like the wine which glides off of grapes ripening in a basket [if someone recites a teaching in his name].

[E]   R. Haninah bar Papai and R. Simon [explained the verse cited above].

[F]   One said as follows, "Compare this [case in the verse] to one who drinks [spiced] conditon-wine."

[G]   And the other said, "Compare this [case in the verse] to one who drinks aged wine." Even though he finished drinking, the taste remains on his lips. [So too, one who recites Torah. The words remain on his lips after his death. When others repeat the tradition in his name, his lips move along with theirs.]

[H]   [The following relates to Ps. 61:4 cited above at A]: Every generation has its scoffers. What did the wiseacres of David's generation do? They would go before David's windows and say to him, "David, when will you build the Temple? When shall we go to the house of the Lord?"

[I]   And he would say, "Even though they intend to anger me, I affirm that inwardly I am happy [as this verse implies], 'I was glad when they said to me, "Let us go to the house of the Lord'" [Ps. 122:1].

[J]   [The next is a related teaching regarding David:] "When your days are fulfilled [and you lie down with your fathers, I will raise up your offspring after you, who shall come forth from your body, and I will establish his kingdom]" [2 Sam. 7:12]. Said R. Samuel bar Nahami, "God said to David, 'David, I have apportioned for you a full life-span. I have not apportioned for you a shortened life-span.

[K]   ' "Why will Solomon your son build the Temple if not to offer the sacrifices there?

[L]   ' "[Nevertheless I will not shorten your life to hasten the building of the Temple because you perform good deeds for me.] The deeds of justice and charity which you perform are more beloved to me than sacrifices.' "

[M]   And what is the basis for this in Scripture? "To do righteousness and justice is more acceptable to the Lord than sacrifice" [Prov. 21:3].

[VI.A]   Piska: *And at the breaks [between the paragraphs of the* Shema'*] one may [interrupt to] extend a greeting out of respect and respond [to another person's greeting]* [M. 2:1D]. For what purpose may one respond? Out of fear or out of respect [as well]? Let us deduce the answer from the following: *And in the middle [of the paragraphs] one may extend a greeting out of fear and respond* out of fear [so PM's version], *the words of R. Meir* [M. 2:1E]. That implies that in the preceding rule one may [stop to] greet [another person] out of respect and respond [to a greeting] out of respect [during his recitation].

[B]   *"And in the middle [of one's recitation of one of the paragraphs of the* Shema'*] one may extend a greeting out of fear and respond," the words of R. Meir* [M. 2:1E]. For what purpose may one respond? Out of fear or [also] out of respect?

[C]   Let us deduce the answer from the following: *R. Judah says, "In the middle [of the paragraphs] one may greet [another person] out of fear and respond [to a greeting] out of respect"* [M. 2:1F]. That implies that in the preceding rule, he may greet [another person] out of fear and respond [to a greeting] out of fear.

[D]   Until now we spoke of [a case of interruption in] the middle of the paragraph. What about [one who is reciting and is in] the middle of a verse [may he interrupt]?

[E]   R. Jeremiah would remain silent [in such an instance].

[F]   R. Jonah would speak.

[G]   R. Huna [and] R. Joseph [say], "'And you shall talk of them' [Deut. 6:7]. From here [we learn] that you have permission to speak [in the middle] of [reciting] them [i.e., interrupt even in the middle of a verse as R. Jonah did]."

Unit **I** scrutinizes M. through a series of Amoraic statements. Two related issues emerge here. First, what is the status of the blessings before and after the *Shema'?* And second, what is the extent of the intention or concentration one needs to have while reciting the *Shema'?* The section also includes at F–I, a brief comparison of the content of the first and second paragraphs of the *Shema'.*

Unit **II** presents and discusses various customs for reciting the *Shema'* which are related indirectly to the issue in M. concerning the recitation of the liturgy.

Unit **III** gives us a sustained analysis of the duration of the interval which counts as an interruption to invalidate the performance of a ritual. The recitation of the *Shema'* is the main concern of the unit, but the discussion ranges well beyond that issue.

Greeting one who is greater than you is one of M.'s paradigmatic examples of social situations which might cause a person to interrupt his recitation of the *Shema'.* Unit **IV**'s traditions about the obligation a student has to greet his teacher relate indirectly to M.'s interest in greetings.

Unit **V** goes off on a tangent, first taking up the problem of attributing a saying to its author, then on to related topics. Unit **VI** takes up the second half of the M. and works through its implications.

2:2

[A]   *These are the breaks [in the* Shema'*]:*

[B]   *Between the first blessing and the second [of those which precede the scriptural passages of the* Shema'*].*

[C]   *Between the second blessing and [the paragraph which begins]
       "Hear, O Israel" [Deut. 6:4–9].*

[D]   *Between [the two sections which begin] "Hear, O Israel" [ibid.]
       and "And it shall come to pass if you shall hearken" [Deut.
       11:13–21].*

[E]   *Between [the two sections beginning] "And it shall come to
       pass" and "And God said to Moses" [Num. 15:37–41].*

[F]   *Between [the two sections] "And God said" and "True and up-
       right" [the blessing that follows the Scriptural passages].*

[G]   *R. Judah said, "Between [the two sections] 'And God said' and
       'True and upright,' one may not interrupt."*

[H]   *Said R. Joshua b. Qorha, "Why does [the recitation of] 'Hear, O
       Israel' precede [the recitation of] 'And it shall come to pass'?*

[I]   *"So that one should first accept upon himself the yoke of the
       kingdom of heaven [by reciting the first paragraph] and after-
       ward [accept] the yoke of the commandments [by reciting the
       second paragraph]."*

[J]   *"[Why does the recitation of] 'And it shall come to pass' [precede
       the recitation of] 'And God said'?*

[K]   *"For 'And it shall come to pass' is recited both by day and
       night. 'And God said' is recited only by day." [The principle is
       that a more frequent requirement takes precedence over a less
       frequent requirement.]*

[I.A]   Said R. Levi, "The scriptural basis for R. Judah [in G] is [the
        following]. It says, 'I am the Lord your God' [Num. 15:41].
        And it is written 'The Lord is the true God'" [Jer. 10:10].
        [Thus Scripture links together 'true' and 'Lord your God'].

[II.A] R. Hiyya in the name of R. Yohanan, "Why did they say, 'A
        person should put on tefillin, then recite the *Shema'*, then pray'?
        So that he may accept the yoke of the kingdom of heaven com-
        pletely [i.e., he recites the *Shema'* while wearing the tefillin
        which contain the verses of the *Shema'* on a parchment.]"

[B]   Rab said, "One recites the *Shema'*, and then puts on his tefillin,
        and then prays [reciting the eighteen blessings]."

[C]   A teaching [in a baraita] contradicts Rab: Lo, one who was oc-
        cupied with burying a corpse, when it comes time for him to

recite the *Shema'*, lo, he moves [at least four cubits] to a clean
place, and then puts on his tefillin, and then recites the *Shema'*,
and then prays.

[D]   A teaching [in the Mishnah] supports Rab: *A person should first*
accept upon himself the yoke of the kingdom of heaven [i.e.,
recite the Shema'*] and then accept upon himself the yoke of the*
commandments [e.g., the obligation to wear tefillin] [M. 2:2I].

[III.A]   Said R. Yannai, "[One who wears] tefillin must have a clean
body."

[B]   Why did they not make a presumption concerning them [that
one may trust any person who wears tefillin that he keeps the
commandments, such as the laws of cleanness]? Because of the
impostors.

[C]   [Some people put on tefillin as a ruse to deceive their fellows, as
in the following story:] One time a person entrusted an article to
his fellow [to watch for him]. And later he denied [having received it]. He said to him, "It was not you that I trusted [when I
gave you the article]. I trusted the [tefillin] upon your head."
[I thought that it was a sign that you were trustworthy. I was
misled.]

[D]   After recovering from an illness, R. Yannai used to wear them
[his tefillin, all day long] for three days to show that illness
cleanses [the body. His reference above in A to a "clean body"
should be understood figuratively—"clean of sin."] What is the
Scriptural basis for this practice? "[Bless the Lord . . .] who for-
gives all your iniquity, who heals all your diseases" [Ps. 103:3].
[The verse juxtaposes sin and disease. This suggests that disease
removes sin.]

[E]   Rabban Yohanan b. Zakkai never took off his tefillin. Not in the
summer. Not in the winter. And R. Eliezer his disciple also
acted accordingly. In the winter when R. Yohanan could tolerate
it, he wore both [the tefillin of the head and the arm]. But in the
summer when he could not tolerate it [because of the heat], he
wore only the tefillin of the arm.

[F]   [But how is Yohanan's practice permissible?] Is it not forbidden
[to wear tefillin constantly] lest they be exposed to one's nakedness [when one is in the bathhouse or latrine]?

[G]   Said R. Hiyya bar Abba, "He wore undergarments inside [the
latrine and did not expose his nakedness]. And when he went to

the baths, when he reached the bath-attendant, he removed them [the tefillin]."

[H]   Said R. Yitzhak, "He wore them until he reached Jacob the Thermasarius [the attendant outside of the bathhouse]. And when he returned from bathing, he [Jacob] gave them back to him."

[I]   And when he gave them to him, Yohanan would tell this to him: Two arks went along with the Israelites in the desert—the ark of the Eternal [containing the tablets of the law] and the ark of Joseph [i.e., the coffin containing the bones of Joseph].

[J]   The nations of the world said, "What is the nature of these arks?"

[K]   Israel said to them, "This is Joseph's coffin and this is the ark of the Eternal."

[L]   And the nations of the world ridiculed Israel and said, "Is it possible that a coffin goes alongside the ark of the Eternal?"

[M]   And Israel said, "It is because this person [Joseph] kept [the commandments of the Torah] which this one [God] wrote [on the tablets of the law]."

[N]   And why did [Yohanan] tell this [story] to him [Jacob]?

[O]   Said R. Haninah, "He wanted to tell him a teaching of Torah."

[P]   Said to him R. Mana, "Did he have no other teaching of Torah to tell him?" But rather [this tradition is relevant because Jacob made him wait to get his tefillin back]. He wanted to chastise him saying, "Joseph merited being the progenitor of the tribe from which kings descended only because he kept God's commandments. And we merit all of our honors only because we keep God's commandments. And you wish to disrupt us from keeping his commandments. [Hurry up and give us back our tefillin.]"

[IV.A]   In what way does one recite the blessings over them [the tefillin]?

[B]   R. Zeriqan in the name of R. Jacob bar Idi, "When one puts on the tefillin of the arm what does he say? 'Blessed . . . who sanctified us with his commandments and commanded us concerning the commandment of tefillin.' When he puts on the tefillin of the head what does he say? 'Blessed . . . who sanctified us with his commandments and commanded us concerning the commandment of putting on tefillin.'" [B. Berakhot 60b (also 42b) gives

different blessings. For the head: "Concerning the commandment of tefillin." For the arm: "to put on the tefillin." Later
practice follows this.]

[C]   "When he [who wears tefillin all day] takes them off [at the end
of the day] what does he say? 'Blessed . . . who sanctified us
with his commandments and commanded us to keep his
statutes.'"

[D]   And this accords with the one who holds the view that the verse,
"[You shall therefore keep this ordinance at its appointed time
from day to day" (Exod. 13:10)] refers to the statute regarding
tefillin [mentioned in Exod. 13:9]. [Accordingly, there is a special commandment to remove the tefillin after the appointed
time, at the end of the day.] But according to the one who holds
the opinion that the verse refers only to the statutes of Passover
[Exod. 13:6–8, and that tefillin may be worn at night], it [the
obligation to recite a blessing] does not apply. [He has no obligation to remove them at night and so does not recite any blessing
when he removes them.]

[E]   R. Abahu in the name of R. Eleazar, "One who puts on tefillin at night violates a positive commandment. And what is the
scriptural basis? "You shall therefore keep this ordinance at its
appointed time from day to day" [Exod. 13:10]. "[From] day"—
and not at night. "To day"—[the repetition of the phrase comes]
to exclude Sabbaths and festivals [as a time for wearing tefillin].

[F]   But lo, R. Abahu sat and taught at night with his tefillin on.
[This does not contradict the preceding because] they were
on [his head] sideways and fastened on his arm as if for safe-
keeping [but not fastened the way one would fulfill the commandment. So Abahu did not act improperly.]

[G]   [Alternatively] it is possible to say that [the prohibition against
wearing tefillin at night] applies only to one who puts them on
[at night]. But if they were on him already during the day, he is
permitted [to continue wearing them at night].

[H]   (L omits: [Alternatively] it is possible to say that the obligation to wear them persists until pedestrian traffic ceases in the
marketplace [at night].)

[I]   It is possible to say that we derive the rule [that tefillin are not to
be worn on Sabbaths and holidays] from the following: "And it
shall be to you as a sign" [Exod. 13:9]—[you should wear] that

which can serve as a sign for you. [This verse comes] to exclude [one from wearing tefillin] on Sabbaths and festivals. [These days are] entirely "signs" [of sanctity. Wearing tefillin on these days is not an effective sign of sanctity because these days are completely holy to begin with. In Exod. 31:17, for instance, the Sabbath day itself is called a "sign."]

[J]   Is this exclusion not also derived from the [next verse], "From day to day" (Exod. 13:10)]? [Why have we two verses teaching the same thing?] We need both, in accordance with this opinion of R. Yohanan, "Concerning any matter [of practice] which is not clearly evident [from a direct reference in a verse], we bring support for it from several places."

[V.A]   We learned there, *Women and slaves [and minors] are exempt from [the obligations of] the recitation of the* Shema' *and [wearing] tefillin* [M. 3:3A].

[B]   Whence [do we learn the exemption for] women? "And you shall teach them to your sons" [Deut. 11:19] and not to your daughters. Whoever is obligated [to perform the commandment] to study Torah is obligated [to perform the commandment] to wear tefillin. Women who are not obligated to study Torah are not obligated to wear tefillin.

[C]   They asked: Lo, Michal daughter of Kushi used to wear tefillin. And Jonah's wife used to go up to Jerusalem on the pilgrimages, and the sages did not object.

[D]   R. Hezekiah in the name of R. Abahu, "They sent the wife of Jonah home and the sages objected to Michal the daughter of Kushi's actions."

[VI.A]   We learned: **One who enters a bath house, [when he stands] in a place where people stand dressed, may recite the *Shema'* or Prayer (Y. has the reading 'wear tefillin') there, and it goes without saying that he may extend a greeting there. He may put on his tefillin, and it goes without saying that he need not remove them [if he enters wearing them].**

[B]   **[When he stands] in a place where most people stand naked, one may not extend a greeting, and it goes without saying that he may not recite the *Shema'* or Prayer there. And he must remove his tefillin, and it goes without saying that he may not put them on.**

[C]   **[When he stands] in a place where some stand naked and some stand dressed, one may extend a greeting and one may not recite the *Shema'* or Prayer. And one need not remove his tefillin, but he may not put them on. [T. 2:20.]**

[D]   He may not put them on until he goes completely outside the bath house. And this supports that which R. Yitzhak said concerning R. Yohanan, "He used to wear them until he reached Jacob the Thermasarius." [See above **III.**]

[VII.A]   R. Jeremiah posed a question before R. Zeira, "If a bath house is used for bathing in the summer months but not in the winter months, [does it have the status of a bath house in the winter with respect to the recitation of the *Shema'* and the Prayer and wearing the tefillin?]"

[B]   He said to him, "[It has the status of a] bath house even when not in use for bathing. And a latrine [has the status of a latrine] even when [it is not in use and] contains no waste matter. [One may not recite the *Shema'*, the Prayer, or wear tefillin in that place]."

[C]   Mar Uqba said, "A swine is like a moving latrine [and one may not wear tefillin or pray near it]."

[D]   R. Jonah asked, "What is law regarding [reciting the Prayer or wearing tefillin near] dried waste matter on the seashore?"

[E]   Said R. Ammi the physician, "R. Jeremiah taught, 'One removes it with a cloth [before praying nearby].' But they do not rely on his teaching." [P.M. gives alternative explanations.]

[VIII.A]   R. Zeira in the name of R. Abba bar Jeremiah, "[While wearing tefillin] one may eat a snack but not a regular meal, and one may take a nap but not a regular sleep."

[B]   [This teaching accords with another.] One authority teaches that one recites the blessing [for wearing tefillin] once a day, and another teaches [that one recites the blessing for tefillin] twice.

[C]   [P.M. interprets the text as follows:] According to the one who says "twice" it makes sense. [He takes them off when he eats his regular meal and recites the blessing when he puts them back on.] But according to the one who says "once" how is it possible [that he not recite a blessing when he puts on his tefillin after eating?] When he ate he surely did not have on his tefillin!

[D]   Said R. Zeira, "[The one who says one recites the blessing "once"] holds the view of Abba bar Jeremiah [in A] who says that one may eat a snack [without removing his tefillin and this is what he does. Thus he need not remove his tefillin to eat, and does not put them back on with another blessing]."

[E]   R. Zeira in the name of R. Abba bar Jeremiah, "One may not enter the water closet while carrying his scrolls or wearing his tefillin."

[F]   When R. Yohanan was carrying his scrolls he would give them to another person [to hold when he entered the water closet]. When he was wearing his tefillin he would stand with them on [in the water closet].

[G]   A teaching disputes Abba bar Jeremiah: "A person may enter the water closet with his scrolls or tefillin."

[H]   Said R. Zeira, "Abba bar Jeremiah's view agrees with that teaching as well. [He may continue to wear them in the water closet] if he will yet [have some time left to] wear them [while it is still day]. [He must remove them] if he will not [have any time left to] wear them [while it is still day]. [We reason that] since he fulfills no commandment with them [by wearing them at night when he comes out], we should [not permit him] to degrade them [by wearing them into the water closet]."

[I]   At first they used to give them [tefillin] to their associates [when they entered the water closet]. But some [unscrupulous individuals] used to take the [tefillin] and flee. They decreed that they may put them into crevices [in the walls of the facility]. But when a certain incident occurred, they decreed that one may enter with them on. [A student left his tefillin in a crevice. A harlot stole them, came to the study hall and proclaimed, "Look what so and so gave me as my payment." The student, distraught, took his own life by leaping from a roof. B. Ber 23a.]

[J]   R. Jacob bar Aha in the name of R. Zeira said, "That is [he may enter with them] only if there will be time left in the day to wear them [when he comes out]. But if there will be no time left in the day to wear them [after he is finished], he is forbidden [to enter with them]. For since he fulfills no commandment with them [when he comes out at night wearing them] why should he [be permitted] to degrade them [by wearing them into the water closet]?"

[K]   Meyasha, the grandson of R. Joshua b. Levi, said, "Whoever wishes to follow the best practice should make a pouch the size of a handbreadth [for his tefillin] and place them [in it and hang it on his chest] near his heart. What is the Scriptural basis for this? 'I keep the Lord always before me'" [Ps. 16:8].

[L]   They said there [in Babylonia]. "Whoever is not [as pure as] Elisha the Winged-one [see story in b. Shabbat 130a: His tefillin changed miraculously into the wings of a dove in order to protect him from the Romans who sought to kill him for wearing tefillin,] should not wear tefillin [all day long, rather just during the recitation of the *Shema'* and the Prayer]."

[IX.A]   R. Zeira in the name of R. Abba bar Jeremiah, "A person should not enter a cemetery and relieve himself there. But concerning one who did so Scripture says, 'He who mocks the poor [i.e., the dead] insults his Maker'" [Prov. 17:5].

[B]   *dylm':* Once R. Hiyya the great and R. Jonathan were walking in front of the coffin of R. Simeon bar Yose bar Leqonia, and R. Jonathan walked over some graves.

[C]   Said to him R. Hiyya the great, "[Because of what you are doing] they [the dead] shall say, 'Tomorrow they shall join us [in the grave]. But now they trample upon us.'"

[D]   He said to him, "Do they [the dead] know anything [about what the living do]? Is it not so written, 'The dead know nothing'" [Qoh. 9:5].

[E]   He [Hiyya] said to him, "You know how to recite [Scripture] but you do not know how to interpret [the verse]: 'For the living know that they will die' [ibid.] refers to the righteous who are called 'the living' even when they are dead; 'And the dead know nothing' [ibid.] refers to the wicked who are called 'the dead' even when they are alive."

[F]   And whence do we know that the wicked are called 'the dead' even when alive? For it is written, "For I have no pleasure in the death of the dead" [Ezek. 18:23]. Can a dead person die? Rather this refers to the wicked who are called the dead even when alive.

[G]   And whence do we know that the righteous are called 'the living' even when dead? For it is written, "'This is the land which I swore to Abraham, to Isaac, and to Jacob saying,'" [Deut. 34:4]. What does 'saying' teach us? [It means] He [God] said to him,

"Go and tell the forefathers that all that which I contracted with you I have done for your descendants after you." [He is told to go and speak with the forefathers as if they were still alive.]

[X.A] [The unit first cites three traditions of R. Idi, then deals with the subject of prayer.] [A scribe] who connected two letters together [in a scroll]—there is one opinion that it is valid, and there is another opinion that it is invalid.

[B] R. Idi in the name of R. Simeon in the name of R. Yohanan [says there is no dispute]. The ruling that says it is valid [refers to a case of one who connected them together] at the bottom. And the ruling that says it is not valid [refers to a case of one who connected them together] at the top.

[C] For example: two words [whose last two letters are connected together at the bottom, we would say that it is valid. And if they were connected at the top, it should be judged invalid.] But in the case of two words [whose last two letters were connected at the center, in such a case] we have a doubt [whether the scroll is valid].

[D] R. Idi b. R. Simeon in the name of R. Yohanan [L has Yosa], "A person should not stand on a high place and pray." What is the Scriptural basis for this? Said R. Abba b. R. Papi, "Out of the depths I cry to thee, O Lord" [Ps. 130:1].

[E] Said R. Idi b. R. Simeon in the name of R. Yohanan, "A person should not stand up to pray if he needs to relieve himself." What is the Scriptural basis for this? "Prepare to meet your God, O Israel" [Amos 4:12].

[F] Said R. Alexander, "'Guard your feet when you go to the house of God' [Qoh. 4:17]—[means] guard yourself from the drops which fall from between your legs [when you urinate]."

[G] This [Idi's statement] refers to urination. But regarding defecation, if he can restrain himself, he may do so [and pray].

[H] R. Jacob bar Abaye in the name of R. Aha, "'Guard your feet when you go to the house of God'—[means] guard yourself so that when you are called to the house of God [i.e., after you die], you are pure and clean."

[I] Said R. Abba, "'Let your fountain [mqwrk] be blessed' [Prov. 5:18]—[means] may your being called [mqr'] to the grave be blessed."

[J]   Said R. Berekhiah, "'There is a time to be born and a time to die' [Qoh. 3:2]. [This implies that] happy is the person whose hour of dying is like the hour of his birth. [That is] just as at the hour of his birth he is clean [of sin] so at the hour of his death he should be clean [of sin]."

Unit **I** comments on Mishnah, and unit **II** expands upon its general theme, the order and conjunction of the rituals. Unit **III** is a diverse collection of materials whose unifying concern is proper and improper places for one to wear tefillin. The Talmud continues with traditions regarding tefillin in units **IV, V,** and **VIII.**

Unit **IV** continues the digression from the main concern of M., with traditions regarding the blessing for wearing tefillin and the time one may wear them. Unit **V** briefly considers who may wear tefillin, citing first a reference in M. The unit does not resolve whether women may wear tefillin.

After citing the relevant T. passage, unit **VI** adds a brief remark which connects T. with the Talmud's earlier discussion of the practices associated with wearing tefillin.

At unit **VII** the Talmud turns to some traditions concerning prayer in or near a bath house or latrine, continuing the concern raised in its citation of Tosefta. Unit **VIII,** a collection of traditions regarding tefillin, completes Y.'s interest in the matter.

Unit **IX's** miscellaneous tradition and its accompanying story have only a tangential connection to our context through their reference to waste matter.

The last collection at unit **X** presents short teachings on the customs one must observe to prepare for prayer. It provides us with an appropriate conclusion to a long rich series of materials on a variety of subjects and brings us back to our main theme, practices for the recitation of prayer.

2:3

[A]   *One who recites the* Shema' *but does not articulate it [out loud] fulfills his obligation.*

[B]   *R. Yose says, "He did not fulfill his obligation."*

[C]   *If he recited but was not careful about [pronunciation of] the letters [of each word]—*

[D]   *R. Yose says, "He fulfilled his obligation."*

[E]   *R. Judah says, "He did not fulfill his obligation."*

[F]   *One who recites it backwards [i.e., recites the verses or para-graphs out of order] does not fulfill his obligation.*

[G]   *One who recited and erred—he must return to the place where he erred [and repeat his recitation].*

[I.A]   Rab said, "In both [disputes A–B and C–E] we follow the le-nient ruling," [i.e., the anonymous law (A) in the first, and Yose (D) in the second].

[B]   [Why must Rab tell us this?] Without this [explicit statement] do we not say [that the principle is that in any case of a dispute between] an anonymous rule and R. Yose, the law follows the anonymous rule? [Moreover, the principle is that in any dispute between] R. Yose and R. Judah, the law follows R. Yose. So why does Rab have to say that in both disputes we follow the lenient ruling? [It is self-evident.]

[C]   But it is because he [Rab] learned that R. Hiyya [in another version, identified by P.M. with T. 2 : 13] taught [the equivalent of M.'s anonymous rule] in the name of R. Meir. [And the prin-ciple is that in a dispute bewteen Meir and Yose, we follow Yose.] Therefore [Rab] had to [explicitly] say, "In both disputes we follow the lenient ruling [to teach us that we follow the anonymous rule of A in M., not Yose]."

[II.A]   It was taught: "If one recited the Prayer but did not articulate it—he fulfilled his obligation." For whom is it necessary to state this law? For R. Yose. Which [ruling of] R. Yose [appears to contradict this]? That which we learned [in M.], *One who re-cites the* Shema' *but does not articulate it fulfills his obligation. R. Yose says, "He does not fulfill his obligation."*

[B]   [It was taught elsewhere: *All are fit to recite the Megillah except for the deaf-mute, idiot, and minor* (M. Meg. 2 : 4).] Said R. Matna, "[The law that a deaf-mute may not recite] is according to R. Yose [who says in B of our M. that one must articulate his recitation]."

[C]   Said R. Yose [the Amora], "[If not for Matna's teaching] I would have assumed that the rabbis and R. Yose were in dispute only regarding the *Shema'*. For it is written concerning that, 'Hear [O Israel]' [Deut. 6 : 4] [i.e., aloud]. But [I would assume that] they were not in dispute concerning other religious obligations. Since R. Matna said that [the rule in M. Meg. 2 : 4] accords with

R. Yose's view, [I see that he holds the same opinion whether for the *Shema'* or] for all other religious obligations. [Where one must recite, Yose holds he must articulate the words in order to hear them.]"

[D]   What is the Scriptural basis for R. Yose's ruling? "And give heed [*wh'znt*] to his commandments" [Exod. 15:26]—[this means] let your ears ['*znyk*] hear what your mouth speaks.

[E]   Said R. Hisda, "[M. Meg 2:4 does not accord with Yose's view.] The deaf-mute should not appear there [in M. Meg. 2:4's list. It appears there mistakenly] as part of a familiar idiom ["deaf-mute, idiot and minor" which often appear together as a triplicate in M.] [S.H. omits the words which follow: "According to Judah."]

[F]   Said R. Yose [the Amora], "It makes sense that R. Hisda will admit that [M.] Terumot [1:2] follows R. Yose: [*The deaf person who can speak but not hear shall not set aside heave-offering. But if he set it aside, his heave-offering is valid.* The argument is, first, according to R. Judah we need not initially prohibit the deaf person from setting aside the heave-offering. And, second, according to Yose one can be more lenient regarding heave-offering since he must only recite a blessing when he separates it. Reciting a blessing is a rabbinic obligation, not derived explicitly from the Torah. Accordingly, Yose rules that the recitation of the blessing by a deaf person is effective. And so] said R. Haninah in the name of R. Hisda, "[M. Ter. 1:2] is in accord with [the view of] R. Yose."

[G]   Said R. Yose b. R. Bun, "We are compelled to conclude [by virtue of another argument] that it [M. Ter. 1:2] is in accord with R. Yose. For Mishnah first listed five, *[Five shall not set aside heave-offering. And if they set it aside, their heave-offering is not valid: the deaf-mute, the idiot, the minor, and he who sets aside heave-offering from that which is not his own, and a gentile who sets aside heave-offering from that which belongs to an Israelite]* [M. Ter. 1:1], and [the deaf person who can speak] was not included with them.

[H]   "And if you argue that it is because the heave-offering which he separates is not valid, [and that of the deaf person who speaks is valid] lo, M. lists five more, *[Five shall not set aside heave-offering. And if they set it aside, their heave-offering is valid:*

*the mute, the drunk, the nude person, the blind person, and
one who suffered a seminal emission shall not set aside heave-
offering. But if they set it aside, their heave-offering is valid]*
[M. Ter. 1:6], and [the deaf person who speaks] is not included
with them [in the list] either. You must at last conclude that this
[rule] is in accord with R. Yose [and therefore taught separately
at M. Ter. 1:2]."

[**III.**A] The following [phrases in the *Shema'*] require special care
[for their pronunciation lest one combine two words together]:
'*l lbbk, 'l lbbkm, 'śb bśdk, w'bdtm mhrh, hknp ptyl, 'tkm m'rṣ*
[in each case the last letter of the first word and the first letter of
the second word are identical].

[B] R. Haninah in the name of R. Aha [added], "'*śr nśb' 'dny* [the
second and the third words might combine]."

[C] R. Samuel bar Haninah in the name of R. Hoshaiah, "[In the
blessing before the *Shema'*, one must take care to say], 'Who
formed light and created darkness [*hwšk*] [cf. Isa. 45:7] so that
he should not say, 'Who formed light and created brightness
[*nwgh*].'" [One must contrast light and darkness. The word
nwgh is an ambiguous term which can mean brightness or
darkness.]

[D] R. Haggai in the name of R. Abba bar Zabda, "[One should
say,] 'They sang [*šrw*] to you there' and not 'They praised you
[*hllw*] there.'" [In the blessings after the Scriptural passages of
the *Shema'* one must also take care in recitation. The phrase
referred to is not found in traditional Prayer books. P.M. explains, in light of A, that one might run *hllw lk* together to
become *hllwk*.]

[E] R. Levi, R. Abdima of Haifa in the name of R. Levi bar Sisi,
"One must enunciate *lm'n tzkrw*, 'So that they shall remember,'
[so it does not sound like *lm'n tskrw*, 'So they shall hire,' i.e.,
perform commandments for reward]."

[F] R. Jonah in the name of R. Hisda, "One must enunciate *ky l'wlm
hsdw*, 'His mercy is forever,' [so it does not sound like *hšdw*, his
suspicions, or *hs dw*, the mercy of a dualistic divinity]."

[G] It was taught: They do not permit [the following persons] to
pass before the ark [as leaders of Prayer]: neither residents of
Haifa, nor of Bet Shean, nor of Tibon because they pronounce

the letter *heh* like the letter *ḥet* and the letter *ʿayin* like the letter *ʾaleph*. But if any [person from these towns] is able to enunciate properly, he is permitted [to lead the Prayers].

[**IV**.A] Piska. *One who recites it backwards does not fulfill his obligation* [M. 2:3F]. R. Jonah said, "R. Nahman bar Ada taught [the following]." And R. Yose said, "Nahman Saba taught [the following]." "[Scripture says, 'And these words . . .] shall be' [Deut. 6:6]—the way they are [ordered in Scripture] so they shall be [in your recitation of the *Shemaʿ* and not in a different order]."

[B] It was taught: **So too regarding the Hallel, [and the recitation of the Prayer,] and the recitation of the Megillah** [one who recites in the wrong order does not fulfill his obligation] [T. 2:3].

[C] This makes sense regarding the recitation of the Megillah. For it is written therein, "According to what was written" [Esther 9:27]. [This implies that one must recite it in the order things appear in Scripture.]

[D] But what about the [order for the recitation of] Hallel? [What basis is there in Scripture to justify the requirement to recite it in order?] Because it is written [in the Hallel itself], "From the rising of the sun to its setting the name of the Lord is to be praised" [Ps. 113:3]. What may you deduce from this? [That one must recite the verses in order, just as the day has its order.]

[E] Said R. Abun, "[Not only must one recite the verses in order within each paragraph, but the paragraphs themselves] also must be recited in the correct order. [The original order of the Psalms conveys a logical progression in their praises as follows:]

[F] "When Israel went forth from Egypt" [Ps. chap. 114], [refers to the events of] the past.

[G] "Not to us, O Lord, not to us" [Ps. chap. 115], [refers to the events of] the present generations.

[H] "I love the Lord, because he has heard my voice and my supplications" [Ps. chap. 116], [refers to the future events of] the messianic age.

[I] "Bind the festal procession with branches" [Ps. 118:27], [refers to the future events of] the age of Gog and Magog. [The word "bind" is an allusion to the time following the festival; bind over or hold over the festival to celebrate it in the future.]

[J] "Thou art my God and I will give thanks" [Ps. 118:28], [the use of the future tense refers to] the future age [after the messianic conflict and triumph]."

[V.A] R. Aha in the name of R. Joshua b. Levi, "Also when the Prayer was ordained, they ordained it according to [a logical] order [as follows]:"

[B] The first three blessings and the last three blessings are praises of God. And the middle blessings [deal as follows with] the needs of all creatures:

Grant us knowledge.

Now that you have granted us knowledge, accept our repentance.

Now that you have accepted our repentance, forgive us [our sins].

Now that you have forgiven us, redeem us.

Now that you have redeemed us, heal our sickness.

Now that you have healed our sickness, bless our years [with plenty].

Now that you have blessed our years, gather us together.

Now that you have gathered us together, judge us in righteousness.

Now that you have judged us in righteousness, defeat our opponents.

Now that you have defeated our opponents, exonerate us in judgment.

Now that you have exonerated us in judgment, build your House for us, and hear our entreaties, and accept us into it.

[C] But should it not be [in a different order] from "First build the House, then hear our entreaties, and accept us into it"? [Rather only after hearing our entreaties, God should respond by building the Temple.] But [the reason for the variation is that] according to the order of the [following] verse, that is the order of the teaching [by which they decreed the order for the text of the Prayer:] "These I will bring to my holy mountain [i.e., build the House], and make them joyful in my House of Prayer [i.e., hear their entreaties]; their burnt offerings and their sacrifices will be accepted on my altar; for my House shall be called a House of Prayer for all peoples" [Isa. 56:7].

[D] Said R. Jeremiah, "One hundred and twenty elders, and among them more than eighty prophets, ordained this Prayer [of Eighteen Blessings]."

[E]   And why did they see fit to juxtapose [the third blessing] "O
       Lord Holy God" with [the fourth] "Gracious giver of knowl-
       edge"? In accord [with the verse of the prophet], "They will
       sanctify the Holy One of Jacob" [Isa. 29:23]. What is written
       following that? "And those who err in spirit will come to under-
       standing" [Isa. 29:24]. [After sanctification comes
       understanding.]

[F]   [And why did they juxtapose the fourth blessing, concerning]
       knowledge with [the fifth blessing, regarding] repentance? [In
       accord with this verse,] "Make the hearts of his people fat, and
       their ears heavy, and shut their eyes; lest they see with their eyes
       and hear with their ears and understand with their hearts, and
       turn and be healed" [Isa. 6:10]. [After understanding comes
       repentance.]

[G]   [And why did they juxtapose the fifth blessing regarding] repen-
       tance with [the sixth regarding] pardon? [In accord with this
       verse,] "Let him return to the Lord, that he may have mercy
       on him, and to our God, for he will abundantly pardon" [Isa.
       56:7]. [After turning to repent comes pardon.]

[H]   [And why did they juxtapose the sixth and seventh blessings re-
       garding] pardon and redemption? [In accord with this verse,]
       "Bless the Lord . . . who forgives all your iniquity, who heals all
       your diseases, who redeems your life from the Pit" [Ps. 103:
       3–4]. [After forgiveness comes redemption.]

[I]   [But in accord with this verse] one should say [the eighth bless-
       ing concerning] the healing of the sick before [the seventh
       blessing concerning redemption].

[J]   Said R. Aha, "Why did they ordain 'Redeemer of Israel' as the
       seventh blessing? To teach you that Israel will be redeemed only
       in the seventh year [the sabbatical year]."

[K]   R. Jonah in the name of R. Aha, "'A Song of Ascents. When
       the Lord restored the fortunes of Zion' [Ps. 126:1] is the sev-
       enth song of ascents to teach you that Israel will be redeemed
       only in the seventh year."

[L]   Said R. Hiyya bar Abba, "Why did they ordain [the blessing
       concerning] healing the sick as the eighth blessing? It is a refer-
       ence to circumcision which is on the eighth day. In accord with
       [this verse], 'My covenant with him was a covenant of life and

peace'" [Mal. 2:5]. [The covenant, whose symbol is the circum-cision, is associated with life and, thereby, with healing.]

[M] Said R. Alexander, "Why did they ordain the blessing, 'Who blesses the years' as the ninth blessing? In accord with [this verse,] 'The voice of the Lord breaks cedars' [Ps. 29:5] [the ninth use of the term 'voice' in this psalm]. For in the future He will break [the hold of] those who set the prices [too high in order to extort money from the people and He will bring pros-perity]." [The teaching plays on the word for cedars, 'rzym, which may also mean the tradesmen who set the prices of goods.]

[N] R. Levi in the name of R. Aha bar Haninah, "Why did they juxtapose [the ninth and tenth blessings,] 'Who blesses the years' and 'Who gathers the dispersed of thy people Israel'? In accord with [this verse:] 'But you, O mountains of Israel, shall shoot forth your branches and yield your fruit to my people Israel; Why? For they will soon come home'" [Ezek. 36:8]. [Prosperity is linked to the gathering of exiles.]

[O] [As to the order of the remaining blessings:] Once the exiles have been gathered in [the tenth blessing], then justice is done [the eleventh], then the arrogant are humbled [the twelfth bless-ing], then the righteous are happy [the thirteenth blessing].

[P] And it was taught concerning this: One includes the references regarding the heretics and the wicked in the blessing 'Who humbles the arrogant' [12].

[Q] [And one includes references] to the proselytes and the elders [in the blessing] 'Trust of the righteous' [13].

[R] [And one includes reference] to David [in] 'Who rebuilds Jerusa-lem' [14, based on this verse:] "Afterward the children of Israel shall return and seek the Lord their God and David their king" [Hos. 3:5]. [After they return to Jerusalem, they shall seek David.]

[VI.A] [The reference to David in the preceding leads to this digression regarding the Messiah.] The rabbis said, "If this Messiah–king comes from among the living, David will be his name; if he comes from among the dead, it will be David himself."

[B] Said R. Tanhuma, "I say that the Scriptural basis for this teach-ing is, 'And he shows steadfast love to his Messiah, to David'" [Ps. 18:50].

[C]   R. Joshua b. Levi said, "Semah is his name."

[D]   R. Yudan son of R. Aybo said, "Menahem is his name."

[E]   Said Hananiah son of R. Abahu, "They do not disagree. The numerical value of the letters of one name equals the numerical value of the other. Semah [= 138] is equal to Menahem [= 138]."

[F]   And this [following story] supports the view of R. Yudan son of R. Aybo.

[G]   Once a Jew was plowing and his ox snorted once before him. An Arab who was passing and heard the sound said to him, "Jew, Jew. Loosen your ox, and loosen your plow [and stop plowing]. For today your Temple was destroyed."

[H]   The ox snorted again. He [the Arab] said to him, "Jew, Jew. Bind your ox, and bind your plow. For today the Messiah-king was born."

[I]   He said to him, "What is his name?"

[J]   [The Arab replied,] "Menahem."

[K]   He said to him, "And what is his father's name?"

[L]   He [the Arab] said to him, "Hezekiah."

[M]   He said to him, "Where is he from?"

[N]   He said to him, "From the royal capital of Bethlehem in Judea."

[O]   He [the Jew] went and sold his ox and sold his plow. And he became a peddler of infants' clothes [diapers]. And he went from place to place until he came to that very city. All of the women bought from him. But Menahem's mother did not buy from him.

[P]   He heard the women saying, "Menahen's mother, Menahem's mother, come buy for your child."

[Q]   She said, "I want to choke this enemy of Israel. For on the day he was born, the Temple was destroyed."

[R]   He [this Jew] said to her, "We are sure that on this day it was destroyed, and on this day [of the year] it will be rebuilt. [Do not abandon the child. Provide for him.]"

[S]   She said to him [the peddler], "I have no money."

[T]   He said to her, "It is of no matter to me. Come and buy for him and if you have no money, pay me when I return."

[U]   After a while he returned. He went up to that place.

[V]   He said to her, "What happened to the infant?"

[W]   She said to him, "Since the time you saw him a spirit came and carried him up and took him away from me."

[X]   Said R. Bun, "Why must we learn this [that the Messiah was born on the day that the Temple was destroyed] from [a story about] an Arab? Do we not have explicit Scriptural evidence for it? 'Lebanon with its majestic trees will fall' [Isa. 10:34]. And what follows this? 'There shall come forth a shoot from the stump of Jesse' [Isa. 11:1]. [Right after an allusion to the destruction of the Temple, the prophet speaks of the Messiah.]"

[VII.A]   [Now we return to the discussion begun in unit V regarding the Prayer.] Said R. Tanhuma, "Why did they ordain 'Who harkens to Prayer' as the fifteenth [in the standard service it is the sixteenth] blessing [of the Prayer]? In accord with the verse, 'The Lord sits enthroned over the flood' [Ps. 29:10]. [This is the fifteenth occurrence of the Lord's name in the Psalm.] He [hears our prayers and] withholds punishment from the world [as he withholds another deluge]."

[B]   [Why is the blessing concerning] the Temple service [juxtaposed] to the blessing of Thanksgiving [the standard service's seventeenth and eighteenth blessings]? [In accord with this verse,] "He who brings thanksgiving as his sacrifice honors me; to him who orders his way aright I will show the salvation of God!" [Ps. 50:23]. [The verse links Thanksgiving and the Temple service.]

[C]   And [the Prayer] concludes with the blessing for peace because all [the priestly] blessings conclude with [the word] 'Peace.'

[D]   Said R. Simeon b. Halafta, "There is no stronger way to conclude one's blessings than with [the word] 'Peace.' And what is the Scriptural basis for this? 'May the Lord give strength to his people! May the Lord bless his people with peace!'" [Ps. 29:11].

[VIII.A]   *One who recited and erred, he must return to the place where he erred [and recite again]* [M. 2:3G]. **If one errs and skips from the first phrase, 'And you shall write them' [Deut. 6:9] to the**

second phrase, 'And you shall write them' [Deut. 11:20], he
returns to the first phrase [and recites to the end]. If one errs,
and does not know where he erred, he returns to the first
place he knows clearly [that he recited]. [Cf. T. 2:5.]

[B]   *dylm':* Once R. Hiyya, R. Yasa, and R. Ammi went off to set up
the marriage canopy for R. Eleazar. They heard R. Yohanan's
voice.

[C]   [They said,] "He may speak of some new subject. Who will go
down to hear it from him?"

[D]   They said, "Let R. Eleazar go down for he is the most indus-
trious scholar [among us]."

[E]   He went down and came back and told them, "This is what R.
Yohanan said, 'One who resided and [his attention lapsed and]
he found himself reciting "That your days . . ." [Deut. 11:21],
the presumption is that he recited it straight through [to that
place properly].'"

[F]   R. Lya [perhaps La or Ila], [and] R. Yasa in the name of R. Aha
the great, "One who was reciting the Prayer, and found himself
reciting the blessing, 'Who harkens to Prayer' [the sixteenth],
the presumption is that he recited straight through [to that
place]."

[G]   R. Jeremiah in the name of R. Eleazar, "One who was reciting
the prayer and his concentration lapsed, if he knows that he
can go back and concentrate, he should go back and recite
the Prayer. And if not, he should not go back and recite the
Prayer."

[H]   Said R. Hiyya the great, "In all my days I never concentrated
[properly on my Prayer. P.M. explains that he was involved
deeply in his study.] One time I wanted to concentrate and I
meditated. And I said to myself, 'Who goes up first before the
king? The *Arkafta* [a high dignitary in Persia (Jastrow, p. 73)]
or the Exilarch?'" [To induce the proper state of mind to help
him concentrate on his prayers he thought about the Persian
hierarchy.]

[I]   Samuel said, "I count the birds [or clouds, to help me induce
the proper state of mind]."

[J]   R. Bun bar Hiyya said, "I count rows of bricks [in a building
to aid me in achieving the proper state of mind]."

[K]   Said R. Matna, "I consider myself lucky. For when I reach the
       Thanksgiving blessing [the eighteenth], I bow instinctively. [I
       need employ no special means to maintain the proper state of
       mind for my Prayer.]"

Unit **I** cites a teaching of Rab regarding the decision of the law
disputed in the M., then challenges the teaching, and finally
supports it on the basis of a reference to a source in Tosefta.

Unit **II** examines Yose's view that one who does not properly
articulate a formula does not thereby fulfill his obligation. On
the basis of this lemma, the Talmud explores whether Yose
stands behind other rulings in M. Matna and the Amora Yose
argue the issue. The unit concludes that one anonymous law in
M. Terumot accords with Yose's view.

Unit **III**.A, B, and E provide further traditions on the pronunciation of elements of the *Shema'*, a subject in M. C–D and
F give us further rules on pronouncing other formulae. G ends
the unit with a statement about public recitation by persons
with strong regional accents.

Unit **IV** first cites Tosefta and seeks Scriptural bases to justify the requirement to recite the *Shema'*, Megillah, and Hallel
in their correct order. The last teaching about the order of the
paragraphs of the Hallel also provides an important eschato-
logical interpretation of the liturgy.

Because of M.'s interest in reciting the *Shema'* in the correct
order, the redactor introduced next unit **V**. The entire section
deals with the order of the paragraphs of the Prayer of Eighteen
Blessings and provides verses to justify the organization of the
Prayer.

The story at unit **VI** gives us some insight into the Talmud's
theology but it has no connection to the subject matter of our M.
After the digression of unit **VI**, unit **VII** completes the analysis
begun in unit **V** of the order of the blessings of the Prayer of
Eighteen.

Unit **VIII** deals with rules concerning one who errs in his
recitation and with the subject of concentration during prayer.
B–F speak of the presumptions one may make about his regular
recitation of prayers. If a person's mind wanders, how much can
he assume he recited once he redirects his attention? G deals
with the case of lapsed concentration. The remainder of the unit
discusses the mental devices some rabbis used to enhance their
concentration.

2:4

[A]   *Craftsmen may recite [the* Shema'*] from atop a tree or atop a scaffold—something which they are not permitted to do for the [recitation of the] Prayer.*

[I.A]   We must emend the Mishnah as follows: Workers may recite [the *Shema'*] from atop a tree and craftsmen from atop a scaffold.

[B]   And it was taught: **[Workers may recite [the *Shema'*] from atop a tree,] and they may recite the Prayer from atop an olive tree or from atop a fig tree.**

[C]   **But from all other kinds of trees one must come down to recite the Prayer below.**

[D]   **And the householder must always come down and recite the Prayer below** [T. 2:8]. [Though craftsmen are accustomed to the height, they are not as adept as fruit pickers who work in the trees and so may not recite the *Shema'* while up in a tree.]

[E]   And why [does T. say workers need not come down from] atop an olive tree or a fig tree?

[F]   R. Abba and R. Simon both say, "Because it is a great trouble [to the householder to have his workers take the time to come down from these trees to recite the *Shema'* or recite the Prayer and then to go back up.]"

[G]   It was taught: **The porter—even with his burden on his shoulder, lo, he may recite the *Shema'*.**

[H]   **But when he is [loading or] unloading, he may not [start to] recite because he cannot concentrate [properly].**

[I]   **In any case he may not recite the Prayer until he unloads.**

[J]   **But if his burden is [less than] four qabs, he is permitted [to recite the Prayer while it is on his shoulder]** [T. 2:7].

[K]   Said R. Jonathan, "This is so if he balanced his load."

[L]   What is meant by "balanced his load"? [It means he placed] two bundles behind him and one in front of him.

[M]   It was taught: One may not gesture with his eyes and recite [the *Shema'* at the same time. This action shows that he is not concentrating.]

[II.A]   It was taught: **Workers who were working with the house-holder [and stopped to eat], lo, they recite [two blessings after eating].**

[B]   [They say] the first blessing and then include the [third blessing] concerning Jerusalem in [their second] concerning the Land and conclude [their second blessing with the usual conclusion for the second blessing] concerning the Land.

[C]   **But if they were working with him [in return for a] meal or if the householder was eating with them, lo, they recite four blessings** [T. 5 : 24].

[D]   Said R. Mana, "That [rule in T. 5 : 24] implies that one may not do work at the time he is reciting a blessing. For if this is not so, why did we have to say that he may do work and recite the blessings [at the same time]?" [According to Tosefta, the special rule is that the servants recite a shorter version of the blessings following the meal.]

[III.A]   R. Samuel bar R. Yitzhak in the name of R. Huna, "A person may not stand and recite the Prayer while he holds coins in his hands." [He is concerned not to drop them and will not concentrate on his prayer.]

[B]   (GRA adds: "And if they were wrapped around him in a pouch" [see Luncz, p. 21b, n. 10]) in front of him he is forbidden [to recite the Prayer], in back of him, he is permitted [to recite the Prayer for they are out of sight and out of mind.]

[C]   R. Yasa used to bind them [in a pouch] and hold them in his hand [while praying].

[D]   And we learned in accord with this: Said R. Yitzhak, "'And bind up the money in your hand' [Deut. 14 : 25]—specifically in your hand." [One who binds up money in this way will not worry.]

[E]   R. Yose bar Abun instructed R. Hillel, his son-in-law, as follows: R. Hezekiah and R. Jacob bar Aha were sitting in one place and R. Jacob bar Aha had with him some coins. The time came to recite the Prayer and he tied [the coins up] and gave them to R. Hezekiah [to hold for him. He watched to see what Hezekiah would do.]

[F]   He [Hezekiah] tied the ends [adding knots to the pouch] and bound them with a strap.

[G]   He [Jacob] said to him, "How [with these actions, do you account for the verse,] 'In your hand.' [No matter how well you tie it, to properly guard it, you must have it in your hand.]"

[IV.A]   Said R. Hanina, "Even one [priest] who is carrying the water [of the sin-offering] on his shoulders, lo, he may recite the *Shema*ʿ and recite the Prayer." [The law is that if one diverts his attention from this water, it becomes unfit. Since the rule is that he still may recite the *Shema*ʿ and recite the Prayer while carrying the water, we conclude that these latter acts do not require one's concentration.] [Cf. M. Parah 7:9.]

[B]   R. Huna said, "Does the recitation of the *Shema*ʿ and the recitation of the Prayer not require concentration?" [When he concentrates on his recitation, he diverts his attention from the water and it should be rendered unfit.]

[C]   Said R. Mana, "I posed this question before R. Pinhas, 'Even if one says [rhetorically], Does the recitation of the *Shema*ʿ require concentration? [it implies that only the first verse does, and that is why the water remains fit, if he recites the *Shema*ʿ while he is carrying it]. Can we [then] say, Does the recitation of the Prayer not require concentration? [It certainly does throughout. And according to Hanina the water should be unfit.]'"

[D]   Said R. Yose, "I can uphold it [Hanina's rule] according to that which R. Jacob bar Aha said in the name of R. Yohanan: 'You are forced to say that [the case here is one of a priest who was carrying the water] during the last part of the Water-ritual. There is no support in the Torah [to say that diverting one's attention at this point renders the water unfit].' [Since it is a rabbinic law, not a direct Torah law, that one must not divert his attention while carrying the water of the sin-offering, the rabbis could allow a person to recite the Prayer or recite the *Shema*ʿ while performing this ritual.]"

Unit **I**, A–N, cite and discuss the relevant Tosefta passage, followed by a single miscellaneous rule inserted here without regard for the redactional context. Unit **II** cites T. concerning the blessings some workers may recite while they serve at the meal and adds to its some remarks.

Unit **III** takes up how one deals with a subject not broached directly in M.—the distraction of guarding one's money from theft during the recitation of one's prayers.

Unit **IV** asks about concentration and diversion during recitation based on the rules for a Temple rite which requires uninterrupted concentration.

2:5

[A]   *A bridegroom is exempt from the recitation of the Shema' from the first night [after the wedding] until after the Sabbath*

[B]   *if he did not consummate the marriage.*

[C]   *Once: R. Gamaliel recited [the Shema'] on the first night after his marriage.*

[D]   *His students said to him, "Did our master not teach us that a bridegroom is exempt [from the recitation of the Shema' on the first night]?"*

[E]   *He said to them, "I cannot listen to you. [For I do not wish] to suspend myself from accepting the yoke of the kingdom of heaven [i.e., reciting the Shema'] even for a short time."*

[I.A]   R. Eleazar b. Antigonos in the name of R. Eliezer of the house of R. Yannai, "This means that [a bridegroom] is permitted to have initial intercourse [with his virgin bride] on the Sabbath." [M. 2 : 5A allows the bridegroom until after the Sabbath to consummate the marriage. This implies that he may consummate the marriage on the Sabbath, even though they presume this act will cause bleeding, which is not permitted on the Sabbath.]

[B]   Said R. Haggai before R. Yose, "You could explain [that the case in M. concerns one who married] a widow. Intercourse with her would not cause bleeding [as it might for a virgin and, accordingly, it is permissible on the Sabbath]."

[C]   And, lo, we learned [M. Niddah 10 : 1]: *[A girl . . . who reached the age of menstruation and was married . . . the House of Hillel says, "They wait until after the Sabbath,] four days* [to see if she bleeds after intercourse]." And do you wish to say that [the statement,] "They wait four days" [refers there to a case of one who marries] a widow [who then must wait after having intercourse with her to see if she will bleed]? [This inference makes no sense. You must say that both M. Niddah and our M.'s case refer to the instance of one who marries a virgin. We then may conclude on the basis of our M. that one is permitted to engage in the first intercourse with a virgin on the Sabbath.]

[D]   Said R. Jacob bar Zebedi, "I posed this question before R. Yose, [As to the theory of the law of the Sabbath,] what is the difference between this case [of one who engages in the first act of intercourse with a virgin,] and the case of one who breaks a barrel [on the Sabbath] to eat raisins that are inside?" [In the first instance, he may violate the Sabbath by causing a wound, but this is incidental to the main purpose of the act of having intercourse. In the second case, he may violate the Sabbath by breaking the vessel, but this is incidental to the main purpose of his act, to get the raisins to eat from the barrel. Should not both actions be permissible on the Sabbath because the forbidden action is incidental to the main intent of the action? M. Shabbat 22:3 says, *A person may break a barrel to eat from it raisins as long as he does not intend to make a vessel out of the broken barrel.*]

[E]   He [Yose] said to him, "Consider the latter part of M.'s rule, *As long as he does not intend to make of it a vessel.* Here [in the case of one who has intercourse] he does intend to make of her a 'non-virgin.' So he is like one who intended to make a vessel [by breaking a barrel in the case of M. Shabbat]." [Yose argues that the comparison is not valid because the cases are not parallel. In the case of intercourse one cannot separate the act from the result. But one can say that he breaks a vessel for another purpose, in order to get some object out of it or to make a container.]

[F]   R. Yitzhak bar Mesharshia [said], "One may pose this question: What is the difference [as regards the theory of the law] between this case [of having intercourse with a virgin on the Sabbath] and the case of one who breaks open an abscess on the Sabbath?" [M. Eduyot 2:5 says, *One who breaks open an abscess on the Sabbath—in order to make an opening—he is liable; but in order to let out pus—he is free of liability.*]

[G]   He said to him, "Consider the latter part of M.'s rule, *As long as he does not intend to make an opening* [he is not liable to punishment for violating the Sabbath] [M. Shabbat 22:3]. Here [in the case of intercourse] he does intend to make of her a 'non-virgin.' He is like one who intended to make [an opening for the abscess (Y. reads: 'a vessel')]." [As above, Yose responds that the objection is not valid.]

[H]   It was taught, "A person should not have initial intercourse [with his wife] on the Sabbath, because it may cause her to bleed. And others permit."

[I]   Said R. Yose of the house of R. Abun, "The reasoning of the ruling of 'others' is that he [the husband] has intention to perform the act [of intercourse]. The wound comes about on its own." [It is in the category of an unintended forbidden result of a permitted action. One is not liable for that on the Sabbath. Cf. B. Ketubot 10b.]

[J]   Asi said that it is forbidden.

[K]   Benjamin of Ginzak came and said in the name of Rab that it is permissible.

[L]   Samuel heard and got angry at him and Benjamin died.

[M]   And they said about him, "Blessed is the one who was smitten."

[N]   And about Rab they said, "No ill befalls the righteous" [Prov. 12:21].

[II.A]   Samuel said, "All of those laws at the beginning of the last chapter of M. Niddah [regarding intercourse with a child] are laws [for study] but not for practice."

[B]   R. Yannai abstained [after his first intercourse] with a child whom he married who had not reached the age of menstruation. [He imposed a stringency on himself and assumed that the bleeding was due to menstruation. Because Yannai's practice does not follow the law of M. Niddah 10:1, it shows that Samuel's statement in A is correct.]

[C]   They posed a question before R. Yohanan, "Is one permitted to have intercourse a second time [with his newlywed wife on the Sabbath]? [Even the second act may cause bleeding.]

[D]   "[But why is this an issue at all?] We say that we do not presume [in such a case that] the bleeding [from the first intercourse] results from [a wound caused by] penetration. [In accord with Yannai, Yohanan's teacher, we assume it was menstrual blood.] Shall we then permit him to have intercourse [with her] a second time on the Sabbath? [We rule stringently on these matters and she is unclean as a menstruant.]"

[E]   In what case is there uncertainty [about whether or not to permit the husband to engage in a second act of intercourse on the Sabbath]? [In a case] where on the days which intervened [after the first act of intercourse] she was clean [i.e., there was no bleeding. If she did bleed after the first act, and it was menstrual blood, in any case she will be clean on a subsequent Sabbath. The uncertainty is whether they fear that the second act of intercourse may cause bleeding on the Sabbath because of irritation.]

[F]   Said R. Abahu, "I was an attendant at the wedding of R. Simeon bar Abba. He asked R. Eleazar, 'Is one permitted to have intercourse a second time [on the Sabbath]?' And he permitted him, for he ruled in accord with Samuel. For Samuel said, 'One may enter through a tight opening on the Sabbath even if he dislodges pebbles [for this is an unintended result of his act].'" [So too one may have intercourse even if it causes bleeding.]

[G]   Said R. Haggai, "I was an attendant at the wedding of R. Samuel of Cappadocia. He asked R. Yoshiah [whether he could have intercourse a second time on the Sabbath] and he shied away [from answering the question]. He asked R. Samuel bar R. Yitzhak. He said to him, "How can you tell which is menstrual blood and which is blood of virginity?" [It is forbidden to have intercourse with her because of the possibility of menstrual uncleanness.]

[H]   It was taught [in support of this]: "A bride is forbidden to her husband for seven days. And he is forbidden to take a cup from her in order to recite a blessing. [She is unclean and he may have no contact with her.]" The words of R. Eliezer. What is R. Eliezer's reason? [He believes that] some menstrual blood will certainly come out with the blood of virginity.

M.'s case implies that a certain action may be performed on the Sabbath. The Talmud in Unit I analyzes the implications of that inference, based on a variety of sources and arguments. This unit shows how quickly the Talmud may diverge from the main subject of M. and take up one of its incidental implications.

Unit II further develops and extends the discussion of the issues introduced in I. The unit deals first with the issue of intercourse with a child. It then brings up the question of whether the second act of intercourse with one's newlywed wife may be permitted on the Sabbath. Through this case the section investigates aspects of the connection between intent and action in the realm of Sabbath law and looks into various presumptions regarding the rules of uncleanness.

2:6

[A]   *[Gamaliel] bathed on the first night after his wife died.*

[B]   *[His students] said to him, "Did not our master teach us that a mourner is forbidden to bathe?"*

[C]   *He said to them, "I am not like other men. I am of frail constitution."*

[I.A]   Who taught that a mourner is forbidden to bathe all of the seven days [of mourning]? R. Nathan.

[B]   R. Ammi was bereaved and he asked R. Hiyya bar Ba [for a ruling]. And he ruled [that a mourner is forbidden to bathe] all of the seven days in accord with R. Nathan.

[C]   R. Yose was bereaved and he asked R. Ba bar Kohen. (S.H. omits, "regarding R. Aha.")

[D]   He said to him, "Did not [the master] teach us as follows, 'R. Ammi was bereaved and he asked Resh Laqish [for a ruling]. And he ruled in accord with R. Nathan [that a mourner is forbidden to bathe] all of the seven days'?"

[E]   He said to him, "Perhaps there were two cases of bereavement [suffered by Ammi]. We speak of [the ruling received by R. Ammi from] R. Hiyya bar Ba and you speak of [a ruling he received from] Resh Laqish."

[F]   And furthermore [in response to Yose] from the following [we see that a mourner is forbidden to bathe all seven days]: R. Hama the father of R. Oshaia was bereaved. He asked the rabbis [for a ruling] and they forbade him [to bathe all seven days].

[G]   R. Yose asked, "Which 'rabbis' were these? The rabbis here or the rabbis of the south? If you say it refers to the rabbis here, that is fine. If you say it refers to the rabbis of the south, that means that even though all the great rabbis were here in front of him, he went and asked the lesser rabbis [of the south].

[H]   "And if you say [it means Hama asked] the rabbis of the south, [their rulings contradict each other]. Some permit [bathing as in

the following] and some forbid [as in the answer received by
Hama]."

[I]   For it was taught, "In a place where they were accustomed to
bathe after [burying] the coffin, they may bathe. And in the
south they [were accustomed to] bathe."

[II.A] Said R. Yose of the House of R. Abun, "Whoever permits such
bathing [i.e., right after the burial] makes it [just as permissible
for the mourner to engage in it throughout the seven days] as
eating and drinking [are permitted]."

[B]   That which we have been discussing up to now has been recrea-
tional bathing. But nonrecreational bathing is permitted in
accord with [this incident concerning] Samuel bar Abba: He had
sores on his skin. They went and asked R. Yasa whether he may
bathe. He said to them, "In a case where if he does not bathe he
may die, he may bathe even on the Ninth of Ab and even on the
Day of Atonement."

[C]   They saw R. Yose b. R. Hanina immerse himself [in a ritual
bath while he was a mourner] and they did not know whether he
did so on account of [uncleanness because of] an emission, or
whether he did so in order to cool himself off. For, bathing in
cold water is not [considered to fall into the category of] bathing
[and is permitted for a mourner].

[D]   R. Ba ruled in accord with this teaching: R. Aha ruled, "[Regard-
ing] one who came off the road [on a major fast day] whose feet
were sore—he is permitted to bathe them in water."

[III.A] It was taught, "A mourner and a banished person who were
walking on the road are permitted to wear leather shoes. And
when they come to a city, they should remove them. And so too
[people may do the same] on the Ninth of Ab, and so too on a
public fast day" [cf. M. Ta'an. 1:6].

[B]   It was taught, "In a place where they were accustomed to greet
mourners on the Sabbath, they may greet them. And in the
south they would greet them."

[C]   R. Hoshia the great went to a place where he saw mourners on
the Sabbath and he greeted them.

[D]   He said to them, "I do not know the custom in your town, but
peace be with you in accord with the custom of my town."

[E]   R. Yose of the house of R. Halafta was praising R. Meir before the townsfolk of Sepphoris.

[F]   "He was a great man, a holy man, a modest man. Once he saw mourners on the Sabbath and he greeted them."

[G]   They said to him, "Is this how you praise him?"

[H]   He said to them, "What's the matter?"

[I]   They said to him, "[Why did you praise him by saying that] he saw mourners on the Sabbath and greeted them?"

[J]   He said to them, "You should know that was his strength. [He taught a positive approach to life through his own actions.]

[K]   "This incident teaches us that there may be no mourning on the Sabbath. [This is] in accord with what is written, 'The blessing of the Lord makes rich' [Prov. 10:22], this refers to the blessing of the Sabbath; 'And toil ['ṣb] adds nothing to it' [ibid.], this refers to mourning. As it says, 'The king is grieving [n'ṣb] for his son'" [2 Sam. 19:2].

Units **I** and **II** add stories and rules relevant to M.'s main point concerning the custom of not bathing during the period of mourning. Unit **III** extends the discussion to other customs for the period of mourning, including the practice of the mourner not wearing shoes, and of others not greeting the mourner.

2:7

[A]   *When Tabi [Gamaliel's] servant died, he accepted condolences on his account.*

[B]   *[His students] said to him, "Did you not teach us that one does not accept condolences for slaves?"*

[C]   *He said to them, "My slave Tabi was not like other slaves. He was proper."*

[I.A] [B says that one does not accept condolences for slaves in general. It does not specify that they must be one's own slaves. This seems to imply that] one may accept condolences for unrelated free-men. [And we know that this is not the practice. The Talmud answers,] this is how the Mishnah stated the law, *One does not accept condolences for slaves*. [But one should not draw any general inferences from the way the rule was stated.]

[B] It was taught that one time the maidservant of R. Eliezer died, and his students came to him to extend condolences to him, but he did not wish to accept [their condolences]. He went into the courtyard to avoid them, and they followed him. [He went] into the house, and they followed him.

[C] He said to them, "It seems to me that you did not take my mild hint [when I went out to avoid you the first time] and you did not take my more heated hint [when I went in to avoid you the second time].

[D] "Have they not said, 'They do not accept condolences on account of slaves because slaves are [one's property] as are animals'?

[E] "If for unrelated free-men they may not accept condolences, they surely may not for slaves." [Eliezer disputes Gamaliel's teaching.]

[F] [To] one whose slave or animal died—[to comfort him] you say to him, "May God restore your loss."

[II.A] When R. Hiyya bar Adda, the nephew of Bar Qappara, died Resh Laqish accepted [condolences] on his account because he [Resh Laqish] had been his teacher. We may say that [this action is justified because] a person's student is as beloved to him as his son.

[B] And he [Resh Laqish] expounded concerning him [Hiyya] this verse: "My beloved has gone down to his garden, to the beds of spices, to pasture his flock in the gardens, and to gather lilies" [Song of Sol. 6:2]. It is not necessary [for the verse to mention, 'To the beds of spices']. [It is redundant if you interpret the verse literally, for most gardens have spice beds.]

[C] Rather [interpret the verse as follows:] My beloved— this is God; has gone down to his garden—this is the world; to the beds of spices—this is Israel; to pasture his flock in the gardens—these are the nations of the world; and to gather lilies—these are the righteous whom he takes from their midst.

[D] They offer a parable [relevant to this subject]. To what may we compare this matter [of the tragic death of his student]? A king

had a son who was very beloved to him. What did the king do?
He planted an orchard for him.

[E]   As long as the son acted according to his father's will, he would
search throughout the world to seek the beautiful saplings of
the world, and to plant them in his orchard. And when his son
angered him, he went and cut down all his saplings.

[F]   Accordingly, as long as Israel acts according to God's will, he
searches throughout the world to seek the righteous persons of
the nations of the world and bring them and join them to Israel,
as he did with Jethro and Rahab. And when they [the Israelites]
anger him, he removes the righteous from their midst.

[G]   Once R. Hiyya bar Abba and his associates, and some say it was
R. Yose b. Halafta and his associates, and some say it was R.
Aqiba and his associates, were sitting discussing Torah under a
certain fig tree. And each day the owner of the fig tree would
awaken early and gather [the ripe figs].

[H]   They said, "Perhaps he suspects [that we are taking his figs].
Let us change our place."

[I]   The next day the owner of the fig tree came and said to them,
"My masters, you have deprived me of the one commandment
which you were accustomed to fulfill with me [i.e., under my
tree]."

[J]   They said to him, "We feared perhaps you suspected us [of
taking your figs.]"

[K]   The next morning he [thought he would] let them see [why he
picked the figs early]. He waited until the sun shone upon them
and his figs got worm-eaten.

[L]   At that time they said, "The owner of the fig tree knows when it
is the right time to pick a fig, and [at that time] he picks it."

[M]   So too God knows when it is the right time to take the righteous
from the world, and [at that time] he takes them.

[N]   When R. Bun bar R. Hiyya died [at a young age], R. Zeira came
up and eulogized him [by expounding this verse]: "Sweet is the
sleep of a laborer [whether he eats little or much; but the surfeit
of the rich will not let him sleep]" [Qoh. 5:12]. It does not say
whether he sleeps [little or much] but rather whether he eats
little or much. [Even though R. Bun died young and did not

study for too many years, he will still have a sweet repose in the world to come.]

[O]   To what [story] may [the life of] R. Bun bar R. Hiyya be compared? [To this story.] A king hired many workers. One worker excelled in his work. What did the king do? He took him and walked with him back and forth [through the rows of crops and did not let him finish his day's work]. Toward evening, when all the workers came to be paid, he gave him a full day's wages along with [the rest of] them.

[P]   The workers complained and said, "We toiled all day, and this one toiled only two hours, and he gave him a full day's wages!"

[Q]   The king said to them, "This one worked [and accomplished] more in two hours than you did in a whole day."

[R]   So R. Bun toiled in the study of the Torah for twenty-eight years, [and he learned] more than an aged student could learn in a hundred years.

[S]   When R. Simon bar Zebid died, R. Ilya came up and eulogized him [by expounding as follows]: Four things are essential for the [existence of the] world. But if they are lost, they can be replaced [as we see from the following verse], "Surely there is a mine for silver, and a place for gold which they refine. Iron is taken out of the earth, and copper is smelted from the ore" [Job 28 : 1–2]. If these are lost, they can be replaced.

[T]   But if a disciple of the sages dies, who shall bring us his replacement? Who shall bring us his substitute? "But where shall wisdom be found and where is the place of understanding?" [Job 28 : 12]. "It is hid from the eyes of all living" [Job 28 : 21].

[U]   Said R. Levi, "If the hearts of Joseph's brothers failed them when they found [something valuable—the money in their bags] as it is written, 'At this their hearts failed them' [Gen. 42 : 28], how much moreso should we [feel deeply saddened] who have lost [someone valuable—] R. Simon bar Zebid."

[V]   When R. Levi bar Sisi died, Samuel's father came up and eulogized him [by expounding]: "The end of the matter; all has been heard. Fear God . . ." [Qoh. 12 : 13].

[W]   To what [may the life of] R. Levi bar Sisi be compared? [To the story of] a king who had a vineyard, and in it were one hundred vines, which produced one hundred barrels of wine each year.

[As his estate dwindled], he was left with fifty, then forty, then thirty, then twenty, then ten, then one [vine]. And still it [alone] produced one hundred barrels of wine. And he loved this vine as much as the whole vineyard.

[X] In this way was R. Levi bar Sisi beloved to God as much as all other persons together. This is as it is written, "For this is the whole of man [ibid.]." (Var.: Meaning [he loved] this one as much as all mankind [for he was a great God-fearing person].)

[III.A] [The young] Kahana was a prodigy [in rabbinic learning]. [According to legend R. Yohanan caused Kahana to die. Yohanan then prayed and he was resurrected. Cf. Rashi on B.Q. 117b.] When he arrived here [in the Land of Israel], a scoffer saw him and said to him, "What did you hear up in heaven?"

[B] He said to him, "Your fate is sealed." And so it was. He died.

[C] Another [scoffer] met him and said, "What did you hear up in heaven?"

[D] He said to him, "Your fate is sealed." And so it was.

[E] He [Kahana] said, "What is this? I came here to [gain] merit [and study Torah]. And now I have sinned. Did I come here to kill the inhabitants of the Land of Israel? I must go back to whence I came."

[F] He went before R. Yohanan. He said to him, "Where should a person go whose mother mocks him and whose stepmother honors him?"

[G] He said to him, "He should go to whomever honors him."

[H] So Kahana went back to [Babylonia] whence he came.

[I] They came and told R. Yohanan, "Behold Kahana has gone off to Babylonia."

[J] He said, "How could he go without asking permission?"

[K] They said to him, "From the words you spoke to him, he took it that he had permission [to go back to Babylonia]."

[L] When R. Zeira came here [to Israel], he went to have some of his blood let. [Afterward] he went to buy a liter [i.e., a dry measure] of meat from the butcher [to restore his strength].

[M] He said to him, "How much is this liter?"

[N]   He said to him, "Fifty coins and one blow with an iron."

[O]   He said to him, "Take sixty and spare me the blow. Take seventy and spare me the blow. Take eighty and spare me the blow. Take ninety and spare me the blow."

[P]   He got as far as, "Take one hundred and spare me the blow." [And he gave up.]

[Q]   He said to him, "Do as you are accustomed. [Smite me.]"

[R]   That evening he came to the meeting house. He said to the rabbis, "What is the meaning of this evil practice? Must a person who eats a liter of meat first receive a blow with an iron?"

[S]   They said to him, "Who does this?"

[T]   He said to them, "That butcher."

[U]   They inquired after him. They found that he had died, and they encountered his funeral procession.

[V]   They said to him [Zeira], "Rabbi, did you have to go so far [in your anger toward him as to kill him]?"

[W]   He said to them, "Honestly I was not angry at him. I thought it was the custom [to receive a blow]."

[X]   When R. Yasa came here [to Israel] he went once to get a haircut. He wanted thereafter to go bathe in the hot springs of Tiberias. He met a wise guy who smacked him on the neck with a staff. He said, "What a weak neck this man has."

[Y]   [At that very time] an archon [magistrate] was judging a bandit. He [the wise guy] went to stand [hiding] behind a column to laugh at him.

[Z]   The magistrate said, "Who was with you [during the theft]?"

[AA]   He [the bandit] looked around and saw this man laughing and said, "That one who is laughing was with me."

[BB]   They seized him, and tried him, and he confessed to a murder he had committed.

[CC]   When the two of them [the convicted criminals] came out bearing beams [on which to be hanged] they encountered R. Yasa coming from the bath. He [the wise guy] said to him [to Yasa], "Your soft neck has made it hard for me. [It is on account of you that I am going to be put to death.]"

[DD]   He said to him, "That is your own bad luck. Is it not written, 'Now therefore do not scoff lest your bonds be made strong'" [Isa. 28:22]?

[EE]   R. Pinhas, R. Jeremiah in the name of R. Samuel bar R. Yitzhak: "Scoffing brings hardship upon a person. For first it brings punishment and later it brings destruction. First it brings punishment, as it is written, 'Now therefore do not scoff lest your bonds be made strong' [ibid.]. And later it brings destruction, as it is written, 'For I have heard a decree of destruction from the Lord God of hosts upon the whole land' [ibid.]."

Unit **I** develops the main point of M. 2:7, the practices for mourning for one's slaves. E reverses the opening lemma in A and draws the opposite inference from a general rule to a custom regarding slaves.

Unit **II** continues the theme of unit **I**, traditions regarding accepting condolences, with the idea that a teacher may mourn his student. The unit presents several exemplary eulogies. Each draws on verses and parables to extol the virtues of the respective rabbinic leaders.

Unit **III** brings together several stories of rabbis who came from Babylonia to the Land of Israel and through their anger caused death. The unit's link to the context is simply that the eulogies above are attributed to rabbis who came to Israel from Babylonia as in the preceding material.

2:8

[A]   *A bridegroom—if he wishes to recite the* Shema' *on the first night [after his wedding]—he may recite.*

[B]   *Rabban Simeon b. Gamaliel says, "Not all who wish to take [the liberty of reciting] the name [of God by reciting the* Shema' *and its blessings] may do so."*

[I.A]   It was taught: In all matters [of religious obligations] entailing pain [such as a fast], anyone who wishes to single himself out [to observe them] may do so. A disciple of the sages may observe them and will receive a blessing. [Y. in **I** and **II** understands M. 2:8B to mean: Not everyone who wishes to assume upon himself the title (disciple of the sages) may do so.]

[B]   And in all matters [of religious obligation] entailing benefit [such as wearing a special Prayer shawl], not everyone who wishes to single himself out [to observe them] may do so. A disciple of the sages may do so unless they appoint him an administrator of the community [lest people suspect him of taking graft].

[C]   It was taught: They may move over to walk on the sides of the road [on private property] to avoid [walking on] the hardened clay of the roads. And at a time when one sinks into [the mud of the road, he may move over to walk on the private fields on the side of the road] even to a field filled with crocuses [though it may cause considerable loss to the owner].

[D]   Said R. Abahu: Once Rabban Gamaliel and R. Joshua were walking on the road and moved over to walk on the sides of the road on account of the hardened clay of the road. And they saw R. Judah b. Pappos who was sinking into the mud as he came toward them.

[E]   Said Rabban Gamaliel to R. Joshua, "Who is this who singled himself out [as so righteous a person who does not traverse private property even though he is sinking in the mud]?"

[F]   He [Joshua] said to him, "It is Judah b. Pappos whose every action is for the sake of heaven."

[G]   He [Gamaliel] said to him, "Is it not taught, 'In all matters entailing benefit not everyone who wishes to single himself out may do so. A disciple of the sages may do so unless they appointed him administrator of the city'!?" [Even in this matter, where Judah was permitted to benefit by leaving the road, he chose to act righteously. This seems to be a haughty attitude.]

[H]   He [Joshua] said to him, "Behold it is taught, 'In all matters [of obligations] entailing pain anyone who wishes to single himself out may do so. A disciple of the sages may observe them and he will receive a blessing." [Judah did not act in a haughty way. He followed the rule, since walking in the mud is a matter that entails pain.]

[II.A]   Said R. Zeira, "[A disciple of the sages may follow a course of action that will entail for him pain] only if he does not cause others ridicule."

[B]   [The following story illustrates this:] Once R. Meyasha [var: Yasa] and R. Samuel bar R. Yitzhak were sitting and eating in one of the upstairs' synagogues. And it came time to pray. R. Samuel bar R. Yitzhak got up and prayed [interrupting his meal].

[C]   R. Meyasha said to him, "Did not Rabbi teach, 'If they started [eating], they do not interrupt [to pray]'?

[D]   "And [did not] Hezekiah teach, 'Anyone who is exempt from an obligation and performs it is called a simpleton?'"

[E]   He [Samuel] said to him, "Lo we learned, *A bridegroom is exempt. . . . A bridegroom—if he wishes to recite . . . he may recite*" [M. 2:7–8].

[F]   He [Meyasha] said to him, "Does this not apply only to R. Gamaliel [while we would regard another who acted in this way as a simpleton]?"

[G]   He [Samuel] said to him, "I can explain [my actions in interrupting my meal to pray] as did R. Gamaliel.

[H]   "For R. Gamaliel said, *'I cannot listen to you. [For I do not wish] to suspend myself from [accepting] the yoke of the kingdom of heaven even for a short time'*" [M. 2:5]. [Samuel considered Prayer to be a special case and he prayed, even if it caused him inconvenience, even in the presence of others].

Units **I** and **II** extend the main idea of M., that one should not perform religious acts that appear to be excessive. As its example, unit **I** introduces the issue of what lengths one must go to in order to avoid trampling on private property. Unit **II** makes more general observations, drawing directly on our M. for its illustration.

3 Yerushalmi Berakhot Chapter Three

3:1

[A] *He whose deceased relative is lying before him [not yet buried], is exempt from the obligations to recite the Shema' and to wear tefillin.*

[B] *The [first set of] pallbearers, and the [next people] who replace them, and the [next people] who replace their replacements— whether they go [in the procession to the cemetery] before the bier, or they go behind the bier—*

[C] *if they are needed to [carry] the bier, they are exempt [from reciting the Shema' and wearing tefillin].*

[D] *And if they are not needed to [carry] the bier, they are obligated [to recite the Shema' and to wear tefillin].*

[E] *Both are exempt from [reciting] the Prayer [of Eighteen Blessings].* [Y. printed ed. continues here with M. 3:2–6, given below at the appropriate places.]

[I.A] It was taught, *[He whose deceased relative is not yet buried, is] exempt from [the obligations to recite the Shema' and to wear] tefillin* [M. 3:1A]. [Related to this we learned in a baraita:] "A mourner does not put on tefillin on the first day of mourning. On the second day he may put on tefillin. Throughout the entire seven days of mourning, if a new person comes [to console him,] he removes [the tefillin while that person remains with him because it is as though the presence of a new person renews the mourner's grieving]," the words of R. Eliezer.

[B] R. Joshua says, "On the first and second days he does not put on tefillin. On the third day he puts on tefillin. And if a new per-

son comes [to console him] he does not remove them [cf. b.
M.Q. 21a]."

[C]   [Now, to raise a question:] If on the second day he does not
put on tefillin [in accord with Joshua], do we need to say [in
M. 3:1A], *He whose deceased relative is not yet buried is exempt from . . . tefillin?*

[D]   [The answer is, it is redundant. However,] because they taught
[in the M.] this rule concerning the [recitation by a mourner of
the] *Shema'*, they taught [together with it that rule] concerning
the tefillin as well.

[E]   R. Zeira, R. Jeremiah in the name of Rab, "The law follows
R. Eliezer with regard to putting on tefillin [i.e., he may put
them on the second day]. And [the law follows] R. Joshua with
regard to taking them off [i.e., from the third day he does not
have to remove them if someone new comes to console him]."

[F]   R. Zeira asked, "What if he puts on tefillin on the second day
in accord with R. Eliezer's rule? Can he act in accord with
R. Joshua and not remove them [if someone new comes to console him] while [at the same time] he follows R. Eliezer [and
wears them on the second day]?" [This appears to be a self-
contradictory position.]

[G]   Said R. Yose b. R. Bun, "In truth, the law follows R. Eliezer
with regard to putting on tefillin [i.e., he may do so] on the
second day. And while following R. Eliezer, we act in accord
with R. Joshua and do not remove them on the second day
either."

[H]   Then why, if this is true, do we not just say, "The law follows
R. Eliezer [with regard to putting them on]?" [Then we could
infer that the law follows Joshua and that one does not remove
them following the third day. It would be clearer for Rab (E) to
say only that we follow Eliezer with regard to putting on tefillin.
This then would imply that we do not follow his opinion with
regard to taking them off. Why does Rab also add that we follow
Joshua's view, thereby leaving unresolved the issue of what the
practice is on the second day? The Talmud leaves this objection
unresolved.]

[II.A]   Said R. Bun, "It is written, 'That all the days of your life you
may remember the day when you came out of the Land of

Egypt' [Deut. 16:3]. On days when you are taking care of the
living [you must recite the *Shema'* and remember the Exodus],
but not on days when you are taking care of the dead." [The
verse is used to support the exemption of a mourner from the
obligation to recite the *Shema'*.]

[C]   It was taught, "If he [a mourner] wished to be strict with himself [and recite the *Shema'*], they do not allow him to." Why? Is
it out of respect for the dead or because there will be no one else
to bear his burden [assisting in the interment while he recites]?

[D]   What is the difference [with regard to the law between these two
explanations]? [The difference is apparent in a case where] there
was another to bear his burden for him. If you say the reason he
may not recite [the *Shema'*] is out of respect for the dead, [in
this case] he is still forbidden to recite. But if you say the reason
is because no one else will bear his burden, lo, [in this case]
there is someone who will bear his burden [and he should be
permitted to recite].

[E]   But it was taught, "[A mourner] is exempt from taking the lulab." [They do not perform a burial on the festival day. Accordingly, he could not be exempt from taking the lulab only because
of his involvement in the burial. This proves that one is exempt
from the obligation to recite out of respect for the dead.]

[F]   [This is not probative.] We may explain that this refers to [a case
of one who is exempt from taking the lulab on] an intermediate
day of the festival [on which burial is permitted. It could be that
he is exempt out of respect for the dead or because of his involvement in the burial. This case is no proof one way or the
other.]

[G]   But it was taught, "[A mourner] is exempt from the obligation
of hearing the blasts of the shofar." In this case can you say it
refers to an intermediate day? No, it must refer to a festival day
[because the shofar is sounded on the New Year festival days
only. Accordingly, the reason one does not recite the *Shema'* must
be out of respect for the dead, and not because he is involved
with the burial.]

[H]   Said R. Haninah, "[From this case of the shofar on the New
Year there is still no proof one way or the other.] Because [even
on the festival] one is obliged to bring a coffin and shrouds [for
the deceased] in accord with that which was taught [M. Shab.

24 : 2]: *They may await nightfall at the Sabbath limit to see to the business of a bride or of a corpse, to bring for it a coffin and a shroud, flutes and weepers.*

[I]   "[Even on the festival day, as on the Sabbath, he may have tasks to do for the deceased. It is no different from an ordinary case of] one who has a burden to bear [for the burial. On the New Year festival either reason for the exemption from his obligation may apply and we have no proof one way or the other.]" [The question remains unresolved. If there is someone who will attend to his tasks for him, we do not know whether the mourner is exempt.]

[**III.A**]   When do they turn over the beds [making them lower to the floor in a house of mourning, as a sign of mourning]?

[B]   "When the body is taken out through the courtyard gate," the words of R. Eliezer.

[C]   And R. Joshua says, "When the stone is set in place [closing the burial chamber]."

[D]   When R. Gamaliel died, as soon as they went out through the courtyard gate [with the body,] R. Eliezer said to his students, "Turn over the beds."

[E]   When the stone was set in place R. Joshua said, "Turn over the beds."

[F]   They said to him, "We have already turned them over in accord with [the words of the] Elder [Eliezer]."

[G]   On the Sabbath eve one turns the beds upright [again] and after the Sabbath one turns them over [since they do not permit one to show signs of mourning on the Sabbath].

[H]   It was taught: The state-bed [a low bed, see below] may be left upright and need not be turned over.

[I]   R. Simeon b. Eleazar says, "One detaches the straps [from the bed], and that is enough [of a sign of mourning]."

[J]   R. Yosa in the name of R. Joshua b. Levi, "The law follows R. Simeon b. Eleazar."

[K]   R. Jacob bar Aha in the name of R. Yose, "In the case of a bed with a curtain frame, it is enough [of a sign of mourning] to detach it."

[L]   What is the difference between a bed [*mth*] and a state-bed
       [*drgš*]?

[M]   Said R. Jeremiah, "A bedstead on which the girths [interlaced
       straps] are drawn over the frame is called a bed. And a bedstead
       [which is lower] on which the girths are now drawn over the
       frame [but are attached in another way] is called a state-bed
       [Jastrow, p. 1022, s.v. *šrg*]."

[N]   But was it not taught, *The bed and cot [become susceptible to
       uncleanness] after they are rubbed over with fish skin [to smooth
       them? Before that time, they cannot be used, because they are
       too rough]* [M. Kel. 16 : 1]. If they are girded over the top [of
       the frame, thus covering the top of the frame,] what purpose is
       served by rubbing [the bed frame to smooth it]?

[O]   Said R. Eleazar, "We may solve this problem [as follows: Mish-
       nah refers to] those cots from Caesarea which have openings [for
       the straps to go through. Since the top of the frame is exposed,
       rubbing it with skin serves the purpose of finishing it for use.]"

[P]   What is the basis for [the custom of] turning over the beds?

[Q]   R. Qerispa in the name of R. Yohanan, "[They justify the prac-
       tice based on the verse] 'And they sat with him near to the
       ground' [*l'rṣ*] [Job 2 : 13]. It does not say, 'On the ground' but,
       'Near to the ground,' implying they sat on something close to
       the ground. From here we see that they slept on beds which
       were turned over."

[R]   Bar Qappara [explained the custom as follows], "[God] says, 'I
       had a fine likeness of myself in your house and you caused me to
       turn it over [to the ground, to die, through your sins]. Now [as a
       sign for this] you shall turn over your beds.'"

[S]   [Some interpret this explanation of Bar Qappara differently:
       Not, "You caused me to turn it over,"] but, "You forced [his
       likeness from the world]." As in the saying, "May the agent of
       sin be forced [away]." [So now you are forced to turn over your
       beds. P.M. explains that this is just a semantic difference.]

[T]   R. Jonah and R. Yose both [taught] in the name of R. Simeon b.
       Laqish: One said, "Why does one sleep on an overturned bed?
       So that if he should awaken at night, he will remember that he is
       a mourner."

[U]   And the other said, "Since he sleeps on an overturned bed, he
       will awaken at night and remember that he is a mourner."

[IV.A] A mourner must eat at the house of his fellow until the corpse of
       his deceased relative is buried. And if he has no fellow [with
       whom he can eat], he should eat in a stranger's house. And if he
       has no stranger's house [nearby in which to eat] he should con-
       struct a partition [in his own house] and eat there. And if he
       cannot construct a partition, he should turn his face to the wall
       [of his own house] and eat.

[B]   And he [the mourner before the body is buried] may neither
       recline and eat, nor eat and drink a full meal, nor eat meat, nor
       drink wine. And they do not [count him in the quorum] to ex-
       tend the invitation [to recite the blessing over the meal as a
       group]. And if he recited the blessing [over the meal], others do
       not respond [to it] 'Amen.' And [when he hears] blessings of
       others, he does not respond [to them] 'Amen.'

[C]   All of these [rules] apply during the week. But on the Sabbath
       he may recline and eat, and he may eat meat and drink wine,
       and he may eat and drink a full meal, and they may [count him
       to establish the needed quorum in order] to extend the invitation
       to recite the blessing of the meal, and if he recited a blessing,
       others may respond 'Amen,' and for the blessings of others, he
       may respond 'Amen.'

[D]   Said Rabban Simeon b. Gamaliel, "Once I have permitted [the
       mourner] to do all this, I may as well obligate him to keep all the
       commandments of the Torah. For if I permit him [to partake
       fully] of temporal life [by eating and drinking on the Sabbath],
       should I not surely permit him [to partake fully] of eternal life
       [by keeping all the commandments on the Sabbath]?"

[E]   R. Judah b. Pazzi in the name of R. Joshua b. Levi, "The law
       follows Rabban Simeon b. Gamaliel."

[F]   Once it [the body] has been given over to the [burial] associa-
       tion, [the mourner] may eat meat and drink wine. Once it was
       given over to the corpse-bearers, it is as if it was given over to
       the [burial] association.

[G]   When R. Yosa died, R. Hiyya bar Wawa [i.e., Abba] took it
       upon himself to mourn [for his teacher]. Even so he ate meat
       and drank wine [before the body was buried].

[H]   When R. Hiyya bar Abba died, R. Samuel bar R. Yitzhak took it upon himself to mourn [for his teacher]. Even so he ate meat and drank wine [before the body was buried].

[I]   When R. Samuel bar R. Yitzhak died, R. Zeira took it upon himself to mourn [for his teacher]. But he ate [only] lentils. That tells us that we act according to the custom [of a place. What one eats if he accepts upon himself mourning for his teacher is not fixed by law.]

[J]   As R. Zeira was dying, he instructed his disciples saying, "Do not take it upon yourselves to mourn for me today but wait until tomorrow to begin mourning." [This accords with P.M.'s second explanation. He wanted to delay them to be sure that they would not get carried away in their mourner's meal, get drunk, and act foolishly, as in the following story.]

[K]   R. Yitzhak the son of Rab [R: son of R. Hiyya] at Toba [P.M.'s reading] suffered an untimely bereavement. R. Mana and R. Yudan went up [to console him], and they had some good wine, and they drank until they became silly.

[L]   The next day when they wished to visit him [Yitzhak] again, he said to them, "Rabbis, is this how a person acts toward his associate? The only thing we missed yesterday was to get up and to dance [and we would have had a time of festivity rather than of mourning]."

[V.A]   It was taught: They drink ten cups [of wine] in a house of mourning—two before the meal, and five during the meal, and three after the meal.

[B]   Regarding these three after the meal—over the first [they recite] the blessings following the meal, over the second [they recite a blessing concerning the] acts of loving-kindness [of those who came to console the mourners], and over the third [they recite a blessing] to console the mourners themselves. [So P.M. Cf. M. Semahot, ch. 14. T. 3:23–24 refers to two blessings: "Comforting the mourners" and "merciful works." The present text directs that one recite each of these blessings over a cup of wine.]

[C]   When Rabban Gamaliel died, they added another three [cups]—one for the Hazzan [sexton] of the Congregation, one for the Head of the Congregation [to praise them for their public service], and one for Rabban Gamaliel [because he permitted people to perform a simple inexpensive funeral].

[D]   And when the court saw that people were getting drunk [on account of the extra three cups], they issued a decree forbidding [people to drink] these cups, and [the custom] reverted to its previous state [i.e., ten cups].

[VI.A]   May a priest render himself unclean [by coming into proximity or contact with a corpse, by participating in his teacher's funeral] out of honor to his master?

[B]   R. Yannai the younger's father-in-law died. He had been both his father-in-law and his master. He [Yannai] asked R. Yose [whether he could take part in the funeral and render himself unclean]. And [R. Yose] forbade him.

[C]   R. Aha heard this and said, "His students may become unclean on his account." [He considered one's master to be equivalent to one's father.]

[D]   R. Yose [died and his] students became unclean on his account [by taking part in his funeral], and [before the funeral], they ate meat and drank wine.

[E]   Said R. Mana to them, "You cannot have it both ways. If you are mourners, why did you eat meat and drink wine? And if you are not mourning, why did you render yourselves unclean?"

[F]   May a priest render himself unclean in order to honor [i.e., study] the Torah?

[G]   R. Yose was sitting and teaching, and a corpse was brought up [to the study hall for a eulogy]. To [all those priests studying there] who went out, so as not to become unclean, he did not say anything. And to all those who remained seated, he did not say anything. [For he was in doubt about this matter.]

[H]   R. Nehemiah, son of R. Hiyya bar Abba said, "My father would not pass under the arch at Caesarea [even though this was the shortest way for him to go to study Torah, for the arch could transmit the uncleanness of a corpse as a tent]." R. Ammi [L. omits: would pass under the arch].

[I]   R. Hezekiah and R. Kohen and R. Jacob bar Aha were walking in the plazas of Sepphoris [R: Caesarea]. When they reached the arch, R. Kohen separated from them. And when they reached a clean area, he rejoined them.

[J]   He [Kohen] said to them, "What were you discussing [in my absence]?"

[K]   R. Hezekiah said to R. Jacob bar Aha, "Do not tell him anything."

[L]   [And this story does not prove anything because we do not know] whether [he instructed Jacob to remain silent] because he was angry that he [R. Kohen] left, because [a priest] is permitted to become unclean in order to study Torah, or whether [Hezekiah told Jacob to be silent] because [he did not wish to be detained by a lengthy] discussion. [S.H.: He wanted to go ahead to finish his own lesson.]

[VII.A]   It was taught: A priest is permitted to go out of the Land of Israel, and thereby render himself unclean, for monetary judgments, for capital judgments, for sanctifying the new moon, for intercalating the year, and for saving a field from seizure by a gentile. And he may go out even with a claim to contest [the seizure]. [The principle is that all lands outside of Israel are unclean with a form of uncleanness decreed by the rabbis.]

[B]   **[And a priest may leave Israel] to study Torah and to get married. R. Judah says, "If he has somewhere to study [in Israel], he may not render himself unclean [by leaving the Land]."**

[C]   **R. Yose says, "Even if he [the priest] has somewhere to study [in Israel], he may render himself unclean [and leave Israel to study]. For one may not be worthy enough to learn from all persons. [He may need a different teacher.]"**

[D]   **They said concerning Joseph the priest that he used to go out and defile himself [by leaving the Land of Israel] to follow his teacher to Sidon.**

[E]   **But they said: a priest should not leave the Land of Israel [to get married on the chance that he may find a wife. He may leave] only if he was promised a bride [in a place outside of the Land of Israel] [Tos. A.Z. 1:8–9].**

[VIII.A]   May a priest render himself unclean in order to recite the priestly blessing [in a synagogue in which there is uncleanness]?

[B]   Magbilah the brother of R. Abba bar Kohen said in the presence
       of R. Yose in the name of R. Aha, "A priest may render himself
       unclean to make the priestly blessing."

[C]   R. Aha heard this and said, "I never told him any such thing."

[D]   He [Aha] retracted, "It could be that he heard me teach [and
       misinterpreted] that which R. Judah b. Pazzi said in the name of
       R. Eleazar, 'Any priest who stands in the synagogue and does
       not raise his hands [to recite the priestly blessing] violates a posi-
       tive commandment.' And he [Yose] concluded that to perform
       this positive commandment [to bless the people] one may over-
       ride a negative commandment [to avoid uncleanness]. [But this
       is a grave error.] I never said any such thing. Bring him before
       me and I shall flog him."

[E]   R. Abahu was sitting and teaching in the synagogue of the city
       gate in Caesarea.

[F]   And there was [in the synagogue] a corpse [for a funeral]. When
       it came time [to recite] the priestly blessing [his students who
       were priests] did not ask him [whether they should stop study-
       ing to recite the blessing. For once they stopped studying they
       would then have to leave, since they thought one may continue
       to render himself unclean in the presence of a corpse only to
       study Torah, but not in order to recite the priestly blessing.]
       When it came time for eating, they asked him [whether to stop
       studying].

[G]   He said to them, "You did not ask me [whether to stop study-
       ing] for the priestly blessing! You now ask me [whether to stop
       studying] in order to eat?"

[H]   When they heard this, they ran [back to study, duly chastised.
       So S.H. P.M.: They scurried out.]

[I]   Said R. Yannai, "A priest may defile himself in order to see
       the emperor. When the emperor Diocletian came here, they
       saw R. Hiyya bar Abba [a priest] walking over Tyrian graves in
       order to see him."

[J]   [This accords with the following teaching:] R. Hezekiah and
       R. Jeremiah in the name of R. Yohanan [said], "It is an obliga-
       tion to see great royalty [even a gentile king], so that when the
       royalty of the House of David [the Messiah] comes, one will

know how to distinguish between one kind of royalty and another [i.e., between the ordinary king and the Messiah]."

[K]   May a priest render himself unclean in honor of a patriarch [by attending his funeral]?

[L]   When R. Judah, the patriarch, died, R. Yannai announced, "For today, the [prohibition against becoming unclean applicable to members of the] priesthood is suspended [i.e., priests may come to the funeral]."

[M]   When R. Judah II, the patriarch, grandson of Judah I the patriarch, died, R. Hiyya bar Abba pushed R. Zeira into the synagogue in the vineyard near Sepphoris [where the funeral was held] and rendered him unclean. [The room transmitted the corpse-uncleanness as a "tent."]

[N]   When Nehorai, the sister of R. Judah II, the patriarch, died, R. Haninah sent for R. Mana, [a priest, to attend the funeral], and he did not come.

[O]   He [Mana] said to him, "If we do not render ourselves unclean on their account when they are alive [i.e., we remove ourselves from having relations with women when they menstruate], all the moreso [shall we take care not to render ourselves unclean on account of women] when they are dead."

[P]   Said R. Nasa, "[When a woman of stature such as a sister of the patriarch dies], we may render ourselves unclean for her, just as [we may render ourselves unclean] for a neglected corpse for which we are obliged to defile ourselves." [So a priest may render himself unclean for the sister of the patriarch.]

[Q]   May a priest render himself unclean in order to honor his father or mother [in their lifetime, e.g., to visit them outside the Land of Israel]?

[R]   [This case may clarify the matter.] R. Yosa heard that his mother was going to Bozrah. He went to ask R. Yohanan whether he may go out [of the Land of Israel with her].

[S]   He said to him, "If you wish to go [to protect her] on account of the dangers of the road [in her travels], then go. If you wish to go in order to honor your mother, then I do not know whether to allow you to go or not."

[T]   Because [Yosa] pressured R. Yohanan [about this issue] he said, "If you have decided to go, then come back in peace."

[U]   Said R. Samuel bar R. Yitzhak, "R. Yohanan is still in doubt concerning this issue."

[V]   R. Eleazar heard this and said, "You could not have better permission than that [which Yohanan gave to Yosa saying, 'Come back in peace']."

[W]   May a priest render himself unclean for the public honor?

[X]   [This will clarify the question.] It was taught: If there were two alternative routes [for going to console a mourner], one longer [and through an area which is] clean, the other shorter but [passing through] unclean [precincts]. If the majority of people goes by way of the longer route, he [a priest] should go by way of the longer route. And if not, he may go by the way of the shorter [unclean] route out of deference to the public honor.

[Y]   This is the case for uncleanness ordained by the rabbis. But [how do we know the same law applies in] a case of uncleanness ordained in Scripture?

[Z]   Based on what R. Zeira said, "The public honor is so important. In some instances it [even temporarily] overrides prohibitions [against becoming unclean]. As in the case, [for instance, of the obligation to bury an unknown corpse]. That is to say, [for the sake of the public honor one may render himself unclean] even with [a form of uncleanness] prohibited by Scripture."

[IX.A]   R. Jonah, R. Yose the Galilean, in the name of R. Yasa bar R. Hanina, "They do not inquire into decisions of law in the presence of a coffin of the dead." [This is disrespectful to the dead, for they can no longer learn.]

[B]   [This case appears to contradict the following ruling:] But lo, R. Yohanan inquired of R. Yannai in the presence of the coffin of R. Samuel b. Yozadak, "If one consecrated to the Temple treasury his [animal previously designated for a] burnt-offering [what is the outcome]?" [Must he pay its value to the treasury? Or did he have no right to consecrate an animal which was already sanctified for use as a sacrifice on the altar? Clearly this is a question requiring a decision of law.]

[C]   And he [Yannai even] answered him! We may say that [in this case] they were far [from the bier], or that they already had completed the service.

[D]   But, lo, [another apparent contradiction:] R. Jeremiah inquired of R. Zeira [about a legal ruling] in the presence of the coffin of R. Samuel bar R. Yitzhak [and he answered him]!

[E]   We may say that [when he asked him a question while] he was far[from the coffin], he answered him. [When he asked him a question while] he was close [to the coffin], he would not answer him.

[F]   It was taught: The pallbearers are prohibited to wear sandals, lest the [strap of the] sandal of one of them break and as a result he be prevented from performing his obligation [of carrying the bier].

[G]   R. Zeira fainted while speaking. They came and tried to lift him up and found he was too weak.

[H]   They said to him, "What is causing this?"

[I]   He said to them, "Because we came to [study laws which deal with the subject of death and mourning, I became weak,] in accord with the verse, '[It is better to go to the house of mourning than to go to the house of feasting; for this is the end of all men,] and the living will lay it to heart' [Qoh. 7:2]. [When I study these subjects, it makes my heart faint.]"

Unit **I** begins to deal with M., first citing a baraita of a dispute between Eliezer and Joshua about when one may put on tefillin again after the funeral of his relative, and then working through its implications. Unit **II** discusses the possible reasons for the exemption of the mourner from certain commandments, presenting two alternatives, and appropriate cases to determine which is correct.

Other practices during the period of mourning are presented in units **III** through **V**, all tangential to M. Unit **III** first gives general rules regarding the custom of lowering the beds in a house so that the mourners may sit and sleep close to the ground, then spells this custom out for different kinds of beds, and further explains the custom.

Unit **IV** discusses where and when a mourner may eat after the funeral, and what he may eat when he mourns for his relative, or for his teacher. Unit **V** follows this with rules for the number of cups of wine one must drink in the house of mourning after the funeral and a brief excursus on the subject relating to a new custom instituted after Gamaliel's death.

Units **VI–VIII** move off to another topic, whether a priest may render himself unclean under certain circumstances: to mourn his teacher (**VI**), or to go outside Israel to study Torah. Unit **VII** cites an appropriate Tosefta on this last subject. Unit **VIII** continues the discussion with two instances of priests who render themselves unclean in a synagogue, followed by stories of priests doing so to see the emperor, the patriarch, or the sister of the patriarch. On this subject the Talmud also inquires whether a priest may render himself unclean to leave Israel out of respect for his parents, or to conform to the common practice in consoling a mourner.

Unit **IX** gives us the last of several related issues on the subject of practices of mourners, whether one may discuss Torah in the presence of a coffin. The unit concludes with a short general story about Zeira who said he was physically affected by studying these rules and stories about mourning.

3:2

[A]   *Once they [the mourners] have buried the deceased and returned [from the grave site]—*

[B]   *if they have time to begin and complete [the recitation of the* Shemaʻ*] before they reach the line [of those who come to console the mourners]—they may begin.*

[C]   *And if not—they may not begin.*

[D]   *And those who stand in line—the innermost [closest to the mourners] are exempt [from the recitation of the* Shemaʻ*] and the outermost are obligated [to recite].*

[I.A]   It was taught: They do not bring out the deceased [for burial] close to [the time of] the recitation of the *Shemaʻ*, unless they do so some time before or after [the appointed time for recitation] so that they may [have enough time to] recite [the *Shemaʻ*] and the Prayer [of Eighteen Blessings at their appointed hours].

[B]   But was it not taught [in the Mishnah], *Once they buried the deceased and returned?* [This implies that they apparently took out the body for burial close to the time for recitation.]

[C]   We may resolve the contradiction [as follows: Mishnah speaks
        of] those who thought they had enough time [to finish the burial
        before the time for the recitation of the *Shema'*] but [because
        of unexpected delays it turned out that they] did not have
        enough time.

[II.A] It was taught, **The one who eulogizes and all those who par-
        ticipate in the eulogy, may interrupt to recite the *Shema'*, but
        may not interrupt to recite the Prayer. One time the rabbis
        interrupted [a eulogy] to recite the *Shema'* and the Prayer**
        [T. 2:11J–K].

[B]   But was it not taught in the Mishnah, *If they have time to begin
        and complete [the recitation] before they reach the line, they
        may begin?* [Surely they are not allowed to interrupt the service
        or eulogy!]

[C]   [The contradiction may be resolved by explaining that] the Mish-
        nah refers to [a eulogy given on] the first day [i.e., the day of the
        funeral]. What the Tanna taught [in Tosefta] refers to [a eulogy
        given on] the second day [i.e., the day after the funeral, when
        one may interrupt the eulogy to recite the *Shema'* or Prayer.]

[III.A] Said R. Samuel bar Abdoma, "One who enters a synagogue and
        finds [the congregation] standing and praying—if he knows that
        he can begin and finish reciting [the Prayer] before the leader
        begins [his recitation], so that he can respond 'Amen' to it—he
        may [go ahead and recite the] Prayer. But if not—he may not
        [recite the] Prayer [at that time, but he must wait until the
        leader is finished]."

[B]   To which 'Amen' do they refer [in this teaching]? [This is a dis-
        pute between] two Amoraim.

[C]   One said, "The 'Amen' following [the third blessing], 'The holy
        God.'"

[D]   The other said, "The 'Amen' following [the sixteenth blessing],
        'Who harkenest unto prayer' [the last of the intermediate thir-
        teen blessings]."

[E]   Said R. Pinhas, "They do not dispute one another. The one who
        holds [that Samuel refers to] the 'Amen' following 'The holy
        God' [so rules] for the Sabbath [when the intermediate thirteen
        blessings are omitted]. And the one who holds [that Samuel
        refers to] the 'Amen' following 'Who harkenest unto prayer'

[so rules] for weekdays [when one recites the intermediate blessings]."

[IV.A]   It was taught: **R. Judah says, "If they [who came to console the mourners] all were standing in a single line, those who stand there for the sake of honor [to be first to console the mourners], are obligated [to recite the** *Shema'*].

[B]   "[Those who stand there] for the sake of the mourner, are exempt [from reciting the *Shema'*]."

[C]   **Once they have gone down to [hear the] the eulogy, those who can see the faces [of the mourners] are exempt [from reciting]. And those who cannot see the faces [of the mourners] are obligated [to recite]** [T. 2:11].

[D]   [T.'s distinction between those who can and cannot see the mourners does not contradict M.] That which was taught in the Mishnah, *Those who stand in the line—the innermost are exempt and the outermost are obligated,* is a later teaching. And that which we learned [in Tosefta], **Those who stand there for the sake of honor are obligated, [those who stand there] for the sake of the mourner are exempt,** is an earlier teaching. [The earlier practice, reflected in T., was for the mourners to stand in place and the consolers to stand in one line and pass before the mourners. Those who demanded the honor of going first to console the mourners were obligated to recite. And those who put the honor of the mourners first and were willing to await their turn in line were exempt from the obligation to recite. The later practice was for the consolers to all stand in several lines and for the mourners to pass before them, as M. indicates.]

[E]   And that [distinction between early and late teachings] accords with that which was taught elsewhere, *And when he [the high priest] consoles the others [i.e., the mourners], it is the practice of the people to pass one after the other, and the prefect of the priests places him [the high priest] between himself and the people* [M. San. 2:1]. [This M. passage implies that the mourners stood while those who came to console them passed before them, contrary to our Mishnah]. This is an earlier [L: later] teaching, [and our Mishnah is a later teaching and it is authoritative].

[F]   Said R. Hanina, "At first the families [of those who came to console the mourners] used to stand and the mourners passed before them [in accord with our M.]. When contention [between those vying for places to stand] increased in Sepphoris, R. Yose b. Halafta ordained that the families [of those who came to console] should pass, and the mourners should stand still." [Cf. b. San. 19b, another version of this teaching.]

[G]   Said R. Simeon of Tosfa [alt. in the Tosefta], "[According to Yose b. Halafta] the situation has reverted to the old way [to accord with the earlier teaching as reflected in T., i.e., the consolers pass before the mourners. Simeon expresses disapproval of Yose's decree.]

Unit I develops a contradiction between a baraita and M. and proceeds to resolve it. Likewise, unit II displays a discordance between M. and T. then harmonizes it. The subject of unit III reminds the Talmud of another parallel instance. B–E expands the unit with an explanation of A. Finally, unit IV resolves a conflict of opinion between M. and T. by declaring that T.'s ruling represents an older law, and that M.'s expresses the more recent ruling.

3:3

[A]   *Women, slaves and minors are exempt from the [obligation of the] recitation of the Shema', and from [wearing] tefillin.*

[B]   *And they are obligated [to recite the] Prayer [of Eighteen Blessings],*

[C]   *in the [obligation to post] a mezuzah [on the doorpost],*

[D]   *and [to recite] the blessing following the meal.*

[I.A]   Whence [do we learn] that women [are exempt from the obligation to recite the *Shema'*]? [From this verse,] "And you shall teach them to your sons" [Deut. 11:9]. [This implies that the obligation applies] "to your sons," and not to your daughters.

[B]   Whence [do we learn] that slaves [are exempt from the obligation to recite the *Shema'*]? As it says, "Hear O Israel: The Lord is our God, the Lord is one" [Deut. 6:4]. Whoever has no master except God [is obligated]. The slave is excluded [from the obligation to recite the *Shema'*], because he has another master.

[C]   Whence [do we learn] that minors [are exempt from the obligation to recite the *Shema'*]? [From the verse,] "That the law of
the Lord may be in your mouth" [Exod. 13:9]. At the time you
can regularly [observe these commandments, you will be obligated to wear tefillin and to recite the *Shema'*. Minors cannot
regularly observe them so they are not obligated].

[D]   *And they are obligated in [reciting the] Prayer* [M. 3:3], so that
each and every person may ask for mercy for him or herself.

[E]   . . . *[and to post a] mezuzah,* as it is written, "And you shall
write them on the doorposts of your house and on your gates"
[Deut. 6:9] [implying that the obligation falls upon even the
women, slaves, and minors in your house].

[F]   . . . *and [to recite] the blessing following the meal* [M. 3:3 B],
as it says, "And you shall eat and be full and you shall bless the
Lord your God" [Deut. 8:10]. [All those who eat are obligated
to recite the blessings.]

[II.A]   It was taught elsewhere in the Mishnah, *For all positive religious
obligations that are restricted to a specific time—men are obligated [to perform them] and women are exempt. And for all
positive religious obligations that are not restricted to a specific
time—both men and women alike are obligated* [M. Qid. 1:7].

[B]   What is a positive religious obligation that is restricted to a specific time? For instance: [dwelling in a] sukkah, [taking a] lulab,
[hearing the] shofar, and [wearing] tefillin.

[C]   And what is a positive religious obligation that is not restricted
to a specific time? For instance: [returning] a lost item, send-
ing away the mother bird from the nest [before taking the off-
spring], [building] a guard-rail [on the roof of your house], and
[wearing] fringes [on your four-cornered garment].

[D]   R. Simeon exempts women from the commandment [to wear]
fringes [on a four-cornered garment] since it is a positive religious obligation that is restricted to a specific time, because a
covering that one wears at night is exempt from fringes. [The
obligation applies only by day.]

[E]   Said R. Layya, "The reason the rabbis [dispute Simeon and
hold that the obligation to wear fringes is not restricted by time
and that women are obligated and may fulfill the obligation] is
because if a [specific] garment were designated for use [both] by
day and night, one would be obligated to have fringes on it."

[The obligation to wear a garment with fringes may continue to be fulfilled even at night.]

[**III**.A] It was taught: Any commandment from which a person is exempt [because he already fulfilled it]—that person may exempt others from their obligation [by performing it again on their behalf]—except for [the obligation to recite] the blessing following the meal.

[B] And it was taught in the Mishnah, *Anyone who is not obligated [to perform a religious obligation] may not free others from their obligation* [M. R.H. 3:8]. Lo [this implies] if he was once obligated, even if he is already free from his obligation, he may free others [by performing the action on their behalf]. [Why then can he not do so for the blessing of the meal?]

[C] Said R. Layya, "The [obligation to recite the] blessing of the meal is different. For it is written concerning it, "And you shall eat and be full and you shall bless the Lord your God" [Deut. 8:10]. [Only one] who ate [together with others and has not yet recited the blessing] may recite the blessing [on behalf of the others]."

[**IV**.A] R. Yose and R. Judah b. Pazzi were sitting [and discussing the obligations of reciting blessings]. They said, "Is it not reasonable [that with regard] to the recitation of the *Shema'*, each person must speak it distinctly from his own mouth, just as it is reasonable [that with regard to] Prayer, each person should ask for mercy on his own behalf." [Why, then, does the M. obligate women, slaves, and minors in the Prayer and exempt them from the *Shema'?*]

[B] [Yose and Judah asked further:] What is the difference between the [obligation to recite blessings for the commandment to dwell in a] sukkah and [the commandment to take hold of the] lulab?

[C] For the sukkah, one needs to recite a blessing only on the first night. For the lulab, one needs to recite a blessing each of the seven days. [And why must we distinguish between the two obligations? So M.H.'s explanation.]

[D] R. Yose and R. Aha were sitting and [discussing this same question]. They said, "What is the difference between [the two religious obligations—to dwell in a] sukkah and [to take hold of] a lulab?

[E] "[The commandment to dwell in a] sukkah applies by night and day [throughout the festival]. [The commandment to take hold of a] lulab applies only by day." [Accordingly, as C directs, one recites a blessing for the sukkah only once, when he enters it the first night, and the blessing applies throughout the festival without interruption. But each day he takes hold of the lulab, after the night interrupts, and hence he recites the blessing again.]

[F]   R. Jacob of the South objected, "Lo, the commandment to study Torah applies by night as well as by day! [Yet we recite a new blessing each day for Torah study.]"

[G]   What is the resolution of this problem? [The explanation is as follows.] Can one suspend himself from dwelling in the sukkah? [No. Because when one eats and sleeps there, he fulfills his obligation]. But can one not suspend oneself from the study of Torah? [He must interrupt his study in order to sleep or eat. So he must recite a new blessing each morning].

[V.A] It was taught, **Truly they said: a woman may recite a blessing for her husband, a son may recite a blessing for his father, a slave may recite a blessing for his master** [T. 5:17].

[B]   We may grant that a woman may recite a blessing for her husband and that a slave may recite for his master, but a son for his father? [A minor has no religious obligations. How can he exempt his father?] [L: omits B.]

[C]   Did not R. Aha say as follows in the name of R. Yose b. R. Nehorai: "All that they said about a minor [performing religious obligations should not imply that he has any obligation to fulfill them. Rather he does them] so that one may train him." [How then can a minor recite a blessing on behalf of his father?]

[D]   You may resolve this question [by stipulating that the case under discussion is one in which the father] responds 'Amen' after the blessing. [P.M.'s version omits the word 'Amen.' His reading is, "The father repeats the blessing after the son."]

[E]   This accords with that which was taught elsewhere [M. Sukkah 3:10]: *Whoever has his slave, or wife, or a minor recite [the Hallel] for him, must repeat after them what they say.*

[F]   *And let this be an embarrassment for him* [i.e., it is an insult to him that he does not know how to recite it himself. Luncz explains that only for the Hallel must he repeat word for word. For the blessing of the meal it suffices if he responds 'Amen.' As

indicated, P.M. insists that he must repeat even the meal blessing word for word.]

[G]   Truly they said, "And let it be an embarrassment for a twenty
year old who needs a ten year old [to recite for him]."

The first unit provides verses to support M.'s exemptions. Unit
II introduces the concept that women are exempt from positive
religious obligations restricted to a specific time and discusses
its implications. The Talmud then goes on to ask in unit **III**
whether one who is exempt from an obligation and nevertheless
performs the action can thereby exempt others.

In unit **IV** the question turns to whether one must recite several blessings for the same religious obligation, repeated over
several days, or whether one suffices. Unit **V** closes with a citation of a passage from T. The issue is, can a child perform an
obligation on behalf of an adult? The Talmud looks at the legal
implications of whether one who is not obligated can exempt a
person who is required to perform the action. The last discussion ends with reference to the social disgrace suffered by a
person who is so illiterate that he needs a child to recite on his
behalf.

3:4

[A]   *One who has discharged semen may silently meditate [the*
Shemaʿ] but may not recite the blessings [because the rabbis
deem him to be unclean].

[B]   *Neither [may he recite those blessings] before nor after [the*
Shemaʿ].

[C]   *And [regarding the blessings] for the meal—one [who suffered*
such a discharge] may recite the blessings after it, but may not
recite the blessings before it.

[D]   *R. Judah says, "He may recite the blessings before and after*
[the Shemaʿ and the meal]."

[I.A]   What [words] does he meditate? [Those of the] blessings. [But
he must recite out loud the scriptural passages of the *Shema*ʿ.
Alternatively, P.M. interprets this comment to refer to Mishnah's rule in C regarding the recitation of the meal blessing.]

[B]   The rule of our Mishnah applies only to a case where there is no water [of a miqveh bath available for immersing oneself. But if a miqveh is available, one may not even meditate before he goes into it.]

[C]   And this accords with the ruling of R. Meir. As it was taught: **One who has discharged semen who does not have water [of a miqveh available] to immerse himself in—**

[D]   **"Lo, he may recite the *Shema'* [to himself] but not out loud, and he may not recite the blessings before it or after it," the words of R. Meir.**

[E]   **And sages say, "He may recite the *Shema'* out loud, and recite the blessings before it and after it"** [T. 2:13].

[F]   It was taught: **One who was ill and discharged semen, upon whom was poured nine *qabs* of water—**

[G]   **(T. MS omit: and a clean person [who suffered a discharge] upon whom was poured three logs of drawn water, he has purified himself [with this action and may recite] but)**

[H]   **he cannot exempt others from their obligation until he has gone into a pool of forty seahs [of water].**

[I]   **R. Judah says, "In either case [he must go into a pool of] forty seahs [even before he may recite for himself]"** [T. 2:12].

[II.A] R. Jacob bar Aha, R. Yosa in the name of R. Joshua b. Levi, "The discharge of semen [which renders one unclean, referred to in Mishnah] refers only to that resulting from sexual intercourse."

[B]   R. Huna said, "Even if he [discharged semen as a result of] dreaming about having intercourse, [he is unclean]." That must mean only [if he dreamed of intercourse] with a woman.

[C]   R. Jonah and R. Yose both said, "Even [if he dreamed] of something else [and discharged semen, he is unclean]."

[D]   It was taught in the Mishnah, *On the Day of Atonement it is forbidden to eat, drink, wash, anoint oneself, wear shoes, or have sexual intercourse* [M. Yoma 8:1].

[E]   And concerning this it was taught, **Those who have discharged semen may immerse themselves privately as is their practice on the Day of Atonement** [T. Kippurim 4:5, following the reading of the first printed edition].

[F] And does this not contradict R. Joshua b. Levi who says [in A] that the only discharge of semen which causes uncleanness is that [which results] from sexual relations [which is forbidden on the Day of Atonement]?

[G] We may resolve the contradiction as follows: The case is that he had intercourse while it was yet day [on the eve of the Day of Atonement] and he forgot and did not immerse himself.

[H] But was it not taught, "Once they saw R. Yose b. Halafta immerse himself privately on the Day of Atonement." Can you imagine that such a holy person [had intercourse while it was yet daytime and] forgot [to immerse himself before sundown]? [This implies that Joshua b. Levi was wrong. The discharge of semen in circumstances other than sexual intercourse also renders one unclean.]

[IIIA] Said R. Jacob bar Abun, "They only ordained that one must immerse himself [after discharging semen] so that the Israelites should not act [in their sexual behavior] like roosters. [That is, they should not] have sexual intercourse, get right up and go to eat."

[B] R. Haninah was passing the gate of the bathhouse at daybreak. He said, "What are those early-morning dippers doing here? Why don't they go and study?" [They need not immerse themselves before studying.]

[C] Regarding those [who immerse themselves] in the morning he said, "Whoever has work to do should go and do it [and not spend time needlessly immersing himself]."

[D] May one meditate [about matters of Torah] while in the outhouse?

[E] Hezekiah said, "It is permissible."

[F] R. Yose said, "It is forbidden."

[G] Said R. Zeira, "All the difficult [thought] problems I have had I have worked out while in there."

[H] Said R. Eleazar bar Simeon, "All the difficult [legal] problems concerning [the legal matter of] 'One who immersed himself on the selfsame day' I have worked out while in there."

[I] R. Aha in the name of R. Tanhum b. R. Hiyya, "In the days of R. Joshua b. Levi they tried to abolish this [different related practice of] immersing oneself [before engaging in intercourse] on account of some Galilean women who were abandoned because [their husbands abstained from intercourse with them in the winter so they would not have to immerse themselves in] the cold water [of the bath].

[J]   "Said R. Joshua b. Levi to them, 'Do you wish to abolish something which keeps the people of Israel from sinning?'"

[K]   How does it keep [the people of] Israel from sinning? Once a vineyard keeper wanted to have sexual relations with a married woman. Before they were able to find a place in which to immerse themselves, people passed by [and saw them] and prevented the sin.

[L]   And one time a man came to have sexual relations with the gentile maid of Rabbi. She said to him, "If the gentleman will not immerse himself, then neither will I."

[M]   He said to her, "Are you not like an animal anyway? [Immersion has no relevance to you because you are a non-Jew.]"

[N]   She retorted, "Do you not know that one who has sexual relations with an animal is put to death by stoning? As it says, 'Whoever lies with a beast shall be put to death'" [Exod. 22:19].

[O]   Said R. Hiyya bar Abba [Wawa], "They only established this practice of immersing oneself [after engaging in sexual relations] on account of [concern that people should spend more time engaged in] study. For if you were to say it is always permissible [for a man to have intercourse with his wife and then go and study even without immersing himself afterward] one will say, 'I will go satisfy my [sexual] needs, then I will come to fulfill my [spiritual] need to study.' But since you say it is forbidden [to study after intercourse unless one immerses himself], he will come and fulfill his need to study [first and not so easily be diverted]."

[P]   There [in Babylonia] they said, "It is even forbidden to go and listen to words of Torah [after intercourse unless one first immerses himself]."

[Q]   Said R. Judah bar Titus, R. Aha in the name of R. Eleazar [in accord with the above statement], "[Our practice is consonant with that of] ancient times. [When the Israelites first heard the words of the Torah at Sinai, they were clean, as it says,]

'Be ready by the third day; do not go near a woman'" [Exod. 19:15].

[IV.A]   It was taught: **Zabim** and **Zabot** [those persons who suffer discharge], **Nidot** and **Yoldot** [menstruating women and women after childbirth] may recite from the Torah, [Prophets and Writings] and may study [Mishnah,] Midrash, *halakhot* and *aggadot.*

[B]   And one who has discharged semen is forbidden [to engage] in all [those activities].

[C]   R. Abba bar Aha in the name of Rabbi, "He may study *halakhot* but he may not study *aggadot* [lest he become too involved in his study and forget to immerse]" [T. 2:12].

[D]   It was taught in the name of R. Yose: **One may study routine** *halakhot* **as long as he does not cite the Mishnah [lest he become too involved in his study]** [T. 2:12]. Some say, "[One may study when he is unclean on account of an emission] as long as he does not mention the divine names [in the texts]."

[E]   R. Zeira raised a question before R. Yosa, "Did [you] my master not study with me a chapter each night [even after you had intercourse with your wife and before you went to immerse yourself]?"

[F]   He said to him, "Yes." [This accords with **III.B**, above.]

[G]   R. Hiyya bar Abba studied a chapter each night with R. Nehemiah his son.

[H]   The next morning he would say, "Whoever has work to do should go and do it [and he need not delay to immerse himself]." [P.M. says this accords with **III.A** above.]

[V.A]   Once a man [who had suffered a seminal emission] rose to recite from the Torah in Nisibis. When he came to [reading] a divine name he began to mumble [because he had not yet immersed himself and thought that he was not allowed to pronounce the name, as we saw above].

[B]   Said to him R. Judah b. Beterah, "Open your mouth and speak clearly, for words of Torah are not susceptible to uncleanness." [He told him that one need not immerse himself before studying Torah after previously having suffered an emission.]

[C]   Said R. Jacob bar Aha, "There [in Babylonia] they follow [the opinion of] R. Ilai concerning the disposition of the first shearings, and [the opinion of] R. Josiah concerning mixed kinds in a vineyard, and [the opinion of] R. Judah b. Beterah concerning those who discharged semen.

[D]   "They follow R. Ilai concerning the disposition of the first shearings, as it was taught: R. Ilai said, 'The law of the first shearings applies only in the Land of Israel.'

[E]   "They follow R. Josiah concerning mixed kinds in the vineyard, as it was taught: R. Josiah says, 'One is not liable [for mixed kinds] until he sows wheat, barley, and grapes in one throw of the hand.'

[F]   "And they follow R. Judah b. Beterah concerning those who discharged semen, as it was taught: R. Judah says, 'The words of Torah are not susceptible to uncleanness.'"

[VI.A] R. Yose bar Halafta was walking down a path at night and a donkey driver was walking behind him. He came to a watering hole.

[B]   He [the donkey driver] said to him, "I need to go into the water."

[C]   He said to him, "Do not endanger yourself!"

[D]   He said to him, "On account of [having intercourse] with a menstruating woman and with a married woman I must go into the water."

[E]   Even so he [Yose] said to him, "Do not endanger yourself!"

[F]   [He went in the water anyway.] When he did not listen, Yose said to him [to warn him], "You shall go down and you shall not come up." And so it was.

[G]   R. Yose b. Yose was travelling on a ship. He saw someone lowering himself by rope to go down into the water [to immerse to purify himself].

[H]   He said, "Do not endanger yourself!"

[I]   He said to him, "I need to eat."

[J]   He [Yose] said to him, "Eat!"

[K]   "I need to drink."

[L]   He said to him, "Drink!"

[M]   When they came to port he [Yose] said to him, "[Out] there I
permitted you [to eat and drink] only because of the mortal danger [you faced in lowering yourself into the water]. But here you
are forbidden to taste a thing before you immerse yourself."

[N]   Said R. Yannai, "I understand that some are lenient and some
are strict in this matter [of immersing oneself after discharging
semen]. And all who are strict shall live a long, good life."

[O]   [To what does Yannai refer?] Some are lenient, and permit a
person to wash in drawn water. Some are strict and permit immersing oneself only in a pool of fresh water.

Unit **I** cites the Tosefta passage relevant to M. Unit **II** introduces
Joshua b. Levi's lemma as a comment to M.'s rule. The Talmud
proceeds then to analyze the statement, trying to show that a
statement elsewhere in M. contradicts it. Failing that, the Talmud shows Joshua to be wrong by relating stories of the
behavior of the rabbis.

Unit **III** brings into the discussion immersion practices ordained by the rabbis. The Talmud refers to two separate
requirements. It first discusses the custom of immersing oneself
after engaging in sexual relations and before engaging in other
activities, such as eating or studying. D–H intrudes on the flow
of the unit, but is only linked to the context because one of the
rabbis worked out problems relating to immersions while he was
sitting in the outhouse.

Sections I–O turn to another requirement, immersion before
engaging in sexual relations. This ordained action keeps people
from sinning, as the stories illustrate. At P–Q the Talmud turns
back to the issue of immersing after sexual relations.

Unit **IV** first cites those T. passages relevant to the issue of
immersing after emissions. It then gives us two cases indicating
that immersion after sexual relations is optional. Unit **V** extends
the notion that some immersions are not compulsory to the case
of one who had suffered a seminal emission.

Finally, unit **VI** provides stories to substantiate the notion
that sometimes too much diligence in seeking to immerse can
lead one to endanger his life. Sections A–F suggest that in some
cases one should not immerse after sexual relations. Sections

G–M follow on the same subject but presents a less definitively negative attitude toward the requirement to immerse oneself. The end of the unit remarks about some contradictory practices and seeks to explain them.

All told the Talmud here revolves closely around the main themes of M.—adding and digressing but then returning to the main issues.

3:5

[A]   *One who was standing and reciting the Prayer [of Eighteen]*

[B]   *and remembered that he had discharged semen,*

[C]   *should not interrupt [his recitation]*

[D]   *but should shorten [the Prayer].*

[E]   *One who went down to immerse himself [in a ritual bath]—*

[F]   *if he has time to come up [out of the bath] and cover himself and recite [the Shema'] before the sun rises—*

[G]   *he should come up and cover himself and recite.*

[H]   *And if not, he should submerge himself [partially] in the water to cover himself and recite.*

[I]   *But one may submerge himself neither in foul water, nor in water used for soaking [flax].*

[J]   *[And one may not pray near a chamber pot] until one mixes into it [some fresh] water.*

[K]   *And how far must one move away from [undiluted urine] and from excrement [before praying]?*

[L]   *Four cubits.*

[I.A]   The Mishnah [A–D refers to one who was praying with others] in public [and remembered that he had suffered a seminal emission]. But a person praying by himself [who remembered that he had suffered a seminal emission] must interrupt. And this accords with the view of R. Meir [as preserved in T.].

[B]   **(One who had discharged semen who does not have water [of a miqveh available] in which to immerse himself—**

[C]   "Lo, he may recite the *Shema'* [to himself] but not out loud, and he may not recite the blessings before it or after it," the words of R. Meir.

[D]   And sages say, "He may recite the *Shema'* out loud, and may recite the blessings before it and after it") [T. 2:13].

[E]   But according to the view of R. Judah [who rules leniently in M. 3:4D, and accords with the view of the sages in T. 2:13], even in the case of a person praying by himself, he need not interrupt if he has no water available to immerse himself in [T. 2:13]. But if he has water available, even R. Judah would admit that he must interrupt [his recitation to immerse himself].

[F]   [Concerning] a sick person who had intercourse [does he have to immerse himself? If he immerses himself in a pool, he may die]. Said R. Ammi, "If he initiated the intercourse, let him immerse himself and face death! But if he suffered an accidental discharge, we do not trouble him [to immerse himself]."

[G]   R. Haggai in the name of R. Abba bar Zabda, "In either case we do not trouble him."

[H]   A sick person who had normal intercourse, must [wash with] nine *qabs* of water. A healthy person who had normal intercourse, must [immerse himself in a pool of] forty *seahs* [of water].

[I]   A sick person who suffered an accidental discharge is not troubled [to wash]. A healthy person who suffered an accidental discharge must wash with nine *qabs* of water.

[J]   R. Zabdi [Zebediah] son of R. Jacob bar Zabdi in the name of R. Jonah, "In a city whose spring is far away, lo, one may recite the *Shema'*, and go down and immerse himself, and come up and recite the Prayer.

[K]   "And for an exceptional person [P.M.: an obese person who has difficulty going to immerse himself] they permitted him to follow this practice [of immersing himself after reciting the *Shema'*, as was prescribed for residents of a city whose] spring is far away."

[II.A]   Piska: *And if not, he should submerge himself in the water and recite* [M. 3:5H]. The Mishnah refers to [a case of a pool of] cloudy water.

[B]   But it is forbidden [to go into a pool of] clear water [to cover one's nakedness in order to recite]. But if he can cloud [the clear water] by stirring it with his feet, he may cloud it [and is permitted to recite in such water].

[III.A]   It was taught, **[Before praying] they move away [four cubits] from human excrement, and [four cubits] from canine excrement if they use [that substance] for tanning hides** [T. 2 : 16].

[B]   R. Jeremiah in the name of R. Zeira, "[Before praying] one must move away four cubits from a decomposing animal carcass."

[C]   Said R. Abina, "And does not a rule in the Mishnah imply this?: *And how far should one distance oneself from it [urine, water used for soaking or by extension, any foul-smelling substance] and from excrement? Four cubits* [M. 3 : 5K]. [Why does Jeremiah need to repeat this as a special rule?]"

[D]   Said R. Ammi, said R. Shammai, "We may resolve this [question by explaining that one might think Mishnah refers here only to] water used for soaking laundry [which is foul-smelling because of the dirt found in it—S.H.]" [So Zeira's rule is not necessarily redundant.]

[E]   Said to him R. Mana, "If it refers to water used for soaking laundry, Mishnah already taught [a rule about that in M. 3 : 5I]: *Neither in foul water, nor in water used for soaking.* [M.'s rule is not specific and may include water which is foul smelling because of excrement in it or because of other substances. This implies that one may not pray near any foul-smelling object. Accordingly, Zeira's rule is redundant after all.]"

[IV.A]   It was taught: **A child who is able to eat an olive's bulk of grain [i.e., sufficiently weaned to eat solid foods]—we must move away from his excrement and urine four cubits [before we pray].**

[B]   **And if he is not able to eat an olive's bulk of grain [but is still nursing]—we need move away neither from his excrement nor from his urine [in order to pray]** [T. 2 : 16].

[C]   They raised this question before R. Abahu: Why must we move away [four cubits] from the [child's] excrement and urine [before we pray]?

[D]   He said to them, "Because his thoughts may be evil." [P.M.

suggests that there is an association between the odor of urine and evil thoughts. A child's urine may have a bad odor as soon as he can have evil thoughts.]

[E]   They said to him, "But he is only a child! [How can he have evil thoughts?]"

[F]   He said to them, "Does not the verse say, 'For the imagination of man's heart is evil from his youth'" [Gen. 8:21]? [And "youth" may imply infancy in accord with that which] R. Yudan said, "The word meaning 'from his youth' is written [without the vowel and may be read *n'ryw*]—from the time he moves [*nn'r*] and enters the world [i.e., from birth]." [This verse supports Abahu's assertion that infants may have evil thoughts.]

[G]   R. Yose bar R. Haninah said, "We must move away four cubits from animal droppings [before we may pray]."

[H]   R. Samuel bar R. Yitzhak said, "This rule only applies to soft ones and only to those of an ass."

[I]   R. Hiyya bar Abba said, "[It refers only to that which the animal eliminates] right after coming in off the road."

[J]   Levi said, "We must move away four cubits from the excrement of a swine [before we may pray]."

[K]   And so it was taught: We must move away four cubits from swine excrement, and four cubits from marten excrement, and four cubits from chicken excrement.

[L]   R. Yose bar Abun in the name of R. Huna, "This last rule only [applies to the excrement of] red chickens [which has a foul odor]."

[M]   It was taught: We must move away four cubits from a [source of a] foul odor.

[N]   Said R. Ammi, "From a foul odor which is dissipating, one must stand away four cubits."

[O]   And the rule [of M. that one must move away four cubits] applies [if the source of the odor is] behind him. But if it is in front of him, he must move away so he can no longer see it.

[P]   This accords with the story of R. Lya [Ilai] and [his] colleagues who were sitting before an inn in the evening. [They smelled an odor but could not see its source.]

[Q] They said to him, "May we discuss Torah here?"

[R] He said to them, "Since we would be able to see what is in front of us if it were daytime, in this case it is forbidden [for us to discuss Torah here]."

[V.A] It was taught: **A chamber pot—one must stand four cubits away from it whether it contains excrement or urine.**

[B] **[The chamber pot] of the bedroom—if one poured some water into it, one may recite [the *Shema'*] near it. If not—one may not recite [near it]** [T. 2:16].

[C] R. Zakkai said, "If one poured a quarter-log of water into it—he may recite. If not—he may not recite."

[D] But what does [Zakkai mean by] the amount of a quarter-log? [He means one must add] one quarter-log [of water] for each quarter-log [of urine]. The same rule applies whether it is a small pot or a large pot.

[E] **R. Simeon b. Gamaliel said, "[Near the pot] behind the bed one may recite. [Near the pot] in front of the bed one may not recite."**

[F] **R. Simeon b. Eleazar said, "Even in a large house of ten [cubits] by ten [cubits] one may not recite unless he covers the pot or places it under the bed"** [T. 2:16].

[G] R. Jacob bar Aha in the name of R. Hiyya bar Abba [Wawa], "R. Haninah of Tartiah ruled in accord with R. Simeon b. Eleazar."

[H] R. Benjamin bar Yapet in the name of R. Yohanan, "One may dilute a small amount of excrement with spittle [and may then pray near it]."

[I] R. Zeira [and] R. Jacob bar Zabdi were sitting where they could see some excrement. R. Jacob bar Zabdi got up and spit on it.

[J] Said to him R. Zeira, "[That is of use only for a brief instant,] until the spit dries."

[VI.A] One must place a box containing scrolls at the head of the bed, not at the foot of the bed. [It is not befitting scrolls to lie about in a bedroom.]

[B] R. Abun in the name of R. Huna, "This rule applies when the bed is ten handbreadths high, as long as the cords of the bed do not touch the box."

[C]   R. Yasa in the place of R. Samuel bar R. Yitzhak taught in accord with R. Huna.

[D]   A person may not engage in sexual relations if there is a Torah scroll in the house with him.

[E]   R. Jeremiah in the name of R. Abahu, "If it is wrapped in a cover or placed up in a window recess ten handbreadths high—it is permitted."

[F]   R. Joshua b. Levi [said], "He must make an enclosure for it."

[G]   A person may not sit on a bench upon which a Torah scroll is resting.

[H]   Once R. Eliezer was sitting on a bench upon which a Torah scroll was resting, and [when he noticed it], he recoiled from it as one would recoil from a serpent.

[I]   If the Torah was resting on some other object, it is permissible [to sit on the same bench with a Torah scroll].

[J]   How thick [must the object be on which the Torah rests]?

[K]   R. Abba in the name of R. Huna, "A handbreadth."

[L]   R. Jeremiah in the name of R. Zeira, "Any thickness."

[M]   A saddlebag full of scrolls, or in which there were [human] bones—he must set them behind him and he may ride [on the same animal with them].

[N]   Tefillin—one must hang them over the head of the bed, and one may not hang them at the foot of the bed.

[O]   R. Samuel, R. Abahu, R. Eleazar, in the name of R. Haninah, "Rabbi used to hang his tefillin at the head of the bed."

[P]   R. Hezekiah in the name of R. Abahu, "One should not hang them like a basket [i.e., with the straps above and the container dangling below]. Rather the tefillin [must hang] above and the straps [may dangle] down."

[Q]   R. Halafta b. Saul taught, "One who breaks wind while wearing his tefillin—this is a bad sign for him." [But the same does not apply to one who sneezes.] This accords with that which has been said, "[Breaking wind] below [is a bad sign]. But [sneezing] above is not."

[R] This accords with that which R. Haninah said, "I saw Rabbi yawn, and sneeze and cover his mouth with his hand [to yawn during his recitation of the Prayer]. But I did not see him spit."

[S] R. Yohanan said, "Even spitting [is permitted] if it serves to clear one's throat."

[T] Spitting in front of oneself is forbidden. Behind is permitted. To his right is forbidden. To his left is permitted. This follows what is written, "A thousand may fall at your side; [ten thousand at your right hand]" [Ps. 91 : 7] [i.e., the right side is more important].

[U] Everyone agrees that one who needs to spit into his jacket [or a handkerchief is permitted to do so, but he] is forbidden [to spit anywhere else during his recitation of Prayer—P.M.].

[V] R. Joshua b. Levi said, "Spitting in the synagogue is like spitting in [God's] eye."

[W] R. Jonah used to spit and then smooth over it [with his foot].

[X] R. Jeremiah, R. Samuel bar Halafta in the name of R. Ada b. Ahavah, "One who prays should not spit until he moves four cubits [from the place in which he prays]."

[Y] Said R. Yose b. R. Abun, "Likewise one who spits should not pray until he moves four cubits [from the place he spit]."

[VII.A] It was taught: **One who is praying should not urinate until he moves four cubits [from the place he prays].**

[B] **And likewise, one who urinates should not pray until he moves four cubits [from the place he urinates]** [T. 2 : 19].

[C] Said R. Jacob bar Aha, "It is not only the case that one must actually move away four cubits. But it is also sufficient if he waits [before praying in that place] the amount of time it would take to move away four cubits."

[D] Said R. Ammi, "If you insist that one should actually move away four cubits [from a place where someone urinated long before], then I could say [about every single place that maybe] someone urinated there [before and it should be forbidden to pray anywhere.]" [Ammi supports Jacob bar Aha's comment.]

[E]   R. Abba in the name of Rab, "[It is forbidden to pray near] excrement until it is as dry as a bone and near urine as long as it is moist."

[F]   Geniva said, "As long as the outline of the urine is discernible [on the ground, one may not pray nearby]."

[G]   Samuel said, "[One may not pray near excrement] until its [outer] surface hardens."

[H]   Samuel bar Abba [Wawa] in the name of R. Yohanan, "Until its [outer] surface hardens."

[I]   R. Jeremiah, R. Zeira in the name of Rab, "It is forbidden [to pray] near excrement even if it is dry as a bone."

[J]   Samuel said, "Until its surface hardens."

[K]   Simeon bar Abba [Wawa] said in the name of R. Yohanan, "Until its surface hardens."

[L]   Said Hezekiah, "R. Abba rules more strictly regarding urine than regarding excrement."

[M]   R. Mana said to him [Hezekiah], "Do you refer to Geniva's statement?"

[N]   He said to him [Mana], "[Even aside from that,] it is forbidden [to pray near excrement] until it is dry as a bone because it is tangibly present. [But urine even though] it is not tangibly there [even if it is merely moist, it is still forbidden to pray nearby. This is a stricter ruling.]"

Unit **I** cites T., correlates it with the rules in M., and continues with rules about immersion for those who are sick or for whom the immersion pool is far off. Unit **II** continues with a simple exegesis of a line of M. At unit **III** the Talmud turns to T. again, followed by a rule attributed to Zeira. This subject occupies the interest of the Talmud as it tries to determine whether, and finally shows that, the law is redundant, and that it may be inferred from M.

Unit **IV** cites the relevant T. and examines the implication regarding the status of a child's excreta. The Talmud introduces a side-point, that a child may have evil thoughts, to justify its conclusion regarding the law of praying near its wastes. The unit

continues with rules regarding different kinds of waste matter
and rules for praying near it, before it turns back directly to M.
to interpret the meaning of its rule.

Unit **V** again introduces appropriate T. passages and examines
their implications. The issue centers on how to dilute waste
matter so that one may pray near it. **VI** is truly tangential to all
that precedes it, surveying several different subjects. Taking off
on T.'s issue of where one may put one object in a bedroom, the
Talmud discusses this issue with reference to tefillin. Other rules
for tefillin and scrolls follow before the unit goes on to regulations for comportment during prayer and in the synagogue.

Unit **VII** continues with citations of T. and rules that develop
its concerns regarding the kinds of waste materials near which
one may recite one's prayers.

3:6

[A]   *A Zab who had a [seminal] emission, and a Niddah who dis-*
       charged semen [after intercourse], and the woman who had
       intercourse and then had a menstrual discharge, must immerse
       themselves [in a ritual bath to remove the uncleanness caused by
       the emission or intercourse before they can recite the Shemaʿ.
       They must do this even though they remain unclean on account
       of their more severe condition of uncleanness.]

[B]   *And R. Judah exempts them [from the requirement of immers-*
       ing themselves because in his view nothing is accomplished
       through the immersion. They remain unclean by virtue of the
       more severe uncleanness.]

[I.A] Thus far [from M. we understand that] if a *Zab* experienced an
       emission, [Judah exempts him from immersion]. [Does this im-
       ply that] one who had [previously] experienced an emission and
       then suffered the flow of a *Zab* may immerse himself? [Does the
       immersion have any effect if afterwards he remains unclean from
       the more severe form of uncleanness?] [From M. we deduce that
       Judah thinks that one who is severely unclean as a *Zab* cannot
       become further unclean due to an emission, and is not required
       to immerse himself to cleanse himself of the latter, rabbinically
       ordained uncleanness caused by an emission. But does Judah
       exempt a person from immersing himself if he first becomes
       unclean due to an emission, and then becomes severely unclean

due to the flow of a *Zab?* In such a case, according to Judah, does the individual have to immerse himself to remove the first uncleanness?]

[B]   Let us deduce the answer from the following: *The woman who had intercourse and then saw a menstrual discharge must immerse herself.*

[C]   *R. Judah exempts.* And what is Judah's reasoning? Is it because he reasons, "What good is immersing oneself [in this case since even if she removes the lesser uncleanness of the nocturnal emission, the severe uncleanness remains]?" Or is it because [he holds that] lesser uncleanness does not persist in the presence of more severe uncleanness [and therefore there is no moderate uncleanness to remove here, it is gone, and there is no reason for him to immerse himself]?

[D]   In what instance is there a practical difference between these alternative lines of reasoning? [In our case above, in A,] one who [first] suffered an emission [then later came into the category of *Zab*].

[E]   If your reasoning is "What good is immersing oneself [because the more severe uncleanness persists]?"—here it [the immersion] is effective. [The person initially was required to immerse himself to remove the lesser uncleanness. And by immersing himself he may fulfill this requirement.]

[F]   So the basis must be that moderate uncleanness does not persist in the presence of severe uncleanness. [This is our problem.]

[G]   This is only the case where the lesser uncleanness follows the severe uncleanness [and cannot therefore change the status of a person who is already severely unclean].

[H]   Is it also so in a case where the lesser uncleanness precedes the severe uncleanness [and when the person becomes severely unclean, that action suspends the moderate uncleanness, so there is no need for him to immerse himself on account of the lesser uncleanness]?

[I]   We may deduce [the solution] from the following [in our M.]: *A woman who had intercourse and then had a menstrual discharge must immerse. . . . And R. Judah exempts.*

[J]   This [M.] we say is parallel to our case. [The lesser uncleanness precedes the more severe uncleanness. We may then conclude that Judah exempts her from immersing herself because severe uncleanness suspends lesser uncleanness. Hence there remains no obligation for her to immerse herself.]

This long unit has one item on its agenda—the substantive analysis of Judah's exemption. It proposes that one may defend his position on the basis of two possible arguments, and then goes on to see which works best based on a close examination of the limited sources. This section represents the Talmud's most abstract level of reasoning.

4 Yerushalmi Berakhot
Chapter Four

4:1

[A]   *The Morning Prayer [may be recited] until midday.*

[B]   *R. Judah says, "Until the fourth hour [of the day]."*

[C]   *The Afternoon Prayer [may be recited] until the evening.*

[D]   *R. Judah says, "Until midafternoon."*

[E]   *The Evening Prayer has no fixed rule.*

[F]   *And the prayers of the Additional Service [may be recited] throughout the day.*

[G]   *R. Judah says, "Until the seventh hour."*

[I.A]   It is written, "To love the Lord your God, and to serve him with all your heart and with all your soul" [Deut. 11:13]. Is there [such a thing as] a service of the heart? And what is it? It is prayer.

[B]   And so it says, "[The king said to Daniel,] 'May your God, whom you serve continually, deliver you'" [Dan. 6:17]. And was there [such a thing as] a service in Babylonia? And what was it? It was prayer.

[II.A]   **One might think that he may combine the three [Prayer Services] together. It was said concerning Daniel, "And he got down upon his knees three times a day [and prayed and gave thanks before his God]" [Dan. 6:10].**

[B]   **One might think that he may pray facing any direction he wishes. [On the contrary,] Scripture states, "[He went to his** house where] he had windows in his upper chamber open toward Jerusalem" [Dan. 6:10].

[C]   One might think [that they prayed in this way] only after they came to the Diaspora. [On the contrary,] Scripture states, "As he had done previously" [ibid.].

[D]   One might think that he may recite the three [daily prayers] at any time he wishes. David already stated, "Evening and morning and noon [I utter my complaint and moan]" [Ps. 55:17].

[E]   One might think that he must raise his voice and pray. It was stated concerning Hannah, "Hannah was speaking in her heart" [1 Sam. 1:13] [T. 3:6].

[F]   One might think that he may just meditate [during Prayer]. [On the contrary,] Scripture states, "Only her lips moved" [ibid.].

[G]   What does that mean? That she spoke with her lips [i.e., articulated the words quietly—P.M.].

[H]   Said R. Yose bar Haninah, "From this verse [ibid.] you learn four things.

[I]   "'Hannah was speaking in her heart': from this you learn that Prayer requires concentration. [The heart was considered to be the source of thought.]

[J]   "'Only her lips moved': from this you learn that one must mouth the Prayer with one's lips.

[K]   "'And her voice was not heard': from this you learn that one may not raise his voice and pray.

[L]   "'And Eli took her to be a drunken woman': from this you learn a drunken person is forbidden to pray."

[M]   A teaching of Hanan bar Abba conflicts [with Yose bar Haninah's teaching that one may not pray aloud]. [According to the following story, he heard Rab pray out loud.] For Hanan bar Ba said to the associates, "Let me tell you about something good which I saw Rab do. [He bowed in a certain way during his prayer,] and I described this in front of Samuel, and he got up and kissed me on the mouth."

[N]   [And this is what Rab did. When he said,] "Blessed art Thou," he bowed. When he mentioned the name [of God, "O Lord,"] he straightened up. [Rab straightened before reciting the name of God.]

[O] Samuel said, "I will tell you that the basis for this [Rab's action is the verse,] 'The Lord lifts up those who are bowed down'" [Ps. 146:8]. [Accordingly, when one who is bowed down recites the name of the Lord, he should straighten up.]

[P] Said R. Ammi, "This does not make sense [because another verse says,] 'He bowed in awe of my name'" [Mal. 2:5].

[Q] Said R. Abin, "If it was written in the verse, 'At my name [bšmy]' he bowed, very well [that would contradict Rab's practice.] But is it not written, 'He bowed in awe of my name?' [That could mean] previously, before he mentioned the name, he was already bowing down." [It could then be said that when he mentioned God's name he straightened up. That is not a contradiction of Rab's custom.] [Cf. above, M. 1:4 IX.]

[III.A] R. Abba bar Zabdi used to pray [reciting the Eighteen Blessings] in a loud voice.

[B] When R. Yonah prayed in a synagogue, he prayed quietly. And when he prayed at home, he prayed in a loud voice so that his family would learn from him how to pray.

[C] Said R. Mana, "My father's family learned how to pray from him."

[IV.A] Whence did they derive the [obligation to recite daily] three prayers? R. Samuel bar Nahmani said, "They parallel the three changes people undergo each day.

[B] "In the morning a person must say, 'I give thanks, Lord, my God and God of my fathers, for you have brought me forth from darkness into light!'

[C] "In the afternoon a person must say, 'I give thanks to you, Lord, my God and God of my fathers, for just as I have merited seeing the sun [rise] in the east, now may I merit seeing it [set] in the west.'

[D] "In the evening he must say, 'May it be thy will, Lord, my God and God of my fathers, that just as I have been in darkness before and you have brought me forth to light, so shall you once again bring me forth from darkness to light.'"

[E]   R. Joshua ben Levi said, "They learned the [obligation to recite the three daily] prayers from the [actions of the] patriarchs.

[F]   "[They derived the obligation to recite] the Morning Prayer from [the action of] our forefather Abraham: 'And Abraham went early in the morning to the place where he had stood before the Lord' [Gen. 19:27]. And 'standing' must refer to [the recitation of the] Prayer. As it says, 'Then Phineas stood up and prayed' [Ps. 106:30].

[G]   "[They derived the obligation to recite] the Afternoon Prayer, [from the action of] our forefather Isaac: 'And Isaac went out to meditate in the field in the evening' [Gen. 24:63]. And 'meditation' must refer to [the recitation of the] Prayer. As it says, 'A prayer of one afflicted, when he is faint and pours out his meditation before the Lord' [Ps. 101:1].

[H]   "[They derived the obligation to recite] the Evening Prayer, from [the action of] our forefather Jacob: 'And he came to [wypg'] a certain place, and stayed there that night because the sun had set' [Gen. 28:11]. And [the Hebrew term for] 'coming to' [pgy'h] must refer to [the recitation of the] Prayer. As it says, 'Let them intercede [ypg'w] with the Lord of hosts' [Jer. 28:18]. And it says, 'As for you, do not pray for this people, or lift up cry or Prayer for them, and do not intercede [tpg'] with me, for I do not hear you'" [Jer. 7:16].

[I]   And our rabbis said: The [obligation to recite three daily] Prayers is derived from the [comparison to the order of the] daily sacrifices.

[J]   The [obligation to recite the] Morning Prayer [is derived] from the daily morning sacrifice: 'The one lamb you shall offer in the morning' [Num. 28:4].

[K]   The [obligation to recite the] Afternoon Prayer [is derived] from the daily evening sacrifice: 'And the other lamb you shall offer in the evening' [ibid.].

[L]   For the Evening Prayer, they found no support. So they just taught [that one is obliged to recite it] without elaborating [on the sources of the obligation]. This is as we learned, *The Evening Prayer has no fixed rule. And the Additional Prayer may be recited throughout the day* [M. 4:1].

[M]   Said R. Tanhuma, "[The Evening Prayer also had a parallel in the sacrificial service of the Temple.] They established it parallel to the consumption [by burning] of the fats and entrails. For they were consumed on the altar throughout the night."

[V.A]   From words in Scripture, R. Judah [M. 4:1B] derived [his rule, that one may recite the Prayer until the fourth hour of the day]. As R. Ishmael taught, "'When the sun grew hot, it [the manna] melted' [Exod. 16:21]—that was at the fourth hour."

[B]   Must you say it was at the fourth hour? Or [can you not argue that it was rather at the sixth hour [i.e., at noon]?

[C]   When it says, "In the heat of the day" [Gen. 18:1], lo, this implies [it was at] the sixth hour [in the middle of the day].

[D]   We may then infer that "when the sun grew hot, it melted" refers to [a slightly earlier time of day—] the fourth hour.

[E]   And you may expound upon the verse, "Morning by morning [they gathered it]" [Exod. 16:21, the first part of the verse cited above,] as follows. Just as the word "morning" here [ibid.] [means until] the fourth hour [one may gather the manna], so also "morning" elsewhere ["The one lamb shall you offer in the morning" in Num. 28:4] means until the fourth hour [one may offer the morning sacrifice. Accordingly, until the fourth hour one may recite the Morning Prayer].

[F]   [According to C–D why does "when the sun grew hot" refer to the fourth hour and "the heat of the day," refer to the sixth hour?] At the fourth hour, it is hot in the sun, and it is cool in the shade. At the sixth hour, it is hot in the sun, and it is hot in the shade.

[G]   Said R. Tanhuma, "What does 'in the heat of the day' mean? A time when no creature can find shade."

[H]   R. Yasa would pray at the third hour. R. Hiyya bar Abba [Wawa] would pray at the third hour.

[I]   R. Berekhiah Hamuniah would recite the *Shemaʿ* and pray after the third hour.

[J]   But lo, it was taught, *One who recites from here onwards, has not lost [the purpose of the act entirely since he is] like one who recites from the Torah* [M. 1:2]. [But if he recites this late, he does not fulfill his obligation even according to Joshua who says he may recite, *Until the third hour* (M. 1:2E)!]

[K]   Let us say that in this case he [Berekhiah] had already accepted
        the yoke of heaven [i.e., recited the *Shema'*] in its proper time.
        [He was repeating it later.]

[L]   Alternatively, R. Judah [M. 4:1B] derived [his rule, *Until the
        fourth hour*] from a testimony [described in M. Eduyot].

[M]   As R. Simon in the name of R. Joshua b. Levi said, "In the days
        of Seleucid rule they used to lower down [over the wall, from
        the besieged Temple of Jerusalem,] two vessels of gold. And in
        return they [the besiegers] sent back up two lambs [for the daily
        sacrifice].

[N]   "One time they lowered down two vessels of gold and in return
        they sent back up two goats [instead of lambs]. At that very time
        the Holy One revealed to them two lambs in the Temple Store.
        Based on that event [when they offered the sacrifice late in the
        morning], *R. Judah b. Baba testified that the daily morning sac-
        rifice is to be offered at the fourth hour*" [M. Eduyot 6:1].

[O]   Said R. Levi, "[The following event occurred] also during [the
        period of subjugation to] these wicked rulers [i.e., Rome]. They
        would lower down two vessels of gold, and in return they [the
        Romans] used to send back up two lambs. At the end [of the
        siege] they sent down two vessels of gold and they [the Romans]
        sent back up two pigs. They had raised them less than half way
        up the wall, and a pig became stuck in the wall. And the wall
        shook. And the pig sprang [away, alt.: and the land shook for]
        forty parsangs away from the Land of Israel. At that very time,
        because of the sins [of Israel], the daily sacrifice was suspended,
        and the Temple was destroyed."

[VI.A] What is the basis for the rule of the rabbis [*The Morning Prayer
        may be recited until midday* (M. 4:1A)]? The verse says,
        "There are two [sacrifices] each day" [Num. 28:3]. [This im-
        plies that] you should divide the day into two equal parts.

[B]   And how does R. Judah interpret this phrase? He says, "Two
        each day" serves as the Scriptural basis for the obligation [to
        bring two daily sacrifices. It does not teach us anything regard-
        ing the time for the sacrifice].

[C]   Or, "Two each day"—[you may say he explains] they serve as
        two defenders [of Israel] through each day [one the first half, the
        other the second half].

[D]   Or, "Two each day"—[You may say he explains] they should be slaughtered for the sake of use that day [as a daily sacrifice, not another day].

[E]   Or, "Two each day"—[you may say he explains] they should be slaughtered [outside] in the daylight. [These are possible alternative interpretations in support of Judah's view against the view of the sages.]

[F]   This [last alternative] accords with that which was taught: *The daily morning sacrifice was slaughtered in the northwestern corner, near the second ring [of the altar], in the daylight.*

[G]   *And the evening sacrifice was slaughtered in the northeastern corner, near the second ring, in the daylight* [M. Tamid 4:1].

[H]   And this is done [i.e., they are slaughtered in different places] so that they will know which of them was slaughtered in the morning and which in the evening [when the remains are later burned on the altar].

[VII.A]   R. Hiyya in the name of R. Yohanan, "[In the afternoon, if one has not yet recited both] the Afternoon Prayer and the Additional Prayer [on a Sabbath or festival]—the Afternoon Prayer takes precedence. [He must recite it first.] You must say [this rule applies only] when there is not enough time left in the day to recite both [prayers]. But if there is enough time to recite both, the Additional Prayer takes precedence."

[B]   R. Zeira in the name of R. Yohanan, "Even if there is enough time left in the day to recite both prayers, the Afternoon Prayer takes precedence."

[C]   R. Nathan bar Tobiah in the name of R. Yohanan, "Even if there is enough time left in the day to recite both prayers, the Afternoon Prayer takes precedence."

[D]   But was it not taught, "One who recited the Afternoon Prayer in advance of the Additional Prayer fulfilled his obligation"? [This rule applies to] an action in the past [post facto]. But [ab initio] to begin with [this rule] does not apply. [This appears to contradict A, Yohanan's teaching—P.M.] [The Additional Prayer takes precedence.]

[E]   You may resolve this contradiction [by explaining that this baraita refers to a case where one prays] before the proper time for

the Afternoon Prayer [i.e., before six and one-half hours of the
day have elapsed. In some cases one may recite the Afternoon
Prayer before the Additional Prayer.]

[F]   [And] this accords with [the following:] R. Joshua b. Levi would
instruct his students, "If you are going to have a big meal [and
fear it may last into the night], and if it is past the sixth hour of
the day before you go to the meal, then you should recite the
Afternoon Prayer before you go to the meal." [You may pray a
little bit early to avoid possibly missing the time for the Prayer
later, when you are involved in the meal. Yohanan above may
refer to a case such as this one.]

[VIII.A] [*The Afternoon Prayer . . . R. Judah says, "Until midafternoon."*
M. 4 : 1D]. And when is midafternoon? Ten and three-quarters
hours into the day. [The 'short measure of afternoon' begins at
nine and one-half hours into the day (about 3:30 P.M.), with day
finishing at 6:00 P.M. The midafternoon by this reckoning is
about 4:45 P.M. And note that the length of an "hour" is ad-
justed according to the seasonal variation in the amount of
daylight.] [See T. 3 : 1.]

[B]   It was taught there, *The Daily Sacrifice is slaughtered at eight
and one-half hours, and offered on the altar at nine and one-
half hours.*

[C]   *On Passover eve it was slaughtered at seven and one-half hours,
and offered on the altar at eight and one-half hours, whether it
fell on a weekday or on the Sabbath* [M. Pes. 5 : 1].

[D]   R. Jeremiah posed this objection, "Here [in the baraita in A]
you specify the time for the Afternoon [Sacrifice and Prayer] as
two and one-half hours before sunset. And here [in M. Pes.
cited in B–C] you specify the time for the Afternoon [Sacrifice
and Prayer] as three and one-half hours [before sunset]."

[E]   Said R. Yose, "The [rule for the] Afternoon Prayer is not to be
connected to [the rule for] the Afternoon Sacrifice [which is
slaughtered at eight and one-half hours]. Rather [the rule is con-
nected] to [the law for bringing the Afternoon] Incense Offering
[which takes place one hour after the Daily Sacrifice is offered
upon the altar, at nine and one-half hours. The time at which
the Incense Offering is brought is also the time for the recitation
of the Afternoon Prayer, i.e., from nine and one-half to twelve
hours.]"

[F]   What is the Scriptural basis [for this calculation]? "Let my
       Prayer be counted as incense before thee, and the lifting up of
       my hands as an evening sacrifice" [Ps. 141:2]. You may exclude
       [from your reckoning of the time of afternoon] one hour for its
       preparations [before the incense sacrifice is brought to the altar
       and is lit]. That makes the afternoon [up to] two and one-half
       hours long.

[IX.A] R. Yose b. Haninah used to recite [the Afternoon] Prayer at sun-
       set, so that he would be in fear of heaven all the day long.

[B]   Said R. Yose b. Haninah, "May my lot be cast with those who
       recite their prayers at sunset." What is the Scriptural basis [for
       this practice]? "Therefore, let everyone who is worthy offer
       prayers to thee; at a time they are pressed" [Ps. 32:6]. What
       is "a time they are pressed" [*mṣw'*]? A time in the day [when
       people] are pressed [i.e., at the end of the day—*mṣwyw šl ywm*,
       lit. the squeezing of the day—a word play]. [We follow S.H.
       here. P.M. interprets differently.]

[C]   R. Ada's mother's brother [uncle] used to hold the prayer cloak
       of Rab on the great fast [the Day of Atonement]. He [Rab] said
       to him, "When you see the sun reach the tops of the palm trees,
       give me my prayer cloak so that I may recite the Afternoon
       Prayer." [This implies that Rab asked for his prayer cloak
       early—before the sun was setting.]

[D]   [At the time of day] while the sun is yet at the tops of the palm
       trees there [in Babylonia where the terrain of settlement is level,
       the time when the sun reaches the tops of the trees may be close
       to nightfall, but] it is [often still] daytime here [in the Land of
       Israel where settlements are found on varying terrains and the
       time the sun reaches the tops of the trees may be early in the
       afternoon].

[E]   As R. Yohanan said, "Who says to the deep, 'be dry' [Isa.
       44:27]—this is Babylonia for it is in the lowest part of the
       earth."

[F]   Said R. Yohanan, "Why is it called 'The deep'? Because those
       who died in the generation of the flood sank down there." [This
       verse supports this teaching:] 'Babylon must fall for the slain
       of Israel, as in Babylon have fallen the slain of all the earth'
       [Jer. 51:49].

[G]   It is written, "They found a plain in the land of Shinar and settled there" [Gen. 11:2]. [Shinar is in Babylonia and the Talmud assumes that the incidents in the story of the Tower of Babel took place in Babylonia.]

[H]   Said Resh Laqish, "Why did they call it 'Shinar'? [The explanations which follow are based on word plays.] Because all the corpses of the generation of the flood were dumped there [nn'rw]."

[I]   Another explanation [of the meaning of] "Shinar"—they are dying, choking in the smoke and odor, for they are without oil lamps [nr], without a bathhouse.

[J]   Another explanation of "Shinar"—they are stripped [mnw'rym] of the commandments. [For they are outside the Land of Israel,] without [the obligations to give] heave-offerings or tithes.

[K]   Another explanation of "Shinar"—its officials die as lads [n'rym].

[L]   Another explanation of "Shinar"—it produced an enemy and hater [śwn' w'r] of the Holy One, Blessed be He. And who was that? The evil Nebuchadnezzar [who destroyed the Temple].

[M]   Does Rab [returning to the story above, C, who recited the Afternoon Prayer early, before midafternoon] then follow the rule of R. Judah [against the view of sages, i.e., that one must recite the Afternoon Prayer before nine and one-half hours into the day? Yes, for the following reason:] If you act in accord with the view of the rabbis [and pray later than midafternoon], R. Judah will not agree [that this is proper]. But if you act in accord with the view of R. Judah [and pray only before midafternoon], even the rabbis will agree [that this is proper and you will have satisfied both views].

[X.A]   Whence [do we derive the obligation to recite] the Closing Service [Ne'ilah, on the Day of Atonement and other public fast days]?

[B]   Said R. Levi, "'Even though you make many prayers I will not listen' [Isa. 1:15]. [Only in that instance will he not listen. Ordinarily he would listen.] From here we learn that all those who add more prayers, are answered." [The Closing Prayer is an instance of an added prayer.]

[C]   [It appears that] R. Levi holds the opposite view elsewhere [i.e., that adding prayers may be detrimental].

[D]   There [cf. Y. Bik. 2:1] said R. Abba son of R. Pappi, R. Joshua of Sakhnin in the name of R. Levi, "'In all toil there is profit, but mere talk tends only to want' [Prov. 14:23]. By adding to her prayers, Hannah shortened Samuel's life.

[E]   "[She asked that he live for fifty years. How so?] For she said, ['As soon as the child is weaned, I will bring him, that he may appear in the presence of the Lord,] and abide there forever' [1 Sam. 1:22]. 'Forever' for a Levite means for fifty years. As it is written, 'From the age of fifty years they shall withdraw from the work of the service and serve no more'" [Num. 8:25].

[F]   But [Samuel] lived fifty-two years!

[G]   Said R. Yose b. R. Bun, "[Add] two years [before] he was weaned." [In any case, Hannah's added prayers were heard, and her son Samuel's life was shortened accordingly.]

[H]   Does [Levi] then say [in D that increasing Prayer may be detrimental]? If he does, it is only regarding the Prayer of an individual [such as Hannah]. But regarding communal Prayer [Levi holds the view that adding to it is beneficial, as in B above].

[I]   R. Hiyya in the name of R. Yohanan, R. Simeon b. Halafta in the name of R. Meir, "'As she continued praying before the Lord' [1 Sam. 1:12]—from this we learn that all who add to their prayers are answered. [Even an individual benefits by adding prayers, contrary to Levi's view.]"

[J]   When [does one recite] the Closing Prayer?

[K]   The rabbis of Caesarea [may be: Katzrin] said, "Rab and R. Yohanan disputed this issue."

[L]   Rab said, "At the [time of the] closing of the gates of heaven [i.e., sunset]."

[M]   And R. Yohanan said, "At the [time of the] closing of the gates of the Temple courtyard [after the Incense Offering of the Afternoon Sacrifice]."

[N]   R. Yudan Antordia said, "The Mishnah supports [this view of] R. Yohanan: *On three occasions the priests raise their hands [to*

bless the people] four times during the day—at the Morning
Service, at the Additional Service, at the Afternoon Service, and
at the Close of the Gates—on fast days, on the days of changing
the watch, and on the Day of Atonement" [M. Ta'anit 4 : 1].

[O] Can you say that this refers to the [priests blessing the people
after the] close of the gates of heaven [i.e., after sunset? The text
of M. says they raised their hands four times] during the day. [It
must refer to the (time of the) close of the gates of the courtyard
while it is still day. This supports Yohanan against Rab.]

[P] [But as we saw in **IX**.C above:] R. Ada's mother's brother
[uncle] used to hold Rab's prayer cloak on the great fast [the
Day of Atonement]. He [Rab] said to him, "When you see the
sun reach the tops of the palm trees [in the afternoon], give me
my Prayer cloak so that I may recite the [service of the] Closing
of the Gates." [This implies that Rab asked for his Prayer cloak
early—before the sun was setting.]

[Q] It appears that the opinion of Rab is reversed. There [in L] he
says [the Closing Prayer is to be recited], "At the close of the
gates of heaven [i.e., at sunset]." Here he says [to recite it],
"At the close of the gates of the Temple courtyard [in the
afternoon]."

[R] Said R. Matna, "[There is no contradiction.] Since Rab extended [his recitation of] his Prayer so much, [though he may
have started reciting early] he would continue until the [time of
the] close of the gates of heaven [i.e., sunset]."

[S] [According to the view that one recites it after sunset,] does [the
recitation of] the Closing Prayer exempt one from [the obligation
to recite] the Evening Prayer?

[T] R. Abba and R. Huna in the name of Rab, "[The recitation of]
the Closing Prayer exempts one from [the obligation to recite]
the Evening Prayer."

[U] R. Abba said to R. Huna [by way of objection], "[If one does
not recite the Evening Prayer,] how then does one mention the
Prayer of Divison [the *Habdalah*, Prayer of Separation or Distinction, normally inserted in the fourth blessing of the Evening
Prayer at the conclusion of a holiday]?"

[V] Said R. Yona to R. Abba [by way of another objection], "How
does [reciting a prayer service of] seven [i.e., the Closing Prayer]

exempt one from [the obligation to recite a Prayer of] Eighteen [the Evening Prayer]?"

[W]   Said [R. Abba] to R. Yona, "Did I not already raise one objection?"

[X]   Said R. Yona to R. Abba, "Because of your [weak] objection, shall we invalidate [Rab's ruling]?"

[Y]   Said R. Yose, "[On the contrary.] R. Abba's question is a very good one. R. Yona's question is not a very good one. For in this case, [on the Day of Atonement a person is weak and we may explain that] he be allowed leniency because of the fast. [In this instance they allowed that reciting a Prayer of] seven blessings exempts one from the obligation to recite eighteen blessings."

[Z]   R. Abba bar Mamal said to the associates, "I have learned from all of you that [reciting] the Closing Prayer does not exempt one from [the obligation to recite] the Evening Prayer."

[AA]   [Likewise] R. Simon in the name of R. Joshua b. Levi, "[Reciting] the Closing Prayer does not exempt one from the [obligation to recite the] Evening Prayer."

[BB]   Said R. Yose b. R. Bun and taught R. Hiyya, "A person must recite the Prayer of Eighteen every day—[including the] the evening following the Sabbath, the evening following the Day of Atonement, and the evening following a public fast day [that coincides with the Sabbath. They must recite the Prayer of Eighteen so that they may insert the Prayer of Division formula in the fourth blessing of the Eighteen—P.M.]."

[XI.A] R. Yitzhak bar Nahman in the name of R. Joshua b. Levi, "When the Day of Atonement coincides with the Sabbath, even though [ordinarily they recite] no Closing Prayer on the Sabbath day, [in this case] one inserts a mention of the Sabbath in the Closing service."

[B]   They added to this [the following related teachings], "When the new moon coincides with a public fast day, even though [ordinarily they recite] no Closing Prayer on the new moon, [in this case] one inserts a mention of the new moon in the Closing Prayer."

[C]   R. Simon in the name of R. Joshua b. Levi, "When the Sabbath coincides with Hanukkah, even though [ordinarily they recite] no Additional Service on Hanukkah, [in this case] one inserts a mention of Hanukkah in the Additional Service [of the Sabbath day]."

[D]   They added to this [further teachings], "When the new moon coincides with Hanukkah, even though [ordinarily they recite] no Additional Service for Hanukkah, [in this case] one inserts a mention of Hanukkah in the Additional Service [for the new moon]."

[E]   When a new moon coincides with a fast day [B]—where [in the Closing Service] does one insert a mention of the new moon?

[F]   R. Zeira says, "In the blessing of thanksgiving [the sixth]."

[G]   R. Abba bar Mamal said, "In the blessing of the Temple service [the fifth]."

[H]   R. Abina said, "In a fourth blessing [S.H. and M.H.: fifth blessing]."

[I]   Said R. Abba, "What is the rule in other instances? One inserts [a mention of the day] in the fourth blessing. Here too one inserts [a mention of the new moon] in the fourth blessing." And so it was the practice to act according to R. Abba's statement.

[XII.A]   What passage do they read [from the Torah on the new moon which coincides with a fast day]?

[B]   R. Yose said, "They read the blessings and curses [Deut. 28, the passage usually read on the fast day]."

[C]   R. Mana said to him, "[Do you read the passage for a fast day] in order to inform the people that it is a fast day? They will be bowing over already [to recite the Tahanun Service]. And will they not know it is a fast day [since otherwise that practice is omitted on the new moon]?"

[D]   R. Yose said to R. Mana, "[I stated this rule] to inform you that the practice is to read the passage concerning the blessings and curses. [Indeed, this practice is not intended to be a sign for the people that it is a fast day. Rather it is to lead people to repent. S.H.]"

[E]   R. Yudan of Cappadocia said before R. Yose in the name of R. Judah b. Pazzi, "[On a new moon that coincides with a fast day] they read the passage for the new moon."

[F]　R. Yose arose [to inquire about this] with R. Judah b. Pazzi. He [Yose] said to him [Judah], "Did you learn this from your father?"

[G]　He said to him, "My father said this applied only for the village of Ein Tob. Since they knew for sure that it was the new moon, [since the court which sanctified the new moon was located there,] they read the passage for the new moon. But in all other places they read [the passage for a fast day—] the blessings and curses."

[H]　Jeremiah the scribe asked R. Jeremiah, "On a new moon which coincides with the Sabbath, what [passage from the prophets] do they read?"

[I]　He said to him, "They read the passage [usually read on] the new moon."

[J]　R. Helbo said before R. Ammi, "The Mishnah so teaches: *They interrupt [the regular order of the readings from the prophets on the Sabbath] on all [those Sabbaths which coincide with these holidays]: for new moons, for Hanukkah, and for Purim, [for fast days, for watch days, and for the Day of Atonement]*" [M. Meg. 3:4].

[K]　Yitzhak the merchant asked R. Yitzhak, "On the new moon that coincides with Hanukkah, what [passage from the Torah] do they read?"

[L]　He said to him, "They first read three sections from [the passage for] the new moon and then one section from [the passage for] Hanukkah."

[M]　R. Pinhas, and R. Simon, and R. Abba bar Zemina who cited it in the name of R. Abdima of Haifa, "They [first] read three sections from [the passage for] Hanukkah and then read one section from [the passage for] the new moon to indicate that the fourth [portion] is read only on account of the new moon."

[N]　Bar Shalmaya the scribe asked R. Mana, "Take notice that when the new moon of Hanukkah coincides with the Sabbath, do we not read seven [portions]? Can you possibly contend that anyone will know that 'the fourth is read only on account of the new moon'?" (P.M. omits: "I have asked the scribes [this question].")

[O]   He said to him, "Is that [worthy enough to be] a scribe's question? [It is a foolish objection because they always read seven portions on the Sabbath. How can you compare that to the case of the weekday readings?] [So P.M.]"

[XIII.A]   Rabbi instructed his spokesman Abdan to announce to the congregation, "Whoever wishes to recite the [Saturday] Evening Prayer may do so, even while it is still daytime [after mid-afternoon]."

[B]   R. Hiyya bar Abba [Wawa] instructed his spokesman to announce to the congregation, "Whoever wishes to recite the [Saturday] Evening Prayer may do so, even while it is still daytime."

[C]   Said R. Haninah, "R. Ishmael b. R. Yose took me to a certain inn and said to me, 'Here my father once recited the Evening Sabbath Prayer on the eve of the Sabbath [while it was yet day]'."

[D]   Said R. Ammi, "R. Yohanan disputed [this practice of saying the Sabbath Eve Prayer while it is yet day]." But he had no cause to dispute this. Why? For we are permitted to take [time] from the profane [weekdays] and add it to the holy [Sabbath]. [Reciting the Sabbath Eve Service early is surely permissible.]

[E]   And furthermore [a story supports the practice]: The donkey drivers came from Araba to Sepphoris and said, "R. Haninah b. Dosa already began the Sabbath [while it was still daytime] in his village." [Yohanan surely would not dispute this practice.]

[F]   So concerning what practice did he [Ammi] say [that Yohanan disputed]? Concerning this: For R. Haninah said, "R. Ishmael b. R. Yose took me to a certain inn and said to me, 'Here my father once recited the Evening Prayer of the conclusion of the Sabbath on the Sabbath day.'"

[G]   And even concerning this he [Yohanan] had no cause to dispute [because this was an accepted practice]: For Rabbi instructed Abdan his spokesman to announce to the congregation, "Whoever wishes to recite the [Saturday] Evening Prayer may do so, even while it is still daytime."

[H]   R. Hiyya bar Abba [Wawa] instructed his spokesman to announce to the congregation, "Whoever wishes to recite the

[Saturday] Evening Prayer may do so even while it is still daytime."

[I]   The house of R. Yannai said concerning [the recitation of the Evening Prayer], "They do not require a person [who had not recited the Evening Prayer at night and had already recited the Evening Prayer early, during the day and] who is in bed [at night], to get out in order to recite the Evening Prayer."

[J]   Said R. Zeira, "Whenever I followed this practice [and did not say the Evening Prayer at home at night], I was afraid the whole night."

[K]   You have then only this [one leniency which applies to the recitation of the Evening Prayer]: For Rabbi instructed his spokesman Abdan to announce to the congregation, "Whoever wishes to recite the Evening Prayer may do so, even while it is still daytime."

[L]   R. Hiyya bar Abba [Wawa] instructed his spokesman to announce to the congregation, "Whoever wishes to recite the Evening Prayer may do so, even while it is still daytime."

[XIV.A]   Said R. Jacob bar Aha, "It was taught there: What is the rule concerning the Evening Prayer? Rabban Gamaliel says, 'It is compulsory.' R. Joshua says, 'It is optional.'"

[B]   R. Haninah said, "This dispute [concerning the obligation to recite the Evening Prayer] parallels this dispute [above, unit **X,** whether one who recites the Closing Prayer of the Day of Atonement is exempt from reciting the Evening Prayer].

[C]   "The one who holds [the view that the Evening Prayer is] compulsory, [also holds the view that reciting] the Closing Prayer does not exempt one from reciting the Evening Prayer.

[D]   "And the one who holds [the view that the Evening Prayer is] optional, [also holds the view that reciting] the Closing Prayer exempts one from reciting the Evening Prayer."

[XV.A]   Once a student came and asked R. Joshua, "What is the rule concerning the Evening Prayer?"

[B]   He said to him, "It is optional."

[C]   He came and asked Rabban Gamaliel, "What is the rule concerning the Evening Prayer?"

[D]   He said to him, "It is compulsory."

[E]   He said to him, "But behold, R. Joshua told me that it is optional."

[F]   He said to him, "Tomorrow, when I enter the meeting house, stand and ask me concerning this law."

[G]   The next day this student stood up and asked Rabban Gamaliel, "What is the rule concerning the Evening Prayer?"

[H]   He said to him, "It is compulsory."

[I]   He said to him, "But, lo, R. Joshua told me it is optional."

[J]   Said Rabban Gamaliel to R. Joshua, "Are you the one who said it is optional?"

[K]   He said to him, "No." He said to him, "Stand on your feet and they will testify [that you said it]."

[L]   And Rabban Gamaliel sat and expounded, and R. Joshua stood [in disgrace] until the people cried out.

[M]   And they said to R. Huspit the Meturgaman, "Dismiss the people."

[N]   And they said to R. Zenon the Hazzan, "Begin saying." He began to say. The people began.

[O]   And they stood up and they said to him [Gamaliel], "For upon whom has not come your unceasing evil" [Nahum 3 : 19]?

[P]   They [deposed Gamaliel and] appointed R. Eleazar ben Azariah to [head] the Academy. He was sixteen years old and all his hair had turned grey [cf. M. Ber. 1 : 5].

[Q]   And R. Aqiba sat, troubled [that he had not been selected]. And he said [concerning Eleazar], "It is not that he is more learned in Torah than I. Rather he is of greater parentage than I. Happy is the person who has ancestral merit! Happy is the person who has a 'peg' to hang upon!"

[R]   And what was R. Eleazar b. Azariah's 'peg'? He was the tenth generation [in descent] from Ezra.

[S]   And how many benches were there [in the Academy]?

[T]   R. Jacob bar Sisi said, "There were eighty benches full of scholars besides those who stood behind the partition."

[U]   R. Yose b. R. Abun said, "There were three hundred there besides those who stood behind the partition."

[V]   And this refers to what was taught elsewhere: *On the day that they seated R. Eleazar b. Azariah in the Academy* [M. Zeb. 1:3, M. Yad. 3:5, 4:2].

[W]   And it was taught elsewhere, *This teaching R. Eleazar b. Azariah expounded before the sages at the vineyard at Yavneh* [M.Ket. 4:6]. And was there a vineyard there [where they sat and learned]? Rather this refers to the scholars who were arranged in rows, like [vines in] a vineyard.

[X]   Rabban Gamaliel immediately went to each one's house to appease him. He went to Joshua. He found him sitting and making needles.

[Y]   He said to him, "Is this how you make a living?" He said to him, "Are you finally finding out [how hard it is for us to make a living]? Woe to the generation of which you are the steward." He [Gamaliel] said, "I submit to you."

[Z]   And they sent a fuller to R. Eleazar b. Azariah [to inform him of the reconciliation]. And some say it was R. Aqiba.

[AA]   He said to him [Eleazar], "He who is [a priest authorized] to sprinkle [the water of purification], the son of one who sprinkles, let him sprinkle. He who is neither [a priest authorized] to sprinkle, nor the son of a sprinkler, shall he [have the authority] to say to one who sprinkles, who is the son of one who sprinkles, '[You are unfit for your duties.] Your water is water from a cave, and your ashes are from wood'?" [Shall you, Eleazar, have the authority to replace Gamaliel, the legitimate heir to the patriarchate?]

[BB]   He [Eleazar] said to him, "You have appeased me. Let us go to Rabban Gamaliel's door [and inform him]."

[CC]   Even so they did not depose him [Eleazar] from his high position. Rather they appointed him Chief Judge [*ab bet din*].

In unit **I** the Talmud begins with a brief but crucial tradition that prayer is, "service of the heart." Unit **II** goes ahead to cite the relevant Tosefta passages that deal with the procedures for reciting the Daily Prayer Services. They touch on the issues of the time, articulation, orientation, and place for prayer.

The Talmud adds to this a related teaching and then goes on to derive practices for prayer from the example of Hannah. The unit concludes with a teaching we saw earlier in another context, brought in here because it indicates that one may pray aloud. Unit **III** continues on that same issue.

Unit **IV** deals with the basis for the daily ritual of reciting three prayer services. It first suggests that the practice is based on the natural unfolding of the day. It then posits that the three daily services have distinct historical precedents. The Talmud then suggests that the direct precedents for the Morning and Afternoon Prayers are the sacrifices of the Temple and seeks some source for the legitimacy of the Evening service.

Following this discussion of the background for M.'s subject matter, at unit **V,** the Talmud turns to the exegesis of the M. itself. The section undertakes an extended discussion of Judah's view to show from Scriptural exegesis that morning extends until the fourth hour, and it supplies another source for Judah's law.

Unit **VI** looks first to Scripture for support for the ruling of the rabbis. Unit **VII** departs briefly from the exegesis of the M. to take up the issue of precedence between the obligations to recite the Morning and the Afternoon Prayers.

Unit **VIII** returns to the exegetical task and explains the term "midafternoon" in our M. Having completed its interpretation of M., the Talmud begins next to present materials related to its general themes. Unit **IX,** with intervening digressions, correlates practices of the rabbis for reciting their prayers at different times of day with the rules of our M. Unit **X** leaves the subjects of our M. to introduce an independent unit on the Closing Prayer, recited on the Day of Atonement, and public fast days.

Unit **XI** opens a complex derivative issue, where one makes insertions in the Closing Prayer when two special occasions coincide. Unit **XII** continues this line of interest with several rules about the readings from the Torah and Prophets on days when two occasions coincide.

Unit **XIII** introduces the question of whether one may recite the Evening Prayer while it is still daytime, another issue secondary to our M.'s theme. Several arguments, stories, and testimonies clarify the practice. The Talmud then shows at unit

XIV that you may correlate the independent dispute regarding the obligation to recite the Evening Prayer, with a dispute introduced earlier, at unit **X**, regarding the Closing Prayer.

This reference to the dispute about the obligation to recite the Evening Prayer leads the Talmud to conclude the entire section with Yerushalmi's version of the complex story of the deposition of Patriarch Gamaliel and the installation in his place of Eleazar b. Azariah.

4:2

[A]   *R. Nehuniah b. Haqanah used to recite a short Prayer when he entered the study hall and when he exited.*

[B]   *They said to him, "What is the nature of this Prayer?"*

[C]   *He said to them, "When I enter, I pray that I will cause no offense. And when I exit, I give thanks for my portion."*

[I.A]   When he enters [the study hall], what does he say? "May it be thy will, Lord my God, God of my fathers that I shall not be angry with my associates, and that my associates shall not be angry with me [S.H.]; that we not declare the clean to be unclean, that we not declare the unclean to be clean; that we not declare the permissible to be forbidden, that we not declare the forbidden to be permissible; lest I find myself put to shame in this world and in the world to come [for rendering a wrong decision]."

[B]   And when he exits [the study hall], what does he say? "I give thanks to thee, Lord my God, God of my fathers, that you cast my lot with those who sit in the study hall and the synagogues, and you did not cast my lot with those who sit in the theaters and circuses. For I toil and they toil. I arise early and they arise early. I toil so that I shall inherit [a share of] paradise [in the world to come] and they toil [and shall end up] in a pit of destruction. As it says, 'For thou dost not give me up to Sheol, or let thy godly one see the pit'" [Ps. 16:10].

[II.A]   R. Pedat in the name of R. Jacob bar Idi, "R. Eleazar used to recite three prayers after his recitation of the Prayer [of Eighteen]. What did he say? 'May it be thy will, Lord my God, and God of my fathers, that no person come to hate us, nor that we come to hate any person, and that no person come to envy us, nor that we come to envy any person. And let [the study of] your Torah be our occupation all the days of our lives. And let our words be supplications before you."

[B]   R. Hiyya bar Abba adds [to this prayer recited after the recitation of the Prayer of Eighteen], "And unite our hearts to fear your name. And keep us far from that which you despise. And bring us near to that which you love. And deal justly with us for the sake of your name."

[C]   The house of R. Yannai says, "When one wakes up from his sleep, he must say, 'Blessed are you, Lord, who resurrects the dead. My master, I have sinned before you. May it be thy will, Lord my God, that you give to me a good heart, a good portion, a good inclination, a good associate, a good name, a good eye, and a good soul, and a humble soul and a modest spirit. And do not allow your name to be profaned among us. And do not make us the subject of [evil] talk among your creatures. And do not lead us in the end to destruction. And [do not turn] our hope to despair. And do not make our welfare depend on gifts from other people. And do not make us depend for sustenance on other people. For the beneficence of others is small and their hatred is great. And set our portion with your Torah, with those who do your will. Rebuild your house, your [Temple] courtyard, your city, and your Temple speedily in our days."

[D]   R. Hiyya bar Abba [Wawa] prayed, "May it be thy will, Lord our God, and God of our fathers, that you put in our hearts [the ability] to repent fully before you so that we not be put to shame in the presence of our forefathers in the world to come [after our death, on account of our sins]."

[E]   R. Yudan b. R. Ishmael established the practice that his spokesman say this [Hiyya's Prayer above] after he recited the portion [of Torah].

[F]   R. Tanhum bar Scholasticus prayed, "And may it be thy will, Lord my God, God of my fathers, that you break the yoke of the evil inclination and vanquish it from our hearts. For you created us to do your will. And we are obligated to do your will. You desire [that we do your will]. And we desire [to do your will]. And what prevents us? That bacteria [the evil inclination] which nings following] the Sabbath, and the Day of Atonement, and a infect us [lit.: the yeast which makes the dough rise]. It is obvious to you that we do not have the strength to resist it. So let it be thy will, Lord my God, and God of my fathers, and you vanquish it from before us, and subdue it, so that we may do thy will as our own will, with a whole heart."

[G]   R. Yohanan used to pray, "May it be thy will, Lord my God, and God of my fathers that you imbue our portion [of life] with love and brotherhood, peace and friendship. And bring [our lives] to a happy end and [fulfill] all our hopes. And fill our dominion with disciples. And grant that we may enjoy our portion in paradise [in the world to come]. And provide for us a good heart and a good associate. And grant that we may rise early and find [each day] our hearts' desires. And let our souls' yearnings come before you for [our future] good."

[III.A]   *And when I exit I give thanks for my portion* [M. 4:2]. Said R. Abun, "[I give thanks to] the God who has bestowed upon me understanding and good works."

Unit **I** gives texts for Nehuniah's prayers referred to in M. Unit **II** provides texts of the prayers rabbis recited after their recitation of the Daily Prayer of Eighteen (A–B), and after waking up from sleep (C–G). Unit **III** comments briefly on a line of M.

4:3

[A]   *Rabban Gamaliel says, "Each day one must recite a prayer of Eighteen [Blessings]."*

[B]   *And R. Joshua says, "[It suffices to recite] an Abstract of Eighteen."*

[C]   *R. Aqiba says, "If one is fluent in prayer, he recites a Prayer of Eighteen. And if not, [he recites] an Abstract of Eighteen [Blessings]."*

[I.A]   And why [do they recite] eighteen [blessings]? Said R. Joshua b. Levi, "It corresponds with the first eighteen psalms, from the beginning [of the book] of Pslams until, 'The Lord will answer you in the day of trouble'" [Ps. 20:1].

[B]   But if someone will say to you [that up to that place in the book

of Psalms] there are nineteen psalms, tell him that [Ps. 2]—
"Why do the nations conspire?"—is not counted among them
[as a separate psalm but is considered to be the continuation
of Ps. 1].

[C]   Based on this verse ["The Lord will answer you in the day of
trouble," Ps. 20:1] they said, "One who prays and is not answered, must fast." [God will answer one who fasts.]

[D]   Said R. Mana, "[This verse contains] a hint for a disciple of the
sages that a person must say to his master, '[The Lord will answer you.] May your prayer be heard.'"

[E]   Said R. Simon, "[The eighteen blessings of the Daily Prayer]
correspond to the eighteen vertebrae of the spinal cord. For
when a person stands and prays he must bend them all to bow.
What is the basis in Scripture for this? 'All my bones shall say,
O Lord, who is like Thee?'" [Ps. 35:10].

[F]   Said R. Levi, "[The eighteen blessings] correspond to the
eighteen invocations [of God's name in Ps. 29]: 'Ascribe to
the Lord' [T. 3:25]. R. Huna said, "And if someone will say to
you that there are nineteen [invocations in that psalm], tell him
that the rabbis at Yavneh established a [nineteenth blessing] concerning the heretics." [The twelfth blessing in the Daily Prayer.]

[G]   R. Eleazar b. R. Yose [accordingly] objected before R. Yose,
"Lo it is written, 'The God (El) of glory thunders' [Ps. 29:3] [in
the psalm there is yet another invocation of God's name (El).
They should have established another blessing on its account.]"

[H]   He said to him, "It was taught, **They insert the references to
the heretics and the sinners in the blessing concerning the
slanderers [the twelfth], and the references to the elders and
the proselytes in the blessing concerning the righteous [the
thirteenth], and the reference to David in the blessing concerning the rebuilding of Jerusalem [the fourteenth]** [T. 3:25].
We have enough invocations [in the chapter] for each and every
one of these subjects [and no more]" [P.M. explains this section
differently, based on a variant reading.]

[I]   R. Haninah in the name of R. Pinhas, "[The eighteen blessings]
correspond to the eighteen times that the [names of the] patriarchs Abraham, Isaac, and Jacob are mentioned together in
the Torah."

[J]   And if someone says to you that there are nineteen [instances], tell him that we do not count this one: "And behold the Lord stood above it [or: 'beside him,' and said, 'I am the Lord, the God of Abraham your father and the God of Isaac; the land on which you lie I will give to you and to your descendants" [Gen. 28:13]. [Jacob is not named there.]

[K]   If someone tells you that there are only seventeen [instances], tell him that we do count this one: "And in them let my name [Jacob] be perpetuated, and the name of my father Abraham and Isaac" [Gen. 48:16].

[L]   R. Samuel bar Nahmani in the name of R. Yohanan, "[The eighteen blessings] correspond to the eighteen commands [i.e., the words, 'As the Lord had commanded'] in the passage concerning the building of the Tabernacle [Exod. 38:21 ff.]."

[M]   Said R. Hiyya bar Abba [Wawa], "Only [those commands mentioned] between, 'And with him was Oholiab the son of Ahisamach, of the tribe of Dan' [Exod. 38:23] and the end of the book [are counted, excluding the first command in verse 22]."

[II.A]   Whence [is the source for ordaining the liturgy of] the seven [blessings] for the Sabbath [Prayer]?

[B]   Said R. Yitzhak, "They correspond to the seven mentions of voices in [Ps. 29] 'Ascribe to the Lord.'"

[C]   Said R. Yudan Antoriah [Antordia], "They correspond to the seven invocations of God's name in [Ps. 92], 'A Psalm. A Song for the Sabbath.'"

[III.A]   Whence [is the source for ordaining the liturgy of] the nine [blessings] of the New Year's [Prayer]?

[B]   Said R. Abba of Carthage, "They correspond to the nine invocations [of God's name] in the pasage concerning Hannah [1 Sam. 2]. And [this is an appropriate source because] it is written at the end [of the passage], 'The Lord will judge the ends of the earth' [1 Sam. 2:10]. [This is a reference to the judgment of the New Year]."

[IV.A]   Whence [is the source for ordaining the liturgy of] the twenty-four [blessings] of the fast day [Prayer]?

[B]   R. Helbo and R. Simon bar R. Nahman both say, "They correspond to the twenty-four times that it says in the passage concerning Solomon [1 Kings 8]: song, Prayer, or supplication."

[V.A]   R. Zeira in the name of R. Jeremiah, "An individual who recites the Prayer [of Eighteen Blessings] alone on a public fast day must mention the occasion in his Prayer." Where does he do so? Between [the seventh blessing,] "Redeem us," and [the eighth blessing,] "Heal us."

[B]   And what does he say? "Answer us, O Lord, answer us, in this time and season. For we are in great trouble. Hide not your face from us and forsake not our supplications. For you are the Lord who answers us in times of trouble, who redeems us, and saves us in all our times of distress. 'Then they cried to the Lord in their trouble and he delivered them from their distress' [Ps. 107:28]. Blessed are you who answers us in a time of trouble."

[C]   R. Yannai in the name of R. Ishmael in the name of the house of R. Yannai says, "[An individual who recites the Prayer mentions the fast day] in [the sixteenth blessing regarding] the hearing of prayer."

[D]   R. Jonah in the name of Rab, "Even an individual who ordained for himself a fast day must mention the occasion [in his recitation of the Prayer]."

[E]   Where does he say it? R. Zeira in the name of R. Huna, "[In the same place one inserts a mention] on the Sabbath eve and day [in the fourth blessing]." [S.H.: In the evening, morning, and afternoon services as on the Sabbath eve and day.]

[F]   Said R. Mana, "I was uncertain whether the practice [for inserting a reference to the individual's fast day into the Prayer of Eighteen] followed the view of R. Jeremiah [that it be mentioned as a separate blessing between the seventh and eighth blessings] or the view of R. Yannai in the name of R. Ishmael [that it be inserted into the sixteenth blessing].

[G]   "Then I went to the session [in the study hall] and heard R. Huna in the name of Rab [say], 'Even an individual who declared a fast day for himself must insert [as a separate blessing] a mention of the occasion.'

[H]   "R. Yose objected, 'But lo, this contradicts a teaching: Every day one must recite the Prayer of Eighteen—[including the eve-

public fast day. [One may not add blessings].' [Cf. M. 4 : 1, above.]

[I]   "From Yose's statement that this [rule of Rab] contradicts a [different] teaching, [we can deduce that] he objected [to the interpretation of Rab's view that the mention of a special prayer on an individual's fast day be inserted as a separate blessing between the seventh blessing,] 'Redeem us,' and [eighth blessing,] 'Heal us.' [We should rather interpret that Rab intended for the mention of a fast of an individual to be inserted in the sixteenth blessing, the practice which accords with R. Jeremiah's ruling regarding insertion in prayer on a public fast day.]"

[J]   Said R. Aha bar Yitzhak in the name of R. Hiyya of Sepphoris, "On the ninth day of Ab, an individual [who recites the Prayer of Eighteen] must insert a mention of the occasion."

[K]   What does he say? "Have mercy, Lord our God, out of your bountiful mercy and true loving-kindness, upon us, and upon your nation Israel, and upon your city Jerusalem, and upon Zion your honored dwelling, and upon the city of mourning, ruin, destruction, and desolation, which has been given over into the hands of strangers, which the wicked devastated, foreign legions inherited, and idolaters desecrated. For you gave it as an inheritance to your people of Israel, and bequeathed it as an inheritance to the descendants of Yeshurun. Lo, you destroyed it with fire, and you shall rebuild it in a conflagration. As it says, 'For I will be to her a wall of fire round about, says the Lord, and I will be that glory within her' [Zech. 2 : 5 (RSV)]."

[L]   R. Abdima of Sepphoris posed a question to R. Mana. "Where do they say this Prayer?"

[M]   He said to him, "Do you still not know?" [There is a rule:] all references [like this one] to events of the future [such as the rebuilding of the Temple], you insert in the [seventeenth blessing concerning] the Temple service. And all references to events of the past, you insert in the [eighteenth blessing concerning] Thanksgiving. And the Mishnah alludes to this: *And he gives thanks for the past, and he cries out for the future* [M. 9 : 4C].

[VI.A]   What is the meaning of an *Abstract of Eighteen* [M. 4 : 3C]?

[B]   Rab said, "They say the end of each blessing."

[C]   And Samuel said, "[They say] the beginning of each blessing."

[D]   There is one version [of Joshua's statement in Mishnah], "Seven [blessings], an Abstract of [the Prayer of] Eighteen."

[E]   And there is another version, "Eighteen [blessings], an Abstract of [the Prayer of] Eighteen."

[F]   One who holds the view that the version is, "Seven [blessings], an Abstract of [the Prayer of] Eighteen," accords with Samuel's view. [They omit the closing invocations of the middle blessings and condense the beginnings of the thirteen middle blessings into one.]

[G]   One who holds the view that the version is, "Eighteen [blessings], an Abstract of [the Prayer of] Eighteen," accords with Rab's view. [They shorten the beginning of the text of each blessing and recite the closing blessing formula of each paragraph.]

[H]   R. Zeira sent [a question] to R. Nahum, who was with R. Yannai b. R. Ishmael. He asked him, "What is the meaning of, 'Seven [blessings], an Abstract of [the Prayer of] Eighteen' according to Samuel's view?"

[I]   He said to him, "[It means one should condense the middle thirteen blessings as follows], 'Give us intelligence, accept our repentance, forgive us, redeem us, heal our sickness, bless our years. . . .'"

[J]   Said R. Haggai, "If it was [during] the [winter] rainy season, they add, '[Bless our years] with the blessed rains' [L has 'dew']. If it was [during the season of] the dew [the summer], they add, '[Bless our years] with the blessed dew.'"

[K]   [Continuing F, Nahum's text of the Abstract of Eighteen:] "Gather us for we are scattered, we depend upon you for justice, bring your hand down on the wicked, and all who trust in you shall rejoice in the rebuilding of your city, and in the restoration of your Temple, and in the rejuvenation of [the house of] David your servant. For before we call out to you, you will answer us. As it says, 'Before they call I will answer, while they are yet speaking I will hear' [Isa. 65:24]. Blessed art Thou, O Lord who hears [our] Prayer."

[L]   "And he says the first three [of the eighteen] blessings [before saying this abstract], and he says the last three blessings [after saying this text]. And he says [in conclusion], 'Blessed be the Lord, for he has heard the voice of my supplications'" [Ps. 28:6].

Unit **I** finds indirect support for reciting eighteen blessings in several places: in a parallel to the first eighteen chapters of the book of Psalms, in a comparison with the number of vertebrae in the spine in the human anatomy, in a correlation to the phrases invoking God's name in one particular Psalm, in the eighteen occurrences of the names of the three patriarchs together, and in the number of commands of a chapter in the book of Exodus.

Unit **II** undertakes a similar process, looking for the possible justifications for the Sabbath liturgy of seven blessings, as does unit **III**, for the nine blessings of the New Year's Prayer, and unit **IV**, for the twenty-four blessings of the Prayer for a Fast Day.

The mention of the Prayer for a public fast day brings with it in unit **V** a variety of rules for content and position for the insertion of liturgical additions in the Prayer on such an occasion. Unit **IV** then returns to M.'s subject, giving a dispute regarding the definition of M.'s term, "Abstract of Eighteen."

4:4

[A] *R. Eliezer says, "One who fixes [the recitation of] his Prayer, his Prayer is not supplication."*

[B] *R. Joshua says, "One who goes through a dangerous place should recite a short Prayer [some texts: an Abstract of Eighteen Blessings.]*

[C] *"And he should say, 'God save your people Israel. In all their crises let their needs come before you. Blessed art Thou, O Lord who hears our Prayer and supplications."*

[I.A] R. Abahu in the name of R. Eleazar, "[R. Eliezer means] one should not [recite one's prayers] as if he were reading a letter [i.e., fixed without emotion]."

[B] R. Aha in the name of R. Yose, "[Eliezer means] one must add some new [dimension] each day [to one's prayer]."

[C] Ahitofel used to recite three new prayers each day. R. Zeira said, "Whenever I did this, I would make mistakes [in my prayer]."

[D]   Rather [here is the correct version of the preceding set of teachings, A–C] as R. Abahu said in the name of R. Eleazar, "One should not [recite one's prayers] as if he were reading a letter."

[E]   R. Eleazar used to recite a new prayer each day.

[F]   R. Abahu used to recite a new blessing each day.

[II.A]   R. Yose of Tyre in the name of R. Yohanan, "Before his [recitation of the] Prayer one should say, 'O Lord, open thou my lips, and my mouth shall show forth thy praise' [Ps. 51:15]. And after his [recitation of the] Prayer one should say, 'Let the words of my mouth and the meditation of my heart be acceptable in thy sight, O Lord, my rock and my redeemer'" [Ps. 19:14].

[B]   R. Yudan recited both of these verses before his [recitation of the] Prayer.

[III.A]   One who was praying and he remembered that he had already prayed—Rab said, "He should break off [from praying]."

[B]   And Samuel said, "He should not break off." [He may complete the second recitation of the Prayer.]

[C]   Simeon bar Abba [Wawa] said in the name of R. Yohanan, "O that one might [have the opportunity to] pray all day long [in accord with Samuel]. Why [does Yohanan say that one may pray all day long]? Because [the recitation of the] Prayer never loses its value." [Cf. M.1:1, III.]

[D]   R. Zeira posed a question before R. Yose, "Do we not know that R. Yohanan said, 'One who is in doubt whether or not he prayed, should not pray'?" And he [Yose] did not answer him.

[E]   R. Abahu brought [this teaching] in the name of R. Yohanan, "One who is in doubt whether or not he prayed, should not pray."

[F]   R. Haninah did not say this [version of Yohanan's teaching]. Rather [he gave this version]: They posed a question before R. Yohanan, "One who is in doubt whether or not he prayed, [what should he do]?"

[G]   He said to them, "O that one might [have the opportunity to] pray all day long. Why [does Yohanan say that one may pray all day long]? Because [the recitation of the] Prayer never loses its value."

[**IV.**A] One who was praying on the Sabbath and he forgot [to say] the Sabbath Prayer, but [instead] he said the weekday Prayer— R. Huna says, "[Concerning this case] there is a dispute between R. Nahman bar Jacob and R. Sheshet.

[B] "One said, '[When he remembers] he must break off from reciting [even in the middle of] a blessing.'

[C] "And the other said, 'He should finish [saying] the blessing [he is reciting when he remembers it is the Sabbath].'

[D] "And all agree that he must finish [saying the fourth blessing], 'Who bestows knowledge,' [if that is where he remembers he erred]."

[E] And this [last rule] accords with Rabbi's view. For Rabbi said, "I am surprised that they deleted [the fourth blessing], 'Who bestows knowledge,' from the Sabbath [Prayer]. [For] without knowledge how can there be Prayer?"

[F] Said R. Yitzhak, "Great is knowledge. For it is enclosed between two invocations [of God's names in a verse]. As it says, 'A God of knowledge is the Lord'" [1 Samuel 2:3]. Some say we learn [this teaching] from this verse, 'Then you will understand the fear of the Lord and find knowledge of God' [Prov. 2:5].

[**V.**A] [*One who goes through a dangerous place* (M. 4:4B):] R. Simeon bar Abba in the name of R. Haninah, "All roads are presumed to be dangerous."

[B] When R. Yona would go [on an overnight trip] to an inn, he would first give instructions to his household [concerning his last will and testament].

[C] When R. Mana would go to bathe in a heated bathhouse, he would first give instructions to his household [concerning his last will and testament].

[D] R. Haninah son of R. Abahu, R. Simeon bar Abba in the name of R. Joshua b. Levi, "All sicknesses are presumed dangerous. [One who falls ill should recite the short Prayer of M. 4:4C, *In all their crises*]."

[**VI.**A] R. Aha in the name of R. Asa, "[*In all their crises* (*pršt h'ybwr*) (M. 4:4C)—that short prayer asks that you, God, heed] all that the leader of the prayers asks of you when he goes before the ark ['*wbr lpny htybh*] and places the request for the needs of your people before you." [Aha calls attention to the similarity of the words *'ybwr, 'wbr.*]

[B]   R. Pinhas, R. Levi, R. Yohanan in the name of Menahem the Galilean, "[To invite] one to go before the ark they do not say [to him], 'Come and pray.' Rather they say [to him], 'Come and draw near. Come and make our offerings for us, provide for us, fight for us, make peace for us.'"

[C]   Others say [the text of the short Prayer is as follows]: **"The needs of your people Israel are great and their ability [to express them] is limited. But let it be your will, Lord our God, and God of our fathers, that you provide for each and every creature his needs, and for each and every person that which he lacks. 'Blessed be the Lord, for he has heard the voice of my supplications' [Ps. 28:6]. Blessed art Thou, O Lord who hears [our Prayer]"** [T. 3:7F].

[D]   R. Hisda said, "The practice [for reciting the short Prayer] follows the [teaching of] 'Others' [in C]. [We recite their text of the short Prayer]."

[E]   R. Hisda said, "[The short Prayer consists of] the first three and the last three blessings [of the Prayer of Eighteen with the special text recited between them]."

[VII.A]   There is a Tanna who taught, "One prays and then asks for his [individual] needs."

[B]   And there is a Tanna who taught, "One asks for his [individual] needs and then prays."

[C]   One who holds the view that one prays and then asks for his [individual] needs [bases his view on the opening to Ps. 102, which says,] "A Prayer of one afflicted, when he is faint," and after that [the verse concludes,] "and pours out his complaint before the Lord."

[D]   And one who holds the view that one first asks for his [individual] needs and then prays [bases his view on the verse,] "O Lord my God, hearkening to the cry," and after that, "And to the Prayer" [1 Kings 8:28].

[E]   The view of the sages [does not accord with the preceding but with the view of] R. Zeira in the name of R. Huna, "An individual asks for his needs in the [sixteenth] blessing, 'Who hears our prayer.'"

[VIII.A]   R. Abba, R. Hiyya in the name of R. Yohanan, "A person must pray in a place designated for Prayer [i.e., a synagogue].

[B]   "And what is the basis [in Scripture for this rule]? 'In every place where I cause my name to be remembered I will come to you and bless you' [Exod. 20:24]. It is not written, 'Where you shall [happen to] remember my name.' But rather, 'In every place where I cause my name to be remembered' [i.e., where there is regular service or Prayer—the Temple, and, after its destruction, the synagogue]."

[C]   Said R. Tanhum bar Haninah, "A person must designate for himself a place to pray in the synagogue.

[D]   "And what is the basis [in Scripture for this rule]? 'When David came to the summit where he worshipped God' [2 Sam. 15:32]. It is not written, 'Where he shall worship God.' [The verse implies that he regularly worshiped in that place.]"

[IX.A]   R. Yasa, R. Helbo, R. Berekhiah, R. Helbo of Tobah, in the name of R. Abduma from Haifa, "A person must turn to face a wall to pray. What is the basis [in Scripture for this view]? 'Then Hezekiah turned his face to the wall [and prayed to the Lord]'" [Isa. 38:2].

[B]   What wall did he [Hezekiah] turn to?

[C]   R. Joshua b. Levi said, "He turned to the wall of Rahab. [As the verse says,] 'For her house was built into the city wall' [Josh. 2:15]. He [Hezekiah] recited before it, '[Master of the Universe,] Rahab the harlot saved only two people for you. Look at how many people you saved for her.'

[D]   "In this regard it is written, 'So the young men who had been spies went in, [and brought out Rahab, and her father and mother and brother and all who belonged to her]'" [Josh. 6:23].

[E]   Said R. Simeon bar Yohai, "Even though her family included two hundred people who each married into two hundred [different] families, they all were saved on account of her merits."

[F]   [Hezekiah argued in his prayer,] "My forefathers brought to you so many proselytes [i.e., saved so many souls]. How much more [should I be rewarded on account of their merits]."

[G]   R. Haninah bar Papa said, "He [Hezekiah] turned to the walls of the Temple [to pray, as this verse implies,] 'By setting their threshold by my threshold and their doorposts beside my doorposts, with only a wall between me and them' [Ezek. 43:8]. These were great people. And they were not able to go up and pray in the Temple all the time. And they used to pray in their houses. Yet the Holy one, blessed be He, gave them credit as if they were praying in the Temple.

[H]   "[Hezekiah argued further in his Prayer,] '[Master of the universe,] my forefathers praised you so much [in all their worship in the Temple]. How much more [should you give me credit on their account].'"

[I]   R. Samuel bar Nahman said, "He turned to the wall of the [house of the] Shunammite [woman]. As it says, 'Let us make a small roof chamber with walls' [2 Kings 4:10].

[J]   "[Hezekiah] said before him, 'Master of the universe, [the Shunammite woman] made one small wall for Elisha and you resurrected her son [on its account]. My forefathers praised you so much [and built for you the Temple]. How much more should you grant me life [on their account].'"

[K]   And sages say, "He turned inward to the wall of his heart. [As it says,] 'My anguish, my anguish! I writhe in pain! Oh the walls of my heart' [Jer. 4:19].

[L]   "[Hezekiah] said before him, 'Master of the Universe, I have looked into the 248 bones of my body and have not found even one with which I angered you. How much more should you grant me life [on account of the sincerity of my heart].'"

Unit **I** explains what M. means by "fixing" the recitation of one's Prayer. Unit **II** interjects a rule for reciting introductory and concluding phrases for one's Prayer. Units **III** and **IV** address the issue of one who errs in his recitation, either by repeating his recitation or by reciting the wrong version of the Prayer.

Unit **V** returns to M.'s main subject, providing traditions that define for us what is a dangerous place. Unit **VI** turns to explain the text of M.'s short prayer and to give alternatives in citing T. and Hisda's alternative. After opening at units **V–VI** the question of asking for personal needs in the recitation of the Short Prayer, at unit **VII** the Talmud assembles materials related to the issue of where in the recitation of his Prayer one may ask for his personal needs.

Unit **VIII** discusses the proper places for the recitation of the Prayer under normal circumstances.

Unit **IX** continues with the discussion of the place of Prayer, by raising the issue of the propriety of praying near a wall. The unit then goes off on a related subject, variants of traditions about the prayer that Hezekiah recited near a wall.

4:5

[A]   *One who was riding on an ass should dismount [to recite the Prayer].*

[B]   *If he cannot dismount, he should turn [to face toward Jerusalem].*

[C]   *And if he cannot turn, he should direct his thoughts to the chamber of the Holy of Holies [in the Temple of Jerusalem].*

4:6

[A]   *One who was travelling on a boat or a raft—he should direct his thoughts to [the chamber of] the Holy of Holies.*

[I.A]   It was taught: **One who was riding on an ass—if there is someone who can hold the ass, he should dismount and pray. If not, he may pray where he is.**

[B]   **Rabbi says, "In either case he should pray where he is for that way his mind is more at ease [and he can better concentrate]"** [T. 3:18].

[C]   R. Judah b. Pazzi, in the name of R. Joshua b. Levi, "The law accords with [the view of] Rabbi."

[II.A]   Said R. Jacob bar Aha, "It was taught there: one may not face in any direction [to recite the Prayer], except East." [P.M. and S.H. explain otherwise.]

[B]   Said R. Yose bar Abun, "At first [in ancient times they prayed] 'With their backs to the Temple of the Lord and their faces toward the East, worshipping the sun toward the East'" [Ezek. 8:16].

[C]   It was taught: **A blind man or anyone who is not able to discern directions [whether he faces east or west,] lo, they pray** [by turning their thoughts] toward heaven. As it says, 'And they pray to the Lord [toward the city which thou hast chosen and the house which I have built for thy name]' [1 Kings 8:44] [T. 3:14].

[D]   Those who stand and pray outside the Land of Israel, turn to face the Land of Israel [to pray]. And what is the basis [in Scripture for this rule]? 'And pray to thee toward the land which thou gavest their fathers' [1 Kings 8:48].

[E]   Those who stand and pray in the Land of Israel turn to face Jerusalem. And what is the basis [in Scripture for this rule]? 'Toward the city which thou hast chosen' [ibid. cf. 2 Chron. 6:34] [T. 3:15].

[F]   Those who stand and pray in Jerusalem, turn to face the Temple mount. And what is the basis [in Scripture]? 'And the house which I have built for thy name' [ibid. cf. 2 Chron. 6:32].

[G]   And those who stand and pray on the Temple mount, turn to face the chamber of the Holy of Holies. And what is the basis [in Scripture for this rule]? '[And hearken to the supplication of thy servant and of thy people Israel,] when they pray toward this place; yea, hear thou in heaven thy dwelling place; and when thou hearest, forgive' [1 Kings 8:30].

[H]   It turns out that [when they pray] those who stand north [of the Temple], face south, those who stand in the south, face north, those who stand in the east, face west, those who stand in the west, face east. It turns out that all of Israel prays toward one place [T. 3:16].

[I]   That accords with [the verse], 'For my house shall be called a House of Prayer for all peoples' [Isa. 56:7].

[III.A]   Said R. Joshua b. Levi, "[We find the following phrase in a verse referring to the Temple,] 'The house, that is, the nave in front of the inner sanctuary' [1 Kings 6:17]—[this phrase suggests they stood during prayer in front of] the nave [of the Temple—the place] to which all people faced. [This is a play on lpny/lpnym/pnym//in front of/the inner/face]."

[B]   This [rule that one must pray facing the Temple] applies at a time when the Temple was standing. How do we know [it applies] when the Temple is destroyed [i.e., that all must still face the Temple mount when praying]?

[C]   Said R. Abun, ["We may derive this from the following verse, 'Your neck is like the tower of David] an arsenal [the Hebrew word can be split into two: *tl pyot*] (Song of Sol. 4:4)—that means [we call the Temple mount] a hill [*tel*—implying that even after it stands destroyed as a Tel, it is the place] to which all mouths [*pyot*] pray."

[D]   [One should pray for Jerusalem] in the blessings [of the meal], in the recitation of the *Shema'*, and in the Prayer [of Eighteen].

[E]   In the blessing of the meal [they say, "Blessed art Thou] who rebuilds Jerusalem."

[F]   In the Prayer [of Eighteen they say the blessing concerning] the Lord of David [i.e., "And speedily establish in Jerusalem the throne of David. Blessed art Thou] God of David who rebuilds Jerusalem" [the fourteenth blessing].

[G]   And in the recitation of the *Shema'* [on Sabbaths and Festivals they say at the conclusion of the evening recitaiton], "Who spreads his tabernacle of peace upon us, and upon his people Israel, and upon Jerusalem."

[H]   One verse says, "I will return again to my place" [Hos. 5:16]. And a second verse says, "My eyes and my heart will be there for all time" [1 Kings 9:3].

[I]   How is this possible? [The verses contradict each other.] [You may explain that although] His presence [lit. face] remains above [in heaven, to return later,] but His eyes and heart [are always turned] below [to watch over the place of the Temple].

[IV.A]   *And if not, let him direct his thoughts to the chamber of the Holy of Holies* [M. 4:5C]. To which chamber of the Holy of Holies? R. Hiyya the great, "Toward the [chamber of the] Holy of Holies above [in heaven]."

[B]   R. Simeon b. Halafta said, "Toward the chamber of the Holy of Holies below [in the Temple]."

[C]   Said R. Pinhas, "They do not dispute one another. For the chamber of the Holy of Holies down below is opposite the chamber of the Holy of Holies up above, [as implied in the verse,] 'The place [*mkwn*]; O Lord, which thou hast made for thy abode' [Exod. 15:17]. [Read the verse rather as follows:] Situated opposite [*mkwwn* instead of *mkwn*] thy abode.' [What is situated opposite it? It is, 'The sanctuary, O Lord, which thy hands have established' (ibid.)]."

[V.A]   "[Then Solomon began to build the house of the Lord in Jerusalem on] Mount Moriah" [2 Chron. 3:1]. R. Hiyya the great and R. Yannai [disputed over the reason it was called *mwryh*, Moriah]. One said it was because from that place instruction [*hwryh*] goes forth to the world. The other said it was because from that place fear [*yr'h*] goes forth to the world.

[B]   The ark ['*rwn*]—[what is the explanation of this word]? R. Hiyya the great and R. Yannai [disputed this matter]. One said [it was called '*rwn*] because from there light ['*wrh*] shone forth to the world. And the other said [it was called '*rwn*] because from there curses ['*ryrh*] went forth to the world [to the idolaters—P.M.].

[C]   *Debir*—the Holy of Holies—[what is the explanation of this word]? R. Hiyya and R. Yannai [disputed]. One said [it was called *Debir*] because from there a pestilence [*dbr*] goes forth to the world. And the other said [it was called *Debir*] because from there the utterances [*dybrwt*, the ten commandments] go forth to the world.

[VI.A]   *One who was travelling on a boat or on a raft should direct his thoughts toward the chamber of the Holy of Holies* [M. 4:6]. The term 'raft' [Hebrew: '*sd*'], means the same as the term 'float' ['*skry*'], which means the same as the term rafts [*rpswdwt*] mentioned in the verse, "And we will cut whatever timber you need from Lebanon, and bring it to you in rafts by sea to Joppa" [2 Chron. 2:16].

Unit **I** cites the relevant T. and adds a brief comment. Unit **II** begins with two miscellaneous traditions and then continues with the citation of the appropriate Tosefta passages, which expand on M.'s theme that during the recitation of Prayer, one must orient oneself to face the Temple. Unit **III** continues with traditions that emphasize the continuing centrality of Jerusalem, even after its destruction. The unit proves further the importance of Jerusalem by reminding us of its prominent position in various liturgies.

Unit **IV** comes back to M. and explains the reference to the chamber of the Holy of Holies in the text of M. After the discussion of one specialized phrase, unit **V** digresses to discuss the etymologies of several other phrases.

The Talmud concludes its explanation of terms in M. at unit **VI**.

4:7

[A]   *R. Eleazar b. Azariah says, "The Additional Prayer is said only with the Ḥeber 'yr [congregation or association of the town]."*

[B]   *And sages say, "Both with the Ḥeber 'yr and apart from the Ḥeber 'yr."*

[C]   *R. Judah said in his [Eleazar's] name, "Any place where there is a Ḥeber 'yr [i.e., a place where they recite the Prayer in public] an individual is exempt from [reciting] the Additional Prayer."*

[I.A]   R. Bibi in the name of R. Hannah said, "The law follows R. Judah who said [the law] in the name of R. Eleazar b. Azariah [i.e., M. 4:7C]."

[B]   A dictum of Samuel accords with this statement. For Samuel said, "All my days I never recited the Additional Prayer [because I fulfilled my obligation by virtue of the public recitation of the Service]. Except for one time when the son of the Exilarch died. And the congregation did not recite [the Additional Prayer because they were preoccupied with the loss], and [on that occasion] I recited it myself."

[C]   A dictum of the sages disputes [Bibi's statement]. For R. Jacob bar Idi said in the name of R. Simeon the pious, "[This law applies only] to the shepherds and the field watchmen [who are separated from the communities which assemble for Prayer]. Lo, the Mishnah referred [only] to shepherds and field watchmen. But other people are obligated [to recite the Additional Prayer]."

[D]   A dictum of R. Yohanan accords with this [statement of R. Bibi]. For R. Yohanan said, "I saw R. Yannai standing and reciting [the Morning Prayer] in the marketplace of Sepphoris. And he walked four cubits and [then] recited the Additional Prayer."

[E]   And was there no *Ḥeber 'yr* in Sepphoris? [Surely there was.] You learn from this story three things.

[F]   You learn that [in some respects the marketplace] of Sepphoris is considered to be part of the city of Sepphoris [even though it was situated far from the town].

[G]   You learn that [in this case only] they dispute the ruling of R. Judah who spoke in the name of R. Eleazar b. Azariah [M. 4:7C. Because the marketplace was so far from the city, Yannai recited the Additional Prayer himself].

[H]   And you learn that a person may recite [the Morning Prayer], walk four cubits, and then recite the Additional Prayer.

[I]   Said R. Abba, "Do not take it literally that one must walk four cubits [after reciting the Morning Prayer and before reciting the Additional Prayer]. But even if one pauses for an interval long enough [for a person] to walk four cubits [after reciting the Morning Prayer, he may then recite the Additional Prayer]."

[II.A]   Rab said, "[One who recites the Additional Prayer right after the morning Prayer] must add something new [in the Additional Prayer]."

[B]   Samuel said, "He does not have to add something new."

[C]   R. Zeira posed a question before R. Yose, "What new thing must one add [so as to fulfill his obligation in reciting the Additional Prayer]?"

[D]   He said to him, "Even if he just added [the phrase], 'And let us fulfill our obligations before you of offering the Daily Sacrifices and the Additional Sacrifice,' he fulfilled his obligation."

[III.A]   R. Shila in the name of Rab, "One who already prayed [in private] and later found ten people praying, should pray [again in public] with them."

[B]   R. Zeira and R. Nahman bar Jacob were sitting together. After they had prayed, a [group of ten other people] came to pray. R. Nahman bar Jacob got up to pray [with them].

[C]   R. Zeira said to him, "Didn't we already pray?"

[D]   He said to him, "[Nevertheless] I am going to pray."

[E]   And he went to pray again with them. [He acted in accord with the rule (A) which] R. Shila said in the name of Rab, "One who already prayed in private and later found ten people praying, should pray [again in public] with them."

[F]   R. Aha, R. Jonah, in the name of R. Zeira, "One who had re-
       cited the Morning Prayer and came and found them [a congre-
       gation] reciting the Additional Prayer, should [go ahead and]
       pray with them. One who had not recited the Morning Prayer
       and came and found [a congregation] reciting the Additional
       Prayer—if he knows that he has enough time to begin [reciting
       the Morning Prayer] and finish it, before the leader starts [recit-
       ing the Additional Prayer,] so that he will be able to respond
       'Amen' [to the leader's recitation], he may recite [first the Morn-
       ing Prayer]. But if [he knows he will] not [have enough time], he
       may not recite [the Morning Prayer until the reader completes
       the recitation of the Additional Prayer]."

[G]   Which responses of "Amen" do they refer to [in the case above
       of a person who came to synagogue and found the congregation
       in the middle of reciting the Prayer? Cf. the discussion regarding
       M. 3:2 **III.**]

[H]   [This is disputed by] two Amoraim.

[I]   One said [it refers to] the 'Amen' to be said after [the third bless-
       ing], The Holy God.

[J]   The other says [it refers to] the 'Amen' to be said after [the six-
       teenth blessing], Who Hears Prayer.

[K]   Said R. Pinhas, "There is no dispute [between these parties.
       They refer to different cases.]"

[L]   The one who says [it refers to] the 'Amen' after [the third bless-
       ing], The Holy God, [refers to the recitation of the Prayer on
       the] Sabbath [when they do not recite the thirteen intermediate
       blessings].

[M]   The one who says it refers to the 'Amen' after [the sixteenth
       blessing], Who Hears Prayer, refers to [the recitation of the
       Prayer on a] weekday [when they do recite the intermediate thir-
       teen blessings].

[**IV.A**] It was taught there [cf. b. R.H. 33b]: Rabban Gamaliel said,
       "The leader [of the Prayer, by virtue of his recitation of the
       Prayer] exempts the congregation of its obligation [to recite the
       Prayer]."

[B]   R. Huna the great of Sepphoris in the name of R. Yohanan,
       "The law follows R. Gamaliel with regard to [the prayers of the

New Year's day, the day of] the sounding of the shofar. [This service is long and unfamiliar to the congregation]."

[C] R. Zeira and R. Hisda were sitting together on [New Year's day, the day of] the sounding of the shofar. After they had prayed [by themselves in private, a congregation] came together to pray [together in public]. R. Hisda got up and prayed [again].

[D] R. Zeira said to him, "Didn't we already pray?"

[E] He said to him, "[Nevertheless] I am going to pray."

[F] And he went to pray again with them. [He explained his action as follows:] "When some Jews of the West [i.e., the Land of Israel] came here [i.e., to Babylonia], they said in the name of R. Yohanan, 'The law follows Rabban Gamaliel with regard to the prayers of [the New Year's day] the day of the sounding of the shofar.'

[G] "And I was not concentrating when I first prayed. But if I had been concentrating [at first], I would already have fulfilled my obligation." [In this case, by virtue of the leader's recitation, he fulfilled his obligation. But in other cases, such as one who erred in his recitation, he could not fulfill his obligation through the leader's recitation.]

[H] Said R. Zeira, "Very well. [You acted in accord with the view of] those who taught, that the law follows Rabban Gamaliel [in a case like yours]. But R. Hoshaiah taught that the law follows the sages [in all other cases—S.H.]."

[I] R. Ada of Caesarea in the name of R. Yohahan, "This law [that the leader's recitation exempts members of the congregation from their obligation to recite applies only] to those who are present from the beginning of [the leader's recitation of] the Prayer."

[J] Said R. Tanhum bar Jeremiah, "One may infer this rule from the Mishnah: *This is the order of blessings for the New Year's Prayer.*" (M. R.H. 4:5 implies that one must recite the blessings in the specified order. One who joins the group after the leader begins reciting must later go back and recite the blessings he missed. He does not fulfill his obligation because he recites the blessings out of their prescribed order. M. there continues: *[Blessings that mention] (1) the patriarchs, (2) God's wonders, (3) the sanctity of God's name.*

[K]   *He included [the New Year's blessings concerning] kingship with those, but he does not sound the shofar.*

[L]   *[He recites the blessing concerning] the sanctity of the day and sounds the shofar.*

[M]   *He recites the [New Year's blessing concerning] the remembrances and sounds the shofar.*

[N]   *He [recites the blessings which refer to] the sounding of the shofar and sounds the shofar.*

[O]   *And he says the section concerning the sacrificial order, and the thanksgiving blessing, and the priestly blessing, the words of R. Yohanan b. Nuri.)*

Unit **I** explains that the common practice accords with Judah's view, and gives appropriate support for its claim. The section includes a variety of related side issues. Unit **II** turns to other practical customs, relating to the recitation of the Additional Prayer.

Unit **III** focuses on whether one who recited his Prayer in private must repeat it in public, an issue related to the concern of our **M.** To conclude, unit **IV** extends to the New Year's Prayer, **M.**'s rule about public recitation exempting the individual from his own recitation.

5 Yerushalmi Berakhot
Chapter Five

5:1

[A] *One may stand to pray only with a solemn frame of mind.*

[B] *The ancient saints used to tarry for a while, and then pray so that they could first direct their thoughts [to God].*

[C] *[One who is praying,] even if a king extends to him a greeting, he should not respond; even if a serpent is coiled to strike at his heel, he should not interrupt [his recitation].*

[I.A] R. Jeremiah in the name of R. Abba, "One who comes in off the road [from travelling] is forbidden to pray [right away because the events of his journey distract his thoughts].

[B] "And what is the basis [in Scripture for this]? 'And therefore hear this, you [exiles] who are afflicted, who are drunk, but not with wine' [Isa. 51:21]. [Those who are exiled from their land are distracted as if they were intoxicated.]"

[C] R. Zeriqan, R. Yohanan in the name of R. Eleazar the son of R. Yose the Galilean, "One who is afflicted with anguish is forbidden to pray."

[D] This ruling runs counter to one's intuition [since we would think that anguish is a good justification for prayer]. [It is, nonetheless, the case.] As the same verse says, 'And therefore hear this, you who are afflicted, who are drunk, but not with wine' [ibid.]." [The verse compares an afflicted person with a drunk person. The Talmud infers that just as a drunk person may not pray, so also an afflicted person may not pray.]

[**II.A**]   It was taught: **One may stand to pray neither after conversation, nor after laughter, nor after levity, nor after any trivial matter, but only after words of Torah.**

[B]   **And likewise one may depart from his associate neither after conversation, nor after laughter, nor after levity, nor after any trivial matter, but only after words of Torah. [And one may not depart after words of sorrow or anguish—S.H.] For so we find that the ancient prophets concluded their messages with words of praise and consolation** [T. 3:21].

[C]   Said R. Eleazar, "[All the prophets concluded with praise and consolation] except for Jeremiah who concluded with reproof."

[D]   Said R. Yohanan to him, "Even he concluded [his prophecy] with words of consolation saying, 'Thus shall Babylon sink, [to rise no more, because of the evil that I am bringing upon her. Thus far are the words of Jeremiah]'" [Jer. 51:64].

[E]   Because Jeremiah continues [in chap. 52] to prophesy regarding the Temple, you might argue that he concludes [his prophecy with a message of sorrow,] with the account of [the destruction of] the Temple. [Accordingly] it teaches explicitly that this [at the end of Jer. 51:64] is the conclusion of Jeremiah's message, "Thus far are the words of Jeremiah."

[F]   [And are the concluding words of the prophet Isaiah not words of sorrow and anguish?] He concludes with a description of those who seek to destroy God, can you say these are not words of reproof? "[And they shall go forth and look on the dead bodies of the men that have rebelled against me; for their worm shall not die, their fire shall not be quenched,] and they shall be an abhorrence to all flesh" [Isa. 66:24].

[G]   [Are these not words of reproof? To answer this objection you could say] this refers to those idolaters [who are enemies of God, not to Jews].

[H]   [And does the book of Lamentations not conclude with words of reproof?] As it is written, "Or hast thou utterly rejected us? [Art thou exceedingly angry with us?]" [Lam. 5:22].

[I]   [Here too you may interpret this conclusion as consolation because the writer requests in the verse before,] "Restore us [to thyself, O Lord, that we may be restored! Renew our days as of old!]" [Lam. 5:21] and do not utterly reject us.

[III.A]   Elijah too took leave of Elisha only after speaking words of Torah: 'As they still went on and talked, [*wdbr*] [behold, a chariot of fire and horses of fire separated the two of them. And Elijah went up by a whirlwind into heaven]' [2 Kings 2 : 11].

[B]   [B–E refer to places where the word 'talk,' *dbr* appears.] And what were they talking about? R. Ahawa b. R. Zeira said, "They were discussing the recitation of the *Shemaʿ*. In accord with what is said [in the *Shemaʿ* itself], 'And you shall talk [*dbrt*] of them'" [Deut. 6 : 7].

[C]   R. Judah b. Pazzi says, "They were discussing the creation of the world. In accord with what is said, 'By the word [*dbr*] of the Lord the heavens were made [and all the host by the breath of his mouth]'" [Ps. 33 : 6].

[D]   R. Yudan, son of R. Ayybo, said, "They were discussing the consolations of Jerusalem. As it says, 'Speak [*dbrw*] tenderly to Jerusalem, [and cry to her that her warfare is ended, that her iniquity is pardoned, that she has received from the Lord's hand double for all her sins]'" [Isa. 40 : 2].

[E]   And sages say, "They were discussing [description of the] *Merkabah* [chariot]. In accord with what is said, '[And behold they were walking and talking [*wdbr*], and behold here was] a chariot of fire and horses of fire'" [2 Kings 2 : 11].

[IV.A]   R. Jeremiah said, "One should stand to pray only after [speaking of a] decision of the law."

[B]   R. Jeremiah said, "He who is involved with communal needs is like one who is involved [in the study of] words of Torah. [And he may pray immediately after he finishes serving a communal need.]"

[C]   R. Huna said, "[Before praying one should speak of a law such as the following:] 'A woman who sees [a discharge of] a drop of blood the size of a mustard seed must sit and keep seven clean days [during which he sees no discharge, then immerse herself before resuming regular marital relations].' Then [after reciting this law] one may go and pray." [After reciting this strict decision, one will be able to turn one's attention away from further contemplation of the laws of the Torah.]

[D]   Zeira bar R. Hinenah said, "[Before praying one should speak of a law such as the following:] 'One who lets blood from animals

dedicated to the Temple [and uses the blood for ordinary pur-
poses] has misappropriated Temple property.' This too is one of
the fixed laws [which one may recite to divert his thoughts from
his studying before praying]."

[E]   It was taught: Bar Qappara said, "[Recite this law before praying:] 'The [minimum number of] eleven days [which by law one
must reckon] between one menstrual period and another, is
based on a tradition received by Moses at Sinai.'" [This is a
strict decision of the law: a woman who saw a flow in the eleven
days after the seven days of her menstrual period, must reckon
that to be the flow of a *Zabah*. S.H.]

[F]   It was taught: R. Hoshaia [said,] "[Recite this lenient law before
praying:] 'A person may mix his grain with stalks [before bringing it into his storehouse] as an artifice to free it from the tithing
requirement [since thereby it will resemble grain which has not
been winnowed, and will not become liable to tithes]." [Accor-
ding to Hoshaia, reciting a lenient law puts one in the proper
frame of mind for prayer.]

[G]   [Before he went to pray,] Abdan asked Rabbi, "How many levels of holy things are there?"

[H]   And he said to him, "Four."

[I]   "How many levels of heave-offering are there?"

[J]   He said to him, "Three."

[K]   Then [after speaking of these facts of the law, Abdan] went and
prayed.

[V.A]   R. Hezekiah, R. Jacob bar Aha, R. Yasa in the name of
R. Yohanan, "[Before you recite your Prayer,] this verse should
always be on your lips. 'The Lord of hosts is with us; the God of
Jacob is our refuge. Selah'" [Ps. 46:11].

[B]   R. Yose b. R. Abun, R. Abahu in the name of R. Yohanan and
the associates, "[Before you recite your Prayer, this verse should
always be on your lips,] 'O Lord of hosts, blessed is the man
who trusts in thee!'" [Ps. 84:12].

[C]   R. Hezekiah in the name of R. Abahu, "[After you say those
verses, recite this short prayer,] 'May it be thy will, Lord our
God, and God of our fathers, that You save us in the times of
rebellion, the hard times, the evil times that are approaching and
coming to the world.'"

[VI.A]   *One may stand to pray only with a solemn frame of mind* [M.
5 : 1]. R. Joshua b. Levi said, "[Scripture says,] 'Worship the
Lord in holy array' [*hdrt qdš*] [Ps. 29 : 2]. [You should read
the phrase:] '[Worship the Lord] in fear of the holy' [*hrdt qdš*,
the interpretation rests on a play on words] [i.e., a solemn frame
of mind]."

[B]   R. Yose b. Haninah said, "[Scripture says,] 'Serve the Lord with
fear [i.e., with a solemn frame of mind], rejoice with trembling'
[Ps. 2 : 11]. [How can one rejoice while trembling?]"

[C]   Said R. Aha, "When the day of trembling comes, you shall rejoice. [If you have been pious, when you are judged, you will be
rewarded.]"

[VII.A]   Said R. Joshua b. Levi, "One who is standing and praying must
sit down twice [to pause], once before praying, and once after
praying.

[B]   "Before praying—[as it says,] 'Blessed are those who sit in thy
house, ever singing thy praise' [Ps. 84 : 4]. And after praying—
[as it says], 'Surely the righteous shall give thanks to thy name;
the upright shall sit in thy presence'" [Ps. 140 : 13].

[C]   *The ancient saints used to tarry for a while,* pray a while, and
tarry a while after their Prayer. When did they [have time to]
study Torah? When did they [have time to] do their work?

[D]   Said R. Yitzhak b. R. Eleazar, "Because they were saints, their
Torah study was blessed, and their work was blessed, [and they
were able to complete them expeditiously]."

[VIII.A]   Huna said, "One who prays behind a synagogue is called a
wicked person, as it says, 'On every side the wicked prowl'"
[Ps. 12 : 8].

[B]   R. Huna said, "Anyone who does not enter the synagogue
[during his lifetime] in this world will not enter the synagogue
in the afterlife. What is the basis [in Scripture for this view]?
'On every side [shall] the wicked prowl [*ythlkwn*. In the future,
in the world to come, they will prowl. They will not enter
paradise.]"

[C]   Said R. Yohanan, "It is as if an iron wall surrounds one who
prays at home." [He will be protected and his prayers will
be heard.]

[D]   But another contradictory tradition is ascribed to R. Yohanan:

Elsewhere said R. Abba, said R. Hiyya in the name of R. Yohanan, "A person must pray in a place designated for prayer [i.e., a synagogue, cf. above, 4:4, **VIII**]." And here you say this [in his name]!

[E]   [You may reconcile the discrepancy between them as follows: He said them both, and] the first [teaching] refers to [the prayer of] an individual. [It is better that one pray at home if there is no communal prayer.] The second [teaching] refers to [the prayer of] a congregation. [When there is communal prayer, one must pray in a synagogue.]

[F]   R. Pinhas in the name of R. Yohanan Hoshaia, "It is as if one who prays in the synagogue offered a pure meal offering [at the Temple].

[G]   "What is the basis [in Scripture for this view]? '[They shall declare my glory . . . to my holy mountain Jerusalem, says the Lord,] just as the Israelites bring their cereal offerings in a clean vessel to the house of the Lord'" [Isa. 66:19–20].

[H]   R. Jeremiah in the name of R. Abahu, "'Seek the Lord while he may be found' [Isa. 55:6]. Where may he be found? In the synagogues and study halls. 'Call upon him while he is near' [ibid.]. Where is he near? [In the synagogues and study halls.]"

[I]   Said R. Yitzhak b. R. Eleazar, "Moreover, it is as if God stands next to those [who are in synagogues and study halls]. What is the basis [in Scripture for this view]? 'God has taken his place in the divine congregation; in the midst of the gods he holds judgment'" [Ps. 82:1].

[J]   R. Hisda said, "One who enters the synagogue must go in past [the entrance a space equal to twice the width of the] two doors [of the entrance way]. What is the basis [in Scripture for this view]? 'Happy is the man who listens to me, watching daily at my gates, waiting beside my doors' [Prov. 8:34]. [The verse uses the plural] gates, not gate, and doors, not door, [to imply one must enter beyond the door, at least a space equal to the width of two doors to make room at the entrance or to give himself a chance to settle his thoughts before praying]."

[K]   And concerning one who acts in this way, it is written, "For he who finds me finds life" [Prov. 8:35].

[L]   R. Huna said, "One who is on his way to synagogue must walk quickly. What is the basis [in Scripture for this view]? 'Let us know, let us press on to know the Lord' [Hos. 6 : 3].

[M]   "And when one leaves he must walk slowly. What is the basis [in Scripture for this view]? 'For then thou would number my steps'" [Job 14 : 16].

[N]   Said R. Yohanan, "It is as certain as the covenant that what one studies in a synagogue, one does not quickly forget."

[O]   Said R. Yohanan [var.: Haninah] of Anathoth, "It is as certain as the covenant that what one studies in private, one does not quickly forget. What is the basis [in Scripture for this view]? 'With the secluded is wisdom'" [Prov. 11 : 12].

[P]   Said R. Yohanan, "It is as certain as the covenant that one who learns a homily from a book, does not quickly forget it."

[Q]   Said R. Tanhum, "One who has thoroughly analyzed his studies does not quickly forget. What is the basis [in Scripture for this view]? '[Only take heed, and keep your soul diligently,] lest you forget the things which your eyes have seen, [and lest they depart from your heart all the days of your life]' [Deut. 4 : 9]. [The verse implies that you do not forget what 'your eyes have seen,' i.e., what you have analyzed.]"

[IX.A]   R. Jonah in the name of R. Tanhum b. R. Hiyya, "One who has a bad dream must say, 'May it be thy will, Lord my God and God of my fathers, that all the dreams I have dreamed during this past night or other nights, whether my own dreams, or dreams of others concerning me, if they be for good, may they come to pass and bring for me joy and happiness, blessing and life.

[B]   "But if they be otherwise [i.e., for bad], then just as you changed the bitter waters at Marah to sweet waters, and [just as you changed the bitter] waters of Jericho to sweet waters through [the work of] Elisha, and just as you changed the curse of [Balaam] the son of Beor to a blessing, so, [I pray,] may you change all of [my own] bad dreams, and all other bad dreams concerning me to [bring me] good, blessing, and health, and life, happiness, and joy and peace.

[C]   "Thou hast turned for me my mourning into dancing; thou has loosed my sackcloth and girded me with gladness, that my soul may praise thee and not be silent. O Lord my God, I will give thanks to thee forever' [Ps. 30:11–12]. 'Nevertheless the Lord your God would not hearken to Balaam; but the Lord your God turned the curse into a blessing for you, because the Lord your God loved you' [Deut. 23:5]. 'Then shall the maidens rejoice in the dance, and the young men and the old shall be merry. I will turn their mourning into joy, I will comfort them, and give them gladness for sorrow'" [Jer. 31:13].

[X.A]   *Even if a king extends to him a greeting, he should not respond* [M. 5:1]. Said R. Aha, "This applies only to an Israelite king. But to the greeting of a gentile king, one may return a greeting [lest he be offended and punish you]."

[B]   It was taught: **If one was writing God's name [in a Torah scroll], even if a king extends to him a greeting, he should not respond. If one was writing two or three consecutive divine names**—such as El, Elohim, Yahweh—**lo, he should finish writing one and return the greeting** [T. 3:22].

[C]   R. Yohanan was sitting and reciting before a congregation of Babylonians in Sepphoris. An archon passed by but [R. Yohanan] did not stand before him. The [archon's guards] went to strike him.

[D]   He [the archon] said to them, "Let him be! He is busy paying homage to his creator."

[XI.A]   R. Haninah and R. Joshua b. Levi went before the proconsul of Caesarea. When he saw them he stood up. They [his courtiers] said to him, "Why do you stand up for these Jews?"

[B]   He said to them, "I saw in them the faces of angels."

[C]   R. Jonah and R. Yose went before Ursicinus [the governor] in Antioch. When he saw them he stood up. They [his courtiers] said to him, "Why do you stand up for these Jews?"

[D]   He said to them, "I see their faces in a vision when I go out to battle and [on account of that vision] I am victorious."

[E]   R. Abin went before the king. When he was leaving, he turned his back [on the king to go]. They sought [on account of this affront] to execute him. But they saw two streaks of fire [miraculously] emanating from his back and they let him alone.

[F]   [This fulfills what Scripture] says, "And all the peoples of the earth shall see that you are called by the name of the Lord; and they shall be afraid of you" [Deut. 28:10].

[XII.A]   R. Simeon b. Yohai taught, "And all the people of the earth shall see [that you are called by the name of the Lord; and they shall be afraid of you]' [ibid.]. 'All'—even the spirits and even the demons [shall be afraid of you]."

[B]   R. Yannai and R. Yohanan were walking down the street [Luncz: in the woods] when they saw one [demon]. It greeted them and said to them, "May your peace be increased."

[C]   They said, "It even addressed us in friendly terms! It cannot do us any harm!"

[XIII.A   Resh Laqish was accustomed to becoming deeply absorbed in [thoughts concerning] the Torah. [Once while lost in thought] he wandered out of the Sabbath limit [i.e., more than 2000 cubits from the boundary of the village], and he did not realize it. This fulfills that which Scripture says, 'Be infatuated always with her [the Torah's] love' [Prov. 5:19].

[B]   R. Yudan b. R. Ishmael was accustomed to becoming deeply absorbed in [thoughts of] the Torah. [One time] his cloak fell off him and a serpent stood guard over it.

[C]   His students said to him, "Master, your cloak has fallen."

[D]   He said to them, "Is not this deadly serpent guarding it [that no one touch it]?"

[XIV.A]   Even if a serpent is coiled to strike at his heel, he should not interrupt' [M. 5:1C]: R. Huna in the name of R. Yose, "This only applies to a serpent. But one may interrupt for [fear of] a scorpion. Why? Because it may sting at any time."

[B]   R. Ila said, "This only applies to the case of a serpent that is coiled nearby. But if it is slithering toward him, lo, he may move aside, so long as he does not interrupt his Prayer."

[C]   It was taught [in this regard]: **If one was standing and praying in a wide street or a public place, lo, he may move aside to let an ass or a wagon pass, so long as he does not interrupt his Prayer.**

[D]   **They said concerning R. Hanina b. Dosa that while he was standing and praying, a poisonous lizard bit him, but he did not interrupt his Prayer. They went and found the lizard dead at the entrance to its hole. They said, "Woe to the person who is bitten by the lizard. Woe to the lizard who bit R. Hanina Ben Dosa"** [T. 3:20].

[E]   Regarding this matter of a poisonous lizard which bites a person [they say]—if the person drinks water first, the lizard dies. But if the lizard drinks water first, the person dies.

[F]   His [Ben Dosa's] students said to him, "Master, didn't you feel anything [when the lizard bit you]?"

[G]   He said to them, "I swear! I was concentrating on my Prayer and felt nothing."

[H]   Said R. Yitzhak bar Eleazar, "God created a spring beneath his [Ben Dosa's] feet to fulfill the verse that says, 'He will fulfill the desire of all who fear him, he also will hear their cry, and will save them' [Ps. 145:19]. [God heard Ben Dosa's prayer and created for him a spring of water to drink to save him from the serpent's venom.]"

Through its two rulings, Unit **I** illuminates Mishnah's main idea that the recitation of Prayer must be accompanied by the proper state of mind. To further expand upon M., unit **II** cites the relevant Tosefta passage. Tosefta introduces the new theme of the appropriate words to speak before taking leave of one's fellow. The Talmud adds to that a discussion of the conclusions of several biblical books. Unit **III** continues on this topic with a close analysis of the departure of Elijah from Elisha, with special interest in the subject of Torah which they discussed before separating.

Unit **IV** adds another variation on to T.'s point, that to establish the right frame of mind, one should recite Prayer after engaging in Torah study. It adds that communal service is as good an activity to engage in before Prayer as is study, and then proposes several archetypical laws to contemplate as proper preparation before Prayer. Within the different examples we find psychological insights about establishing states of consciousness. The authorities differ over what kind of rule prepares one for Prayer—lenient, strict, or matter-of-fact.

Unit **V** adds new material, alternative one-line prayers that one must recite to prepare for reciting the Prayer of Eighteen. Unit **VI** returns directly to elucidate M. and provide Scriptural sources for its prescriptive rule. Unit **VII** continues the Talmud's more direct interest in M.'s phrase, "Tarry for a while," with a discussion of its implications.

Unit **VIII** begins an independent, although not entirely inappropriate, section on rules regarding the importance of prayer in a synagogue. It deals at length with various statements about the necessity of synagogue attendance and then adds various other rules for the etiquette of attending the synagogue. The unit ends with a short section on the value of study in the synagogue.

Unit **IX** goes off on a tangent with a short supplement regarding the prayers to recite if one has a bad dream, indirectly relevant here. Unit **X** does come back to cite and explain the next line of M., cite T., and add new material relevant to M. Unit **XI** digresses from the previous interest in rabbis confronting officials, with other traditions on the same general topic. As long as the Talmud is on the subject, it interjects one short unit on the confrontation between the rabbis and another force, demons. **XIII** comes back somewhat to the main issue of M., concentration on one's Prayer. This unit gives us some materials regarding rabbis lost in their contemplation of the Torah.

The last reference to a serpent conveniently returns us in unit **XIV** to the M. itself. After two comments on the text of M., this section cites T.'s tradition and story about Ben Dosa. The remaining material deals with that incident.

5 : 2

[A]   *They mention the [liturgical formula that deals with the] "wonders of the rains" [i.e., "Who causes the winds to blow and the rain to fall" during the rainy season] in [the second blessing of the Prayer of Eighteen, called] "The Resurrection of the Dead."*

[B]   *And they [add during the winter the phrase, "Grant us dew and rain for blessing," to] ask for rain in [the ninth blessing, called] "The Blessing of the Years."*

[C]   *And [they insert] the Prayer of Division [recited at the conclusion of a Sabbath or Festival day] in [the fourth blessing of the Prayer of Eighteen on Saturday night, called] "Endower of Knowledge."*

[D]   *R. Aqiba says, "One says it as a separate fourth blessing."*

[E]   *R. Eliezer says, "[One inserts it] in the 'Thanksgiving,' [the name of the eighteenth blessing of the Prayer of Eighteen]."*

[I.A]   [Why do they mention the rain in the blessing that deals with resurrection?] Just as resurrection [restores] life to the world, so too does rainfall [restore] life to the world.

[B]   R. Hiyya bar Abba derived [the association between rain and resurrection] from the following: "After two days he will revive us; on the third day he will raise us up, that we may live before him. Let us know, let us press on to know the Lord; his going forth is sure as the dawn; he will come to us as the showers, as the spring rains that water the earth" [Hos. 6:2–3].

[C]   It is written [elsewhere], "Now Elijah the Tishbite of the settlers in Gilead, said to Ahab, 'As the Lord God of Israel lives, before whom I stand, there shall be neither dew nor rain in these years, except by my word" [1 Kings 17:1]. [This provides a link between rain and resurrection, since the story that follows in Scripture deals with the resurrection of a child.]

[D]   R. Berekhiah [said regarding this verse], "R. Yasa and the sages [disputed]. One said, 'He [God] listened to [Elijah] about [withholding] both the dew and the rain.' The other said, 'He listened to him about [withholding] the rains but not about the dew.'"

[E]   The one who said, "He [God] listened to him about [withholding] the rains but not about the dew," derived his teaching from the following, "[After many days the word of the Lord came to Elijah; in the third year, saying,] 'Go, show yourself to Ahab; and I will send rain upon the earth.'" [1 Kings 18:1].

[F]   And, according to the one who said, "He listened to him about [withholding] both the dew and the rain," [we may ask the following question]. Where does Elijah [later] nullify his vow [1 Kings 17:1] to withhold the dew? [The verse in ch. 18 says only that God will send rain.]

[G]   R. Tanhuma of Idrea, "It can be argued that if one nullifies one part of a vow, one thereby nullifies the entire vow."

[H]   Or [you may say Elijah nullified his vow concerning withholding the dew elsewhere,] as it says in the story of the child of the woman of Zarephath, "Then he stretched himself upon the child three times and cried to the Lord, 'O Lord my God, [let this child's soul come into him again]'" [1 Kings 17:21].

[I]   [And what does this story have to do with Elijah's vow?] Said R. Judah b. Pazzi, "[It may be understood through the following parable:] Someone stole a physician's satchel. After [the thief] leaves, his son [later] is stricken, he returns [to the physician]. And he says to him, 'My lord physician, treat my son.'"

[J]   He says to him, "Return my satchel to me. For in it are all kinds of medications. Then I shall be able to treat your son."

[K]   Thus did God tell Elijah, "Go and nullify your vow concerning [withholding] the dew. For the dead will come to life only through the dew. Then I shall resurrect the son of the Zarephath woman."

[L]   And whence [was it taught] that the dead come to life only through the dew? "Thy dead shall live, their bodies shall rise. O dwellers in the dust, awake and sing for joy! For thy dew is a dew of light, and on the land of the shades thou wilt let it fall" [Isa. 26:19].

[M]   Said R. Tanhum of Idrea, "[Interpret the end of this verse literally as follows:] 'And the land will give forth its surety' [i.e., the dead will rise from their graves]."

[N]   R. Jacob of the village of Hanan in the name of Resh Laqish, "[God said,] 'When your ancestor Abraham acted according to my will, I swore to him that I would never withhold the dew from his descendants.' What is the basis [in Scripture for this statement]? '[From the womb of the morning,] the dew will come to your youth.' Thereafter Scripture says, 'The Lord has sworn and will not change his mind'" [Ps. 110:3–4].

[O]   Said R. Judah b. Pazzi, "[God said,] 'That [dew] that I gave as a bequest, [which may be nullified], to Abraham, I give as a gift, [which can never be nullified to his descendants].' [As it says,] 'May God give you of the dew of heaven, [and of the fatness of the earth, and plenty of grain and wine]'" [Gen. 27:28].

[P]   Said R. Samuel bar Nahmani, "When Israel sins and does evil deeds, the rains are withheld. When they bring an elder, such as R. Yose the Galilean, to intercede for them, the rains fall again.

[Q]   "But the dew does not fall on account of the merit of any living being. What is the basis [in Scripture for this view]? 'Then the remnant of Jacob shall be in the midst of many peoples like dew from the Lord, like showers upon the grass, which tarry not for [the sake of] men nor wait for the [merit of] sons of men'" [Micah 5:7].

[II.A]   R. Zeira in the name of R. Haninah, "If one was standing [and praying before the congregation] in the [winter] rainy season, and he mentioned [in error] the request for dew, they do not make him repeat the Prayer. [If one was praying for the congregation in the summer season when they pray for] dew, and he mentioned [in error] the request for rain, they make him repeat the Prayer."

[B]   But lo, it was taught: [In the summer season] the sages did not obligate a person to mention the dew and the winds [in his Prayer]. But if he wishes to mention it, he may do so.

[C]   [These are different cases. If one omits the request for dew in the summer, he need not repeat the Prayer. But one who erroneously requests rain in the summer must repeat the Prayer.] For one who requests a curse [i.e., rain out of its season] is different from one who neither prays [for dew], nor requests a curse [of summer rain].

[D]   [R. Zeira in the name of R. Haninah, "If one was standing and praying for the congregation] in the rainy season, and he mentioned the request for dew, they do not make him repeat the Prayer." But it was taught: **If one did not ask [for the rains] in the [ninth blessing, i.e.,] the Blessing of the Years, or if one did not mention the wonders of the rains in [the second blessing, i.e.,] the Resurrection of the Dead, they make him repeat [his recitation of the Prayer]** [T. 3:9].

[E]   [These two rulings are not contradictory. In T.'s case] he mentions neither dew nor rain [so he must repeat. In R. Zeira's case he mentions one, and thus need not repeat.]

[F]   R. Zeira in the name of R. Haninah, "If [by error] one did not ask [for rain] in the [ninth blessing], the Blessing of the Years, he may say [the formula] in [the sixteenth], Who Hears Prayer.

[G]   "And likewise if [by error] one did not mention the wonders of the rains in the [second blessing], the Resurrection of the Dead, he may say [the formula] in [the sixteenth], Who Hears Prayer."

[H]   [But why tell us both rules? The second is obvious!] For [one who omits] the request [for rains] that are essential [to sustain life] from the ninth [blessing] may still [request the needed rains in the sixteenth blessing], Who Hears Prayer. The mention [of the rain in the second blessing serves as a supplement to the praise of God's attributes. Because the dew is] a luxury, surely [if one forgets to recite the formula in the second blessing he need not repeat the Prayer. He may insert the formula in the sixteenth blessing].

[I]   But, lo, it was taught: **If one did not ask for the rains in the [ninth blessing] concerning the Blessing of the Years, or if one did not mention the wonders of the rains in [the second blessing] concerning the Resurrection of the Dead, they make him repeat [his recitation of the Prayer]** [T. 3:9]!

[J]   Said R. Abdimi the brother of R. Yose, "[In T.'s cases] he did not [remember soon enough even to] say the formula in the [sixteenth blessing], Who Hears Prayer."

[K]   [They make him repeat his recitation of the Prayer.] What must he repeat? This accords with that said by R. Simeon b. Abba [Wawa] in the name of R. Yohanan, "[Concerning one who forgot to mention the occasion of the new moon in the Prayer for the] new moon, if he began to walk away [after completing his recitation of the Prayer and only then remembered that he had omitted the formula], he must repeat the whole Prayer from the beginning. But if not [i.e., if he remembers before he walks away,] he must repeat from [the seventeenth blessing], the Temple Service, [and insert thereafter the mention of the occasion]."

[L]   Also in the present case, if he walks away [after completing the Prayer, then remembers,] he must repeat the Prayer from the beginning. But if not [i.e., if he remembers before he walks away], he must repeat [the seventeenth blessing], the Temple Service [after again reciting the sixteenth blessing] Who Hears Prayer [and insert the request for rain].

[III.A]   Once in Nineveh they [Luncz: the inhabitants of Naveh] had to declare a fast day after Passover [and to pray for rain]. They went and asked Rabbi [what to do regarding the Prayer]. Rabbi told them, "Go and do so [declare a fast day] but do not change the structure of the Prayer [by adding a special mention of rain]."

[B]   Where then do they recite [the request for rain]? R. Jeremiah thought they should recite it in [the sixteenth blessing], Who Hears Prayer.

[C]   Said to him R. Yose, "Did not R. Zeira say in the name of R. Huna [Haninah], 'If one did not request rain in [the ninth blessing], the Blessing of the Years, or if one did not mention rain in [the second blessing], the Resurrection of the Dead, they make him insert it in [the sixteenth blessing], Who Hears Prayer'? [Only post facto, if one forgot, did the sages permit insertion of the formula in the sixteenth blessing. But ab initio, they required one to insert the formula earlier in the structure of the Prayer!] And Rabbi said, 'Go and do so [insert the formula] as long as you do not change the structure of the Prayer.' [He implied that they may change the regular practice and insert the formula in the sixteenth blessing.]"

[D]   According to R. Yose, where do they insert [the request for rains in this special case of a fast day declared after Passover]? They insert it in the six [special blessings which they add to the Prayer on a fast day]. This [solves the problem] for the congregation, which recites the six additional blessings. [But what of] an individual, who does not recite the six [additional blessings in his private Prayer]? Where [does he insert the request for rain]?

[E]   Said R. Haninah, "Did not R. Zeira say as follows in the name of R. Huna, 'An individual inserts a request for his personal needs in [the sixteenth blessing], Who Hears Prayer'? And this [request for rain] is also a personal need."

[IV.A]   *And [they insert] the Prayer of Division in [the fourth blessing], Endower of Knowledge.*

[B]   *R. Aqiba says, "One says it as a separate fourth blessing."*

[C]   *R. Eliezer says, "In the 'Thanksgiving'"* [M. 5:2C–E].

[D]   Simeon bar Abba posed this question to R. Yohanan, "How is it possible that the sages engage in a dispute over such a common practice?" He said to him, "Because [over the generations the Prayer of Division was] removed [from the Prayer-liturgy and recited primarily] over a cup [of wine as a separate ritual], they forgot [where it was to be inserted] in the Prayer."

[E]   From his [Yohanan's] statement we deduce that one's primary [obligation is to recite the Prayer of Division] over a cup of wine [as a separate ritual].

[F]   R. Jacob bar Idi in the name of R. Yitzhak the great, "If one recited [the Prayer of Division] over a cup of wine, he must [still] recite it in the Prayer [of Eighteen]. [For they say it over wine only] for the sake of the children [in his household who do not recite the Prayer, so they may hear the recitation of the Prayer of Division]."

[G] From his [Yitzhak's] statement we deduce that one's primary [obligation is to recite] the Prayer of Division in the Prayer [of Eighteen].

[H] R. Zeira, R. Judah in the name of Samuel, "If one recited it over a cup he [also] must recite it in the Prayer [of Eighteen]. If one recited it in the Prayer [of Eighteen], he [also] must recite it over a cup."

[I] From his [Samuel's] statement we deduce that one's primary [obligation is to recite] the Prayer of Division in both ways [over a cup of wine and in the Prayer of Eighteen].

[V.A] *R. Eliezer says, "[One inserts it] in the 'Thanksgiving'* [M. 5:2E]." R. Yohanan in the name of Rabbi, "We incline to accept R. Eliezer's view in the case of [the recitation of the Prayer of Division] between the Sabbath and a festival day that falls immediately thereafter."

[B] R. Yitzhak the great in the name of Rabbi, "The law follows R. Eliezer [in the case of the recitation of the Prayer of Division] between a Sabbath and festival day."

[C] R. Yitzhak bar Nahman in the name of R. Haninah b. Gamaliel, "The law follows R. Eliezer in all cases."

[D] R. Abahu in the name of R. Eleazar, "The law follows R. Eliezer in all cases."

[E] Said R. Jacob bar Aha, "It is not on account of the two [independent] traditions [that I accept this as the law,] but because R. Yitzhak bar Nahman and R. Eleazar both [transmitted the tradition] in the name of [the Tanna] R. Haninah b. Gamaliel [that], 'The law follows R. Eliezer in all cases.'"

[VI.A] *And [they insert] Prayer of Division in [the fourth blessing] Endower of Knowledge, the words of the sages.*

[B] *R. Aqiba says, "One says it as a separate fourth blessing"* [M. 5:2C–D].

[C] R. Jacob b. Aha in the name of Samuel says, "[They say it in place of] the fourth blessing."

[D] Said R. Yudan, "He recites the formula of the [regular fourth] blessing and afterward [he recites] the Prayer of Division."

[E]   And this accords with [a tradition ascribed to] Rabbi. For Rabbi says, "I am amazed that they eliminated the [fourth blessing], Endower of knowledge, [from the Prayer of Eighteen] on the Sabbath. Without knowledge how can there be prayer?"

[F]   Likewise without knowledge, [Rabbi would argue,] how can there be Prayer of Division? [One must say both the regular fourth blessing and the Prayer of Division.]

[G]   Said R. Yitzhak b. R. Eleazar, "[One recites] the Prayer of Division and afterward he recites the formula of the [regular fourth] blessing."

[VII.A] R. Eleazar b. R. Hoshaiah, "[One's recitation of the Prayer of Division is effective] so long as he mentions no fewer than three forms of division," [i.e., "He who divides sacred from profane, light from darkness, Israel from the nations, the seventh day from the six days of creation"].

[B]   Said R. Yohanan, "They said, 'One who usually says fewer [forms of division in the Prayer of Division] should say no fewer than three, and one who usually adds more should say no more than seven divisions.'"

[C]   Levi said, "One's recitation of the Prayer of Division [is effective] as long as he mentions 'divisions' that appear in the Torah."

[D]   Nahum b. R. Simai went and said in the name of his father, "Even if one says a single 'division,' [his Prayer of Division is effective]."

[E]   And said R. Abahu, "One must close [the Prayer of Division with a blessing that mentions] 'division,'" [i.e., "Blessed art Thou, O Lord, who divides the sacred from the profane"].

[F]   R. Mana posed a question: According to this [i.e., the view of Abahu in light of the position of Nahum, is one's Prayer of Division effective if he says nothing more, but just] opens with "[Blessed art Thou, Lord our God, king of the universe,] who divides sacred from profane," and immediately closes repeating, "[Blessed art Thou, O Lord,] who divides sacred from profane"?

[G]   Said R. Yose b. R. Bun, "[Mana, why do you raise such a question?] Is this not one of those blessings that opens with the formula 'Blessed art Thou' and closes with the formula 'Blessed

art Thou'?" [Accordingly the blessing surely would be effective
in the form given above.]

[VIII.A]   R. Eleazar b. Antigonos, in the name of R. Eleazar b. R. Yannai,
"[R. Yitzhak b. Eleazar's ruling above, VI, 'One recites the
Prayer of Division and afterward he recites the formula of
the (regular fourth) blessing'] implies that before one recites the
Prayer of Division [on Saturday night], it is forbidden for him
to perform labor.

[B]   "For you can say that [this law], 'Before one recites the Prayer of
Division, it is forbidden for him to perform labor,' is parallel to
[this law], 'Before one recites the Prayer of Division, it is forbidden for him to ask for his needs.'" [Because one must recite the
Prayer of Division toward the beginning of the Prayer of Eighteen, we may infer that one may neither make petition nor
perform labor, before reciting the Prayer of Division.]

[IX.A]   R. Zeira, R. Eleazar bar Antigonos [L: his son] in the name of
R. Yannai, in the name of R. Judah, his son, "If one did not
recite the Prayer of Division at the termination of the Sabbath,
he may recite the Prayer of Division [later in the week,] even on
the following Thursday."

[B]   What you say applies to [the blessing of division,] "Who divides
sacred from profane, ..." But "Who creates the light of the
fire," [recited over the light,] may be recited [only if he says the
Prayer of Division] right away [at the close of the Sabbath day,
but not later in the week].

[X.A]   R. Zeira in the name of R. Judah, R. Abba in the name of Abba
bar Jeremiah, "Even [at the conclusion of] a festival day that
falls in the middle of the week, one says [the same formula in
the Prayer of Division], 'Who divides the seventh day from the
six days of creation.'"

[B]   Said R. Zeira to R. Judah, "[How can one say this?] Do the six
days of the week precede [the festival]?"

[C]   He said to him, "[One may say, 'Who divides the clean from the
unclean.'] Are there clean and unclean objects before him? [One
speaks of the division of the categories not of the division of
actual time or objects.]"

[XI.A]   R. Jeremiah, R. Zeira in the name of R. Hiyya bar Ashi, "One
must say [in the Prayer of Division in the fourth blessing of the

Evening Prayer], 'May the six days, the days of creation, that are approaching us, begin for us in peace.'"

[B]   R. Abba adds, "And may we hear on them sounds of joy and happiness."

[C]   R. Hezekiah in the name of R. Jeremiah [would add], "Cause us to understand and teach us."

[D]   R. Hezekiah in the name of R. Jeremiah, "Those who respond 'Amen' to the blessings of the Prayer of Division must look at the cup [when its blessing is recited] and look at the light [when its blessing is recited]."

[E]   R. Hezekiah in the name of R. Jeremiah, "One must hold the four species [of the lulab on Sukkot] in the manner in which they grow."

The Talmud begins with a direct examination of the rules of M. It first wants to know why it is appropriate to insert the blessings at the locations in the Prayer stipulated by M. Two verses are suggested as basis for the practice. The unit then goes on to examine further implications of the second verse and completes the section dealing with the links between dew, rain, and resurrection.

Unit **II** takes up the derivative issue of what one must do if he deviates from the practices set out in M. Unit **III** turns to special cases for inserting the prayer for rain. Unit **IV** returns to the discussion of the M. text, and presents a variety of materials about practices for the recitation of the Prayer of Division.

Unit **V** discusses Eliezer's view in M. **VI** does the same for Aqiba's opinion. Unit **VII** presents a short collection of traditions on the content of the Prayer of Division itself. Units **VIII–XI** then elucidate other rules regarding the Prayer of Division. The unit concludes with three rules attributed to Hezekiah, the first two about the Prayer of Division, and the third concerning another subject.

5:3

[A]   *They silence one who says [in leading the Prayer of Eighteen], "May thy mercy reach [even] the nest of a bird," or "May thy name be invoked for the good," or "We give thanks, we give thanks." [These are not sanctioned liturgical formulae, because they have heretical overtones.]*

[B]   *He who goes before the ark [to lead the recitation of the Prayer of Eighteen] and erred, they replace him with another.*

[C]   *And one may not decline at that time [if asked to replace the one who errs].*

[D]   *Whence does [the replacement] begin [to recite]?*

[E]   *From the beginning of the blessing in which [the previous leader] erred.*

]I.A]   R. Pinhas in the name of R. Simon, "[One who recites, 'May thy mercy reach the nest of a bird'] is like one who reproaches God's traits [saying], 'Thy mercy reached a bird's nest, but thy mercy did not reach so-and-so.'"

[B]   R. Yose in the name of R. Simon, "[One who recites that formula] is like one who limits God's nature [saying], 'Thy mercy reaches only to a bird's nest [not beyond].'"

[C]   One version of the Mishnah reads, "Upon ['l] a bird's nest," and one version of the Mishnah reads, "Until ['d] a bird's nest."

[D]   One who holds [that the correct version is] "upon" supports the view of R. Pinhas.

[E]   And one who holds that [the correct version is] "until" supports R. Yose.

[F]   Said R. Yose b. R. Bun, "It is not good to imply that God's traits [are derived from his attribute of] mercy. [In this regard] those who translate ['And whether the mother is a cow or a ewe, you shall not kill both her and her young in one day' [Lev. 22:28] as follows]: 'My people, children of Israel, just as I am merciful in heaven, so shall you be merciful on earth: A cow or a ewe, you shall not kill both her and her young in one day,'—that [also] is not good—for it implies that God's traits [are derived from his attribute of] mercy."

[II.A]   *"We give thanks, we give thanks," they silence him* [M. 5:3A]. Said R. Samuel bar R. Yitzhak, "'. . . for the mouth of liars will be stopped' [Ps. 63:11]. This applies only in public [prayer]. But for an individual it is supplication [to repeat phrases in one's recitation of the Prayer of Eighteen]."

[**III**.A] *He who goes before the ark and erred, [they replace with another]* [M. 5:3B]. R. Yose b. Haninah in the name of R. Haninah b. Gamaliel, "If he erred in reciting one of the first three blessings [of the Prayer of Eighteen, the new leader] goes back to the beginning [and repeats the entire Prayer]."

[B] Ada bar bar Hannah, Genivah in the name of Rab, "If he erred in reciting one of the last three blessings, [of the Prayer of Eighteen, the new leader] goes back to [the seventeenth blessing], 'The Temple Service.'"

[C] R. Helbo, R. Huna in the name of Rab, "If he erred in the first three blessings, [of the Prayer of Eighteen, and they replace him, the new leader] goes back to the beginning. If he erred in the last three blessings, [the new leader] goes back to [the seventeenth blessing], 'The Temple Service.' If he erred and is not sure where he erred, [the new leader] goes back to the place he is certain [he recited correctly]."

[**IV**.A] R. Aha and R. Judah b. Pazzi were sitting in a certain synagogue. A person got up before the ark [to lead the Prayer of Eighteen] and he skipped a blessing. They went and asked R. Simon [what to do about this case].

[B] R. Simon said to them in the name of R. Joshua b. Levi, "If a leader of the Prayer [of Eighteen] skipped two or three blessings, they do not make him repeat [the Prayer of Eighteen]."

[C] We find that there is a teaching that contradicts this [ruling of Joshua b. Levi], "They do not make anyone [who skips a blessing] repeat, except for one who did not say [the second blessing], 'Who resurrects the dead,' [the twelfth blessing], 'Who humbles the arrogant,' and [the fourteenth blessing], 'Who builds Jerusalem.' I say [one who omits these blessings] is a heretic."

[D] Samuel the younger went before the ark and skipped [the twelfth blessing], 'Who humbles the arrogant.' When he finished, he turned and looked at them [in the congregation to see what they would say].

[E] They said to him, "The sages did not take into account one such as you [when they said that one who omits this blessing is a heretic]." [Samuel was credited with the original formulation of that blessing.]

[**V**.A] R. Jacob bar Aha, R. Simeon bar Abba in the name of R. Eleazar,

"If there was a doubt whether he mentioned the new moon [in the Prayer of Eighteen], they make him repeat it."

[B] From where [in the Prayer] does he repeat? Simeon bar Abba [Wawa] in the name of R. Yohanan, "If he already started to walk away, he must repeat [the whole Prayer of Eighteen] from the beginning. But if not, he repeats from [the seventeenth blessing], The Temple Service, [and inserts the mention of the new moon thereafter]."

[C] Said R. Judah b. Pazzi, "One who turns his attention away [from the Prayer of Eighteen after finishing his recitation] is the same as one who started to walk away [after finishing his recitation of the Prayer of Eighteen]."

[D] [And what of one who began to doubt whether he omitted mention of the new moon while reciting] the supplications after the Prayer [of Eighteen, before he starts to walk away]? It is a question [whether he must repeat from the beginning, as if he had walked away, or he may repeat from The Temple Service, as if he had not yet walked away.

[VI.A] R. Abba son of R. Hiyya bar Abba, R. Hiyya in the name of R. Yohanan, "If while one was reading [for the congregation] from the Torah he was struck dumb, the one who takes his place should start [reading] from the place where the first [reader] started.

[B] "For if you say he should start from the place where the first one stopped [when he became mute], then [there is a problem concerning the blessings recited by each over the verses he reads]. [If he starts where the first reader stopped, it turns out that] they recited a blessing before [reading] the previous verses, but they did not recite a blessing after [reading them because the reader became dumbstruck].

[C] "And they recited a blessing after [reading] the latter verses, [which the new reader reads], but they did not recite a blessing before reading them. [They relied on the initial blessing of the previous reader.] And it is written, 'The law of the Lord is perfect, reviving the soul'" [Ps. 19:7]. All [the reading] must be perfect [i.e., complete with a blessing before and after each portion].

[D] It was taught: **They do not permit two persons to read from the Torah while another one translates** [T. Meg. 3:20].

[E]   Said R. Zeira, "[This is prohibited] because of [a problem in reciting] the blessing. [Two persons may not recite the blessings for the same portion.]"

[F]   But, lo, it was taught [in the second half of the Tosefta passage], **They do not permit two persons to translate while one reads from the Torah.** Can you say it [is prohibited] because [two persons may not recite] the blessing [over the same portion? Here only one recites a blessing.] Rather [the reason they do not permit these practices is based on the principle that] one ear cannot hear [clearly] two voices [at the same time].

[G]   It was taught [contrary to D]: Two persons may read [together from the same portion in] the Torah. [Because the Torah reading is important, people will pay attention.] But two may not read [together] the portion from the prophets. [It is less important and people will not listen as carefully—P.M.]

[H]   Said R. Ulla, "[Several persons] may be called to read from the Torah, but not to read from the prophets."

[VII.A]   Said R. Joshua of the South, "Concerning three things—too much or too little of them is bad; but a moderate amount of them is good: [They are] yeast, salt, and unwillingness [to serve as leader of the Prayer of Eighteen when called upon].

[B]   "At the first [request by the official of the congregation to a person to lead the Prayer of Eighteen], one may express unwillingness. At the second request, one may express indecision. And at the third request, one should hurry to go [recite]."

[C]   R. Huna was sitting in a certain synagogue. The Hazzan went and tried to impose upon one person to go up [before the ark to lead the Prayer of Eighteen]. He would not accept [the call to go]. [R. Eleazar got angry.]

[D]   Afterward the person went to R. Eleazar and said, "Please master, do not be angry at me. Because I could not gather up [enough strength] I did not go up."

[E]   He [Eleazar] said to him, "I was not angry with you. I was angry at the person who tried to impose upon you [to lead the Prayer of Eighteen]."

[VIII.A]   Batyty [was leading the Prayer of Eighteen] and he was struck dumb while reciting the [liturgy preceding the *Shema*], "And the Ophanim [and the holy Hayyot with a noise of great rushing, raise themselves up toward the Seraphim and over against them offer praise and say, 'Blessed be the Glory of the Lord from his place.'" This is the standard version.]

[B]   They went and asked R. Abun [where the leader who replaces him should commence reciting the service.]

[C]   R. Abun in the name of R. Joshua b. Levi said to them, "The person who replaces him should commence from the place where the first stopped."

[D]   They said to him, "But, lo, we learned, *'[He should commence] from the beginning of the blessing in which the [previous] erred'"* [M. 5:3E].

[E]   He said to them, "Since [when he recited, 'And the Ophanim'] the congregation [already] answered, 'Blessed be the Glory of the Lord from his place,' it is as if this [place in the service] is the beginning of a blessing."

The Talmud begins in units **I–III** with explanations of M.'s rules. From unit **III.B** down to unit **VI**, the Talmud looks into various applications of the rules. Units **VII–VIII** add further materials about practices to follow when one replaces a leader who errs in his recitation.

5:4

[A]   *He who goes before the ark [to lead the Prayer of Eighteen] shall not answer 'Amen' after the [blessing recited by the] priests [in the eighteenth blessing of the Prayer].*

[B]   *Because of the confusion [which might arise by virtue of engaging in such an act].*

[C]   *And if [the leader] is the only priest present [at the service], he should not raise his hands [to recite the Priestly Blessing].*

[D]   *But if he is sure that he can raise his hands [to recite the blessing] and return to his [recitation of the] Prayer [of Eighteen without becoming confused], he is permitted [to raise his hands].*

[I.A] It was taught: **He who leads the liturgy of the *Shema'*, and he who goes before the ark [to lead the recitation of the Prayer of Eighteen], and he who raises his hands, and he who reads the Torah, and he who reads from the prophets, and he who recites a blessing over any of the commandments of the Torah, should not respond 'Amen' to his own blessing. And if he so responds, lo, he is a boor** [T. Meg. 3:27].

[B] [There are two versions of the last sentence of the preceding teaching.] One Tanna taught, "He is a boor."

[C] The other Tanna taught, "He is a sage."

[D] Said R. Hisda, "The one who holds the view, 'He is a sage,' [refers to a case wherein] he answers at the conclusion [of all the liturgy, e.g., after reciting the entire Prayer of Eighteen].

[E] "The one who holds the view, 'He is a boor' [refers to a case wherein] he answers 'Amen' to each and every blessing [e.g., each blessing that he recites in the Prayer of Eighteen]."

[II.A] Said R. Hanina, "[If three persons walk down the road,] two Israelites and one a priest, they permit the priest to walk in the middle [as a sign of respect for his status].

[B] "When is this so? When they are all equal in status. But if one of them [the Israelites] is a disciple of the sages, they permit this associate to walk in the middle."

[C] Said R. Joshua b. Levi, "In my entire life, I have never recited the blessings [for meal] when in the presence of a priest. And [when there was no priest present] I never allowed an Israelite to recite a blessing in my presence [because I, a Levite, took precedence over an Israelite]."

[III.A] R. Judah b. Pazzi in the name of R. Eleazar, "Any priest who stands in the synagogue [during the recitation of the Prayer of Eighteen] and does not raise his hands [to recite the Priestly Blessing] violates a positive precept of the Torah." ['Thus shall you bless the people of Israel' (Num. 6:23).]

[B] When R. Judah b. Pazzi was weak [and could not raise his hands to recite the Priestly Blessing] he would bandage his head [to show that he was ill] and remain behind the pillar [in the synagogue when the other priests went up to recite the Priestly Blessing].

[C]   R. Eleazar [when he was weak and could not raise his hands] would go outside [the synagogue when the other priests went up to recite the blessing].

[D]   R. Aha, R. Tanhuma b. R. Hiyya in the name of R. Simlai, "In a city comprised entirely of priests, they all raise their hands [to recite the Priestly Blessing]. [No one remains in the congregation in front of them when they go to the front of the synagogue to recite the blessing.] For whom [then] do they recite the blessing? [They recite] for their brethren in the north, for their brethren in the south, for their brethren in the east, and for their brethren in the west. And who respond 'Amen' to their blessings? The women and children [in the synagogue]."

[E]   Abaye b. R. Benjamin taught, "Those who stand behind the priests [while they recite the Priestly Blessing] are not included in the blessing."

[F]   Those who stand in front of the priests—said R. Hiyya bar Abba [Wawa], "Even [if they stand behind] an iron wall, the blessing will reach through to them."

[G]   [And what of] those who stand off to the sides? Let us derive the answer from the following: *If the priest intended to sprinkle in front of him [the purification water with a hyssop onto those who are unclean on account of corpse uncleanness], and he [inadvertently] sprinkled behind him, or if he intended to sprinkle behind him, and he sprinkled in front, his [act of] sprinkling is not valid. [But if he intended to sprinkle directly] in front, and he sprinkled to the sides in front, his [act of] sprinkling is valid* [M. Parah 12:2].

[H]   From this we may deduce [the principle] that even those who stand off to the sides [during the recitation of the Priestly Blessing] are included in the blessing.

[I]   Said R. Hisda, "The Hazzan [who leads the recitation of the Prayer] must be an Israelite [so that he can call out the invitation to the priests to recite the blessing, 'Priests!']"

[J]   R. Nahman bar Jacob said, "If there is only one priest [reciting the blessing, the Hazzan] calls out, 'Priest.' If there are two [or more] he calls out, 'Priests.'"

[K]   Said R. Hisda, "Even if there is but one priest, he calls out,

'Priests' [i.e., plural]. For [in this invitation to the priest to recite the Priestly Blessing] he calls out to the [collective] tribe [of
priests to exercise their obligation to bless the nation]." [Cf. Y.
Git. 5:9.]

Unit **I**'s citation of a Tosefta passage regarding saying 'Amen' to
one's own blessings, takes us away from the subject of M.'s
rules. Unit **II**'s rules about giving priority to a priest, go off in
another direction. The Talmud comes back to the subject matter
of M. at unit **III** with a collection of rules for the recitation of
the Priestly Blessing.

5:5

[A]   *He who recites the Prayer and erred, it is a bad sign for him.*

[B]   *And if he is an agent of the congregation [to lead the Prayer], it
is a bad sign for them that appointed him.*

[C]   *[The principle is that] a person's agent personifies him [i.e.,
stands in his stead].*

[D]   *They said concerning R. Haninah b. Dosa that he used to pray
for the sick and could say who would live and who would die.*

[E]   *They said to him, "Whence do you know?"*

[F]   *He said to them, "If my prayer is fluent, then I know it is
accepted.*

[G]   *"And if not, then I know it is rejected."*

[I.A]   R. Aha bar Jacob said, "[It is only a bad sign if one errs in the
first blessing,] The Patriarchs."

[II.A]   Once Rabban Gamaliel's son fell ill and he sent two students to
R. Haninah b. Dosa in his town [to find out from him what his
son's fate would be]. He [Haninah] said to them [the students],
"Wait for me while I go up to the attic [to pray]."

[B]   He went up to the attic, came down, and said to them, "I am
certain that Rabban Gamaliel's son has recovered from his
illness."

[C]   [The students] made note [of the time of day that this happened]. [Later they confirmed that] at that very moment [back in Gamaliel's town, his son recovered] and asked for food.

[III.A]   Said R. Samuel bar Nahmani, "If you concentrate during your prayer, it is like good news for your prayers are heard. And what is the basis [in Scripture for this view]? 'Thou wilt strengthen their heart [to concentrate], thou wilt incline thy ear [to their prayer]'" [Ps. 10:17].

[B]   Said R. Joshua b. Levi, "If a person feels that [his prayers] flow smoothly from his lips, it is like good news, for his prayers are heard. What is the basis [in Scripture for this view]? 'He creates the fruits of the lips. Peace, peace, to the far and to the near, says the Lord; and I will heal him'" [Isa. 57:18–19].

After unit **I** briefly comments on M., unit **II** supplements the story of Ben Dosa's prognostic powers and unit **III** supports the idea of the passage with Scriptural references.

6 Yerushalmi Berakhot
Chapter Six

6:1

[A] *What blessings do they recite over produce?*

[B] *Over produce of the tree he says, "[Blessed art Thou, O Lord our God, King of the Universe,] creator of the fruit of the tree."*

[C] *Except for wine, for over wine he says, "[Blessed art Thou, O Lord our God, King of the Universe,] creator of the fruit of the vine."*

[D] *Over vegetables [produce that grows in the ground] he says, "[Blessed art Thou, O Lord our God, King of the Universe,] creator of the fruit of the ground."*

[E] *Except for bread, for over bread he says, "[Blessed art Thou, O Lord our God, King of the Universe,] who brings forth bread from the earth."*

[F] *And over [salad] greens he says, "Creator of the fruit of the ground."*

[G] *R. Judah says, "Creator of diverse kinds of herbs."*

[I.A] **[One may not taste anything until he recites a blessing.] It is written, "The earth and all therein is the Lord's" [Ps. 24:1]. One who derives any benefit from the world without first reciting a blessing, has committed a sacrilege. [He may not derive any benefit] until [he fulfills all the obligations] that permit him [to derive benefit, i.e., recites the proper blessings] [T. 4:1].**

[B] Said R. Abahu, "It is written, '[You shall not sow your vineyard with two kinds of seed,] lest the whole yield be forfeited to the sanctuary, the crop which you have sown and the yield of the vineyard' [Deut. 22:9]. The [produce of the] entire world is [sacred] like [the fruits of such] a vineyard. How does one redeem it? [By reciting] a blessing."

[C]   R. Hezekiah, R. Jeremiah, R. Abun in the name of R. Simeon b. Laqish, "I say to the Lord, 'Thou art my Lord; I have no good apart from you' [Ps. 16:2]. If you eat and recite the blessings [for the meal], it is as if you have eaten of your own produce." [Only God bestows good upon you, i.e., "apart from you" implies "without you," that is, God has no claim against you—P.M.]

[D]   Another interpretation of, "I have no good apart from you": My goodness will endure in your body. ["Apart from you" implies that it will not depart from you quickly.]

[E]   Another interpretation of, "I have no good apart from you": May all that is good be combined together, and be bestowed upon you. ["Apart" (*bl*) implies let goodness not be apart, but be mixed (*bll*) together for you.]

[F]   Said R. Aha, "What does, 'apart from you [*bl 'lyk*]' mean? Only with your consent [*mbl'dyk*] will I bring good into the world." As it says, "[Moreover Pharaoh said to Joseph, 'I am Pharaoh, and] without your consent [*mbl'dyk*] no man shall lift up hand or foot [in all the Land of Egypt]'" [Gen. 41:44].

[G]   R. Hiyya taught, "'An offering of praises' [the verse uses the plural form, *hlwlym*] [Lev. 19:24]—this teaches that a blessing must be recited before and after [eating of the produce of the land]."

[H]   On this basis R. Aqiba used to say, "A person may not taste a thing until he recites a blessing."

[II.A] R. Haggai and R. Jeremiah went to a [grocery] store [to inspect its scales for accuracy]. R. Haggai eagerly recited a blessing [over this obligation to examine the scales. He said the blessing, "Who sanctified us with his commandments and commanded us to sanctify the weights and the scales and to establish the measures"—S.H.].

[B]   R. Jeremiah said to him, "You have acted very well. For blessings must be [recited] for the performance of all the commandments."

[C]   And whence [do we find support in Scripture] that blessings must be recited over all the commandments?

[D]   R. Tanhuma, R. Abba bar Kahana in the name of R. Eleazar, "[Scripture says,] 'I will give you the tables of stone, with the Torah and the commandment, which I have written for their instruction' [Exod. 24:12]. Scripture juxtaposes the Torah with the commandments. [This teaches that] just as a blessing must be recited over the recitation of the Torah, so also a blessing must be recited over the performance of the commandments."

[III.A]   R. Yohanan ate olives and recited blessings before and after. And R. Hiyya bar Abba [Wawa] stared at him.

[B]   Said to him R. Yohanan, "Babylonian, what are you staring at? Don't you know that blessings must be recited before and after eating any food of the seven kinds of produce [of the Land of Israel]?"

[C]   [The Talmud explains:] He knew the law. So what was his question? [He had a doubt whether one should recite a blessing over the olive] because [when you remove] the olive's pit, it leaves you with less [than an olive's bulk of volume, i.e., less than the minimum volume for which one recites a blessing.]

[D]   And did R. Yohanan not know that [when you remove] the olive's pit, you are left with less [than the minimum volume]?

[E]   R. Yohanan acted as he did because [he held the opinion that a minimum bulk is not required for a piece of] food in its [full] natural form. [One must consume a minimum of an olive's bulk only for cut up or processed food.]

[F]   From R. Yohanan's words we may conclude that if one ate even a single grape or pomegranate seed, a blessing must be recited before and after it.

[IV.A]   **"Over wine when it is in its natural state [thick, undiluted] they recite, 'Blessed [art Thou, O Lord our God, King of the Universe,] creator of the fruit of the tree.' And they may not wash their hands with it."** [T. has, "may."]

[B]   **"Once the wine has been diluted, they say over it, 'Blessed [art Thou, O Lord our God, King of the Universe,] creator of** the fruit of the vine.' And they may wash their hands with it," the words of R. Eliezer. [T. has, "may not."]

[C]   And sages say, "Both over natural [thick wine] and over diluted [wine] they say, 'Blessed [art Thou, O Lord our God, King of the Universe,] creator of the fruit of the vine.' And they may wash their hands with it" [T. 4 : 3]. [T. has "may not."]

[D]   Said R. Abba, "[They may wash with undiluted wine according to Eliezer because such action] is not considered destruction of food [since the raw wine is not ready for consumption—P.M.]."

[V.A]   R. Jacob bar Zabdi in the name of R. Abahu, "Over olive oil one recites, 'Blessed [art Thou, O Lord our God, King of the Universe,] creator of the fruit of the tree.'"

[B]   Said R. Hiyya bar Papa before R. Zeira, "Does not our Mishnah imply [that one should recite a different blessing over the oil? For it says,] *Except for wine, for over wine he says, '[Blessed art Thou, O Lord our God, King of the Universe,] creator of the fruit of the vine'* [M. 6 : 1C]. And is wine not squeezed [from grapes? Since we recite a different blessing over wine, should we not recite a different blessing over oil squeezed from olives?]

[C]   "[This is not a valid inference because] the Mishnah specifies, *Except for wine.* [This implies that with regard to the blessing that we recite we make no similar distinction] for other liquids. Even if the produce is squeezed, [we treat the juice or oil] as if it were [the fruit] intact [and we recite for it the same blessing]."

[VI.A]   R. Abba said, "Rab and Samuel both say, 'Over a cooked vegetable one says, "[Blessed art Thou, O Lord our God, King of the Universe,] for all came into being by his word."'"

[B]   R. Zeira in the name of Samuel, "Over cooked turnip-heads, if [one eats them when] they are intact [in their original form], one says, 'Creator of the fruit of the ground [vegetables].' If he grinds them up [to eat them] one says, 'For all came into being by his word.'"

[C]   Said R. Yose, "Does not our Mishnah imply [that one should recite a different blessing over ground-up vegetables. For it says,] *Except for bread, for over bread he says, '[Blessed art Thou, O Lord our God, King of the Universe] who brings forth bread from the earth'* [M. 6 : 1E]. And is bread not [made from] ground [grain? Since we recite a different blessing over bread should we not recite a different blessing over cooked vegetables if they are ground up, contrary to R. Abba's citation of the ruling of Rab and Samuel above?]

[D]   "[This is not a valid inference because] the Mishnah specifies, *Except for bread.* [This implies that with regard to the blessing we recite, we make no similar distinction] for other foods. Even if the food is ground up, [we treat it] as if it were intact [and we recite for it the same blessing.]"

[VII.A]   R. Hiyya bar Abba [Wawa] in the name of R. Yohanan, "Over a pickled olive one recites, 'Creator of the fruit of the tree.'"

[B]   R. Benjamin bar Yefet in the name of R. Yohanan, "Over a cooked vegetable one recites, 'For all came into being by his word.'" [And the same rule should apply to a pickled vegetable, contrary to Hiyya bar Abba.]

[C]   Said R. Samuel bar R. Yitzhak, "A tradition in the Mishnah supports the ruling of R. Benjamin bar Yefet: *[These are the greens with which one may fulfill his obligation on Passover. . . . One may fulfill his obligation] neither with pickled, nor with marinated, nor with cooked vegetables* [M. Pes. 2 : 6]. If indeed they [the cooked vegetables] are [to be treated as if they were] intact, a person should be able to fulfill his obligation with them on Passover." [Since he cannot, we deduce that neither pickled nor cooked vegetables are treated as if they were intact, supporting Benjamin's version of R. Yohanan's teaching that they recite over both of them 'For all,' and contradicting Hiyya's version that they recite over pickled olives, 'Creator of the fruit of the tree.']

[D]   Said R. Zeira, "Who knows R. Yohanan's teaching better? R. Hiyya bar Abba [Wawa] or R. Benjamin bar Yefet? Is it not R. Hiyya bar Abba [Wawa] [who was Yohanan's best disciple]?"

[E]   Furthermore the following [supports Hiyya bar Abba's version of Yohanan's teaching]: We saw the great rabbis going to get refreshments [to eat]. They took lupine [to eat] and recited over it, "[Blessed art Thou, O Lord our God, King of the Universe,] creator of the fruit of the ground [vegetables]." And are not lupine [generally eaten] cooked? [Yet what they recited accords with Hiyya and appears to contradict the proof against Hiyya from the ruling in Mishnah Pesahim (C).]

[F]   And if you argue that the ruling in the Mishnah deals with a different issue, [that one cannot fulfill his obligation on Passover by eating cooked vegetables] since the Torah specified that [the herbs one eats on Passover] must taste bitter, [we may respond as follows].

[G]   Cooked [vegetables like] lupine, once they are [thoroughly] cooked, lose their bitterness. [Accordingly, aside from this special consideration for bitter herbs for Passover, Hiyya is right. Cooked and uncooked vegetables fall into the same category. One recites the same blessing before eating either. See P.M.]

[H]   Said R. Yose b. R. Bun, "There [really] is no dispute [between Hiyya and Benjamin over Yohanan's ruling. For Hiyya's version applies to] an olive. Because one normally eats it raw, even when it is pickled we treat it as [if it is] intact [and recite over it 'Creator of vegetables']. [And Benjamin's version applies to] green vegetables. Once you cook them, they change [so you recite over them, 'For all came into being by his word']."

[VIII.A]   R. Jacob bar Aha said, "R. Nahman disputed with the sages [over the correct formula for the blessing recited over bread]."

[B]   R. Nahman said, "Who brings forth [hmwsy'] bread from the earth," [indicating past and continuous action].

[C]   And sages said, "Brings forth [mwsy'] bread from the earth," [indicating continuous and future action].

[D]   This dispute parallels the following dispute: [What is the meaning of the term] lepet [relish that one eats with bread]? R. Haninah bar Yitzhak and R. Samuel bar Immi disputed.

[E]   One said lepet means there was [l' pt] no [need for this] food [in the past. In paradise, bread grew from the ground fully seasoned.]

[F]   And the other said lepet means there will be [l' pt] no [need for this] food in the future, [in messianic times—see Jastrow, p. 716 s.v. lpt]. [As the verse in Psalms says,] "May there be abundance of grain in the land; on the tops of the mountains may it wave" [Ps. 72:16]. [May there be no need in the future for you to have relish with your bread.]

[G]   R. Jeremiah recited the blessing, "Who brings forth [hmwsy'] bread from the earth," before R. Zeira, and he [Zeira] praised him.

[H]   Why did he act in accord with the view of R. Nahman [var.
       Nehemiah, see **IX**.A below] [and not in accord with sages]? [He
       did so] in order not to elide the consonant sounds [at the end of
       one word and the beginning of the next: *mlk h'wlm—mwṣy'* in
       the blessing formula].

[I]   Why then did he not say also *lhm—hmn h'rṣ [adding a letter H*
       to separate the two consonants *Mem*] so as not to elide the con-
       sonant sounds [between two words elsewhere in the same bless-
       ing]? [The Talmud gives no answer.]

[IX.A] According to the view of R. Nehemiah [over wine], one recites,
       "Who creates [*hbwr'*] the fruit of the vine."

[B]   And according to the view of the sages, one recites, "Creator of
       [*bwr'*] the fruit of the vine."

[X.A] R. Zeriqin said, "R. Zeira posed this question: One who took
       lupine to eat and recited the blessing over it, and dropped it,
       [before eating it, when he goes to take another piece to eat] what
       does he do? Must he recite the blessing a second time before
       eating it [since it is a different piece]? How does this case differ
       from the case of one who drinks from a [flowing] channel of
       water [where the water over which he recites the blessing flows
       by and he then drinks other water]?

[B]   "[But these are different situations.] We may say there [in the
       case of one who drinks from a channel], he had in mind when he
       recited the blessing [that it should apply to the water which will
       flow down the stream]. But here [in the case of one who dropped
       the lupine over which he recited a blessing], he initially did not
       have in mind to eat another piece. [Accordingly, he should recite
       the blessing again.]"

[C]   R. Hiyya taught, "They recite the blessing over bread only right
       at the time they break the bread [to eat it, but not before lest
       after they recite the blessing, they are distracted and do not get a
       chance to eat the loaf over which they recited the blessing]."

[D]   Said R. Hiyya bar Abba [Wawa], "This accords with what was
       said concerning one who took a radish [var. a round loaf of
       bread] and recited the blessing over it but [unexpectedly] did
       not get a chance [to eat it]. [Later when he does eat it] he must
       recite the blessing over it a second time [before eating it]."

[E]   Said R. Tanhum bar Yudan, "[In such a case where one recited a blessing but was not able to eat,] he must say, 'Blessed be his glorious name for ever and ever,' [after he recites the unnecessary blessing] so that he does not invoke the Divine Name in vain."

[XI.A]   What is the minimum quantity [of bread] for which [before eating it] one recites the blessing?

[B]   R. Hanina and R. Mana [disputed this matter].

[C]   One said, "An olive's bulk."

[D]   And the other said, "Even less than an olive's bulk."

[E]   The one who said, "An olive's bulk" accords with what was taught elsewhere [M. Menahot 6:5]: *[All meal-offerings that are made ready in a vessel must be broken into pieces. . . .] And all of them must be broken into pieces the size of an olive [or larger].*

[F]   The one who said "Even less than an olive's bulk" accords with what R. Ishmael taught, [There was no prescribed minimum measure, as in M. Menahot 6:7]: *Even if he grinds them into meal* [that is acceptable, implying that even a small amount of meal is enough. Cf. B. Men. 75b.]

[G]   It was taught: **This is the general rule: All [those foods over which] after eating one recites three blessings [i.e., grace after meals], one recites over them before eating, "He who brings forth bread from the earth"** [T. 4:7E–G].

[H]   [From this we may infer] all those foods over which after eating one does not recite three blessings, one does not recite over them before eating, "He who brings forth bread from the earth."

[I]   They objected [accordingly]: Behold, one who ate less than an olive's bulk of bread does not recite three blessings after eating and therefore should not recite the blessing before eating, "He who brings forth bread from the earth." [This contradicts the view above in D, that one recites the blessing before eating even less than an olive's bulk.]

[J]   [In response to this question] R. Jacob bar Aha says, "[The general rule in Tosefta was formulated] to exclude other categories of bread." [Over bread not made from the five principal grains, one does not recite the three concluding blessings after eating, and thus does not recite before eating, the blessing, 'He who brings forth.' But T.'s general rule was not formulated to exclude from the requirement to recite the blessing before eating a person who ate less than an olive's bulk.]

[XII.A] R. Abba in the name of Rab, "It is forbidden for those who are seated to taste even a morsel, until the one who recites the blessing [on behalf of all assembled at the meal] tastes first."

[B] R. Joshua b. Levi said, "[Those who are assembled] may drink even before he [who blesses on their behalf] drinks."

[C] This is not a dispute [for the cases of eating and drinking are different]. Rab's [dictum applies in a case where] all assembled partake from a single loaf. [They must wait for the leader to break bread before they eat.]

[D] R. Joshua ben Levi's [dictum applies to a case where] each of those assembled had his own cup in his hand. [They need not wait for the leader before they drink.]

[E] It was taught: **The one who recites the blessing [before eating] stretches forth his hand first [to partake of the food]. But if he wished to give the honor [of partaking first] to his teacher or to one who is greater than he in [mastery of] Torah, he may do so** [T. 5:7C].

[F] When Rab broke bread, he used to partake [of the bread quickly] with his left hand and [at the same time] distribute [pieces to those assembled] with his right hand. [From this we may infer that he who recites the blessing must hurry to partake first—P.M.]

[XIII.A] R. Huna said, "[After reciting the blessing over the bread, but before partaking of it,] he who says [aloud to others some command related to the meal such as], 'Take [this food] and recite the blessing,' 'Take [that food] and recite the blessing,'—this is not a [significant] interruption between the recitation of the blessing [and partaking of the food. Therefore he need not recite another blessing.] [But he who says after reciting the blessing and before partaking of the food,] 'Give fodder to the oxen'— this does constitute a [significant] interruption [because it is not directly related to the meal. Therefore he must subsequently recite another blessing for the food.]"

[B] R. Huna said, "Over *shattita* [a mixture made of barley flour and honey] and over ground *murta* [made of myrrh-gum] one recites the blessing, 'For all came into being by his word.'"

[C]   R. Huna said, "[What should one do if] he forgot and put something into his mouth without first reciting a blessing? In the case of liquid, he should spit it out [and recite the blessing]. In the case of solid food, he may hold it in one side of his mouth [and recite the blessing]."

[D]   R. Yitzhak bar Mari in the presence of R. Yose b. R. Abun in the name of R. Yohanan, "Even in the case of solid food, he must spit it out [and recite the blessing]. As it is written, 'My mouth is filled with thy praise, and with thy glory all the day' [Ps. 71:8]. [One's mouth should not be filled with food when he recites a blessing.]"

[XIV.A]   **He who chews grains of wheat, recites over them [the blessing], "Creator of types of seeds."**

[B]   **If one baked or cooked [a dish using pieces of wheat bread in his recipe]—as long as the pieces remain intact, he must recite over [the dish] before eating, "He who brings forth bread from the earth," and he must recite over it three blessings [i.e., grace] after eating. [It has the same requirements as the bread itself.]**

[C]   **If the pieces do not remain intact [in the dish], he must recite over it [before eating], "Creator of types of grains," and must recite over it after eating one blessing which is an abstract of the three blessings [T. 4:6].**

[D]   What minimum size must the pieces be [to be considered 'intact']? R. Yose b. R. Abun, Kahana bar Malkiah in the name of Rab, "At least [the size of] olives."

[E]   **He who chews grains of rice, recites over them the blessing, "Creator of types of seeds."**

[F]   **If one baked or cooked [a dish using pieces of rice loaves in his recipe], even if the pieces remain intact he recites over [the dish] before eating, "Creator of types of grains," and he need not recite a blessing over it after eating. [It has the same requirements as the rice loaves themselves] [T. 4:7].**

[G]   R. Jeremiah says, "[One recites over this type of dish,] 'Creator of the produce of the earth [vegetables].'"

[H]   Bar Marina in the presence of R. Zeira, and in the presence of R. Hiyya bar Abba [Wawa] recited the blessing [over such a dish], "For all came into being by his word."

[I]   R. Simeon the Pious says [over such a dish one recites], "Creator of kinds of delicacies."

[J]   Said R. Yose b. R. Abun, "There is no dispute [among these four views concerning the blessing for this dish]. He who holds the view that one must recite, 'Creator of types of grains' [i.e., T. 4:7 above] refers to a dish into which one mixed [rice cakes with grains of the five primary kinds].

[K]   "He who holds the view that one must recite, 'Creator of vegetables' [i.e., Jeremiah] refers to a dish made solely [of rice cakes].

[L]   "He who holds the view that one must recite, 'For all things came into being by his word' [i.e., Bar Marina] refers to a dish [of rice cakes] which was cooked.

[M]   "And he who holds the view that one must recite, 'Creator of kinds of delicacies' [i.e., Simeon] refers to a dish [of rice cakes] which was scrambled [together with eggs and other foods and spices]."

[XV.A]   The preceding discussion refers to [the blessing one recites at] the outset [before eating a dish made with rice cakes]. What about after [eating? What blessings does one recite?] R. Jonah in the name of R. Simeon the Pious, "[One says, 'Blessed art Thou, Lord our God, King of the Universe,] who created all kinds of delicacies to delight with them all living souls. Blessed art Thou, O Lord, for the land and for its delicacies.'"

[B]   R. Abba bar Jacob in the name of R. Yitzhak the great, "When Rabbi used to eat meat or eggs he used to say [afterward], 'Blessed [art Thou, O Lord our God, King of the Universe,] who created many souls to give life through them to all living things. Blessed art Thou, O Lord, who lives forever!'"

[C]   The preceding refers to [the blessing recited] after [eating meat or eggs]. What [does one recite at] the outset [before eating]? Said R. Haggai, "[Blessed art Thou, O Lord our God, King of the Universe] creator of many forms of life."

[D]   R. Yose objected [to the rule of R. Haggai], "Lo, the Mishnah disputes this: *Over vinegar, or over unripe fruit, or over edible locusts one recites, 'For all [things] came into being by his word'* [M. 6:3B]. Are not locusts a form of life? [Yet one recites over them, 'For all.' Haggai was wrong.]"

[E]   R. Simeon the Pious' ruling [i.e., in A, one recites after eating a dish made from rice cakes the blessing, "Who created kinds of delicacies,"] accords with Rabbi's ruling [i.e., in B, one recites after meat or eggs, "Who created many souls"]. And both accord with R. Gamaliel's ruling [in the following passage].

[F]   For it was taught: **This is the general rule. . . . R. Judah says in his [Gamaliel's] name, "All [dishes] that are made from the seven kinds [of produce of the Land of Israel], but not of kinds of breadstuff, or made of kinds of breadstuff, but not baked into a loaf, Rabban Gamaliel says, 'One recites three blessings after eating it.'**

[G]   **"And sages say, 'One blessing!'**

[H]   **"And all dishes that are made neither from the seven kinds, nor from kinds of breadstuff, Rabban Gamaliel says, 'One recites [before and] after it [one blessing].'**

[I]   **"And sages say, '[One recites a blessing before eating, and one recites after it] nothing.'"** [T. 4:15. Both Simeon's and Rabbi's opinions above accord with the latter view of Rabban Gamaliel that one recites a blessing after eating such dishes.]

[XVI.A]   R. Jacob bar Idi in the name of R. Hanina, "Over all foods that resemble porridge [flour cooked in water], or resemble dumplings [dough cooked in boiling water—P.M.], and are made of one of the five [major] kinds of grain, one recites [before eating it], 'Creator of types of grains.' And one recites after eating it one blessing, which is an abstract of three blessings."

[B]   And over all foods that resemble porridge, or resemble dumplings, but are not made of one of the five kinds of grain [what blessing does one recite after eating]?

[C]   Said R. Jonah, "R. Zeira sent [this question] to those of the house of R. Yannai and they told me [the answer], but I am not certain what they told me."

[D]   And what is the answer?

[E]   Said R. Yose, "It makes sense that one should recite, 'For all came into being by his word' [over foods like porridge or dumplings]."

[F]   R. Jeremiah posed the question, "What blessing does one who eats porridge recite after eating?"

[G]   Said R. Yose, "[Jeremiah never knew the answer to this question.] For this reason R. Jeremiah never in his life ate porridge. He had a doubt that perhaps one should not [recite one blessing which is an abstract of three, but rather, 'Creator of many souls']."

[XVII.A]   Why does one conclude [the blessing after eating, which is an abstract of three,] with mention of the Land, ["Blessed art Thou, O Lord, for the land, and for the sustenance"]?

[B]   They formulated it [this blessing] like the blessing of the laborers, [which also concludes with mention of the land, as we see in the following passage.]

[C]   For it was taught: **Laborers [who ate] while they were working with the householder, recite two blessings [after eating instead of four, to save time]. They recite the first blessing, and they include [the mention] of Jerusalem in the blessing for the Land [i.e., in the second], and they conclude with [the blessing] for the Land.**

[D]   **But if they were working with him in exchange for their meals, or if the householder were eating with them, lo, they recite [all] four blessings** [T. 5:24].

[E]   Members of the house of R. Yannai established a standardized formula [for the conclusion of all blessings that were abstracts of three, i.e., "Blessed art Thou, O Lord, for the land, and for the sustenance." Regardless of whether one recited the blessing after eating foods made from the five types of grains, or after eating foods of the seven kinds of produce of the Land of Israel, the conclusion was to be the same.]

[F]   Does one mention the occasion [of a Sabbath, festival, or new moon] in [the abstract of three blessings]?

[G]   Said R. Abba bar Zimna, "R. Zeira used to mention the occasion in [the abstract of three blessings]."

[H]   Said R. Jeremiah, "Since R. Zeira was scrupulous in this practice, we too should be scrupulous in the practice [and mention the occasion in the abstract.]"

[XVIII.A]   It was taught: **[When a person has before him several foods to eat—] one should recite the blessing over the breadstuff that is of the highest quality.**

[B]   How so? [If one has before him] a [whole] fine loaf and a whole homemade loaf [of the same grain], he says [the blessing] over the whole fine loaf.

[C]   [If one has] a piece of a fine loaf and a whole homemade loaf, he says [the blessing] over the whole homemade loaf.

[D]   [If one has] wheat bread and barley bread he says [the blessing] over the wheat bread.

[E]   [If one has] a piece of wheat bread and a whole barley bread, he says [the blessing] over the piece of wheat bread.

[F]   [If one has] a barley bread and a spelt bread, one says [the blessing] over the barley bread.

[G]   But is not spelt bread better [quality] than barley bread?

[H]   But this [grain, i.e., barley] is one of the seven kinds [of produce of the Land of Israel, mentioned in Deut. 8:8] and that [grain, i.e., spelt] is not one of the seven kinds [T. 4:15].

[I]   R. Jacob bar Aha in the name of R. Zeira, "This [last rule (H)] accords with R. Judah: *[If one had before him many different kinds of foods—], R. Judah says, 'If among them there are foods of the seven kinds [of produce of the Land of Israel], one must recite the blessing over that [food]'"* [M. 6:4].

[J]   [If one has before him to eat] an unclean bread and a clean bread, R. Hiyya bar Abba [Wawa] said, "One says [the blessing] over the clean bread."

[K]   [If one has before him] an unsoiled [ritually] unclean bread and a soiled [ritually] clean bread, R. Hiyya bar Ada in the name of R. Aha, "One may recite the blessing over whichever one he chooses."

[XIX.A]   R. Jacob bar Aha in the name of Samuel, "One recites over palm-marrow [the edible part of the branch of the palm tree], 'Creator of the fruit of the tree [as if it were a fruit].'"

[B]   Taught R. Halafta b. Saul, "[They recite over the marrow,] 'For all came into being by his word.'"

[C]   Taught R. Joshua, "[They recite over marrow,] 'Creator of kinds of herbs [as if it were an herb].'"

[D]   A teaching of R. Hoshaia contradicts this [view of Joshua]: "These are the species of herbs [over which one recites 'Creator of kinds of herbs']: globe artichoke, mallow, *dymw'* [a teardrop shaped herb], and boxthorn."

Unit **I** proposes several Scriptural sources for the idea that one must recite blessings before eating, the basic principle of Mishnah's laws in this chapter. It first cites the relevant Tosefta passage, then gives alternatives, with expansions before it supplies a third source. Unit **II** gives a Scriptural source for the practice of reciting blessings before performing the various commanded rituals, a point secondary to the immediate context of the Mishnah.

Unit **III** prematurely begins to set forth specific rules for blessings before and after eating foods of the seven kinds, one of Mishnah's main points later in the chapter. Unit **IV** comes back to the present concern with a citation of the relevant materials from Tosefta, followed by a brief comment. The Talmud continues probing Mishnah's main issue, the rules of blessings for kinds of foods. Unit **V** deals with the blessings for olives and olive oil; unit **VI** turns to the formulae for cooked vegetables; unit **VII** discusses pickled olives and other vegetables.

Unit **VIII** comes back to a more direct exposition of Mishnah's concerns with a discussion of the form for the blessing over bread. Unit **IX** does the same more briefly for wine.

At unit **X** the Talmud asks about the act of reciting a blessing over foods. It raises a secondary, and more complex, issue, namely, what one does if he recites and then does not immediately eat the food. Interruption and diversion are a common theme of the tractate, as is the next issue, raised in unit **XI**, concerning the minimum quantity of food to eat to obligate oneself to recite a blessing.

Unit **XII** asks how people begin eating at the meal after the recitation of the initial blessing, the first of several sections concerned with rules of table etiquette. Unit **XIII**.A continues on a similar vein. Sections B–C round out the triplicate of traditions ascribed to Huna on the general subject of blessings. Section D returns to the application in practice of rules for reciting blessings.

Unit **XIV** cites T.'s complement to M., thereby turning to a new, but related, set of concerns—blessings one recites over processed foods that fall between two or more of the main categories that define the necessary blessings for the substances.

Unit **XV** adds further to clarify this issue, turning to the requirement for the blessing after eating processed mixtures. Related to
this, unit **XVI** discusses the blessings one recites for cooked
foods made of flour or dough.

Unit **XVII** begins the discussion of the conclusion of the text
of the short blessing, the abstract of three, which one recites
after some meals. This new subject is only and remotely relevant
to the first Mishnah of the chapter. Unit **XVIII** cites and adds
a few comments to the lengthy Tosefta passage regarding the
priorities one must give to types of foods with regard to the
blessings recited before eating them.

Unit **XIX** concludes with a ruling about palm marrow, which
raises the issue of how one defines fruit with regard to the blessings one recites.

6:2

[A]   *If over the fruit of trees one [by error] recited the blessing,
      "Blessed [art Thou, O Lord our God, King of the Universe,]
      creator of the fruit of the ground," he fulfilled his obligation
      [to recite a blessing over the food because trees do grow in the
      ground].*

[B]   *If over vegetables [one by error recited the blessing, "Blessed
      art Thou, O Lord our God, King of the Universe,] creator of
      the fruit of the trees," he did not fulfill his obligation [because
      produce of the ground does not grow on trees].*

[C]   *If over any [fruits of vegetables] one [by error] recited, "For all
      came into being by his word," he fulfilled his obligation.*

[I.A] R. Hezekiah in the name of R. Jacob bar Aha, "This [rule,
       M. 6:2A,] accords with the view of R. Judah. For R. Judah
       considers [the trunks of] trees to be like stalks [of grain. Just as
       grains of wheat are fruits of the ground even though they grow
       off the ground on stalks, so too fruits of trees are fruits of the
       ground even though they grow off the ground on branches]."
       [Cf. M. Bik. 1:1. Judah says one may bring fruits of trees
       as first fruits and recite over them the formula of avowal of
       Deut. 26:5ff. even though Scripture specifies that you should
       bring, "The first fruits of your ground" (Exod. 23:19). In
       Judah's view the formula, "Fruits of the ground," may apply to
       fruits of trees.]

[B]   Said R. Yose, "Everyone agrees that fruits of trees are included in [the category of] fruits of the ground [vegetables], but fruits of the ground are not included in [the category of] fruits of trees."

[C]   R. Huna said, "Excluding [from the general rule of M. 6:2A] wine and bread." Mishnah itself implies [this exclusion], *Except for wine. For over wine one recites, 'Creator of the fruit of the vine.' Except for bread. For over bread one recites, 'Who brings forth bread from the earth'"* [M. 6:1]. [As to their blessings, wine and bread are different from fruits and vegetables. One may not substitute another formula of blessing for their prescribed formula.]

[II.A] It was taught: **R. Yose says, "Anyone who alters the formula [for blessings] established by the sages does not fulfill his obligation."**

[B]   **R. Judah says, "[If one ate] any food which was changed from its natural state [through any processing], and he changed [var.: he did not change] [the formula of] the blessing, he fulfilled [var.: did not fulfill] his obligation"** [T. 4:5B–C].

[C]   **R. Meir says, "Even if one said, 'Blessed be He who created this object. How beautiful it is,' he fulfilled his obligation"** [T. 4:4F].

[D]   R. Jacob bar Aha in the name of Samuel, "The law accords with the view of R. Meir."

[E]   A tradition concerning Rab supports this [conclusion]: A Persian [Jew] once came before Rab [and asked], "I ate a loaf of bread but because I did not know which blessing to recite over it, I said, 'Blessed be He who created the loaf of bread.' Did I fulfill my obligation?" He [Rab] said to him, "You did, [in accord with the view of R. Meir]."

[III.A] R. Judah in the name of Abba bar bar Hannah, "Bar Qappara and two of his students once stayed over with a certain householder at an inn in the village of Birkata. He brought before them chicken, and plums, and leeks [porret].

[B]   "They said, 'If we recite the blessing over the leeks, we will exempt [ourselves from the obligation to recite the blessing over] the plums [since one can fulfill his obligation for both with the blessing for vegetables, 'Creator of the fruit of the ground'].

But we shall not exempt [ourselves from the obligation to recite the blessing over] the chicken. [It requires a different blessing, 'for all.']

[C]   "'And if we recite the blessing over the plums ['Creator of the fruit of the tree'] we shall exempt [ourselves from the obligation to recite the blessing for] neither one [i.e., the leeks] nor the other [i.e., the chicken].'

[D]   "One student jumped in and recited over the chicken the blessing, 'For all came into being by his word.' His associate laughed at him.

[E]   "Bar Qappara said to them, 'He [who jumped to bless] should not have been so gluttonous, but you [who laughed] should not have mocked him. What he did, was out of gluttony. Why did you mock him? [His choice of blessing was acceptable.]'

[F]   "And he said to that [student who jumped in to bless], 'Is there not a sage present? Is there not an elder present? [You should have waited to see what I would do.]'"

[G]   They said [concerning these students] that before the year was out, they died [because of their misconduct].

[H]   Said R. Yose, "Two lives have been lost. Do we not learn something from this incident?"

[I]   What is the resolution of this issue? It makes sense that one should recite [first] the blessing over the leeks ['Creator of the fruit of the ground']. [Because the blessing over the chicken,] 'For all came into being by his word,' is secondary to it [and should be recited over the chicken after the former blessing].

Units **I–II** take up M.'s main issue, the difference between fruits and vegetables and their respective blessings. Through its story, unit **III** then raises a secondary concern, namely, which takes precedence when one eats foods of two or more categories at the same meal?

6:3

[A]   *Over something that does not grow in the earth, one says [the blessing], "For all came into being by his word."*

[B]   *Over vinegar, and over unripe fruit, and over edible [i.e., per-*
       mitted] locusts, one says [the blessing], "For all came into being
       by his word."

[C]   *R. Judah says, "Over anything which is accursed [i.e., results*
       from a destructive effort], one does not recite a blessing."

[I.A] If one's wine turned to vinegar, he says, "Blessed be the true
       judge." If he goes to drink it, he says, "For all came into being
       by his word."

[B]   If one saw locusts, he says, "Blessed be the true judge." If he
       goes to eat them he says, "For all came into being by his word."

[C]   If one saw fruit that did not ripen, he says, "Blessed be the true
       judge." If he goes to eat them he says, "For all came into being
       by his word."

       The Talmud adds several more specific cases to the rules of M.

       6:4

[A]   *If one had before him many kinds [of food]—*

[B]   *R. Judah says, "If among them there is a food of the seven kinds*
       [of foods of the Land of Israel], one must recite the blessing over
       that [food first]."

[C]   *And sages say, "[One may recite the blessing] over any [food] he*
       wishes."

[I.A] R. Joshua b. Levi said, "Concerning what case do R. Judah and
       sages dispute? [A case] where one had in mind [when he ate
       many kinds of produce] to eat bread [thereafter]. But if he had
       no intention of eating bread [thereafter], all would agree [with
       Judah] that if [among the varieties of produce] there is a food of
       the seven kinds, one must recite the blessing over that food."
       [The reason for this rule is based on the principle that to in-
       crease one's prayers, one should, where possible, eat the food for
       which after eating it one recites the longest blessing. The bless-
       ing recited after eating is connected to the blessing one recites
       before eating. The food one eats and the blessing one recites
       before eating determine which blessing one recites after eating.
       In general the law is that where one eats bread, he recites the full

grace after meals. Where one does not eat bread, and where one recites the blessing over one of the seven kinds of produce before eating, he recites after eating the abstract of three blessings. Otherwise, where one recites a blessing over any other food before eating, he recites the short blessing, "Creator of many forms of life," after he finishes the repast—P.M.]

[B]   Said R. Abba, "One must recite a blessing afterwards. [One must recite the proper blessing after eating the produce, even if one had in mind to eat bread at the same meal after eating the produce.]"

[C]   Said R. Yose, "R. Abba's ruling contradicts R. Joshua b. Levi. For R. Joshua b. Levi said, 'Concerning what case do R. Judah and sages dispute? [A case] where one had in mind to eat bread [thereafter]. But if he had no intention of eating bread [thereafter], all would agree that if there is a food of the seven kinds, one must recite the blessing over that food.'

[D]   "And R. Abba said, 'One must recite a blessing after [eating the produce even if he had in mind to eat bread at the same meal after eating the produce].'"

[E]   If he did not recite the blessing [over the produce right after eating it], then we may consider it to be [a food which is] secondary [to the bread he then eats]. [And the meal blessing which one recites after eating the bread also covers his obligation to recite a blessing after eating foods secondary to the bread. He has no need to recite a separate blessing after eating the produce—following the second explanation of P.M.]

[F]   For it was taught there in the Mishnah: *Over any primary food [main dish] that is accompanied by a secondary food [side dish], one recites the blessing over the primary food and exempts [himself from the obligation to recite the blessing over] the secondary food* [M. 6:7].

[II.A]   Concerning the dessert tray [of assorted nuts and fruits]—
R. Jeremiah in the name of R. Ammi, "One recites the blessing over the lupine [even though he may also have before him fruits of the seven kinds]."

[B]   Said R. Levi, "[This rule is] based on [the verse], 'Do not rob the poor, because he is poor'" [Prov. 22:22]. [The application of the verse here is, "Do not deprive lupine, a common food, of its blessing."]

[C]   This rule applies to one who has in mind to eat bread [after partaking of the dessert tray, for then he may recite the blessing over whichever food he wishes in accord with the view of sages in M. 6:4A]. But it does not apply to one who does not have in mind to eat bread [after the dessert tray, for then he must recite the blessing over a food of the seven kinds rather than over lupine, in accord with the view of Judah in M. 6:4B].

[D]   Rabban Gamaliel Zuga visited the members of the House of R. Yannai. He saw them taking olives [to eat] and reciting blessings both before and after [eating them even if they were going to eat bread afterward].

[E]   He said to them, "Is this any way to act?" [The grace after meals of three blessings which you will recite afterward over the bread should suffice to fulfill your obligation to recite a blessing after eating the olives as well. The Talmud records no response to this question, indicating its approval of Gamaliel's view.]

[F]   R. Zeira sent a question to R. Samuel bar Nahman. [What is the rule in the case where one had before him many kinds of food and did not have in mind to eat bread afterward?—P.M.]

[G]   [Samuel b. Nahman responded as follows:] R. Kahana in the name of R. Abina, "Everyone agrees that if among them there is a food of the seven kinds, he must recite the blessing over it."

[H]   Said R. Zeira, "Very well. This also accords with what we have seen. When the sages went to sanctify the new moon, they used to eat grapes but did not recite a blessing after eating them. Was this not because they had in mind to eat bread afterward [and saying the meal blessing after eating bread sufficed for them to fulfill their obligation to recite a blessing after eating the grapes as well.]"

[III.A]   If one had before him several foods of the seven kinds, over which does he recite the blessing? [What is the order of priority among the foods of the seven kinds?]

[B]   There [in Babylonia] they said, "Whichever appears first in Scripture [in Deut. 8:8, 'A land of wheat and barley, of vines and fig trees and pomegranates, a land of olive trees and honey'] takes priority [with regard to the rule] for reciting a blessing [over these foods]."

[C]   And [the following exception applies to this rule:] those foods mentioned after the word 'land' in the verse [i.e., wheat and olives] take priority over the other foods." [Wheat and olives take priority over foods made from barley, grapes, figs, and pomegranates.]

Unit **I** comments upon M. at some length. Unit **II** adds specific cases to illustrate the general rule of M. Throughout, the Talmud bases its exegesis on the new external assumption that to explain M., one may differentiate between the case of a person who had in mind to eat a meal with bread after eating other foods, and a person who had no such action in mind.

Unit **III** returns to a direct discussion of M.'s rules.

6:5

[A] *If one recited the blessing over wine [which he drank] before the meal, he exempted [himself from the obligation to recite a blessing over] the wine [that he drinks] after the meal.*

[B] *If one recited the blessing over an appetizer [that he ate] before the meal, he exempted [himself from the obligation to recite a blessing over] the appetizer [that he eats] after the meal.*

[C] *If one recited the blessing over bread, he exempted [himself from the obligation to recite the blessing over] the appetizer.*

[D] *If one recited the blessing over the appetizer, he did not exempt [himself from the obligation to recite a blessing over] the bread.*

[E] *The House of Shammai say, "[By reciting a blessing over the appetizer one does] not even [exempt himself from his obligation to recite a blessing over] a potted dish."*

[I.A] Said R. Hisda, "Mishnah teaches [specifically], *If one recited the blessing over wine [that he drank] before the meal, he exempted [himself from the obligation to recite a blessing over] the wine [that he drinks] after the meal* [M. 6:5A]. But, [this implies], if one recited the blessing over wine during the meal, he does not exempt [himself from the obligation to recite a blessing over] wine after the meal."

[B] There [in Babylonia] they said, "Even if one recited the blessing over wine before the meal, he did not exempt wine after the meal."

[C]   But, lo, the Mishnah teaches, *If one recited the blessing over wine [that he drank] before the meal, he exempted [himself from the obligation to recite a blessing over] the wine [that he drinks] after the meal* [M. 6:5A].

[D]   R. Huna and R. Joshua b. Levi resolve this contradiction. One explains [that Mishnah refers to a special case] of one who drinks conditon-wine [a rich wine which is flavored with honey and spices, customarily drunk only on special occasions when it is the focus of the meal. With its blessing one fulfills his obligation to recite a blessing over the wine he drinks after the meal.]

[E]   And the other explains [that M. refers to a case of] one who drinks wine after coming from a bath house [also a special occasion for drinking when the wine is the focus of the meal and by its blessing one fulfills his obligation to recite a blessing over the wine he drinks after the meal. Jastrow has a different interpretation, cf. s.v. *blny*, p. 174.]

[II.A] R. Helbo, R. Huna, Rab in the name of R. Hiyya the great, **"Over a dessert cake [that one eats] after the meal [before he recites the blessings after the meal—P.M.], one is required to recite blessings before and after [eating it, because it is so special.]"** [Cf. T. 5:12].

[B]   Said R. Ammi, "R. Yohanan disputes this."

[C]   Said R. Mana to R. Hezekiah, "In what case does he dispute? Is it only if one ate food of the same kind [of grain as the cakes] during the meal [that later he need not recite another blessing before eating the cakes]?"

[D]   He said to him, "Even if during the meal he did not eat food of the same kind [of grain as the cakes, he still need not recite another blessing before eating the cakes]."

[E]   R. Haggai came [and taught the same rule] in the name of R. Zeira, "Even if during the meal he did not eat food of the same kind, [he need not recite another blessing before eating the dessert cakes]."

[F]   Said R. Haninah, "Bar Sisi [acted as follows:] when the members of the House of the Patriarch sent [premium] Nicolaos dates to him, he set them aside until after he ate his meal, and then recited blessings before and after [he ate them]."

[G]   R. Huna used to eat dates with his bread.

[H]   R. Hiyya bar Ashi said to him, "Do you dispute your master [Rab, cited in A above]? You should set them aside until after you eat your meal, and then recite blessings before and after [you eat them]."

[I]   He said to them, "Both this [the bread] and that [the dates] are essential to my refection."

[J]   R. Yonah and R. Yose went to the feast of R. Hanina of Antonia [alt.: Anath]. They brought before them dessert cakes after the meal.

[K]   They said, "Let us leave aside our own teachings and let us adopt for ourselves the Tannaitic rule.

[L]   "For it was taught: **R. Mana said in the name of R. Judah who said in the name of R. Yose, the Galilean, 'A dessert cake that one eats after the meal requires the recitation of blessings before and after [eating it]'"** [Y.'s version of T. 5:12].

[M]   They [the others at Hanina's feast] said, "Because this [law] is the ruling of individuals, and [since] the rabbis dispute it, let us act in accord with the rabbis."

[III.A] Said Marinus of the House of R. Joshua, "Where one ate from a dessert tray [of nuts and fruits], and ate porridge [made from flour], even if he recites a blessing after [eating from] the dessert tray, he does not exempt [himself from the obligation to recite a blessing over] the porridge."

[B]   Does this accord with the House of Shammai's [ruling in Mishnah 6:5E]? As *The House of Shammai say, [By reciting a blessing over the appetizer one does] not even [exempt himself from his obligation to recite a blessing over] a potted dish."* [The House of Shammai thereby extend the ruling of M. 6:5D.]

[C]   Said R. Yose, "Everyone agrees [that the blessing over fruits and nuts does not suffice for porridge made with flour.]"

[D]   [How then do we explain the House of Shammai's ruling? They dispute M. 6:5C in the following manner:] *If one recited the blessing over bread, he exempted [himself from the obligation to recite blessings over] the appetizer and a potted dish, in accord with the words of the House of Hillel.*

[E]   The House of Shammai say, *"[Reciting a blessing over bread does not even [exempt him from his obligation to recite a blessing over] a potted dish. [M. 6:5E].*

[F]   But *If one recited a blessing over the appetizer first,* everyone agrees that *He did not exempt [himself from the obligation to recite a blessing] over bread* [M. 6:5C] nor [does he exempt himself from his obligation to recite a blessing over] a potted dish.

[G]   R. Abba, son of R. Papa, posed the question, "One who ate porridge [made with flour], who had in mind to [later] eat bread, must he recite a blessing after eating porridge?"

[H]   The rabbis of Caesarea [or Katzrin] answer, "He must recite a blessing after eating it."

In unit **I,** the Talmud goes right into a discussion of the implications of M.'s laws. Unit **II** cites and examines the relevant Tosefta passage. Unit **III** discusses and explains the House of Shammai's position in M.

6:6

[A]   *When they are sitting [together prior to a meal], each person recites the blessings for himself.*

[B]   *When they have reclined [on couches at the meal together], one person recites the blessings for all of them.*

[C]   *When they have brought to them wine during the meal, each person recites the blessing for himself [because they drink by themselves].*

[D]   *[When they have brought to them wine] after the meal, one person recites the blessing for all of them [because they drink together].*

[E]   *And [that person] says the blessing over the incense, even though they bring out the incense only after dinner.*

[I.A]   R. Joshua b. Levi said, "The Mishnah refers to [the feast after] the circumcision of one's son [or some similar special occasion, in making the distinction between sitting and reclining at the meal]. But for the [ordinary meal of a] householder at home [there is] no [such distinction. The householder recites on behalf of his household—P.M.]."

[B]   R. Hiyya taught [in T. 4:8] [that this distinction applies] even for the [ordinary meal of a] householder at home.

[C]   It was taught: **What is the order of the dinner?**

[D]   **When the guests enter, they sit on benches or on chairs while all [the guests] assemble.**

[E]   **Once they all have assembled, and they bring out [water for washing] their hands, each person washes one hand [so that he may hold in it the cup of wine—P.M.].**

[F]   **When [they bring out and] mix the wine, each person recites the blessing for himself.**

[G]   **When they bring out appetizers, each person recites the blessing for himself.**

[H]   **When they get up [from the chairs] and recline [on couches for the meal] and they bring out [water for washing] their hands, even though they each had already washed one hand, they now must wash both hands [to eat].**

[I]   **When they [bring out and] mix the wine, even though they recited a blessing over the first cup, they now recite a blessing over the second cup. [And one person recites the blessing for all of them].**

[J]   **When they bring out an appetizer, [even though they recited a blessing over the first, they now recite a blessing over the second]. And one person recites the blessing for all of them.**

[K]   **[According to custom] a guest may not enter [to join the meal] if he comes after three appetizers are served, [as this is a sure sign that the dinner is under way]** [T. 4:8].

[II.A]   [Because the passage just cited speaks of the order of a meal, the Talmud deems it relevant to discuss here the order of the meal at the conclusion of the Sukkot holiday.] It was taught there: What is [the procedure for leaving] the sukkah on the seventh day [of the festival]?

[B]   When one finishes eating, he does not take apart his sukkah. Rather he takes his utensils out in the afternoon [and brings them into his house to use them inside] in honor of the last day of the festival [i.e., Shemini Aṣeret].

[C]   R. Abba b. Kahana, R. Hiyya bar Ashi in the name of Rab, "A person must render his sukkah invalid [by taking down some essential part of the structure] while it is still day [on the seventh day of the festival to indicate thereby that he is not adding another day to the festival." Then if he wishes, he may dwell in it even on the eighth day.]

[D]   R. Joshua b. Levi says, "One must recite the Prayer of Sanctification in his house [on the eighth day even though he may eat outside in the sukkah]."

[E]   R. Jacob bar Aha, in the name of Samuel, "One who recited the Prayer of Sanctification in one house and decided to eat in another house must recite the Prayer of Sanctification [again in the second house]."

[F]   R. Aha, R. Hanina in the name of R. Joshua [var: Hoshaiah] [in the name of Rab], "Whoever enjoys [eating in] his sukkah may recite the Prayer of Sanctification in his house on the last eve of the festival and go out and eat in his sukkah."

[G]   Said R. Abun, "[Rab and Samuel] are not in dispute. What Rab said [applies to a person] who had in mind [while reciting the Prayer of Sanctification] to eat in another house [e.g., in his sukkah]. What Samuel says [applies to a person] who did not have in mind [while reciting the Prayer of Sanctification] to eat in another house [but later changed his mind]." [This translation follows P.M.'s explanation.]

[H]   Said R. Mana, "Samuel's teaching [that one must recite the Prayer of Sanctification again (E)] accords with R. Hiyya's ruling [that one must render his sukkah invalid on the seventh day (C)]. And R. Joshua's [var.: Hoshaiah's] ruling [that one may recite the Prayer of Sanctification on the eighth night in his house and eat in his sukkah (F)] accords with R. Joshua bar Levi's ruling [that one must recite the Prayer of Sanctification in his house on the eighth night (D)]." [Samuel and Hiyya hold that one must recite in the sukkah where he then eats. But one invalidates the sukkah first lest he appear to add to the Sukkot festival. Hoshaiah and Joshua ben Levi permit one to recite the Prayer of Sanctification in one place and eat in another. Accordingly, one need not invalidate the sukkah because he may recite the Prayer of Sanctification in the house to show that he is not adding to the festival. P.M.'s alternate explanation connects Mana's statement with the views of Hiyya and Joshua ben Levi in unit I. Cf. P.M.]

[I]   Said R. Ammi, "This [T. 4:8] implies that there is a dispute [whether one must recline] for [a meal of] fruits [*pyrwt*]." [See PM's forced explanation. Alternatively, Sirilio reads: "There is an explicit *bpyrws*) dispute," i.e., between Samuel and Hoshaiah.]

[III.A] **They asked Ben Zoma, "Why [does it say],** *When they bring out wine during the meal, each person recites the blessing for himself***"** [M. 6:6C]?

[B]   **He said to them, "It is because [while one eats] his esophagus is not clear. [He may choke if he speaks to respond 'Amen' to the leader's blessing]"** [T. 4:12].

[C]   Said R. Mana, "This implies that during the meal one may not say, 'Bless you' to a person who sneezes, because he may endanger himself [by speaking while eating for his esophagus is not clear]."

[IV.A] *And [that person] says [the blessing] over the incense* [M. 6:6F]. [M. implies that anytime they bring out incense, one person recites the blessing for all.]

[B]   What is the difference between incense and wine? [Why during the meal does each person who drinks wine recite his own blessing?] All [who are present] smell the incense [at once]. But each person tastes his wine [individually.]

[C]   R. Zeira in the name of R. Jeremiah, "One must recite the blessing over the incense when the smoke from it rises up."

[D]   R. Jeremiah wanted to test R. Zeira. He said to him, "What [blessing] does one say over spiced oil?"

[E]   He said to him, "[Blessed art Thou, O Lord our God, King of the Universe,] who provided a good fragrance for spiced oil."

[F]   He said to him, "[You may also say, 'Blessed art Thou, O Lord our God, King of the Universe,] who provided a good fragrance for spice trees.'"

[G]   Yitzhak bar Abba bar Mehasiah and R. Hananel were sitting together [when they smelled the fragrance of spiced oil]. One said, "Blessed [art Thou, O Lord our God, King of the Universe,] who provided a good fragrance for spice trees." And the other said, "Blessed [art Thou, O Lord our God, King of the Universe,] who provided a good fragrance to the grasses of the earth."

[H]   The one who said [the blessing should be], "Grasses of the earth," posed a question to the one who said [the blessing should be], "Spice trees": "Are these [spice plants] really trees?"

[I]   He said to him, "Lo, it is written, 'She hid them with the trees [i.e., stalks] of flax' [Josh. 2:6]. Are these [flax-stalks] really trees? [Scripture calls them, 'trees.' I also call spice-plants, 'trees.']"

[J]   They went to the house of Rab and [heard from] Simeon bar Huna in the name of Rab [that the proper blessing over incense is,] "[Blessed art Thou, O Lord our God, King of the Universe,] who provided a good fragrance for the spice trees."

[V.A]   Geniva said, "[One who rubs his hands with] oil to [remove] the dirt [from them] need not recite a blessing."

[B]   Said R. Yudan, "Even if he holds the oil in his hands [to smell its fragrance before using it to cleanse himself, he need not recite a blessing over its fragrance]."

[C]   R. Helbo, R. Huna in the name of Rab, "One who sprays the inside of his house with oenanthe [an aromatic liquid grape derivative] need not recite a blessing [over the fragrance]."

[D]   Said R. Hisda, "Over all [fragrances] one says, 'Blessed [art Thou, O Lord our God, King of the Universe,] who provided a good fragrance for the spice trees,' except for the fragrance of musk over which one says, '[Blessed art Thou, O Lord our God, King of the Universe,] who provided a good fragrance for all kinds of spices.'"

Unit **I** cites the lengthy complement from Tosefta to our Mishnah. The commentators have difficulty explaining the appearance of the unrelated material concerning the end of the Sukkot holiday at unit **II**. Unit **III** again cites T., adding to it a brief remark. Unit **IV** comments and expands on M., and unit **V** concludes with more material on the blessings for spices and fragrances.

6:7

[A]   *When they bring out for him first a salted relish, and with it bread, he recites the blessing over the salted relish, and exempts [himself from the requirement of reciting a blessing over] the bread, for [in such a case] the bread is secondary to it.*

[B]   *This is the general rule: Over any primary food which is accompanied by a secondary food, one recites the blessing over the primary food and exempts [himself thereby from reciting the blessing over the] secondary food.*

[I.A] R. Samuel bar Nahman in the name of R. Jonathan, "The Mishnah refers to the time before they learned the dinner customs of royalty [to eat a full course dinner with appetizers, a main course and dessert]. And it refers to a place where they make the salted relish the primary food [of the meal]. But [the rule of the Mishnah does not apply to a place where they do not make the salted relish the primary food [of the meal]."

[B]   R. Jeremiah in the name of Rab, "[When one has before him] bread and morsels [made from bread crumbs], one recites the blessing over the morsels, in a place where they serve morsels as the main food [of the meal]. But [this rule] does not apply in a place where they do not serve morsels as the main food [of the meal]."

[C]   R. Simon in the name of R. Simeon b. Laqish "[When one has before him] nut-cakes and bread, one recites the blessing over the nut-cakes in a place where they serve nut-cakes as the main food [of the meal]. But [this rule] does not apply in a place where they do not serve nut-cakes as the main food [of the meal]."

The Talmud expands upon the main issue of M.

6:8

[A]   *"If one ate figs, or grapes, or pomegranates [as the main dish of his meal], he recites over them [after eating them the grace after meals made up of] three blessings," the words of Rabban Gamaliel.*

[B]   *And sages say, "[He recites] one blessing [that embodies the substance of the full grace after meals]."*

[C]   *R. Aqiba says, "Even if one ate cooked vegetables, and that was [the main dish of] his meal, [after eating them] he recites over them three blessings."*

[D]   *One who drinks water to quench his thirst says, "Blessed [art Thou, O Lord our God, King of the Universe,] for all came into being by his word."*

[E]   *R. Tarfon says, "He says, ['Blessed art Thou, O Lord our God, King of the Universe,] Creator of many living things and their needs."*

[I.A]   R. Simon, R. Tadai in the name of R. Joshua, "If one ate on the east side of a fig tree, and then went and ate on the west side, he must recite the blessing [a second time because when he changed his place, it is as if he began a new meal]."

[B]   Abba bar R. Huna said, "[If one drank] aged wine [and then drank] new wine, he must recite the blessing [a second time]."

[C]   If one drank another kind of wine [but both were aged, or both were new], he need not recite the blessing [a second time].

[D]   If one moved to another place [to drink or eat], he must recite the blessing [a second time].

[E]   If one diverted his attention [from drinking and then decided to continue, the rule for that case is] like [the rule for the case of] one who moved to another place. [He must recite the blessing a second time.]

[F]   Rabbi used to recite a blessing over each new barrel of wine which he opened. What did he say? R. Yitzhak the great in the name of Rabbi, "Blessed be He who is good and does good."

[G]   Once R. Aqiba made a feast for his son Simeon. He recited a blessing over each barrel of wine which he opened. And he said, "Good wine! Here's to the life of the rabbis and their students!"

[II.A]   *He who drinks water to quench his thirst says, "Blessed [art Thou, O Lord our God, King of the Universe,] for all came into being by his word"* [M. 6:8D].

[B]   Said R. Jonah, "[He recites the blessing over all water which he drinks] except for medicinal [e.g., laxative,] water."

[C]   Said R. Yose, "[He recites it] over all water that he drinks on account of thirst."

[D]   Said R. Abun, "What blessing does one who drinks medicinal [e.g., laxative,] waters recite? 'Blessed [art Thou, O Lord our God, King of the Universe,] who created healing waters.'"

[E]   [There are two versions:] One Tanna teaches, "*dkrym*-water." And the other Tanna teaches, "*dklym*-water."

[F]   According to the one who holds, "*dkrym*-water," [the term means], "They purge [*dkr*] the bitterness [as laxatives]."

[G]   According to the one who holds, "*dklym*-water," [the term refers to spring water such as that of a spring] that comes out from between two palm trees [*dklym*].

Unit **I** supplies several miscellaneous traditions generally related to the subject of M. Unit **II** takes up M.'s issue of the blessing for water, adding to it considerably.

7 Yerushalmi Berakhot
Chapter Seven

7:1

[A] *Three who ate together are obligated [to designate one person among them] to invite [the others at the meal to recite together the blessings over the meal].*

[B] *One who ate*
(1) Demai [doubtfully tithed produce], or
(2) first tithe from which heave-offering was taken, or
(3) second tithe or heqdeš, [produce given to the Temple], that has been redeemed, or
(4) the servant who ate an olive's bulk [of food], or
(5) the Samaritan [who ate together with Israelites] may be counted [for the quorum] for extending the invitation [to recite together the blessings over the meal].

[C] *But one who ate*
(1) ṭebel [untithed produce], or
(2) first tithe from which heave-offering was not taken, or
(3) second tithe or heqdeš that had not been redeemed, or
(4) the servant who ate less than an olive's bulk, or
(5) the gentile may not be counted [for the quorum] for extending the invitation [to recite together the blessings over the meal].

[I.A] [There [M. 7:4] it says: *[Three who ate together] are not permitted to separate.* [This implies that *if they finished* eating at the same time, they must recite the blessings together.] And here [M. 7:1A] it says, *[Three who ate together] are obligated to invite.* [This implies that once they start eating together, they *must* recite the blessings together, even if they do not finish together. Is this not contradictory?]

[B]   Samuel says, "One [Mishnah refers to a case of three who] started [eating together]. And one [refers to a case of three who] finished [eating together. And they are not contradictory rules.]"

[C]   What is [a case of "three who] began [eating together]"? And what is [a case of "three who] finished [eating together]"?

[D]   Two Amoraim [dispute this]. One said, "When [three persons] had decided to eat together [at the outset, this is a case of 'three who] began [eating together.' And they are obligated to recite the blessings together, as our Mishnah implies.]

[E]   "And when [one or two persons had already] eaten an olive's bulk [and then the other one or two join him, this is a case of 'three who] finished [eating together.' And, as the other Mishnah indicates, they are not permitted to split up to recite the blessings after the meal.]"

[F]   And the other [Amora] said, "When [one or two persons have already eaten] an olive's bulk [and others join, it is also a case of 'three who] began [eating together.' All present do continue eating the major portion of the meal together. Accordingly they are *obligated* to recite the blessings together.]

[G]   "And [if someone joined them] when they had finished eating together [the entire meal] but before they recited the blessings of the meal, this is a case of 'three who] finished [eating together' and in such a case we say they are *not permitted* to separate.]"

[II.A]   R. Abba in the name of R. Huna, and R. Zeira in the name of Abba bar Jeremiah, "It is compulsory for three [who ate together to designate one person from among them to invite the others to recite the blessing after eating]. It is optional for two [to do so]."

[B]   R. Zeira stated this [law] before R. Yasa. He [Yasa] said to him, "I accept only [the law of] the Mishnah: *Three who ate together are obligated to invite.* [Two may not!]"

[C]   [The rulings of] the rabbis here [in the Land of Israel] are consistent. [R. Yasa accords with the principle of R. Yohanan and R. Simeon b. Laqish below.] [And the rulings of] the rabbis there [in Babylonia] are consistent. [R. Abba and R. Zeira accord with Samuel's principle below.]

[D]   Samuel said, "If two [persons entered into a] judgment [as a court], their judgment is valid. [Three is the usual minimum number of judges in monetary cases.] But it is called 'a pre-sumptuous court.'"

[E]   R. Yohanan and R. Simeon b. Laqish both said, "Even if two [persons entered into a] judgment [as a court], their judgment is not valid."

[III.A]   R. Huna said, "Three who ate by themselves and then came together may [designate one among them] to invite [the others to recite the blessings over the meal]."

[B]   R. Hisda said, "[They may join together as a quorum of three] only if each one came from his own group [which had eaten together with a quorum of three]."

[C]   And in accord with the view of R. Zeira and his associates [i.e., R. Yasa, II.B above—in order to join for a quorum] each one [must come from a group of] three who ate the meal together.

[D]   R. Jonah observed concerning R. Huna's [rule in A, that three who ate by themselves may later constitute a quorum if each one had eaten previously with a quorum; this accords in principle with the following:]

[E]   If he [the priest] dipped three hyssop branches individually [in the water of purification mixed with the ashes of the red heifer] and then combined them, he may sprinkle with them [the water, to purify an unclean person].

[F]   R. Hisda said, "Only if each [hyssop branch] comes from its own bunch [of three that previously had been dipped together]."

[G]   And in accord with the view of R. Zeira and his associates [i.e., R. Yasa], each hyssop branch [must come from a group of three] that he dipped [previously in the water] together.

[H]   If you [object] and say, "One cannot derive [rules for sprinkling with] the hyssop branch from [rules for reciting] blessings," [because purity and liturgy are not related realms of the law,] we [may respond that they are related, because we] observed the rabbis discussing [the laws of] the sukkah and deriving [the basis for some of] them from [the laws regarding immersing in] the soft clay [in the pool of a bath]. [Cf. Miq. 7:1.]

[I]   As it was taught there: *If one sets the roofing [of a sukkah] away from the walls [more than] three handbreadths, it is invalid* [M. Sukkah 1:9]. But [if he sets it away] less than this distance, it is valid. May one sleep under it [the open space in the roofing in such a sukkah]?

[J]   R. Yitzhak b. Eliashib responded, "Behold [the rule is that] we may count soft clay as part of [the minimum of forty seahs of liquid needed to fill] a pool, but one still may not dip in [the clay]. So too here—we may count [this space of less than three handbreadths as part of the minimum size] for a sukkah, but one [still] may not sleep under [the space to fulfill his obligation of dwelling in a sukkah]." [A principle derived from one area of the law in purities, may be applied to a totally different legal issue, regarding festivals. Accordingly, principles of the laws of sprinkling of the purification water and ashes of the red heifer can be relevant to the laws of the blessings after eating.]

[IV.A]   If three ate together and one wanted to leave—the house of Rab said, "Let him recite the first blessing and leave."

[B]   What is 'the first blessing'? The house of Rab said, "It is the invitation blessing," [the formula, "Let us recite the blessing"].

[C]   R. Zeira in the name of R. Jeremiah, "It is the [first blessing of the blessings after the meal, which concludes], 'Blessed who provides for all.'"

[D]   R. Helbo bar Hanan in the name of Rab, "It is the [first blessing after the meal], 'Who provides for all.'"

[E]   R. Sheshet objected [to the ruling of the house of Rab]: "Behold a tannaitic teaching contradicts it: 'Two or three [who eat together] are obligated to recite the blessings of the meal [even if each knows and recites only one or two of the blessings—P.M.].'

[F]   "It does not say 'four.' Yet if you consider the invitation-blessing to be the first blessing [of the blessings after the meal], then why not say, 'Two or three or four are obligated'?

[G]   "But we do have a version which teaches 'four.'

[H]   "Now [according to this version] if you say [the first blessing is the paragraph that ends] 'Who provides for all,' we are faced with a question. [Which one is the fourth blessing?]

[I]   "And [to resolve this] you cannot answer that [we may count as the fourth] the blessing, 'Blessed [art thou] who is good and does good.'"

[J]   [For this is a blessing ordained on the authority of the rabbis after the Bar Kokhba revolt.] As R. Huna said, "When they [the Romans] allowed the martyrs of Betar to be buried, the blessing 'Who is good and who does good' was established. 'Who is good' [praises God] because the bodies did not decompose and 'who does good' [praises God] because they allowed them to be buried."

[K]   Said R. Huna, "You may resolve this issue [that 'four' refers to the first three blessings and to the fourth, 'Who is good and does good'] in accord with the view of R. Ishmael. For R. Ishmael said, 'The blessing "Who is good and does good" was ordained on the authority of Scripture.'"

[L]   **[This claim is further supported by the following: All the meal blessings were ordained on the authority of Scripture.] As it is written, "And you shall eat and be satisfied, and you shall bless [the Lord your God for the good land he has given you]"** [Deut. 8:10]—**this refers to the invitation-blessing.**

[M]   **'The Lord your God'—this refers to [the first blessing of the blessings of the meal], Who provides for all.**

[N]   **'For the [good] land'—this refers to [the second] blessing, [concerning] the land.**

[O]   **'For the good [land]'—this refers to [the third] blessing, [concerning] the rebuilding of Jerusalem. As it says, "That goodly hill country and Lebanon"** [Deut. 3:25].

[P]   **'He has given you'—this refers to [the fourth blessing], "Who is good and does good"** [T. 6:1].

[V.A] It is written in the Torah [i.e., one may find a basis in in Scripture concerning the obligation to recite] a blessing before it [i.e., studying Torah]. But it is not written in the Torah [i.e., one can find no basis in Scripture for the obligation to recite] a blessing after it [i.e., studying Torah].

[B]   Where do we find it written in the Torah [i.e., support in Scripture for the obligation to recite] a blessing before it [studying Torah]? "For I will proclaim the name of the Lord. [This implies that when coming to study first one must recite a blessing—] 'Ascribe greatness to our God'" [Deut. 32:3].

[C]   It is written [in the Torah, i.e., one may find a basis in Scripture for the obligation to recite] a blessing after the meal. But it is not written [in the Torah, i.e., one can find no basis in Scripture for the obligation to recite] a blessing before [the meal].

[D] Where do we find it is written [i.e., support in Scripture for the obligation to recite a blessing] after [the meal]? "And you shall eat and be satisfied, and you shall bless the Lord your God" [Deut. 8:10].

[E] And whence that we apply the rule specified for the former [that one must recite a blessing before Torah study] to the latter [to require one to recite a blessing *before* the meal], and that we apply the rule specified for the latter [that one must recite a blessing after the meal] to the former [to require one to recite a blessing *after* Torah study]?

[F] R. Samuel bar Nahmani in the name of R. Jonathan, "We derive it [by inference from a *gezerah shawah*, the presence of the identical word,] God's name [in both verses]. Just as [the word] 'Lord' [Deut. 32:3] is present [in the verse on which we base the obligation to recite a blessing] for the [study of] Torah [and it requires that one recite] a blessing before it [the study of Torah], [the word] 'Lord' [Deut. 8:10] is also present [in the verse on which we base the obligation to recite a blessing] for the meal, [and, by implication, it extends the obligation to recite] a blessing before it [the meal].

[G] "And [vice versa]: just as [the word] 'Lord' is present [in the verse on which we base the obligation to recite a blessing] for the meal [and on the basis of that verse we require that one recite] a blessing after it [the meal], [the word] 'Lord' is also present [in the verse on which we base the obligation to recite a blessing] before the [study of] Torah, [and, by implication, because of the common word we extend to that the obligation to recite] a blessing after it [the study of Torah]."

[H] This solves the problem [of the Scriptural basis of these blessings] according to R. Aqiba [who believes it to be legitimate to extend the law through implication of the presence of the identical word in two verses—*gezerah shawah*]. But according to R. Ishmael, [who does not consider it legitimate to employ this hermeneutical principle to extend the law, what is the basis for reciting these blessings before the meal and after Torah study]?

[I] R. Yohanan in the name of R. Ishmael, "A *qal wahomer* [argument serves as the logical basis to derive the obligation for reciting the blessings]: What [is the case regarding] the meal? One

need not recite a blessing before [the meal, implying that it is a
lighter, less restrictive, ritual] but one still must recite a blessing
after [the meal]. [The case regarding the study of] Torah [is
that] one must recite a blessing before [Torah study, implying
that it is a heavier, more restrictive ritual, surely] it is logical to
conclude that one must recite a blessing after [Torah study].
This solves the problem [of the logical basis for the obligation to
recite a blessing after the study of] Torah.

[J]   "What [can we say regarding the logical basis for the obligation
to recite a blessing before eating] the meal? If [it is the case
regarding] Torah [study] for which one need not recite a blessing
after [Torah study], [that nevertheless] one must recite a blessing
before [Torah study], [then for] the meal for which one must
recite a blessing even after [eating a meal], [it is logical to con-
clude] that one must also recite a blessing beforehand."

[K]   [Regarding the basis in Scripture of the obligation to recite
a blessing before eating a meal], R. Yitzhak and R. Nathan
[disputed].

[L]   R. Yitzhak said [the source is], "Since he must bless the sacrifice; afterward those eat who are invited" [1 Sam. 9:13].

[M]   R. Nathan said [the source is], "You shall serve the Lord your
God, and I will bless your bread and your water" [Exod. 23:25].

[N]   When is it called your bread and your water? Before you eat it.
[After you "serve the Lord" by reciting a blessing.]

[O]   Rabbi says [the logical argument for the obligation to recite a
blessing before eating is as follows]: "If he must recite a blessing
when he has eaten and is full, he surely must recite a blessing
when he is hungry."

[P]   This solves the problem of [the logical basis for the obligation to
recite a blessing before] the meal. What [is the logical basis for
obligation to recite a blessing after the study of Torah]?

[Q]   If you must recite blessings before and after the meal, which
provides only for [your] temporal sustenance, surely [you must
recite blessings before and after] Torah study, which provides
for [your] eternal sustenance [in the World to Come].

[VI.A] R. Zeira posed a question, "To what case shall we compare the
practice of calling three persons [to read from the Torah on Saturday afternoon and Monday and Thursday mornings]? To a

case of three who ate together? Or to a case of three who ate, each one by himself?"

[B]   If we compare it to a case of three who ate together [where one person recites the meal blessings on behalf of all those present], then we shall have to conclude that the first [to read from the Torah] recites the first blessing [before reading, on behalf of all three who read thereafter], and the last [to read] recites the last blessing [after reading, on behalf of all who read prior], and the middle person recites no blessing at all.

[C]   And if we compare it to a case of three who ate, each one by himself [where each one recites his own blessing], then even the middle person [called to the Torah] must recite the blessings before and after [reading his portion].

[D]   Said R. Samuel bar Abdimi, "[Zeira's question implies that] they derive inferences concerning the rules for reciting the blessings over the Torah [reading] from the rules for reciting the invitation-blessing [of the meal] only in the case of public practice.

[E]   "And if [they wish to derive this with regard to] public practice, will you say that an individual [who studies Torah] privately need not recite a blessing?"

[F]   Said R. Abba Mari brother of R. Yose, "They treated [an individual's obligation of reciting blessings over private Torah study] like all of the other commandments of the Torah. Just as one must recite blessings over all of the commandments of the Torah [whether in public or private], one also must recite blessings over this [private Torah study]."

[VII.A]   *One who ate* demai *[produce purchased from an 'am ha'areṣ, a person who may not have separated tithes from it] [may be counted for a quorum]* [M. 7 : 1B]. In accord with this they have said: one who ate produce [of his own] concerning which there was doubt whether or not tithes had been separated from it—they may extend the invitation [to him to join in a quorum for the recitation of the blessings after the meal. Why did the Mishnah not include this law?]

[B]   Said R. Simeon brother of R. Berekhia, "At the time they ordained [the rules of] *demai*-produce the majority of *'amme-ha'areṣ* used to bring [their produce] into their houses [and separate tithes. Hence the case of *demai* is different from the ordinary case of doubt regarding whether tithes have been separated from one's own produce and although one who ate *demai* is accepted, one who had a doubt about his own produce is not.]"

[C] Whence then do we derive [the above rule concerning doubtfully tithed produce (A)]? From the following: *They may invite [to join as a quorum for the recitation of the blessings after the meal on account of] . . . the Samaritan* [M. 7:1B].

[D] And is not the Samaritan a case of doubt [whether he is an Israelite, yet we accept him. Therefore we should also accept a person who ate doubtfully tithed food, A's case.]

[E] Said R. Abba, "We may resolve this issue [as to why Mishnah did not include this law of A] as follows: [Our Mishnah follows the opinion that a Samaritan has the status of a Jew.]

[F] "[And this is a matter of dispute between two Tannaim as follows:] 'A Samaritan has the status of a gentile,' the words of Rabbi.

[G] "R. Simeon b. Gamaliel says, 'A Samaritan has the status of a Jew in every respect.'" [The case of doubt regarding one's own produce is not included in Mishnah because it is different from the case of doubt regarding both *demai* as we saw in B, and the Samaritan, as we see here.]

Unit **I** seeks to harmonize two sentences in M. and in so doing to clarify the obligation to recite collectively the blessings after the meal. Unit **II** discusses the minimum number for the collective recitation. This unit speculates on the implications of the law of M. regarding the meal fellowship in comparison with the laws for the minimum number of judges in a court.

The Talmud's legal comparisons continue in unit **III**. The unit asks under what conditions people who did not eat together can combine together to form a collective for the purposes of reciting the blessings after the meal. In its theoretical speculation, the Talmud cites examples of law from purity rules and from festival laws.

Rab's teaching cited at unit **IV** expands upon M.'s main issue. A discussion of that lemma leads the Talmud to the subject of the authority behind the establishment of the meal blessings. The unit cites a Tosefta passage to prove its point, that the liturgy of four blessings spoken of in the sources does not include the invitation, which is a separate matter.

Unit **V** returns to the approach of the earlier sections—the

comparison between the laws of the meal blessing and another
area of the law, namely, the rules for the blessings one recites
over the study of Torah. The section uses several methods of
comparative deduction, illustrating a moderately involved Talmudic discourse, related in theme to M.

Unit **VI** carries this line of investigation one step further as it
compares the rules for blessings at the public reading of the
Torah with the rules for the recitation of blessings at the meal.

Unit **VII** returns to take up the analysis of the next line of M.
It looks at the secondary implication of M.'s law regarding one
who ate *demai* produce and introduces several additional insights
regarding cases of doubts in its amplification of M.

7:2

[A]   *Women, slaves, or minors [who ate together with adult Israelite
        males] may not be counted [in the quorum] for extending the
        invitation [to recite the blessings over the meal].*

[B]   *What is the minimum amount [that one must eat] so that he may
        be counted [in the quorum] for extending the invitation [to re-
        cite the blessings over the meal]?*

[C]   *At least an olive's bulk.*

[D]   *R. Judah says, "At least an egg's bulk."*

[I.A]   R. Simon in the name of R. Joshua b. Levi, R. Yose b. Saul in
        the name of Rabbi, "They may count in one minor to [be in-
        cluded in] the ten [that they need in order to establish a bigger
        quorum to invoke the name of God in inviting the others in the
        group to recite the blessing of the meal. However one may not
        count a child as one of the three to constitute the basic quorum
        for extending the invitation to others to join as a quorum for the
        recitation of the blessings after the meal. Cf. M. 7:3 below]."

[B]   But behold is it not taught: **One is not strict regarding a minor**
        [T. 5:18]? [This implies that one may count a minor even as one
        of the three needed for the basic quorum.]

[C]   Said R. Yose, "[The following teaching of] R. Simon [in the name
        of R. Joshua ben Levi] accords with this teaching: R. Hanina,
        R. Simon in the name of R. Joshua b. Levi, "[The minor re-
        ferred to] is a minor [in terms] of years [i.e., who is less than
        thirteen years old, but is not a minor in terms of physical signs

of maturity]. For [in most cases of the law] if he is a minor [in this respect], they treat him as a case of doubt [whether or not he is an adult.] [This rendition follows P.M. S.H. explains otherwise based on a parallel in Genesis Rabbah.]

[D]   [But with regard to our law, whether they may count him for the requisite number for extending the invitation to others to join as a quorum for the recitation of the blessings after the meal], they resolve this case of doubt [and do not treat him like a child. That is in T., **One is not strict regarding a minor**—i.e., they treat him like an adult.]"

[E]   R. Judah bar Pazzi in the name of R. Yose, "In a case where nine [persons who ate together] appear to be ten [because they were close together], may they extend the invitation [to recite the blessings over the meal on account of those nine?]

[F]   [Of course not! They must have the] exact number.

[G]   Rather [Judah must mean,] "If there was among them a minor, [they then may regard the presence of nine adults as if they were ten in accord with the rule of A]."

[H]   R. Berekhiah said R. Jacob bar Zabdi asked R. Yose, "It is logical that just as they said there that they may count one minor in the ten, they also should allow them to count one minor in the three. For there, when they count a minor [in the ten], they invoke God's name [on his account]. Here they surely [should allow a minor to be counted in the three, for in this case they] would not even invoke God's name [on his account]."

[I]   He answered him, "Your logic is not sound. [In fact, the opposite of what you argue makes sense.] There [in the case of reciting the invitation with a quorum of ten,] only in order to invoke God's name, [by constituting a quorum of ten,] may they count him!

[J]   "But here [in the case of three,] where they would not [by counting him for the minimum] invoke God's name [for extending the invitation with a quorum of three not as much is gained by counting the child, hence,] they may not count him in."

[K]   It was taught: They may count in a minor or a Torah scroll [with nine adults to reach the quorum of ten].

[L]   Said R. Yudan, "The correct version of the teaching is: They may count in a minor [with six adults to count as one of the seven who read from] the Torah-scroll."

[M]   At what stage may a minor be counted in with adults? R. Abina said, "R. Huna and R. Judah disputed this matter. Both [cited traditions] in the name of Samuel.

[N]   "One said, 'As soon as he knows [how to recite] the form of the blessings.'

[O]   "The other said, 'As soon as he understands to whom he directs his blessings.'"

[P]   Said R. Nasa, "I ate many times with my father R. Tahlifa and with my uncle Hanania bar Sisi, and they did not invite [others to recite the blessing] on my account until I showed signs of puberty." [They did not accept T.'s rule (B).]

[II.A]   Samuel bar Shilat posed this question to Rab, and some say they posed this question to Samuel bar Shilat, "[What is the practice] if nine [people are eating] bread, and one [is eating] vegetables? [Do they designate one of them to invite the others in the group to recite the blessings over the meal with the invocation of God's name, as is the practice with a group of ten who eat bread together?]"

[B]   He said to them, "They invite."

[C]   "[If there were] eight [eating] bread, and two [eating] vegetables?"

[D]   He said to them, "They invite."

[E]   "[If there were] seven [eating] bread, and three [eating] vegetables?"

[F]   He said to them, "They invite."

[G]   R. Abina posed the question. "What about [a case of] half [of those present at the meal who were eating bread] and half [eating vegetables]?"

[H]   Said R. Zeira, "While I was there [in Babylonia], I did not clarify that question. Now I am sorry I did not ask [Rab or Samuel bar Shilat] about it."

[III.A]   R. Jeremiah posed the question: "May one who ate vegetables recite the [invitation and] blessings [for the meal on behalf of those who ate bread]?" [Here Jeremiah raises this question. Elsewhere he treats it as a closed issue.] Jeremiah contradicts himself [as is evident from the end of the lengthy story that follows:]

[B]   It was taught: Three hundred Nazarites went up [to Jerusalem to have their vows annulled] in the time of R. Simeon b. Shetah.

[C]   He [Simeon] found a way out of the vows for one hundred and fifty of them. But he could not find a way out of the vows for [the remaining] one hundred and fifty.

[D]   He went to Yannai the king and said to him, "We have here three hundred Nazarites who must offer nine hundred sacrifices [to fulfill their vows]. If you donate half, I will donate half."

[E]   He [Yannai] sent him four hundred and fifty [animals]. One tale-bearer then went and told Yannai that [Simeon] did not contribute any [animals] of his own. Yannai, the king, heard this and became angry. Simeon ben Shetah feared the consequences and fled.

[F]   After some time, several esteemed individuals from the kingdom of Persia came to visit Yannai, the king.

[G]   When they were sitting and eating, they said to him, "We recall that a certain elder used to be here, and used to speak words of wisdom to us."

[H]   Yannai told them what had happened [to Simeon]. They said to him, "Send for him, and bring him back." He sent for him with assurance [that no harm would befall him].

[I]   And Simeon came back and took his place of honor between the king and the queen.

[J]   Yannai said to him, "Why did you deceive me?"

[K]   Simeon said to him, "I did not deceive you. You gave your part out of your wealth. And I gave my part out of my knowledge of the Torah [by finding a way out of their vows for half the Nazarites,] as it is written, 'For the protection of wisdom is like the protection of money'"[Qoh. 7:12].

[L]   Yannai said to him, "Why then did you flee?"

[M]   He said to him, "I heard that my master was angry at me and I wanted to fulfill this verse: 'Hide yourselves for a little while until the wrath is past' [Isa. 26:20]. And it was said concerning me, 'And the advantage of knowledge is that wisdom preserves the life of him who has it'" [Qoh. 7:12].

[N]   And Yannai said to him, "Why did you take a seat between the king and queen?"

[O]   He said to him, "In the book of Ben Sira it is written, 'The wisdom of a humble man will lift up his head, and will seat him among the great'" [Ben Sira 11:1].

[P]   He [Yannai] said, "Bring him the cup so that he may recite the blessing [after the meal over it]."

[Q]   They brought Simeon the cup and he said, "Let us recite a blessing for the food that Yannai and his associates have eaten."

[R]   Yannai said to him, "Must you persist in your stubbornness? [Are you making fun of us because we did not serve you any food?]"

[S]   Simeon said to him, "What then should I say, 'Let us recite the blessing for the food that we have not eaten'?"

[T]   Yannai said, "Bring him food so that he may eat."

[U]   And so they brought out the food [vegetable—P.M.]. And he ate, and then he said, "Let us recite the blessing for the food that we have eaten."

[V]   Said R. Yohanan, "There are those who dispute Simeon b. Shetah."

[W]   R. Jeremiah said he [Yohanan] refers to the first [account of Simeon's actions in reciting the invitation even though he had not eaten with them].

[X]   And R. Abba said [Yohanan refers to] the second [account of Simeon's action of reciting the invitation at the meal even though he did not eat bread with them. Simeon did not eat the meal with them. How then could he recite the invitation on their behalf?]

[Y]   R. Jeremiah's view here contradicts his view above [at A]. Above he questioned [whether one who ate only vegetables could recite the invitation and blessings for others who had eaten bread]. Here he takes for granted [that Simeon could recite the invitation for Yannai even though he had only eaten vegetables with him—P.M.].

[Z]   [We may explain this contradiction as follows:] Where [Jeremiah] had a question, it was in accord with the ruling of sages. And where [Jeremiah] took the law for granted, it was in accord with the ruling of R. Simeon b. Gamaliel. [The Talmud now spells this out.]

[AA]   As it was taught: **R. Simeon b. Gamaliel says, "When they** arose [from their chairs] and reclined [on their couches] and [one who dips his food] joined them, even though he did not eat an olive's bulk of breadstuff [with them], they may count him [in the quorum] for extending the invitation" [T. 5:20]. [According to this rule, Jeremiah approved of Simeon b. Shetah's action.]

[BB]   And the words of the sages [were as follows]: R. Jacob bar Aha in the name of R. Yohanan, "They may never count him [in the quorum] for extending the invitation unless he has eaten an olive's bulk of breadstuff." [According to this rule, Jeremiah was unclear in A whether one could join with a group if he had eaten only vegetables.]

[CC]   But was it not taught: If two [ate] bread and one [ate] vegetables, they could [constitute a quorum on account of the third to] invite [others in the recitation of the blessings after the meal]?

[DD]   [We must conclude that] this teaching accords with R. Simeon b. Gamaliel. [But sages dispute it.]

The Talmud begins with speculation about one of M.'s main points, the status of the minor, citing first an Amoraic law on the subject, then the relevant Tosefta passage, followed by a discussion of the subject of the minor of moderate length. Unit **II** goes on to examine the implications of B in M., the minimum one must eat to be included in the meal collective. Does one who eats only vegetables count in the reckoning? The lengthy story in unit **III** relates to our context only because of one detail it relates concerning Simeon who ate vegetables and on account of that combined with Yannai and the others who had eaten a full meal. That section concludes with a citation of T. on the subject and an examination of its implications.

7:3

[A]   *How do they invite [the others eating with them to join together to recite the blessings after the meal]?*

[B]   *(1) For three [who ate together the leader] says, "Let us recite the blessings." For three [others] and himself he says, "Recite the blessings."*

[C]   *(2) For ten he says, "Let us recite the blessings to our God."*
For ten and himself he says, "Recite the blessings [to our God]."

[D]   *The same [rule applies] for ten or for ten thousand.*

[E]   *(3) For one hundred he says, "Let us recite the blessings to the*
Lord our God." For one hundred and himself he says, "Recite
the blessings."

[F]   *(4) For one thousand he says, "Let us recite the blessings to the*
Lord our God, God of Israel." For one thousand and himself he
says, "Recite the blessings."

[G]   *(5) For ten thousand he says, "Let us recite the blessings to the*
Lord our God, God of Israel, God of Hosts, who is enthroned on
the cherubim, for the food we have eaten." For ten thousand
and himself he says, "Recite the blessings."

[H]   *And as he recites the blessings, so do they answer after him,*
"Blessed be the Lord our God, God of Israel, God of hosts, who
is enthroned on the cherubim, for the food we have eaten."

[I]   *R. Yose the Galilean says, "The [form of the] blessing they*
recite depends on the size of the congregation, as it says, 'Bless
God in the great congregations, the Lord, O you who are of
Israel's fountain'" [Ps. 68:27].

[J]   *Said R. Aqiba, "What do we find [concerning the form of the*
call to recite the Prayer] in the synagogue? Whether there are
many or few they say, 'Recite the blessings to the Lord.'" [The
same rule should apply for the collective recitation of the bless-
ings after the meal.]

[K]   *R. Ishmael says, "[The form of the call to Prayer is:] 'Recite the*
blessings to the Lord who is blessed.'"

[I.A]   Once [four rabbis] R. Zeira, and R. Jacob bar Aha, and R. Hiyya
bar Abba, and R. Hanina, the associates of the sages, were sitting and eating. R. Jacob bar Aha took the cup and recited [the
invitation to recite the blessings of the meal]. And he said, "Let
us recite the blessings." He did not say, "Recite the blessings,"
[as M. 7:3B says one should say with four persons present].

[B]   R. Hiyya bar Abba said to him, "Why did you not say, 'Recite
the blessings'?"

[C]   He said to him, "Was it not taught: **One is not strict regarding**

the matter [T. reads: a minor]. **Whether one said, 'Let us recite the blessings,' or 'Recite the blessings,' they do not take
him to task for it. But the overscrupulous take him to task for
it"** [T. 5 : 18].

[D]   And R. Zeira was angry because R. Jacob bar Aha had declared [by citing this passage] that R. Hiyya bar Abba was overscrupulous.

[**II.A**]   Samuel said, "I will not exclude myself from the rest [by saying
'recite' instead of 'let us recite']."

[B]   They posed this question: What about the blessing we recite
over the reading of the Torah? [The one who recites] says, "Recite the blessings to the Lord." [He does thereby remove himself
from the rest.]

[C]   Said R. Abin, "Because he continues 'Who is blessed' he does
not remove himself from the rest." [The implication is that, 'He
is blessed by us all.']

III.A]   R. Abba bar Zimna used to serve Zeira. He [once] mixed a cup
of wine for him.

[B]   He [Zeira] said to him, "Take it and recite the blessing [and by
so doing, exempt me from my obligation]. [Crossed out in L: He
said to him.] Have in mind that you will drink another cup."

[C]   For it was taught: The servant recites a blessing over each cup.
But he does not recite a blessing over each piece of bread.

[D]   He [Abba] said to him, "Just as I may have in mind to exempt
you from your obligation with my blessing [over the wine now],
so you should have in mind to exempt me from my obligation
[when you respond] 'Amen' [to my blessing]." [We have a principle: the one who answers "Amen" fulfills the obligation better
than the one who recites the blessing—P.M.]

[E]   Said R. Tanhum bar Jeremiah, "In this regard the Mishnah
teaches: *One who [sounds the shofar while he] is practicing does
not fulfill his obligation [to hear the shofar on the New Year's
day]. And one who hears [the sound of the shofar] from one who
is practicing does not fulfill his obligation* [M. R.H. 4 : 8]." [The
principle operative here is—one who practices does not have in
mind that a person who hears the sounds will fulfill his obligation through these sounds. Accordingly, the servant should have

in mind that the master may fulfill his obligation when respond-
ing "Amen" to the servant's blessing.]

[IV.A]   *For one hundred he says, ["Let us recite the blessings to our
God."]* [M. 7:3E]. Said R. Yohanan, "This is [in accord with]
the words of R. Yose the Galilean. But according to sages, *The
same [rule applies] for ten or for ten thousand"* [M. 7:3D].

[B]   Raba said, "The law follows the [sages'] view which says, *The
same [rule applies] for ten or for ten thousand.*"

[V.A]   Whence [is the Scriptural basis] that ten constitute a congregation? R. Abba and R. Yasa in the name of R. Yohanan, "[Scrip-
ture] uses [the word] 'congregation' in one instance ['The
congregation shall judge . . . and the congregation shall rescue'
[Num. 35:24, 25], and uses [the word] 'congregation' in another
instance ['How long shall this wicked congregation murmur
against me?' (Num. 14:27)].

[B]   "Just as [the word] 'congregation' in the latter instance refers to
ten persons [the twelve spies, excluding Joshua and Caleb], [the
word] 'Congregation' in the former instance refers to ten persons. [And, accordingly, all judgments should take place in the
presence of ten]."

[C]   Said R. Simon, "[Scripture] uses [the word] 'among' in one instance. ['I will be hallowed among the children of Israel' (Lev.
24:32), and] uses [the word] 'among' in another instance, 'Thus
the children of Israel came to buy among the others who came'
[Gen. 42:5].

[D]   "Just as [the word] 'among' in the latter case is a reference to
ten [persons, i.e., the twelve brothers, excluding Joseph and
Benjamin], it also implies ten [are needed in other instances to
make up a congregation for sanctification of God's name]."

[E]   Said to him R. Yose b. R. Bun, "If you base your teaching on
the word 'among,' why, it appears many more times [in Scrip-
ture]! [Rather base your teaching on the words 'The children of
Israel,' which Scripture uses in both the preceding verses.

[F]   "It says here 'Children of Israel' and it says there 'Children of
Israel.' Just as [the words] 'Children of Israel' there refer to ten
[in Gen. 42:5], they also imply ten [persons are needed to make
up a congregation in other instances]."

[VI.A]   How do sages deal with the Scriptural proof of R. Yose the Gali-
         lean [in M. 7:3I]? [They say,] "In the congregation" [Ps. 68:27]
         means in each congregation [shall you bless the same way. It
         does not mean according to the size of the congregation shall you
         bless.]

[B]   Said R. Haninah son of R. Abahu, " 'Congregation,' is written
         mqhlt [instead of *mqhlwt*] in the defective form, [which implies
         the singular, not the plural, to teach that there is one correct way
         to recite the blessing in all instances]." [N.B.: Standard texts of
         Psalms have *mqhlwt*.]

[VII.A] Piska: *Said R. Aqiba, "What do we find [concerning the form of
         the call to recite the Prayer] in the synagogue? Whether there
         are many or few they say, 'Recite the blessings to the Lord.' "
         [The same rule should apply for the collective recitation of the
         blessings after the meal]* [M. 7:3J].

[B]   R. Hiyya bar Ashi came up to read from the Torah. He said,
         "Recite the blessings to the Lord," but he did not say, "who is
         blessed." They tried to silence him.

[C]   Rab said to them, "Let him be. For he is following R. Aqiba's
         practice."

[D]   R. Zeira came up to read from the Torah as a priest in place of a
         Levite. He recited the blessings both before and after reading.
         And they tried to silence him.

[E]   R. Hiyya bar Abba said to them, "Let him be. For that is their
         practice in his place [Babylonia]."

[VIII.A] It is written, 'And Ezra blessed the Lord, the great God [*hgdwl*]'
         [Neh. 8:6]. And how did he magnify [*hgdyl*] Him? He magni-
         fied Him by invoking the divine name.

[B]   R. Matna said, "He magnified Him with a blessing."

[C]   R. Simon in the name of R. Joshua b. Levi, "Why were they
         called the Men of the Great Assembly? Because they restored
         [God's] greatness to its former stature."

[D]   Said R. Pinhas, "Moses ordained the form of the prayer: Great
         and mighty and awesome God. Jeremiah said, 'Great and mighty
         God' [Jer. 32:18] but he did not say 'awesome.' Why did he call
         Him 'mighty?' Because it is fitting to call 'mighty' one who is
         able to witness the destruction of his Temple and keep silent.

[E]   "And why did he not call him 'awesome?' Because 'awesome'
       refers only to the Temple, as it says 'awesome is God in his sanc-
       tuary' [Ps. 68 : 35].

[F]   "Daniel said, 'O Lord, the great and awesome' [Dan. 9 : 4]. And
       why did he not call Him 'mighty?' Because when we, His chil-
       dren, are [in captivity] in chains, how can we call Him 'mighty?'

[G]   "And why did he call Him 'awesome?' It is fitting to call Him
       'awesome' because of the awesome deeds He did [to save] us in
       the fiery furnace.

[H]   "And when the Men of the Great Assembly arose, they returned
       the greatness to its former stature [and ordained that they should
       say,] 'The great and mighty and awesome God'" [Neh. 9 : 32].

[I]   But do men of flesh and blood [i.e., Jeremiah, Daniel] have the
       authority to place a limit on such things [as the praise of God]?

[J]   Said R. Yitzhak b. Eleazar, "The prophets know that God is
       always true and they do not try to flatter [Him]. [They are justi-
       fied when they limit Prayer.]"

Unit **I** begins with a story that directly probes the meaning of
the laws of M., and cites T. as well. Unit **II** continues examining
M.'s main point about the formula for the call to recite the blessings, through a comparison with laws for the blessings over the
recitation in public of the Torah, a comparison familiar to us
from earlier units (e.g., 7 : 1**V–VI**, 7 : 2**I**).

Unit **III** concerning the recitation of a blessing over wine by
a servant is related only distantly to the immediate concerns
of M. and may appear here because it relates to Zeira, who is
mentioned at the end of **I**. Unit **IV** takes up the exegesis of the
meaning in M. D, a line that appears to be a bit out of context.

Unit **V** provides three alternative modes of deriving the Scriptural basis that ten persons comprise a substantial quorum for
matters involving sacred acts. Unit **VI** deals directly with the
meaning of the lemma of Yose the Galilean, and unit **VII** deals
with Aqiba's law as it adds stories in its direct expansion of M.
The last unit, **VIII**, is independent of M. combining exegesis
with history regarding the development of the formula at the
beginning of the Prayer of Eighteen. Aside from the general
relevance of the content to the present tractate, the connection

of this unit to the present context may be the attribution to
Simon, who also appears above in unit **V.**

7:4

[A]   *Three who ate together are not permitted to separate [to recite
the meal blessings, because if they do, they will not have the
minimum quorum of three needed to be able to extend to others
the invitation to recite together the blessings after the meal.]*

[B]   *And so too four, and so too five [who are eating together may
not separate, because if they do, some of them will not be able to
recite the blessings after the meal with a quorum.]*

[C]   *Six [or more] may separate [into two groups of at least three
each] until [they reach] ten.*

[D]   *Ten [or more] may not separate [because they invoke the name
of God in the invitation that they recite with the more substantial quorum of ten, and if they separate, some will not be able to
recite the meal blessings with the fuller invitation formula] until
[they reach] twenty, [then they may separate into two groups
of ten].*

[I.A]   It was taught: One who was sitting and eating on the Sabbath
and forgot and did not mention the Sabbath [in the blessings
after the meal]—Rab says, "He must repeat [his recitation of the
blessings after the meal]." And Samuel says, "He need not
repeat."

[B]   Simeon bar Ba in the name of R. Yohanan, "If one had a doubt
whether he mentioned the new moon, they do not make him
repeat [his recitation of the blessings after the meal]."

[C]   We find a teaching which contradicts this: **Any day on which
there is an Additional Sacrifice [and, accordingly, they recite
the Additional Service], such as the new moon or an intermediate day of the festival, [in the Morning and Afternoon
Services one recites the Prayer of Eighteen] and one says a
prayer corresponding to the occasion [and in the Additional
Prayer one says a prayer concerning the sanctity of the day in
the seventeenth blessing,] the Temple service . . . If one did
not say it, they make him repeat [his recitation of the Prayer]
[T. 3:10].** [This implies that if he forgot to say the appropriate

prayers in the meal blessings, they should make him repeat his recitation of the blessings after the meal.]

[D] **And any day on which there is no Additional Sacrifice [and, accordingly, they do not recite the Additional Service], such as Hanukkah or Purim, [in the Morning and Afternoon Services one recites the Prayer of Eighteen and] says [a prayer] corresponding to the occasion. If he did not say it, they do not make him repeat** [T. 3:10].

[E] Hanan bar Abba and the associates were sitting and eating on the Sabbath. When they finished eating and reciting the blessings, [Hanan] got up and left. When he later returned, he found them reciting the blessings [again]. He said, "Have we not already recited the blessings?"

[F] They said to him, "We recited the blessings. But now we are repeating the blessings because [the first time] we forgot to make mention of the Sabbath."

[G] [Hanan replied,] "But did not R. Ba say in the name of R. Huna, R. Jeremiah of Tobah in the name of Rab: If one forgot and did not mention the Sabbath [in the blessings after the meal], he should say [at the end of the blessings], 'Blessed be he who gave a time for rest to his people Israel'?"

[H] [You may resolve this question as follows:] Here [the associates repeated because in that case they already] turned their attention away [from the blessings]. There [Rab rules they may add a sentence at the end of the liturgy because in that case] they had not yet turned their attention away [from the blessings].

[II.A] It was taught: **Ten people who were travelling on the road [and eating], even if they all eat from the same loaf, each recites the blessings [after the meal] for himself.**

[B] **If they [stopped travelling and] sat down and ate [together], even if each eats from his own loaf, one person recites the blessings for the meal on behalf of all of them** [T. 5:23].

[C] R. Jeremiah invited his associates to recite [the blessings for the meal] when [they were travelling only in a case where] they had stopped [to eat] in an inn [but not by the roadside].

The Talmud ignores M. in favor of T., which it cites and discusses in both units I and II.

7:5

[A]   *Two groups [of people] eating in the same house may combine together for the invitation [i.e., Zimmun, to designate one representative to invite members of both groups to recite the meal blessings only] if some members of each group can see one another.*

[B]   *But, if not, each group by itself [designates its own representative who] invites [the others in the group to recite together the blessings].*

[C]   *"And they may not recite the blessing over the wine [that they drink] unless they dilute it with water," the words of R. Eliezer.*

[D]   *And sages say, "They may recite [the blessing even over undiluted wine that they drink]."*

[**I.A**]   [The ruling at M. 7:5A is obvious. Why does M. teach it?] R. Jonah and R. Abba bar Zimna in the name of R. Zeira, "[We need the ruling in M. 7:5A to teach us the law that two groups may combine together if they can see one another even if they are eating] in two separate houses." [And the phrase in M. 7:5A, "in the same house," applies only to the case of M. 7:5B—P.M.]

[B]   Said R. Yohanan, "[Two groups may combine] only if they had entered [to eat] from the outset with this intention."

[C]   Do we consider the Patriarch's house [where the doors between the rooms may be opened or closed] like one house or like two [with regard to the present law]? We may say [it depends] if it is customary [for people] to pass from one room to the other [during the meal, then the two groups in both rooms] may combine to [constitute a quorum to] extend the invitation [to recite the blessings after the meal.] But if not, they may not combine to extend the invitation.

[D]   R. Berekhiah set up his expounder [interpreter] in the middle hall of the house of study [between the rooms] and he [the expounder] invited [those assembled to recite] on behalf of both groups.

[**II.A**]   *"They do not recite the blessing over the wine unless they dilute it with water," the words of R. Eliezer.*

[B]   *And sages say, "They may recite [the blessing]"* [M. 7:5C–D].

[C]   R. Zeriqa in the name of R. Yose b. Hanina, "The sages will agree with R. Eliezer that one should put [at least] a bit of water into the cup of wine over which one recites the blessing [of the meal]."

[D]   The rabbis customarily [diluted with a bit of water] the cup of wine over which they recited the Prayer of Sanctification.

[E]   R. Yose [b. Haninah's] tradition contradicts [a ruling of] R. Jonah. For R. Jonah used to first take a sip from the cup [after reciting the blessing over it] and then he would prepare it [by diluting it properly for drinking].

[F]   [Now] if you say that [Jonah's wine] was already mixed [when he recited the blessing and after tasting it he diluted it more to suit his taste], lo, it was taught: One who drinks liquids that had been mixed for drinking and left to stand overnight—may his blood be upon his own head [because he puts himself in danger].

[G]   Said R. Yohanan, "This applies [only to liquid] that was left overnight in a metal container."

[III.A]   R. Jeremiah in the name of R. Yohanan, "The ancient [sages] used to ask, 'Can the left hand help the right hand out [to hold the cup] when one is reciting the blessing [after the meal] over a cup of wine?'

[B]   "You learn three things from this question.

[C]   "You learn that one must hold the cup in his right hand.

[D]   "And you learn that one must hold his hand up at least a hand-breadth above the table [and not rest it on the table].

[E]   "And you learn that one must pay attention to the cup [and not put it down and take his mind off it]."

[F]   Said R. Aha, "Three things were said concerning the cup over which one recites the blessing.

[G]   "It must be full.

[H]   "It must be decorated.

[I]   "It must be clean.

[J]   "And all three [are suggested] in one verse, 'O Naphtali, sat-isfied with favor, and full of the blessing of the Lord' [Deut. 33 : 23]. [This implies that for the cup over which one recites 'the blessing of the Lord' one must be] 'satisfied' with decorations.

[K] "'Favor' [implies the cup must be] clean.

[L] "And [when one recites the blessings over the cup it must be] as it implies, 'full.'"

[M] Said R. Haninah, "Since you have gone [and interpreted part of the verse,] what does [the remainder] of the verse mean, 'Possess the lake and the south'?" [It implies that when you follow the advice of the verse], you will be worthy to inherit [a share in] both in this world and in the world to come.

[N] Said R. Eleazar, "One does not recite a blessing over a defective cup. Once he sips it [i.e., a cup which has exactly the minimum], he renders it defective."

[O] You learn from this three things.

[P] You learn that one does not recite a blessing [after the meal] over a defective cup.

[Q] You learn that a cup must contain a minimum quantity.

[R] And you learn that when one sips [a cup which has exactly the minimum], he renders it defective.

[IV.A] Said R. Tanhum bar Yudan, "[If on the Sabbath or festival one had just a single cup of wine] the honor of the day takes precedence over the honor of the night. [He should drink it in the meal he eats during the day.]

[B] "[If one had enough for just a single cup of wine,] [Y. has:] the Prayer of Sanctification of the [Sabbath] night takes precedence over the Prayer of Sanctification of the [Sabbath] day. [T. adds: And the [Prayer of] Sanctification of the [Sabbath] day takes precedence over the honor of the day and the honor of the night]" [T. 3:8].

[C] And what is the honor of the day? R. Yose in the name of R. Jacob bar Aha and R. Eleazar bar Joseph in the name of Rab, "[Reciting the blessing,] 'Creator of the fruit of the vine.'"

[V.A] R. Zeriqan, the brother-in-law of R. Zeriqan, mentioned Hanukkah in the [second blessing of the meal], "For the land," and they praised him.

[B] R. Ba, son of R. Hiyya bar Ba, mentioned "the true judge" [the mourner's blessing] in the [fourth blessing of the meal], "Who is good and does good," and they praised him.

[**VI.A**]   R. Ba, son of R. Hiyya bar Abba, "One who eats while walking should stand still to recite the blessings. One who eats while standing should sit to recite the blessings. One who eats while sitting should recline to recite the blessings. One who eats while reclining should wrap himself in his cloak to recite the blessings.

[B]   "And if he does [wrap himself around], lo, he is like the ministering angels. What is the basis in Scripture for this? 'Above him stood the seraphim; each had six wings: . . . with two he covered his face, and with two he covered his feet.'" [Isa. 6 : 2].

Unit **I** relates directly to M.'s first issue, combining groups together to form the quorum. Unit **II** continues the direct expansion of M., adding several rules concerning mixed wine. Other rules follow in unit **III** regarding the preparation and use of a cup of wine at the occasion of the recitation of the meal blessings. Unit **IV** discusses what to do if one had only a single cup of wine to use for several purposes.

Unit **V** cites T. and works on its implications. Units **V** and **VI** add two independent units with attributions to Ba, the son of R. Hiyya Bar Abba.

8 Yerushalmi Berakhot
Chapter Eight

8:1

[A] *These are the matters disputed by the House of Shammai and the House of Hillel concerning the dinner:*

[B] *The House of Shammai say, "[In the Prayer of Sanctification at the dinner on the eve of the Sabbath or festival] they recite the blessing over [the Sabbath or festival] day, and then they recite the blessing over the wine."*

[C] *And the House of Hillel say, "They recite the blessing over the wine, and then they recite the blessing over the day."*

[I.A] What is the basis of the House of Shammai's view? [They reason that] one uses wine on account of the sanctity of the [Sabbath] day. And one is obligated to recognize the sanctity of the day [through recitation of the Prayer of Sanctification of the Sabbath or festival] before he uses the wine.

[B] And what is the basis of the House of Hillel's view? [They reason that] the presence of wine [at the meal] allows a person to say the [blessing for the] sanctification of the day. [That is, without the wine there is no opportunity to recite the blessing for the day. Therefore one first recites the blessing over the wine.]

[C] Another explanation [to support the view of the House of Hillel]: The [blessing over the] wine is a frequent action. The [sanctification blessing over the day] is not a frequent action. [And the principle is—that which is more frequent takes precedence in the order of performance] [T. 5:25].

[II.A]   Said R. Yose, "[We may deduce that] both [Houses] agree [with regard to the order of the blessing over] the wine and the Prayer of Division [at the conclusion of the Sabbath], the blessing over the wine comes first.

[B]   "[The House of Shammai's above argument does not apply in this case.] The House of Shammai's reason [in the case of reciting the blessings on Friday eve at the meal at the beginning of the Sabbath] was that they use the wine on account of the sanctity of the [Sabbath] day. And here [in the case of the recitation of the Prayer of Division at the conclusion of the Sabbath] they do not use the wine on account of the Prayer of Division, [which marks the end of the Sabbath day. One fulfills his obligation to recite a Prayer of Division when he recites the appropriate words in the Prayer of Eighteen in the Evening Service at the conclusion of the Sabbath. The recitation of another Prayer of Division at home is a secondary requirement.] So the blessing over the wine comes first.

[C]   "The House of Hillel's reason [in the case of reciting the blessings on Friday eve at the meal at the beginning of the Sabbath] was that they first [recite the blessing over] the wine because [reciting it] is a frequent action, and [reciting the blessing for] the sanctification of the day is infrequent. Likewise here [in the case of the recitation of the Prayer of Division at the conclusion of the Sabbath], since [reciting the blessing over] the wine is frequent and [reciting] the Prayer of Division is infrequent, they first [recite the blessing over] the wine."

[D]   Said R. Mana, "[We may deduce the opposite, i.e., that] both Houses agree that with regard to [the blessing over] the wine and Prayer of Division, the Prayer of Division comes first.

[E]   "The House of Shammai's reason [in the case of reciting the blessings on Friday eve at the meal at the beginning of the Sabbath] was that one is already obligated to recite the blessing for the day [when it gets dark on Friday night] before he uses the wine. And likewise here [in the case of the recitation of the Prayer of Division at the conclusion of the Sabbath], since one is obligated to recite the Prayer of Division [when it gets dark on Saturday night] before he obtains the wine, the recitation of the Prayer of Division comes first.

[F]   "And the House of Hillel's reason [in the case of reciting the blessings on Friday eve at the meal at the beginning of the Sabbath] was that the [presence of wine] allows one to recite the blessing for the [sanctification of the] day. But here [in the case of the recitation of the Prayer of Division at the conclusion of the Sabbath], since one does not need wine to enable him to recite the Prayer of Division [because he may fulfill his obligation by reciting a Prayer of Division in the Prayer of Eighteen on Saturday night], the Prayer of Division comes first."

[III.A]   Said R. Zeira, "[We may deduce that] both [R. Yose and R. Mana (P.M.)] agree that one is permitted to recite the Prayer of Division without wine, but one may recite the Prayer of Sanctification of the Sabbath only with wine."

[B]   This is [indeed also] R. Zeira's own view.

[C]   For R. Zeira said, "One may recite the Prayer of Division over beer [if they have no wine]. But one must go searching from place to place [to find wine] in order to recite [the Prayer of] the Sanctification [of the Sabbath day]."

[D]   Said R. Yose b. Rabbi, "This is the custom [in Babylonia] in a place where they have no wine [available for the recitation of the Prayer of Sanctification]: The leader goes before the ark [to recite the Prayer on Friday eve] and he recites the [special Sabbath] blessing, which embodies an abstract of the seven [intermediate blessings of the daily Prayer of Eighteen], and he concludes it by saying, 'Blessed art thou O Lord, who sanctifies Israel and the Sabbath Day.'" [Through this recitation, they fulfill their obligation to recite the Prayer of Sanctification.]

[IV.A]   And a question was raised regarding the view of the House of Shammai: On the Sabbath eve, how should one act? If one was sitting and eating on the eve of the Sabbath, and night fell and the Sabbath commenced, and he had only one cup of wine, you say that he should set it aside until he finishes the meal, and then recite all [the blessings] together over it [i.e., the blessings over the meal, the day, and the wine].

[B]   What do you prefer [that one do, according to the view of the House of Shammai]?

[C]   Should he first recite the blessing over the [Sabbath] day [as they say in Mishnah]? [This makes no sense because] the meal came before it!

[D]   Should he first recite the blessing over the meal? [This makes no sense because] the wine came before it! Should he first recite the blessing over the wine? [This makes no sense because] the [sanctity of the] day came before it!

[E]   Let us deduce [the proper order] from the following: *If they obtained wine after finishing the meal, and they had only one cup: [The House of Shammai say, "They recite the blessing over the wine, and then they recite the blessing over the meal]"* [M. 8:8].

[F]   Said R. Ba, "[That citation from M. 8:8 is no proof] because the blessing over the wine is a short blessing. [In that case we may say that he must recite it first] lest he forget [to recite it after saying the blessing over the meal] and then drink the wine [without a blessing]. But here [in our present case], since he recites the blessings together and recites them over the cup, he will not forget [to recite the blessing for the wine].

[G]   "What should he do to act in accord with the opinion of the House of Shammai? He should first recite the blessing over the meal, and afterward over the day, and afterward over the wine."

[H]   And a question was raised regarding the view of the House of Hillel: At the conclusion of the Sabbath, how should one act?

[I]   If one was sitting and eating on the Sabbath, and night fell and the Sabbath ended, and he had only one cup of wine, you say that he should set it aside until he finishes the meal, and then recite all [the blessings] together over it [i.e., the blessings over the wine, the light, the spices, the Prayer of Division, and the blessings after the meal].

[J]   What do you prefer [that one do, according to the House of Hillel]? Should he first recite the blessing over the wine? [This makes no sense because] the meal came before it!

[K]   Should he first recite the blessing over the meal? [This makes no sense because] the light came before it!

[L]   Should he first recite the blessing over the light? [This makes no sense because] the Prayer of Division came before it!

[M]   Let us deduce [the proper order] from the following: **Said R. Judah, "The House of Shammai and the House of Hillel did not dispute that the blessing over the meal comes first, and the Prayer of Division comes last.**

[N]   **"What did they dispute? [The order of the blessings] over the light and over the spices.**

[O]   **"For the House of Shammai say, 'Spices and then light.'**

[P]   **"And the House of Hillel say, 'Light and then spices'"** [T. 5:30]. [The order is first the meal blessing, then the Prayer of Division.]

[Q]   Raba and R. Judah, "The law accords with the one who says, 'Spices and then light.'" [The House of Shammai.]

[R]   How does one proceed in accord with the opinion of the House of Hillel?

[S]   He first recites the blessing over the meal, and afterward recites the blessing over the wine, and after that recites the blessing over the light.

[V.A]   A festival day that fell on the day after the Sabbath [i.e., on Sunday]: R. Yohanan said, "[The order of the blessings at the meal at the conclusion of the Sabbath is] wine, Sanctification [for the festival], light, Prayer of Division."

[B]   Hanin bar Ba said in the name of Rab, "[The order of the blessings at the meal at the conclusion of the Sabbath is] wine, Sanctification [for the festival], light, Prayer of Division, ['Who sanctified us with his commandments and commanded us to dwell in a] sukkah,' [said on Sukkot,] and ['Who gave us life and kept us alive and brought us to this] season,' [said on the festivals.]"

[C]   R. Hanina said, "[The order of the blessings at the meal at the conclusion of the Sabbath is] wine, light, Prayer of Division, and Sanctification [for the festival]."

[D]   And did not Samuel rule in accord with this opinion of R. Hanina?

[E]   For said R. Aha in the name of R. Joshua b. Levi, "When a king [i.e., the Sabbath] departs and a governor [i.e., the festival] enters, they first accompany the king out—[they recite the Prayer of Division to mark the end of the Sabbath]—and then bring in the governor—[they recite the Prayer of Sanctification for the festival]."

[F]   Levi says, "Wine, Prayer of Division, light, Sanctification."

[G]   It stands to reason that Levi ruled by combining both [the views

of Hanina, because he puts the Prayer of Division before the
Sanctification, and Yohanan, because he juxtaposes the blessing
for the light and the Prayer of Division]." [GRA and Leiden
give an alt. reading; see also Luncz.]

[H]   Said R. Zeira, "R. Yose posed this question before me: 'What is
our practice [in the present case]?'"

[I]   He said to him, "[We act] according to Rab and according to
R. Yohanan [A–B]."

[J]   And so was the decision in accord with Rab and with R. Yohanan.

[K]   And when R. Abahu went south, he acted in accord with R.
Hanina [C]. And when he went to Tiberias, he acted in accord
with R. Yohanan [A]. For one does not act contrary to [the view
of] a person in the place where he is the authority.

[L]   There is no problem if one acts according to the opinion of
R. Hanina [(C) one recites the blessing over the wine, then one
recites the blessing over the light].

[M]   But if one acts according to the opinion of R. Yohanan [A], [why
does he recite the Prayer of Sanctification first]? Why does he
not recite the blessing over the light [as soon as possible after the
blessing over the wine], lest the light go out, as is the practice
[on every regular Sabbath] throughout the year? Here too [on
this special occasion] he should recite the blessing [as soon as
possible] over the light lest the light go out [if the oil is used
up—P.M.]

[N]   How then may one justify R. Yohanan's practice?

[O]   Since he has wine [for his meal we may rest assured that] his light
will not go out. [He will have enough oil. We presume one first
secures enough oil for his lamp and then buys wine for his meal.]

[P]   So why then does he not postpone the blessing over the light
until the very end?

[Q]   In order not to disrupt the routine for [the recitation of the
blessings in the Prayer of Division for] other Sabbaths to come.

Throughout this chapter, the Talmud makes systematic use of
materials collected in Tosefta for the exegesis of Mishnah. Unit I
simply cites T. Unit II examines the ramifications of the rules of
M., and unit III develops further the rules and customs for the

recitation of the blessings of the Prayer of Sanctification and the Prayer of Division. Unit **IV** continues with legal speculation about the views of the Houses. These units are all direct expansions of the concerns of Mishnah. Unit **V** extends the discussion to a new but closely related case, the order of the blessings at a meal on the Saturday night when a festival falls on Sunday.

8:2

[A] *The House of Shammai say, "They wash their hands [before beginning the meal], and then they mix the cup [of concentrated wine with water to prepare it for drinking]."*

[B] *And the House of Hillel say, "They mix the cup, and then they wash their hands."*

[I.A] What is the basis for the [ruling of] the House of Shammai?

[B] **[They first wash their hands] so they do not render the liquids on the sides of the cup unclean [by contact] with their hands, which in turn [through contact] could render [the outside of] the cup unclean.**

[C] What is the basis for the [ruling of] the House of Hillel?

[D] **[They reject the Shammaite position because they hold the view that] the outside of the cup is perpetually unclean. [Since the outside of the cup is already unclean, it makes no difference at what point one washes, whether before or after mixing the cup.]**

[E] **[Why then must one wash after mixing the cup? The explanation is:] Another matter: One must juxtapose washing his hands with the recitation of the blessing [at the beginning of the meal]. [The act of mixing the cup may not intervene]** [T. 5:26].

[F] R. Biban in the name of R. Yohanan, "The opinion of the House of Shammai accords with the view of R. Yose, and the opinion of the House of Hillel accords with the view of R. Meir."

[G] As it was taught there: *[With regard to the laws of uncleanness, the grip is not considered to be part of the cup.] R. Meir says, "This applies [if a person touches the grip with either] clean or unclean hands." [If one holds a cup by the grip, he renders unclean neither the outside nor the contents. Like the House of Hillel, Meir is not concerned about the hands rendering the cup unclean.]*

[H]   And R. Yose says, *"This is true only with regard to [a person who touches the grip with] clean hands." [He is afraid that one who holds a cup by the grip with unclean hands will render unclean the liquids on the outer surface of the cup, just as the House of Shammai fear in our case]* [M. Kelim 25:7–8].

[II.A]   R. Yose in the name of R. Shabbetai and R. Hiyya in the name of R. Simeon b. Laqish, "[To find water to wash one's utensils before kneading dough and separating] the dough-offering, and to [find water to] wash one's hands [before the meal], a person must go up to four miles." ['Mile' refers to 2,000 paces, about 1,470 meters, which is somewhat less than the modern English mile of about 1,609 meters.]

[B]   R. Abahu in the name of R. Yose b. R. Haninah, "This applies to [one who was travelling on the road], who must go ahead [up to four miles to find water]. But [to find water] they do not trouble him to go back [in the direction from which he came on his journey]."

[C]   In what status do they place guards of gardens and orchards [who do not have water available for washing before they eat]? [Do we require that they search for water to wash with before eating] like those who must journey ahead [up to four miles to find water]? [Or do we not require that they search to find water, just as we do not trouble a person to] go back [on his journey. For if the guard leaves his post, thieves may steal the produce]?

[D]   Let us derive the rule from this: *A woman may sit and cut off dough offering while naked [and recite the blessing] because [by sitting down] she can cover herself. But a man may not [separate dough offering and recite the blessing while naked].* [M. Hallah 2:3].

[E]   Now is this not a case of a woman who is sitting in her house? Yet we do not trouble her [to get dressed before separating the dough offering]. Accordingly, here [regarding guards of produce] we do not trouble them [to go search for water to wash with before eating].

[III.A]   It was taught: **[Washing one's hands with] water before the meal is optional.**

[B]   **[Washing one's hands with] water after the meal is compulsory.**

[C]   **But with regard to the first case [i.e., before the meal], one washes and waits. And with regard to the second case [i.e., after the meal], one washes and does not wait [T. 5:13].**

[D]   What does "washes and waits" mean?

[E]   R. Jacob bar Aha said, "One washes twice [i.e., he washes and waits a moment and washes again]."

[F]   R. Samuel bar Yitzhak said, "You say one must wash twice. How can you [also consistently] say [washing before the meal is] optional? [It must be compulsory.]"

[G]   [Washing both before and after the meal is compulsory in accord with the following:] Said R. Jacob bar Idi, "On account of [neglect of] the first [washing before the meal], they came to eat swine's meat.

[H]   "And on account of [neglect of] the second [washing after the meal], a woman [was divorced and] went forth from her house."

[I]   And some say, "[On account of neglect of the second washing after the meal], three persons were killed." [P.M. and S.H. explain these references: The first refers to a story of a butcher who sold both kosher meat to Jews and non-kosher meat to gentiles. A Jew once came to buy meat but did not wash his hands. On account of this the butcher sold him pork. The second refers to a story concerning Judah, Yose, and Meir in b. Yoma 83b. They outwitted a swindler because he had neglected to wash after eating. When the swindler found out that he had been outwitted, he killed his wife in a fit of anger. The third refers to the version of this story in which, after killing his wife in anger, he also killed his son in anger, and then he committed suicide.]

[IV.A]   Samuel went to stay with Rab.

[B]   He saw him eating, with his hands covered [by a napkin].

[C]   He said to him, "What are you doing? [Did you not wash your hands?]"

[D]   Samuel answered, "I am sensitive [and even though I washed my hands, I need to act according to my own habits]."

[E]   When R. Zeira came here [to the Land of Israel], he saw priests eating [heave-offering] with their hands covered [by napkins without first washing!].

[F]   He said to them, "This [nevertheless] accords with the story told of Rab and Samuel [because the priests are more careful, so they need not wash before eating—S.H.]."

[G]   Came R. Yose bar bar Kahana and said in the name of Samuel, "Those who eat unconsecrated food [i.e., ordinary people] must wash their hands [before eating]. But those who eat heave-offering [i.e., priests] need not wash their hands [before eating even unconsecrated food]."

[H]   R. Yose says, "Both [those ordinary persons who eat] unconsecrated food and [those priests who eat] heave-offering [must wash before eating unconsecrated food]."

[I]   R. Yosah in the name of R. Hiyya bar Ashi and R. Yonah, and R. Hiyya bar Ashi in the name of Rab, "[Before eating] heave-offering they [the priests] must wash their hands up to their wrists, and [before eating] unconsecrated food, they [all persons] must wash their hands up to their knuckles."

[J]   Meyasha the grandson of R. Joshua b. Levi said, "Any person who wanted to eat ordinary food with my grandfather, but who did not wash his hands up to his wrists, could not eat with him."

[K]   R. Huna said, "They must wash their hands only [before eating] bread."

[L]   R. Hoshaia taught, "[They wash before eating] anything which can absorb liquid."

[M]   R. Zeira said, "Even when I eat lupine, I wash my hands."

[N]   Rab said, "One who washed his hands in the morning, they do not trouble him to wash again in the afternoon." [He may rely on that washing for eating throughout the entire day.]

[O]   R. Abina instructed donkey drivers [who travel out on the road], "When you are somewhere where there is water for washing, wash your hands [in the morning], and you may rely on that [washing] for [eating throughout] the entire day."

[V.A] R. Zeira went to R. Abahu in Caesarea. He found [Abahu] and he said, "Let us go and eat."

[B]   He [Abahu] gave him a round loaf of bread for slicing and he said, "Sit and recite the blessing."

[C]   He [Zeira] said to him, "The host should know the value of his loaf. [You should recite the blessing.]"

[D]   When they had eaten, Abahu said, "Sit and recite the blessing."

[E]   [Zeira] said to him, "My master surely knows that R. Huna was a great man and he used to say, 'The one who opens [the meal by reciting the blessing] should also close [the meal and recite the blessing at the end of the meal].'"

[F]   The teaching [in Tosefta] disputes R. Huna. For it was taught: **This is the order for washing hands.**

[G]   **For [a group of] up to five people—they start [washing] with the highest in rank.**

[H]   **For more than this—they start [washing] with the lowest in rank [so the important people do not have to wait for long between washing and the meal].**

[I]   **[This is the order for mixing the cup.] In the middle of the meal they start [to mix the cup] from the highest [in rank].**

[J]   **At the end of the meal, they start from the one who recites the blessing [T. 5:6].**

[K]   Do they not do this so that he may [have time to] prepare himself to recite the blessing?

[L]   [However,] if you say that 'the one who opens [the meal by reciting the blessing], should also close [the meal and recite the blessing at the end of the meal],' is he not prepared already?

[M]   Said R. Yitzhak, "We may explain that this is a case wherein the participants came [to join the meal in stages] a few at a time. And some did not know who was to recite the blessing." [Even though they accept Huna's rule (E), 'The one who opens (the meal by reciting the blessing should also close (the meal and recite the blessing at the end of the meal),' they need another way to designate who will recite the blessing since some came to the meal after the first blessing was recited.]

Unit **I** cites Tosefta's exegesis of M. and then correlates the views of the Houses with the opinions of authorities in other cases elsewhere in M. Unit **II** does not further explain M. but instead takes up an issue pertinent to M., the rules for washing one's hands at a meal. Unit **III** continues this interest with an appropriate citation from Tosefta on the same subject and a further discussion of the issue.

The practices of the Amoraim regarding washing for the meal are central concerns of unit **IV**. Unit **V** closes with a story pertinent to a ruling in Tosefta, which the Talmud then cites, about the order of washing hands at the meal.

8:3

[A]   *The House of Shammai say, "[To avoid spreading uncleanness] one wipes his hands on a napkin and places it on the table."*

[B]   *And the House of Hillel say, "[He places the napkin] on the cushion."*

[I.A]   [Leiden cites here M. 8:4, **I.A**.] The Mishnah speaks of a marble table, or a table which may be taken apart, which is not susceptible to uncleanness.

[II.A]   What is the basis for the House of Shammai's view?

[B]   **[He must put the napkin on the table] so that the liquid in the napkin does not become unclean through contact with the cushion, and in turn render unclean the person's hands.**

[C]   And what is the basis for the House of Hillel's view? **[The principle is that] in all cases where there is doubt [whether there was contact between unclean] liquids and one's hands, [the law is that one's hands are considered] clean. [Here there is doubt whether the cushion is unclean, and whether the liquid in the napkin becomes unclean and renders one's hands unclean.]**

[D]   **Another explanation: [According to the House of Hillel there is no need to maintain clean] hands in order to eat unconsecrated food [T. 5:27].**

[E]   And according to the House of Shammai, is it necessary to maintain clean hands in order to eat unconsecrated foods? [Yes, as a precaution, lest priests accidentally eat heave-offering with unclean hands.]

[F]   You may explain [it is necessary] either in accord with R. Simeon b. Eleazar, or with R. Eleazar b. R. Zadok.

[G]   In accord with R. Simeon b. Eleazar, as it was taught: **R. Simeon b. Eleazar says in the name of R. Meir, "One's hands are considered to be unclean in the first degree with regard to** unconsecrated food, and unclean in the second degree with regard to heave-offering" [T. Toh. 1:4].

[H]   Or, in accord with R. Eleazar b. R. Zadok, as it was taught there: *Unconsecrated food, prepared as if it were consecrated food, is to be treated as if it were unconsecrated food.*

[I]   *R. Eleazar b. R. Zadok says, "Lo, it is treated as if it were heave-offering and [accordingly] can become unclean in the second degree and become unfit [for use] in a [third] degree [of uncleanness]"* [M. Toh. 2:8].

[III.A]   It was taught there: *One who anointed himself with clean oil, and became unclean, and went and dipped [in a ritual bath]: The House of Shammai say, "Even though it [the oil] drips from him, it remains clean."*

[B]   *And the House of Hillel say, "It is unclean."*

[C]   *And if the oil was unclean from the outset: The House of Shammai say, "[If there is on him up to] the amount of oil it would take to anoint a little finger, [it is clean]."*

[D]   *And the House of Hillel say, "[If there remains on him] any amount of dripping liquid, [it is unclean]."*

[E]   *R. Judah says in the name of the House of Hillel, "[If there remains on him] any amount which may drip and moisten something else, [it is unclean]"* [M. Ed. 4:6].

[F]   The opinions of the House of Hillel [in our Mishnah and in M. Ed.] are contradictory!

[G]   There [concerning the status of dripping oil] they say, "It is unclean." Here [concerning the status of liquid which may drip from the napkin] they say, "It is clean."

[H]   [We may resolve this contradiction because they are different cases.] There [in the case in M. Ed. the oil] is visible [on his body]. Here [in the case in our M. the liquid] is absorbed in the napkin.

Unit **I** glosses M. Unit **II** cites Tosefta's explanation of the dispute, and then correlates the House of Shammai's view with that of other authorities in M. and T. Unit **III** then finds an ostensible contradiction in the view of the House of Hillel in our M. and in another source. The Talmud ends the section with the harmonization of those traditions.

8:4

[A]   *The House of Shammai say, "[To avoid wasting food] they clean the house [and gather the scraps of food after the meal], and afterward wash their hands."*

[B]   *And the House of Hillel say, "They wash their hands, and afterward clean the house."*

[I.A]   What is the basis for the House of Shammai's view?

[B]   **[They clean the house first] so as not to waste food [by dripping water upon it when cleaning up after washing one's hands, thereby making the food susceptible to uncleanness].**

[C]   And what is the basis for the House of Hillel's view?

[D]   **If the servant is clever, he gathers up the pieces which are larger than an olive's bulk. [Then even if the scraps of food that remain become wet and touch a source of uncleanness, they cannot become unclean, based on the principle that a scrap of food smaller than an olive's bulk cannot become unclean.] And they wash their hands and afterward clean the house [without concern over wasting food] [T. 5:28].**

The Talmud cites Tosefta's explanation of the dispute.

8:5

[A]   *The House of Shammai say, "[The order of the blessings in the service of the Prayer of Division, when it is recited at the meal at the conclusion of the Sabbath is:] Light, meal, spices, Prayer of Division."*

[B]   *And the House of Hillel say, "[The order is:] Light, spices, meal, Prayer of Division."*

[C]   *The House of Shammai say, "[The formula for the blessing over the light is,] 'Who created the light of the fire.'"*

[D]   *And the House of Hillel say, "[It is,] 'Who creates the lights of the fire.'"*

[I.A] It was taught: **Said R. Judah, "The House of Shammai and the House of Hillel did not dispute [concerning the order of the blessings] that the blessing for the meal comes first, and the Prayer of Division comes last.**

[B] **"Concerning what did they dispute? [They disputed over the order of the blessings] for the spices and for the light.**

[C] **"For the House of Shammai say, 'Spices and then light.'**

[D] **"And the House of Hillel say, 'Light and then spices'"** [T. 5:30]. [This version of the dispute is contrary to our Mishnah.]

[E] R. Ba and R. Judah in the name of Rab, "The law follows the one who says, 'Spices and then light' [i.e., the House of Shammai]."

[II.A] **The House of Shammai say, "One holds the cup of wine in his right hand, and the perfumed oil in his left hand. And he says the blessing over the cup of wine, and then he says the blessing over the perfumed oil."**

[B] **And the House of Hillel say, "One holds the perfumed oil in his right hand, and the cup of wine in his left hand. And he says the blessing over the perfumed oil, and smears it on the head of his servant. And if the servant is a disciple of the sages, he smears it on the wall. For it is not befitting a disciple of the sages to go outside perfumed"** [T. 5:29].

[C] Abba bar bar Hannah and R. Huna were sitting and eating and R. Zeira was standing and serving them. He came before them carrying both [the cup of wine and the perfumed oil] in one hand. Abba bar bar Hannah said to him [Zeira], "Has your other hand been cut off?"

[D] And his father [Bar Hannah] got angry at him. He said to him, "Is it not bad enough that you recline, and he stands before you to serve? And besides, he is a priest [and should not be serving you]!"

[E] And [do you not know that] Samuel said, "'One who makes improper use of the priesthood has misappropriated the property of the Temple?' Now [on top of this] you even make fun of him! I decree that he shall sit, and you shall serve him!"

[F] Whence that, "One who makes improper use of the priesthood has misappropriated the property of the Temple"?

[G] R. Aha in the name of Samuel said, "[It is based on this verse:]

'You are holy to the Lord and the vessels are holy' [Ezra 8:28]. Just as one who makes use of the vessels [of the Temple] has misappropriated Temple property, so too one who makes use of the [services of the] priests has misappropriated Temple property."

[III.A] Piska. [The House of Shammai say,] *"Who created [past tense] the light [singular] of the fire"* [M. 8:5C–D]. [One might argue that], according to the view of the House of Shammai, one should say [as a blessing over wine the formula], "Who created [past tense] the fruit of the vine."

[B] And [it makes sense only] according to the view of the House of Hillel that one should say [over wine], "Who creates the fruit of the vine" [as is the accepted practice].

[C] [No. The argument is not valid! Even according to the Shammaites there is a difference between reciting a blessing over light and over wine. The difference is that] wine is renewed each year [in the new crop]. Fire is not renewed at every hour. [And because fire was created once, long ago, its blessing should indicate an action completed in the past: 'created.']

[IV.A] **Fire and mules, though not actually created in the six days of creation, were thought of [by God] during the six days of creation** [T. 5:31].

[B] [When were] mules [first created]? [As it says,] "These are the sons of Zibeon: Aiah and Anah: he is the Anah who found *hyymym* in the wilderness" [Gen. 36:24].

[C] What are *hyymym*? R. Judah b. Simon says, "Mules [Greek: *hemionos*]." And sages say, "Read it *hymsw*, split. [That is, an animal which is] half horse, half ass."

[D] And these are the signs [one should know concerning a mule]: Said R. Judah, "All those with small ears had a horse for a mother, and an ass for a father. [Those with] big ears had an ass for a mother, and a horse for a father."

[E] R. Mana instructed the [servants of the] patriarchate, "If you wish to purchase a mule, buy one with small ears. For its mother was a horse and its father was an ass."

[F] What did Zibeon and Anah do? They mated a she-ass and a male horse and from that union there came forth a mule.

[G]   God said to them, "You have brought into being a creature that will cause damage. So I shall bring upon this man [Zibeon] a creature that will cause him harm."

[H]   What did God do? He mated a snake and a lizard and from that union there came forth a poisonous lizard.

[I]   No man will ever say to you that a poisonous lizard bit him and he survived, or that a mad dog bit him and he survived, or that a she-mule kicked him and he survived. [This last reference is] only to a white she-mule.

[V.A]   **Fire** [T. 5:31]: R. Levi in the name of R. Bezira [or Nezira], "The light created on the first day lasted thirty-six hours: twelve on the Sabbath eve, twelve on the night of the Sabbath, and twelve on the Sabbath day."

[B]   And Adam gazed out [in the primeval night] upon the whole world.

[C]   When the light did not cease, the whole world sang out, as it says, "Under the whole heaven they sang out to Him whose light extends to the corners of the earth" [Job 37:2].

[D]   When the Sabbath ended, darkness began to minister [over the world].

[E]   Adam became frightened and said, "Concerning this Scripture says, 'He [man] will bruise your head, and you [the serpent] shall bruise his heel' [Gen. 3:15]. Perhaps now [that it is dark] he will come to bruise me. [Because] it says [elsewhere], 'In darkness he will bruise me'" [Ps. 139:11].

[F]   Said R. Levi, "At that very time God summoned two flints and he [Adam] struck them against each other and light came forth from them. This is as it is written, 'And the night around me be light' [Ps. 139:11]. And he [Adam] recited the blessing, 'Who creates the lights of the fire.'"

[G]   Samuel said, "We therefore recite the blessing over fire at the conclusion of the Sabbath, for that was when it was first created."

[H]   R. Huna in the name of R. Abahu in the name of R. Yohanan, "They even recite the blessing [over the fire] at the conclusion of the Day of Atonement, for the light 'rested' throughout that day." [That is, it is forbidden to kindle a fire on that day, and so after the day, it is as if fire were created anew.]

Unit **I** cites Tosefta's reflections on M. and adds to them a brief
comment. Unit **II** cites an independent supplement from T. and
appends to that a related story.

At unit **III** the Talmud examines the opinion of the House of
Shammai to see if it leads to a contradiction and finds that it
does not. Unit **IV** cites another supplement from T. and proceeds to develop its theme, which is quite independent of our
M. Unit **V** concludes the discussion of that Tosefta passage.

8:6

[A]   *They recite a blessing [over the light in the Prayer of Division
       Service at the conclusion of the Sabbath] neither over the light
       and spices of gentiles, nor the light and spices [used in honor] of
       the dead, nor the light and spices used before idolatry.*

[B]   *And they do not recite the blessing over the light [in the Prayer
       of Division Service at the conclusion of the Sabbath] until they
       make use of its illumination.*

[I.A] R. Jacob taught before R. Jeremiah, "They may recite a blessing
       over the spices of gentiles."

[B]   Regarding what do they, [the rule in M. and this ruling,] differ?
       This ruling refers to spices used in front of a store [to attract
       customers. One is permitted to recite a blessing over the fra-
       grance of a gentile's spices used for such a purpose.]

[II.A] **Over a lantern, even if it were not extinguished [i.e., it burned
       throughout the Sabbath], they may recite the blessing over it
       [for the light used in the Prayer of Division Service at the end
       of the Sabbath].**

[B]   **[They do not recite the blessing over] a light whose source is
       hidden by a garment, or in a lamp,** or over a light behind a
       glass, **or for any light where they see the flame but cannot
       make use of its illumination, or can make use of its illumina-
       tion but cannot see the flame. They recite the blessing over it
       only if they both can see the flame and make use of its illumi-
       nation** [T. 5:31].

[C]   Five things were said about [the glow of] a glowing coal, and
       five things about [the flame of] a torch. [In the following cases,

the principle is that the flame of a torch is considered to be pure
fire, without any material substance.]

[D]   (1) It is a sacrilege to use [the light of] a glowing coal belonging
to the Temple, but it is neither [a matter of] any [forbidden]
benefit nor a sacrilege to use the light of a torch of the Temple.

[E]   (2) It is forbidden to use [the light of] a glowing coal used for
idolatry. But it is permissible [to use the light of] a torch [used
for idolatry].

[F]   (3) One who vows not to benefit from his associate may not use
[the light of] his glowing coals, but is permitted to use [the light
of] his torch.

[G]   (4) One who takes a glowing coal out to the public thoroughfare
[on the Sabbath] is liable [for punishment]. But one who takes a
torch out is free [from any liability].

[H]   (5) They may recite the blessing [for the light after the Sabbath]
over a torch. But they may not recite the blessing over a glowing coal.

[I]   R. Hiyya bar Ashi in the name of Rab, "If the coals were flaming,
they may recite the blessing over them."

[J]   R. Yohanan of Kerasion [perhaps: Khorazin] in the name of
Nahum bar Simai, "Only if the flame shoots up."

[III.A]   It was taught: [At the end of the Sabbath in the Prayer of Division Service, they may recite the blessing over the light of] a
gentile who lit a light from an Israelite's flame, and [the light
of] an Israelite who lit from a gentile [T. 5:31].

[B]   It makes sense that [they may recite the blessing over the light
of] a gentile who lit it from [the flame of] an Israelite [because the
light of the Israelite was certainly kindled anew after the Sabbath. But from the present ruling that one may use a light of an
Israelite who lit it from the light of a gentile, we may infer that
one may recite the blessing over the light] even of a gentile who
lit a light from another gentile [after the Sabbath].

[C]   But we find that it was taught: They do not recite the blessing
over a light lit by a gentile from the light of a gentile. [The
Talmud suggests that the latter rule is accepted.]

[D]   R. Abahu in the name of R. Yohanan, "They may recite the blessing over a light that emanates from an alleyway populated by gentiles where even one Israelite lives, on account of that one Israelite. [We may presume that the light comes from his house.]"

[IV.A] R. Abahu in the name of R. Yohanan, "They may recite the blessing neither over the spices used on the Sabbath eve in Tiberias, nor over the spices used at the conclusion of the Sabbath in Sepphoris, nor over the light nor over the spices used on Friday morning in Sepphoris, for these are all prepared for another purpose [i.e., for freshening clothes]."

[V.A] [*Nor over the light nor spices of the dead* [M. 8:6]:] R. Hezekiah and R. Jacob bar Aha in the name of R. Yose b. R. Hanina, "Those to which we refer are [the lights and spices] placed over [on top of] the coffin. But over those placed before [and around] the coffin, they may recite the blessing. For I say they are put there for the convenience of the living."

[B] *Nor over the light and spices used before idolatry.* Are those [lights and spices] of gentiles not the same as those of idolatry? We may explain that [the latter] refers to [the light and spices of] an Israelite idolater.

[C] *And they do not recite the blessing over the light until they make use of its illumination.* R. Zeira son of R. Abahu expounded, "'And God saw the light that it was good' [Gen. 1:4]. And after that it says, 'And God divided the light from the darkness' [Gen. 1:5]. [This implies that first he saw the light then he divided. Likewise one should see the light before 'dividing,' i.e., reciting the blessing in the Prayer of Division.]"

[VI.A] Said R. Berekhiah, "Two great men, R. Yohanan and R. Simeon b. Laqish, expounded accordingly, 'And God divided' [means] he permanently divided [light from darkness and put them into separate realms in the world]."

[B] R. Judah b. R. Simon said, "He divided them [set them aside] for Himself [but not for the world]."

[C] And sages said, "He divided them [set them aside] for the righteous [to have light] in the world to come."

[D] They gave a parable: To what may we compare this matter? To a king who had two generals.

[E] One said, "I shall serve by day."

[F]   And the other said, "I shall serve by day."

[G]   The king called in the first and said, "Sir, the daytime is your territory." And he called in the second and said, "Sir, the night-time is your territory."

[H]   This accords with what was written, "And God called the light, day, and the darkness he called night" [Gen. 1:5]. To the light he said, "The day will be your territory." And to the darkness he said, "The night will be your territory."

[I]   Said R. Yohanan, "This is what God said to Job, 'Have you commanded the morning since your days began [as God did in the parable above] and caused the dawn to know its place?' [Job 38:12]. [God asked Job if he knew the secret of] where the light of the six days of creation is stored."

[J]   Said R. Tanhuma, "I shall tell you what is the basis [in Scripture of the teaching of R. Yohanan and R. Simeon b. Laqish, in A]: "Who creates light and makes darkness and makes peace" [Isa. 45:7]. When they [light and darkness] went forth [into the world], God made peace between them [and assigned each to a separate domain]."

[VII.A]   *They do not recite the blessing over the light until they make use of* [y'wtw] *its illumination* [M. 8:6].

[B]   Rab says, "[The correct spelling of 'make use of' is] *y'wtw* [meaning] 'use' [with an aleph]."

[C]   And Samuel says, "[The correct spelling is] *y'wtw* [meaning] 'timely use' [with an ayin]."

[D]   The one who says 'use' [is correct bases his teaching on the verse where we find an appropriate usage,] "Only on this condition will we consent to you [*n'wt*, implying permission to use]" [Gen. 34:15].

[E]   The one who says 'timely' [is correct bases his teaching on the verse where we find an appropriate usage,] "How to sustain with a timely [*l'wt*] word him that is weary" [Isa. 50:4].

[F]   [A similar dispute:] It was taught there [B. Erub. 52b], "How do they extend the Sabbath boundaries [*m'bryn*] of towns?"

[G]   [Commenting on *m'bryn*] Rab said, "[It means] they add a segment [spelled with an aleph, *m'bryn*]."

[H]   And Samuel said, "[It means] they expand the area [*m'bryn,* spelled with an ayin]."

[I]   The one who said, "They add a segment [with an aleph," means literally,] "They add on a limb [to the town]."

[J]   The one who said, "They expand the area [with an ayin," means literally,] "They expand [the boundary outward] as a pregnant woman [expands outward]."

[K]   [A similar dispute:] It was taught there [M. A.Z. 1:1], *Before the festivals* ['ydyhn] *of the idolaters.*

[L]   [Commenting on the meaning of *'ydyhn*] Rab said, "[It means] before their testimonies [idols, spelled with an ayin]."

[M]   And Samuel said, "[It means] before their festivals [spelled with an aleph]."

[N]   The one who said 'festivals' [*'ydyhn*] based his teaching on the verse, "For near is the day of their calamity [*'ydm*]" [Deut. 32:35].

[O]   The one who said 'testimonies' [*'dym*] based his teaching on the verse, "Their testimonies [idols] neither see nor know, that they may be put to shame" [Isa. 44:9].

[P]   How does Samuel explain [the verse cited in defense of] Rab's explanation? He will say that [it means], "Their testimonies [i.e., idols]" will bring shame upon those who worship them on the day of judgment [when they are called upon to testify against the idolaters].

[VIII.A]   *They do not recite the blessing over the light, until they make use of its illumination* [M. 8:6]. R. Judah in the name of Samuel, "[How much illumination must there be in order to recite the blessing over the light?] Enough so that women could spin yarn by its light."

[B]   Said R. Yohanan, "Enough [light] so that one can determine what is in a cup or bowl."

[C]   Said R. Hanina, "Enough [light] so that one could distinguish between two different coins."

[D]   Taught R. Oshaia, "They may recite the blessing [over the light] even if it is [far from them] in a large room of ten by ten cubits."

[E]   R. Zeira used to get very close to the light [to recite the bless-
ing]. His students said to him, "Master, why are you so strict
with us about this? Lo, R. Oshaia taught, 'Even [where the light
is far from a person] in a room up to ten by ten [one may recite
the blessing over the light]'!"

Unit **I** harmonizies an Amoraic rule with M. Unit **II** cites a passage from Tosefta concerning the light used in the Prayer of
Division Service on Saturday night, and expands upon that. Unit
III continues citing and discussing Tosefta. Unit **IV** adds another
tradition attributed to Abahu, who appears in unit **III**, and related to our subject.

At unit **V** the Talmud goes back to the direct explanation of
M., line by line. Unit **VI** briefly digresses to expound in general
upon the subject of the division between light and darkness,
central to the Prayer of Division. At unit **VII** the Talmud comes
back to its exposition of Mishnah, with a dispute that examines
one term in the text. Other materials follow, related to that mor-
phological discussion, but not to the subject of our chapter. Unit
VIII concludes with reflection on the implications of our Mishnah's last rule.

8:7

[A]   *He who ate [a meal] and forgot and did not recite the blessing
[over the meal and left the place where he ate the meal]:*

[B]   *The House of Shammai say, "He must go back to his place
[where he ate] and recite the blessing."*

[C]   *And the House of Hillel say, "He may recite the blessing in the
place he remembers."*

[D]   *And until when [after the meal] may he recite the blessings?*

[E]   *Until he digests the food.*

[I.A] R. Yusta bar Shunam said, "Two Amoraim [interpreted this
Mishnah]. One explained the House of Shammai's view and the
other explained the House of Hillel's view."

[B]   The one who explained the House of Shammai's view [argued as
follows:] if one forgot a purse filled with precious stones and

pearls, would he not go back to get his purse? So in this case as well, *He must go back to his place and recite the blessing.*

[C]   The one who explained the House of Hillel's view [argued as follows:] if a worker were up in a tree or down in a pit, do we trouble him to go back to his place to recite the blessing? [No. That is absurd.] He may recite the blessing in the place he remembers. So, too, [in general,] *He may recite the blessing in the place he remembers.* [We do not trouble him to go back.]

[II.A]   *Until when may he recite the blessings?* [M. 8 : 7D–E].

[B]   R. Hiyya in the name of Samuel, "Until he digests the food." [Texts have, "And sages say." But this reading is problematic.] "As long as he is thirsty on account of the meal."

[C]   R. Yohanan said, "Until he gets hungry [he may recite the blessing]."

Unit **I** opens with an explanation of the first views cited in the M. Unit **II** adds several alternatives to M.'s closing rule.

8:8

[A]   *If they obtained wine after finishing the meal and they had only one cup:*

[B]   *The House of Shammai say, "They recite the blessing over the wine, and then they recite the blessing over the meal."*

[C]   *And the House of Hillel say, "They recite the blessing over the meal, and then they recite the blessing over the wine."*

[D]   *They may answer 'Amen' after an Israelite who recites a blessing. But they may not answer 'Amen' after a Samaritan who recites a blessing, unless they hear the entire blessing [and are certain that he did not say anything unacceptable in the blessing].*

[I.A]   Said R. Ba, "[The House of Shammai reason as follows:] Since [the blessing over the wine] is a short blessing, one may forget and drink [wine without a blessing after reciting the long meal blessing. So he must recite the blessing over the wine first.]. But when he strings it together with another blessing that he recites over the same cup [as in M. 8 : 1B, he may recite it second since],

he will not forget. [Cf. M. 8:1**IV,** above. Some versions omit
this last sentence.]

[**II.**A] [They may answer 'Amen' after an Israelite who recites a blessing. But they may not answer 'Amen' after a Samaritan who
recites a blessing, unless they hear the entire blessing and are
certain that he did not say anything unacceptable in the blessing.
The Mishnah at D seems to imply] that one may answer 'Amen'
after hearing a blessing recited by an Israelite even if he did not
hear [the entire blessing].

[B] But did we not learn [regarding the recitation of a blessing, to
the contrary]? "If one heard [a blessing] and [in the event that
he] did not answer [Amen], he [nevertheless] fulfilled his obligation [to recite the blessing through the other person's recitation
of the blessing]. But [in a case where] he answered [Amen] without hearing [the entire blessing,] he did not fulfill his obligation
[to recite the blessing through the other person's recitation]."

[C] Hiyya the son of Rab said, "Our Mishnah [refers to a case of
one] who did not eat an olive's bulk with those at the meal. [He
was not required to recite the meal blessing. In such a case he
may answer 'Amen' even if he did not hear the whole blessing
because he is not obligated to recite a blessing anyway.]"

[D] It was taught [that one may interpret this rule cited in A not as
a rule regarding the recitation of blessings and the response
'Amen,' but as a rule regarding the responsive recitation of the
Hallel in the synagogue, as follows:] "If one heard [the leader
reciting the verses of the Hallel] but did not answer [by repeating responsively each verse], he fulfilled his obligation. If one
answered but did not hear, he did not fulfill his obligation."

[E] Rab in the name of Abba bar Hannah, and some say Abba bar
Hannah in the name of Rab, "[The rule in C applies] as long as
one answers [the leader] at the paragraph headings [by respond-
ing with the first word of each section, he fulfills his obligation
through the other person's recitation]."

[F] R. Zeira asked, "What are these paragraph headings?" [They
are, e.g.,] "Praise the Lord, praise the servants of the Lord,
praise the name of the Lord" [Ps. 113:1].

[G] They asked this question of R. Hiyya bar Abba, "Whence that if
one heard [the leader reciting the verse of Hallel] but did not

answer [by repeating responsively each verse], he fulfills his obligation?"

[H]   He said, "[I learned this] from what I saw the great rabbis do. When reciting in public [the Hallel on a festival or the new moon], one [group] recited, 'Blessed is he that comes,' and another [group] answered, 'In the name of the Lord' [Ps. 118:26].

[I]   "And [in this manner, each group reciting only half of each verse, members of] both groups fulfilled their obligations [to recite the Hallel]."

[**III.A**]   Taught R. Oshaia, "A person may answer 'Amen,' [upon hearing the blessings after the meal] even if he did not eat [at that meal]. But one may not say, 'Let us recite the blessings to Him of whose bounty we have eaten' [the invitation to recite the blessing over the meal], unless he has eaten [at that meal]."

[B]   It was taught, "They do not answer with an orphaned [isolated] 'Amen,' or with a cut off 'Amen' or with a hasty 'Amen.'"

[C]   Ben Azzai says, "One who answers with an orphaned 'Amen,' his children shall be orphans, with a cut off 'Amen,' his years will be cut off, with a hasty 'Amen,' his soul will be cut down.

[D]   "[But one who answers] with a long 'Amen,' his days and his years will be lengthened with goodness."

[E]   What [case] is an "orphaned 'Amen'"? R. Huna said, "One who was obligated to recite a blessing who responded [to another person's recitation] 'Amen,' but who did not know to whose blessing he answered."

[F]   It was taught, **A gentile who recited a blessing using God's name, they may answer after it, 'Amen.'**

[G]   Said R. Tanhuma, "If a gentile blessed you, answer 'Amen,' as it is written, 'Blessed will you be by all peoples'" [Deut. 7:14].

[H]   A gentile met R. Ishmael and blessed him. He [Ishmael] said to him, "You have already been answered."

[I]   Another gentile met him and cursed him. He said to him, "You have already been answered."

[J]   His students said to him, "Master, how is it that you answered this one in the same way you answered that one?"

[K]   He said to them, "So it is written, 'Those that curse you will be cursed, and those that bless you will be blessed' [Gen. 27:29]. [In both cases, they have already been answered.]"

Unit **I** explains the conception behind Shammai's rule. The discussion in unit **II** focuses on the responsive recitation to blessings of 'Amen' and related rules for the recitation of the Hallel liturgy. Unit **III** concludes with diverse materials on the subject of the recitation of 'Amen.'

9 Yerushalmi Berakhot
Chapter Nine

9:1

[A] *One who sees a place where miracles were performed for Israel says, "Blessed [art Thou, O Lord, our God, King of the Universe,] who performed miracles for our forefathers in this place."*

[B] *[One who sees] a place from which idolatry was uprooted says, "Blessed [art Thou, O Lord, our God, King of the Universe,] who uprooted idolatry from our land."*

[I.A] The Mishnah speaks of miracles that occurred to Israel [as a nation]. But for miracles that occurred only to individuals, one is not required to recite a blessing.

[B] May a person recite a blessing [at places where] miracles occurred to his father or his teacher?

[C] And [may a person recite a blessing at a place where miracles occurred to] a great hero, such as Yoab b. Zeruyah and his associates [2 Sam. 20], or to a person who sanctified God's name [by risking martyrdom], such as Hananiah, Mishael, and Azariah [Shadrach, Meshach, and Abednego, in Dan. chap. 3]? [These questions in B–C are not answered.]

[D] And [when a person comes to a place where a miracle occured on behalf of] one of the tribes of Israel, [may he recite a blessing]?

[E] One who holds the view that you may call every tribe 'a congregation' would say one must recite a blessing [at a place where a miracle occurred to a tribe].

[F] One who holds the view that you may only call all the tribes

together 'a congregation,' would say one need not recite a blessing [at a place where a miracle occurred to just one tribe].

[II.A]   One who sees Babylonia must recite five blessings:
[1] When he sees the Euphrates River, he says, "Blessed [art
Thou, O Lord, our God, King of the Universe,] who is the
creator."
[2] When he sees the statue of Mercury he says, "Blessed [art
Thou, O Lord, our God, King of the Universe,] who is patient."
[3] When he sees [the ruins of] the palace of Nebuchadnezzar he
says, "Blessed [art Thou, O Lord, our God, King of the Universe,] who destroyed this wicked one's house."
[4] When he sees the place of the fiery furnace and the lions' den
[associated with the narratives in Daniel 3 and 6, respectively,]
he says, "Blessed [art Thou, O Lord, our God, King of the
Universe,] who performed miracles for our forefathers in this
place."
[5] When he sees the place from which they quarry gravel [for
idolatrous purposes], he says, "Blessed is He who speaks and
acts; Blessed is He who decrees and upholds his word."

[B]   When one sees Babylonia, he [further] says, "I will sweep it
with the broom of destruction" [Isa. 14:23].

[III.A]   R. Zeira and R. Judah in the name of Rab, "Any blessing that
does not include [a reference to] God's kingdom is not a valid
blessing."

[B]   Said R. Tanhuma, "I will tell you what is the basis [in Scripture
for this rule:] 'I will extol thee my God and King'" [Ps. 145:1].

[C]   Rab said, "One must say, '[Blessed] art Thou ['th]'."

[D]   And Samuel said, "One need not say, 'art Thou.'"

[IV.A]   R. Yohanan and R. Yonatan went to help bring peace to the
villages of the South. They came to one place and found the
leader reciting [in the first blessing of the Prayer of Eighteen
Blessings], "God, the great, mighty, awesome, powerful ['byr],
and valiant ['mys]" [adding these last two terms]. And they si-
lenced him. They said to him, "You do not have the right to add
to the [standard] formula that the sages established for the
blessings."

[B]   [The following traditions support the use of standardized liturgy.]
R. Huna in the name of Rab, "'The Almighty [šdy]—we cannot

find him; he is great in power [and justice, and abundant righteousness he will not violate]' [Job 37:23]. [The verse implies]
we cannot find [adequate words to describe] God's power and
might."

[C]   R. Abahu in the name of R. Yohanan, "'Shall it be told him that
I would speak? Did a man ever wish that he would be swallowed
up?' [Job 37:20]. If a person tries to [fully] describe God's might,
he will be swallowed up [in the process and lost] from the world."

[D]   Said R. Samuel bar Nahman, "Who can utter the mighty
doings of the Lord, [or show forth all his praise]?' [Ps. 106:2].
['Who is better at prayer,' asked the Psalmist,] 'than me or my
associates?'"

[E]   Said R. Abun, "[The question in the verse is rhetorical:] 'Who
can utter the mighty doings of the Lord?' [No one can]."

[F]   R. Jacob of the village of Naburaya in Tyre explained [this verse],
'Praise is due to [dwmyh] thee, O God, in Zion' [Ps. 65:1]: "Silence sums it all up [a reference to the word dwmyh—silence].
As regarding a priceless pearl, all who attempt to praise it, [by
so doing merely] diminish its value."

[V.A]   It was taught: **One who opens [his blessings] with [the invocation of the divine name] 'Lord' [yhwh] and closes his blessing
with the divine name 'Lord,' lo, he is a sage.**

[B]   **[One who opens with the divine name] 'God' ['lwhym] and
closes with 'God,' lo, he is a boor.**

[C]   **One who opens with 'God,' and closes with 'Lord,' lo, this is
a middle way.**

[D]   **One who opens with 'Lord,' and closes with 'God,' lo, this is
another way [heresy]** [T. 6:20].

[VI.A]   The heretics asked R. Simlai, "How many gods created the
world?"

[B]   He said to them, 'Why are you asking me? Go and ask Adam
himself [i.e., look in the verse]. As it says, 'For ask now of the
days that are past, [which were before you since the day that
God created man upon the earth' (Deut. 4:32). It is not written
in the plural form,] 'That *gods* created man upon the earth,' but
[in the singular form,] 'That *God* created man upon the earth.'"

[C]   They said to him, "Is it not written, 'In the beginning God
       ['lhym] created' [Gen. 1:1] [using what appears to be a plural
       noun—'Gods']?"

[D]   He said to them, "It is not written [plural] 'gods created,' but
       [singular] 'God created.'"

[E]   Said R. Simlai, "In every instance that the heretics have raised a
       question [out of Scripture], the answer [to their question] is
       right beside it [in Scripture]."

[F]   [The heretics] returned and asked him, "What is this which is
       written, 'Let us make man in our image, after our likeness'"
       [Gen. 1:26]?

[G]   He said to them, "It does not say, 'The gods created [plural]
       man in their own images' [Gen. 1:27]. But it says, 'So God cre-
       ated [singular] man in his own image.'"

[H]   His [Simlai's] students said to him, "You have deflected their
       question with a straw [i.e., a weak argument]. What will you
       answer us? [How will you explain this verse to us?]"

[I]   He said to them, "At first Adam was created from dust and Eve
       was created from Adam's rib. From that time on [man propa-
       gates] 'in our image, after our likeness.' [That means] a man must
       have a woman, a woman must have a man, and both must have
       the divine presence [together with them in order to propagate]."

[J]   [The heretics] returned and asked him, "What is this that is
       written, 'The mighty one, God, the Lord! The mighty one,
       God, the Lord! He knows.' [Josh. 22:22]? [This appears to im-
       ply that there are three powers in heaven.]"

[K]   He said to them, "It does not say, 'They know.' But it says, 'He
       knows' [supporting the unity, and not the trinity, of God]."

[L]   His students said to him, "Master you deflected their question
       with a straw. How will you answer us?"

[M]   He said to them, "These are three titles for one individual, just
       the same as Basileas Caesar Augustus [are three titles for the
       Roman Emperor]."

[N]   [The heretics] returned and asked him, "What is this that is
       written, 'The Mighty One, God, the Lord, speaks and summons
       the earth'" [Ps. 50:1]? [The verse give three names of God.]

[O]   He said to them, it does not say, 'Speak and summon [plural], but it says speaks and summons [singular].'"

[P]   His students said to him, "Master you deflected their question with a straw. How will you answer us?"

[Q]   He said to them, "These are three titles for one individual, just as artisan, builder, architect [are three titles for one master craftsman]."

[R]   [The heretics] returned and asked him, "What of that which is written, 'For he is a holy God ['lwhym—a plural form modified by a plural adjective]'" [Josh. 24:19]?

[S]   He said to them, "It is not written, 'They [plural] are holy.' But it says, 'He [singular] is a holy God; he is a jealous God'" [ibid.].

[T]   His students said to him, "Master you deflected their question with a straw. How will you answer us?"

[U]   [He answered, as it was taught:] said R. Yitzhak, "He is holy in many ways." [The verse suggests this through the use of the plural form of 'holy.']

[V]   For as R. Yudan said in the name of R. Aha, "The Holy One, blessed be He, His ways are holy, His speech is holy, His throne is holy, the range of His arms is holy. [God is] awesome and majestic in His holiness."

[W]   His ways are holy [as it says,] 'Thy way, O God, is holy' [Ps. 77:13]. His processions are holy [as it says,] 'The processions of my God, my king, into the holy' [Ps. 68:24]. His throne is holy [as it says,] 'God sits on his holy throne' [Ps. 47:9]. His speech is holy [as it says,] 'God speaks in his holiness' [Ps. 108:7]. His arm's range is holy [as it says,] 'The Lord has bared his holy arm' [Isa. 52:10]. God is awesome and majestic in his holiness [as it says,] 'Who is like thee, majestic in holiness, awesome in glorious deeds' [Exod. 15:11].

[X]   [The heretics] returned and asked him [Simlai], "What is this which is written, 'For what great nation is there that has a God so near [plural form of the adjective] to it'" [Deut. 4:7]?

[Y]   He said to them, "It does not say, 'Whenever we call upon them.' But it says, 'Whenever we call upon him' [ibid.]."

[Z]   His students said to him, "Master, you deflected their question with a straw. How will you answer us?"

[AA]   He said to them, "[The plural form of 'near' is used because God] is near to us in many different respects."

[VII.A]   As R. Pinhas said in the name of R. Judah b. Simon, "An idol appears to be nearby, but it is really distant. What is the basis [in Scripture for this statement]? 'They lift it upon their shoulders, they carry it, [they set it in its place, and it stands there; it cannot move from its place. If one cries to it, it does not answer or save him from his trouble]' [Isa. 46:7]. In the end, his god is there with him in his house, and he may cry out to it until he dies, but it cannot hear him and cannot save him from his trouble.

[B]   "But the Holy One, Blessed be He, appears to be distant yet nothing is closer than he."

[C]   As Levi said, "From the earth to the firmament is [equivalent to the distance one may travel in] a journey of five hundred years. And [the distance] from one firmament to the next firmament is [equivalent to the distance one may travel in] a journey of five hundred years. And the width of the darkness of the firmament is [equivalent to the distance one may travel in] a journey of five hundred years. And it is the same for each of the [seven] firmaments."

[D]   And R. Berekhiah and R. Helbo said in the name of R. Abba Semuqah, "Even the hoofs of the beasts [of heaven] are [equivalent to the distance one may travel in] a journey of 515 years. Whence [was this taught? From the verse, 'And their legs were] straight' [Ezek. 1:7] [the numerical value of the Hebrew word for straight—yšrh is 515]."

[E]   See how high the Holy One, blessed be He, is above his world. Yet a person can enter a synagogue, stand behind a pillar, and pray in an undertone, and the Holy One, blessed be He, hears his prayers. As it says, "Hannah was speaking in her heart; only her lips moved, and her voice was not heard" [1 Sam. 1:13]. Yet the Holy One, blessed be He, heard her prayer.

[F]   And so too [does God listen to] all his creatures. As it says, "A prayer of one afflicted, when he is faint [and pours out his complaint before the Lord . . . . Incline thy ear to me]" [Ps. 102:1–2]. [One who prays to God] is like a person who speaks into his fellow's ear and he hears him. And is it possible that a God could be closer to his creatures than this? For he is so close to his creatures [when they pray] it is as if they speak directly into his ear.

[VIII.A]   Regarding this [relationship between God and his people,]
           R. Yudan in the name of R. Yitzhak gave four discourses [in the
           form of parables]:

[B]   [1] A person had a human patron. [One day] they came and told
       him [the patron], "A member of your household has been
       arrested."

[C]   He said to them, "Let me take his place."

[D]   They said to him, "Lo, he is already going out to trial."

[E]   He said to them, "Let me take his place."

[F]   They said to him, "Lo, he is going to be hanged."

[G]   Now where is he and where is his patron [when ultimately he
       needs him]?

[H]   But the Holy One, blessed be He, [will save his subjects, just as
       he] saved Moses from [execution by] the sword of Pharaoh.

[I]   This is in accord with what is written, "He delivered me from
       the sword of Pharaoh" [Exod. 18:4].

[J]   Said R. Yannai, "It is written, 'Moses fled from Pharaoh' [Exod.
       2:15]. Is it possible for a person to flee from the government?
       [No.] But when Pharaoh arrested Moses, he ordered that they de-
       capitate him. But [when they tried to do so,] the sword bounced
       off Moses' neck and broke.

[K]   "This accords with what is written, 'Your neck is like an ivory
       tower' [Song of Sol. 7:4]. This refers to Moses' neck."

[L]   Rabbi said, R. Abyatar [said], "Moreover, the sword bounced off
       Moses' neck, and it fell on Quaestionarius' [the executioner's]
       neck and killed him. This accords with what is written, 'He de-
       livered me from the sword of Pharaoh' [Exod. 18:4]. He deliv-
       ered me, and the executioner was killed."

[M]   R. Berekhiah recited concerning [the story of this incident]
       the verse, "The ransom of the righteous is the wicked" [Prov.
       21:18].

[N]   R. Abun recited, "The righteous is delivered from trouble; and
       the wicked gets into it instead" [Prov. 11:8].

[O]   Taught Bar Qappara, "An angel came down, and took Moses'
       appearance. And they arrested the angel, and Moses escaped."

[P] Said R. Joshua b. Levi, "When Moses fled from Pharaoh, all his people became either dumb, deaf, or blind. He said to the mute ones, 'Where is Moses?' And they could not speak. He asked the deaf ones, and they could not hear. He asked the blind ones, and they could not see.

[Q] "This accords with what the Holy One, blessed be He, said to Moses [when Moses was afraid to go before Pharaoh], 'Who has made a man's mouth? Who makes him dumb, or deaf, or seeing, or blind? Is it not I, the Lord?' [Exod. 4:11].

[R] "[God told Moses,] 'I saved you there [when you fled from Pharaoh]. Shall I not stand up for you now [when you go before Pharaoh to bring down the plagues on Egypt]?'

[S] "In this regard [the verse says], 'For what great nation is there that has a god so near to it as the Lord our God is to us, whenever we call upon him'" [Deut. 4:7].

[T] R. Yudan in the name of R. Yitzhak gave another discourse [in the form of a parable.] [2] A person had a human patron. [One day] they came and told the patron, "A member of your household has been arrested."

[U] He said, "Let me take his place."

[V] They said to him, "Lo, he is already going out to trial."

[W] He said to them, "Let me take his place."

[X] They said to him, "Lo, he is going to be thrown into the water [to be executed]."

[Y] Now where is he and where is his patron?

[Z] But the Holy One, blessed be He, [saves his subjects, just as he] saved Jonah from the belly of the fish. Lo, it says, "And the Lord spoke to the fish, and it vomited out Jonah upon dry land" [Jon. 2:10].

[AA] R. Yudan in the name of R. Yitzhak gave another discourse [in the form of a parable.] [3] A person had a human patron. [One day] they came and told the patron, "A member of your household has been arrested."

[BB] He said to them, "Let me take his place."

[CC] They said to him, "He is going out to trial."

[DD]   He said to them, "Let me take his place."

[EE]   They said to him, "Lo, he is going to be thrown into the fire [to be executed]."

[FF]   Now where is he and where is his patron?

[GG]   But the Holy One, blessed be He, is not like that. He [saves his subjects, just as he] saved Hananiah, Mishael, and Azariah [Shadrach, Meshach, and Abednego] from the fiery furnace.

[HH]   In this regard [it says], "Nebuchadnezzar said, 'Blessed be the God of Shadrach, Meshach, and Abednego, [who has sent his angel and delivered his servants, who trusted in him]'" [Dan. 3:28].

[II]   R. Yudan in the name of R. Yitzhak gave another discourse [in the form of a parable.] [4] A person had a human patron. [One day they came and told the patron, "A member of your household has been arrested."

[JJ]   He said to them, "Let me take his place."

[KK]   They said to him, "He is going out to trial."

[LL]   He said to them, "Let me take his place."

[MM]   They said to him, "He is to be thrown to the beasts [to be executed]."

[NN]   [Now where is he and where is his patron?]

[OO]   But the Holy One, blessed be He, [saves his subjects, just as he] saved Daniel from the lions' den.

[PP]   In this regard [it says], "My God sent his angels and shut the lions' mouths, and they have not hurt me" [Dan. 6:22].

[QQ]   R. Yudan [gave another discourse in addition to the four previous ones in the form of a parable] in his own name: A man has a human patron. When this man faces trouble, he does not suddenly burst in [on his patron to ask for help]. Rather he comes and stands at his patron's gate and calls to his patron's servant or some member of his household. And he [the servant] in turn informs the patron, "So and so is standing at the gate of your courtyard. Do you wish me to let him enter, or shall I let him stand outside?"

[RR]   But the Holy One, blessed be He, is not like that. [God says,]

"If a person faces trouble, he should not cry out to the angels Michael or Gabriel. But he should cry out to me, and I will immediately answer him."

[SS]   In this regard [it says], "All who call upon the name of the Lord shall be delivered" [Joel 2:32 RSV].

[TT]   Said R. Pinhas, "This incident occurred to Rab."

[UU]   He was coming up from the hot spring of Tiberias. He met some Romans. They asked him, "Who are you?"

[VV]   He said to them, "I am a member of [the governor] Severus' [entourage]." They let him pass.

[WW]   That night they came to [the governor] and said to him, "How much longer will you put up with these Jews?"

[XX]   He said to them, "What do you mean?"

[YY]   They said to him, "We encountered a person. He said he was a Jew. We asked him who he was. And he said he was from Severus' [entourage]."

[ZZ]   He [the governor] said to them, "What did you do for him?"

[AAA]   They said to him, "Is it not enough that we let him alone?"

[BBB]   He said to them, "You acted very well."

[CCC]   [The lesson of this story is:] One who relies on the protection of mere flesh and blood may be saved. How much more will one who relies on the protection of the Holy One, blessed be He, [be saved from harm].

[DDD]   In this regard [it says,] "All who call upon the name of the Lord shall be delivered" [ibid.].

[EEE]   Said R. Alexander, "This incident occurred concerning an archon named Alexandrus."

[FFF]   He was presiding over the trial of a thief. He [the judge] asked [the defendant], "What is your name?"

[GGG]   [He responded,] "Alexandrus."

[HHH]   He said to him, "Alexandrus [you are free to go]. Be off to Alexandria."

[III]   [The lesson is] if a man is saved because he invokes the name of a mere human judge, all the more will a person be saved if he invokes the name of the Holy One, blessed be He.

[JJJ]   In this regard [it says,] "All who call upon the name of the Lord shall be delivered" [ibid.].

[IX.A]   R. Pinhas said [concerning this] two [parables], one in the name of R. Zeira, one in the name of R. Tanhum bar Hanilai.

[B]   R. Pinhas in the name of R. Zeira said, "A person has a human patron. If he bothers his patron, the patron will say, 'Did you ever see a fellow who can bother you so much?'

[C]   "But the Holy One, blessed be He, is not like this. Rather he accepts whatever you burden him with.

[D]   "In this regard it says, 'Cast your burden on the Lord and he will sustain you'" [Ps. 55:22].

[E]   R. Pinhas in the name of R. Tanhum bar Hanilai, "A person has a human patron. If his enemies come and seize him at the gate of his patron's courtyard, before he can cry out, before anyone can come forth [to save him], the enemies' sword will sever his neck and kill him.

[F]   "But God saved Jehoshaphat from the sword of the Syrians. As it is written, 'And Jehoshaphat cried out and the Lord helped him. God drew them away from him' [2 Chron. 18:31]. The verse teaches us that just as they were about to decapitate him, 'God drew them away from him.'"

[X.A]   R. Zeira, son of R. Abahu, and R. Abahu in the name of R. Eleazar, "'Happy is he whose help is the God of Jacob, whose hope is the Lord his God.' What follows that verse? 'He made heaven and earth, [the sea and all that is in them, who keeps faith forever]' [Ps. 146:5–6].

[B]   "[Why are these passages juxtaposed? In accord with this parable.] A person has a patron who is a human king. The king may rule over one province, but not over another. Even [a king] who would rule the whole world would rule only over the dry land, but not over the seas.

[C]   "But the Holy One, Blessed be He, rules over the seas, and rules over the land. He can save one from [the perils of] the waters of the seas, and from [the perils of] the fire on dry land.

[D]   "He saved Moses from the sword of Pharaoh. He saved Jonah from the belly of the whale, Shadrach, Meshach and Abednego from the fiery furnace, and Daniel from the lions' den. In this regard [the verse says], 'He made heaven and earth, the sea and all that is in them.'"

[E]   Said R. Tanhuma: Once a boat load of gentiles was sailing the Mediterranean. There was one Jewish child on the boat. A great storm came upon them in the sea. Each person took his idol in his hand and cried out. But it did not help them.

[F]   Once they saw that their cries were of no avail, they turned to the Jewish child and said, "Child, rise up and call out to your God. For we have heard that he answers you when you cry out to him, and that he is heroic."

[G]   The child immediately rose up and cried out with all his heart. The Holy One, blessed be He, accepted his prayer and quieted the seas.

[H]   When the ship reached dry land [at the port], everyone disembarked to purchase his needed staples. They said to the child, "Don't you wish to buy anything?"

[I]   He said to them, "What do you want of me? I am just a poor traveller."

[J]   They said to him, "You are just a poor traveller? They are the poor travellers. Some of them are here, and their idols are in Babylonia. Some of them are here, and their idols are in Rome. Some of them are here and their idols are with them, but they do them no good. But wherever you go, your God is with you."

[K]   In this regard [the verse says], "All who call upon the name of the Lord shall be delivered" [Joel 2:32 RSV].

[XI.A]   Said R. Simeon b. Laqish, "A person has a relative. If [the relative] is rich, he admits [that he is his relative]. And if [the relative] is poor, he denies [that he is his relative]. But not so the Holy One, blessed be He. Even when the Jews are down at their lowest depths, God calls them, 'My brethren and companions.' And what is the Scriptural basis [for this statement]? 'For my brethren and companions' sake [I will say, 'Peace be with you']'"
[Ps. 122:8].

[B]   R. Abun and R. Aha and R. Simeon b. Laqish, "A person has a relative. If [his relative] is [a literate person], a philosopher, he says of him that he is a relative. But the Holy One, blessed be He, calls all of Israel his relatives. In this regard [the verse says], 'He has raised up a horn for his people; [praise for all his saints, for the people of Israel who are near to him [literally: relatives], Praise the Lord'" [Ps. 148:14]! [All people are his kin.]

[XII.A] *[One who sees] a place from which idolatry was uprooted says, "Blessed [art Thou, O Lord, our God, King of the Universe,] who uprooted idolatry from our land"* [M. 9:1]. The Mishnah [speaks of a time when idolatry] was uprooted from every place in the Land of Israel. But if it was uprooted only from one location, one says [a different blessing,] "Blessed [art Thou, O Lord, our God, King of the Universe,] who uprooted idolatry from this place."

[B] If idolatry was uprooted from one location and established in another, when one comes to the place to which it was located, he says, "Blessed [art Thou, O Lord, our God, King of the Universe,] who is patient." And when one comes to the place from which it was uprooted, he says, "Blessed [art Thou, O Lord, our God, King of the Universe,] who uprooted idolatry from this place.

[C] **"May it be thy will, Lord our God, God of our fathers, that just as you uprooted it from this place, so shall you uproot it from all other places. And you shall return the hearts of those who worship it, to worship thee,** and no more shall there be found [in the Land] any worshipper of idolatry" [Y.'s version of parts of T. 6:2].

[D] **[Outside of the Land of Israel one need not say this prayer because the majority of the inhabitants are gentiles.] It was taught: R. Simeon b. Gamaliel says, "Even outside the Land of Israel one must say this [blessing when he comes to the place from which idolatry has been removed]"** [T. 6:2, according to the reading of E.P.].

[E] Said R. Yohanan, "But he who is joined [with all the living has hope]' [Qoh. 9:4]. It is written *ybhr* [literally, will be selected], and it is read *yhbr*—joined with. [If they so choose, the gentiles will be joined with Israel].

[F] "'[But he who is joined] with all the living has hope' [ibid.]. As long as a person lives, there is hope for him [because he can repent and be saved]. Once he dies, his hope is lost. What is the basis [in Scripture for this statement]? 'When a wicked man dies, his hope is lost.'"

[XIII.A]   It was taught: **R. Judah says, "A person must recite three blessings each day: 'Blessed [art Thou, O Lord, our God, King of the Universe,] who did not make me a gentile'; 'Blessed [art Thou, O Lord, our God, King of the Universe,] who did not make me a boor'; 'Blessed [art Thou, O Lord, our God, King of the Universe,] who did not make me a woman.'**

[B]   **"[What is the basis for these blessings?] 'Blessed [art Thou, O Lord, our God, King of the Universe,] who did not make me a gentile,' because the gentiles are of no matter. [As it says,] 'All the nations are as nothing before him' [Isa. 40:17].**

[C]   **"'Blessed [art Thou, O Lord, our God, King of the Universe,] who did not make a boor,' for, *a boor does not fear sin* [M. Abot 2:5].**

[D]   **"'Blessed [art Thou, O Lord, our God, King of the Universe,] who did not make me a woman,' for, women are not obligated to perform the commandments"** [T. 6:18].

[XIV.A]   Said R. Aha, "'But he who is joined with all the living has hope' [Qoh. 9:4]. Even those [soldiers] who stretched forth their hands [to destroy] the Sanctuary have hope. [In what is their hope?] They cannot be brought near [to enter paradise] because they have already stretched forth their hands [to destroy] the Sanctuary. They cannot be driven away [to damnation], because they have repented. [They are not judged and cannot be condemned.] Concerning such persons it is said, '[They shall] sleep a perpetual sleep and not wake, says the Lord' [Jer. 51:39]. [They remain in a state of limbo forever.]"

[B]   The rabbis of Caesarea said [in dispute with R. Aha], "The small [armies] of the gentiles and the other armies of Nebuchadnezzar [who did not directly stretch forth their hands to destroy the Temple], these [are the ones who] will not live [in eternal paradise] but will not be judged [for eternal damnation]. Concerning these persons the verse says, '[They shall] sleep a perpetual sleep' [ibid.]."

[XV.A]   One who passes before a house of idolatry says, "The Lord tears down the house of the proud" [Prov. 15:25].

[B]   R. Yose b. R. Bun in the name of R. Levi, "If one saw [idolaters] offering sacrifices to an idol, he says, 'Whoever sacrifices to any god, save the Lord only, shall be utterly destroyed'" [Exod. 23:20].

[XVI.A] **One who sees a black-, a red-, or a white-skinned person, or a hunchback, or a midget says, "Blessed [art Thou, O Lord, our God, King of the Universe,] who changes the creatures."**

[B]   **[One who sees an] amputee, or the lame, a blind person, or a person afflicted with boils says, "Blessed [art Thou, O Lord, our God, King of the Universe,] the true judge." [T. 6:3].**

[C]   This [second] teaching applies [to those who see handicapped individuals who were born] normal and later were handicapped [—became crippled, blinded or afflicted]. But if one sees a person who was born that way [handicapped] he says, "Blessed [art Thou, O Lord, our God, King of the Universe,] who changes the creatures."

[D]   **One who sees handsome people or beautiful trees says, "Blessed [art Thou, O Lord, our God, King of the Universe,] who created handsome creatures in his world"** [T. 6:4].

[E]   Once R. Gamaliel saw a beautiful gentile woman and recited a blessing on her account.

[F]   But did not R. Zeira in the name of R. Yose bar Haninah, R. Ba, R. Hiyya in the name of R. Yohanan say, "You shall not make marriages [thnm] with them' [Deut. 7:3]. [This means] you shall not attribute beauty [hn] to them!" [A play on the words.]

[G]   What did [R. Gamaliel] say? He did not exclaim, 'Abascanta, may no harm befall you [for you are beautiful]!" But he merely noted that God created beautiful creatures in the world. For even if he saw a beautiful camel, horse, or donkey, he would say, "Blessed [art Thou, O Lord, our God, King of the Universe,] who created beautiful creatures."

[H]   Was it R. Gamaliel's practice to gaze at women? It must have been [that he encountered her along] a winding street, like a narrow passage, and he could not avoid [passing close by and] looking at her.

[XVII.A] When one hears the cock crow, he says, "Blessed [art Thou, O Lord, our God, King of the Universe,] who knows the secrets."

[This accords with the verse,] "Who has put wisdom in the clouds, or given understanding to the cock" [Job 38:36].

[B]   Said R. Levi, "In Arabia they call the goat, *yobla* [in accord with the verse,] 'And when they make a long blast with the ram's horn [*krn hywbl*]' [Josh. 6:5].

[C]   "In Africa they call the menstruating woman a *galmuda* [in accord with the verse,] 'I was bereaved and barren [*glmwdh*]' [Isa. 49:21].

[D]   "And in Rome they call the cock a *skwy* [in accord with the verse,] 'Who has given understanding to the cock [*skwy*].'"

[XVIII.A]   **One who sees a crowd says, "Blessed [art Thou, O Lord, our God, King of the Universe,] who knows the secrets. Just as their faces are different one from the other, so are their opinions different one from the other."**

[B]   **When Ben Zoma saw crowds in Jerusalem [T.: on the Temple Mount] he would say, "Blessed is he who created all these people to serve me. How hard did Adam have to toil, before eating even a morsel. He first plowed, seeded, weeded, irrigated, reaped, made sheaves, threshed, winnowed, separated, grinded, sifted, kneaded, baked, and only then could he eat a morsel. But I arise in the morning and find all this prepared before me.**

[C]   **"See how hard Adam toiled before he had a shirt to wear. He sheared, bleached, separated, dyed, spun, wove, washed, sewed, and only then did he have a shirt to wear. But I arise in the morning and find all this prepared for me. How many craftsmen must rise early and retire late [to prepare my food and clothing]. And I arise in the morning and find all this before me."**

[D]   **And so Ben Zoma would say, "What does an ungrateful guest say? 'What did I take from this householder to eat or drink? I ate just one slice of his bread and drank just one cup of his wine. He expended his energies [to prepare the meal] only on behalf of his wife and children.'**

[E]   **"But the grateful guest says, 'Blessed be this householder. May this householder be remembered for good. How much wine did he bring before me! How many slices [of bread, meat, and cake] did he bring before me! How much energy**

did he expend on my behalf. He expended his energies only for me. And so he says, 'Remember to extol his work, of which men have sung' [Job 36:24]" [T. 6:2].

Unit **I** deals directly with Mishnah's main issue, reciting blessings at sacred places or shrines. The Talmud clarifies the type of shrine included in Mishnah's rule. Must it be a national holy place, or does one recite a blessing even at a local or personal shrine? Unit **II** expands upon the rules regarding the recitation of blessings at certain famous places with a list of blessings one recites upon travelling to Babylonia and viewing its sights along the way.

Units **III** and **IV** turn to another issue, the question of the formula of blessings. Unit **III** specifies that one must include an invocation of God's kingdom in each blessing, and that one must use the second person address. Unit **IV** adds several general traditions about the value of formalized liturgy. These two sections lead up to the citation of Tosefta in unit **V**, rules regarding proper and improper invocations in liturgical blessings.

The reference to heresy at the close of unit **V**, allows the Talmud to introduce as a lengthy digression at unit **VI**, a substantial unit concerning the debate between Simlai and the heretics. This consists of five heretical questions based on verses. Each seems to imply that there exists a plurality of divinities. Simlai gives two levels of answers to each challenge.

Once the subject of heresy is opened, the Talmud sees fit to discuss at unit **VII** the overall negative aspects of idolatry. Unit **VIII** complements unit **VII** by spelling out through parables the value of faith in God, who will protect his subjects. At the end, unit **VIII** adds several related stories which use the same verse as a prooftext. Unit **IX** then adds two more parables in the name of Pinhas, who appears in the section above.

Unit **X** continues the extended homiletical digression with additional stories of God's saving power. Unit **XI** elaborates on the idea that God treats his people better than a person treats his relatives.

At unit **XII**, the Talmud returns at last to comment on the second part of our Mishnah, to explain it, and to cite the relevant Tosefta-passages. Unit **XIII** cites additional Tosefta materials.

Unit **XIV** introduces a tangential tradition, linked to the preceding by virtue of its use of the verse cited above in **XII.D**.

Unit **XV** adds a tradition relevant to M., concerning the blessing to recite at a place of idolatry. At unit **XVI** the Talmud cites more related materials from Tosefta and comments upon them. The curious story about Gamaliel, lightens the overall tone of the present material, after the extended discussion above of heresy and idolatry and faith.

In line with the context of the Talmud's interest, unit **XVII** adds another rule concerning a blessing for the occasion of hearing a cock crow. Finally, unit **XVIII** concludes with the citation of Ben Zoma's grateful homily found in the passage from Tosefta.

9:2

[A]   *For [seeing] meteors, and for earth tremors, and for lightning, and for thunder, and for the winds, one recites, "Blessed [art Thou, O Lord, our God, King of the Universe,] whose power fills the world."*

[B]   *For [seeing] the mountains, and for the hills, and for the seas, and for the rivers, and for the deserts, one recites, "Blessed [art Thou, O Lord, our God, King of the Universe,] the maker of [all of] creation."*

[C]   *R. Judah says, "One who sees the Mediterranean Sea recites, 'Blessed [art Thou, O Lord, our God, King of the Universe,] who made the Mediterranean Sea.'*

[D]   *"[He only recites this blessing] when he sees it [the sea] at intervals."*

[E]   *For the rains, and for good tidings, one recites, "Blessed [art Thou, O Lord, our God, King of the Universe,] who is good and does good."*

[F]   *And for bad tidings one recites, "Blessed [art Thou, O Lord, our God, King of the Universe,] true judge."*

[I.A]   Taught Bar Qappara, "They sound the shofar [and fast and pray] on account of [the fear of the destructive power of] earth tremors."

[II.A]   Samuel said, "The world would be destroyed if a comet passed through the constellation of Orion."

[B]   Someone raised an objection to Samuel's teaching, "I witnessed a comet pass through [the constellation of Orion]."

[C]   He said to him, "It is impossible [for that to occur]. It must have passed above it, or below it."

[D]   Samuel said, "I know the 'byways' of the heavens as well as I know the byways of my city Nehardea. But I do not know about [the path of] this comet."

[E]   And did Samuel ascend to explore the heavens [to learn its byways? No, he learned them by study and observation] in accord with the verse, "Who can number the clouds by wisdom?" [Job 38:37].

[III.A]   Elijah [the prophet] of blessed memory asked R. Nehorai, "Why do earthquakes occur?" He said to him, "On account of the sins of [those who do not separate] heave-offerings and tithes [from their produce]."

[B]   One verse says, "[God protects the Land of Israel], the eyes of the Lord your God are always upon it" [Deut. 11:12]. And a second verse says, "[God] who looks upon the earth and it trembles, who touches the mountains and they smoke" [Ps. 104:32].

[C]   How can one reconcile these two verses? When Israel obeys God's will and properly separates tithes, then "the eyes of the Lord your God are always upon it, from the beginning of the year to the end of the year" [Deut. 11:12], and the Land cannot be damaged. But when Israel does not obey God's will, and does not properly separate tithes [from the produce of the earth], then he "looks upon the earth and it trembles" [Ps. 104:32].

[D]   [Elijah] said to him [Nehorai], "My son, on your life, what you say [about earthquakes] does make sense. But this is the main [reason that there are earthquakes]. When the Holy One, blessed be He, looks down on the theaters and circuses that sit secure, serene, and peaceful [in Israel], and [he looks down] on the ruins of the Temple, he shakes the world to destroy it [and the earth trembles]. In this regard [the verse says], 'The Lord will roar from on high, and from his holy habitation utter his voice' [Jer. 25:30]. [It means he will roar] on account of [the destruction of] his Temple."

[E]   Said R. Aha, "[The earth quakes] on account of the sin of homosexual acts. God said, 'You made your genitals throb in an unnatural act. By your life, I shall shake the earth on account of [the act of] this person.'"

[F]   And the sages said, "[The earth quivers] on account of disputes. [As it says, 'And the valley of my mountains shall be stopped up, for the valley of the mountains shall touch the side of it;] and you shall flee as you fled from the earthquake in the days of Uzziah king of Judah'" [Zech. 14:5]. [Uzziah contested the authority of the priesthood and attempted to enter the Temple and offer an incense offering, cf. 2 Chron. 26:16–23. This dispute caused an earthquake.]

[G]   Said R. Samuel, "An earthquake is a sign of the cessation of kingship. As it says, 'The land trembles and writhes in pain.' On what account? 'For the Lord's purposes against Babylon stand, to make the land of Babylon a desolation, without inhabitant'" [Jer. 51:29].

[IV.A]   Elijah of blessed memory asked R. Nehorai, "Why did God create insects and creeping things in his world?"

[B]   He said to him, "They were created to serve a need. When God's creatures sin, he looks upon them and says, 'Lo, I sustain those creatures that serve no [useful] purpose, all the more must I sustain those creatures that serve some [useful] purpose [even though they sin].'"

[C]   He [Elijah] said to him, "They serve other useful purposes: flies [may be crushed and used as ointment] for a wasp's sting; bed bugs [may be prepared in a potion to remove] a leech; lizards [may be made into an ointment] for sores; snails [may be used to treat] skin eruptions; spiders [may be used in an ointment to treat] a scorpion's bite."

[V.A]   Piska. *[For seeing meteors, and for earth tremors,] and for lightning, [and for thunder, and for the winds, one recites, "Blessed art Thou, O Lord, our God, King of the Universe, whose power fills the world"]* [M. 9:2]. R. Jeremiah and R. Zeira in the name of R. Hasdai, "It is sufficient [if one recites this blessing] once during the day [even if the lightning continues throughout the day]."

[B]   Said R. Yose, "How do we explain [this previous view]? In a case where the storm continues steadily, it is sufficient that he recites the blessing once during the day. But if the storm intermittently ceases, he must recite the blessing each time [there is new lightning or thunder]."

[C]   Support for R. Yose's view comes from the following: **One who was sitting the whole day in a spice dealer's shop recites the blessing [for the fragrance of the spices] only once. One who was going in and out [of the shop throughout the day] recites the blessing each time [he enters]** [T. 5:32].

[D]   R. Aha and R. Hanina came and said in the name of R. Yose, "If the storm continues steadily, it is sufficient that he recite the blessing once during the day. If the storm intermittently ceases he must recite the blessing each time [there is new lightning or thunder]."

[VI.A]   If one were sitting in an outhouse or lavatory [where one is not permitted to recite a blessing, and he hears thunder], if he can go outside and recite the blessing right away [upon hearing the thunder], he must go out. But if not, he need not go out [for the purpose of reciting the blessing].

[B]   R. Jeremiah posed the question, "If one were sitting naked in his house, what should he do [upon hearing thunder]? Should he imagine the house is his garment and stick his head out the window and recite the blessing?

[C]   "If one were sitting naked in a tower, what should he do? Should he imagine the tower is his garment and stick his head out the window, and recite the blessing?" [No answer is given.]

[VII.A]   Piska. *For the winds he recites, "Blessed [art Thou, O Lord, our God, King of the Universe,] whose power fills the world"* [M. 9:2]. The Mishnah speaks of strong winds. But for gentle winds one recites, "Blessed [art Thou, O Lord, our God, King of the Universe,] who made all creation."

[VIII.A]   Said R. Joshua b. Hananiah, "When a wind comes upon the earth, the Holy one, blessed be He, breaks it up on the mountains, and weakens it on the hills and says to it, 'Make sure you do not damage my creations.'"

[B]   What is the basis [in Scripture for this statement]? "For from me proceeds the spirit [wind]" (Isa. 57:16). He weakens it, as it says, "When my spirit [wind] is faint" (Ps. 142:3).

[C]   And why does he do all this [i.e., weaken the winds]?

[D] R. Huna in the name of R. Aha, "I have made the breath [souls] of life [conclusion of Isa. 57:16]—[I weakened the winds] on behalf of [the safety of] those souls which I have made."

[E] Said R. Huna, "In three instances the winds went forth without bounds and sought to destroy the entire world. Once in the time of Jonah, once in the time of Elijah, and once in the time of Job.

[F] "In the time of Jonah [as it says], 'But the Lord hurled a great wind upon the sea' (Jon. 1:4).

[G] "In the time of Job [as it says], 'And behold a great wind came across the wilderness' (Job 1:19).

[H] "Whence in the time of Elijah? 'And behold, the Lord passed by, and a great and strong wind rent the mountains'" (1 Kings 19:11).

[I] Said R. Yudan bar Shalom, "One can argue that the wind [in the time] of Job sought to destroy only him, and the wind [in the time of Jonah] sought to destroy only him. Only the wind in Elijah's time went forth to destroy the entire cosmos. [As it says,] 'And behold the Lord passed by and a great and strong wind rent the mountains, and broke in pieces the rocks before the Lord, . . . but the Lord was not in the wind; and after the wind an earthquake; but the Lord was not in the earthquake; and after the earthquake a fire; but the Lord was not in the fire'" (1 Kings 19:11–12).

[IX.A] Piska: *R. Judah says, "One who sees the Mediterranean Sea recites, 'Blessed [art Thou, O Lord, our God, King of the Universe,] who made the Mediterranean Sea.'"*

[B] *[He only recites this blessing] when he sees it [the sea] at intervals [M. 9:2]. How long is an interval? Thirty days.*

[X.A] Simeon Qamatraya asked R. Hiyya bar Ba, "Because I am a donkey driver and I go to Jerusalem [regularly] throughout the year [to deliver goods], must I rend my garments [each time I go there as a sign of mourning over the destruction of the Temple]?"

[B] He said to him, "If [you return] within thirty days [to Jerusalem], you need not rend your garments. [If you return] after thirty days, then you must rend your garments."

[XI.A] R. Huna, Simeon Qamatraya in the name of R. Samuel bar Nahman, "'And Jonathan the son of Gershom, son of Menasseh [alt. reading in Judges: Moses], and his sons were priests to the tribe of the Danites until the day of captivity of the Land' (Judg. 18 : 30). The letter *nun* [in the name *mnšh*] is suspended [above the other letters]. [This teaches that] if he was worthy, [they called him] Son of Moses [*mšh*, without the *nun*]. But if not, [they called him] Son of Menasseh [who was evil, cf. 2 Kings 21]."

[B]   The associates posed the following question to R. Samuel bar Nahman, "If he [Jonathan] were a priest to a foreign god, why was he granted longevity? [The verse says, "His sons were priests . . . until the day of the captivity of the Land. So they set up Micah's graven image which he made, as long as the house of God was at Shiloh" (Judg. 18 : 30–31).]

[C]   He said to them, "[He was granted longevity] because he acted maliciously toward his idol."

[D]   How did he act maliciously toward his idol? A person would come to him to make an offering to the idol of a bull, a goat, or a ram, and would say to him, "May this be recompense for me."

[E]   He [Jonathan] would say to the person, "What good will this do for you? [This idol] neither sees, nor hears, nor eats, nor drinks, nor does good, nor does evil, nor speaks."

[F]   The person would say to him, "By your life! Then what shall I do [instead]?"

[G]   And Jonathan would say to him, "Go, make and bring to me a container of fine flour, and prepare with it ten eggs, and bring it to me. And he [the idol] shall eat from all that you bring, and I shall seek recompense for you from him." As soon as the person [brought all this and] left, Jonathan ate the food.

[H]   One time a scoundrel came before him [to offer a sacrifice to the idol], and Jonathan told him the same thing ["What good will this do for you, etc."]. He said to Jonathan, "If it is of no use [to offer a sacrifice to the idol] then what are you doing here [serving as its priest]?" He said to him, "This is my livelihood."

[I]   When David became king, he sent for and brought [Jonathan] before him. He said to him, "You are the grandson of that righteous man [Moses]. How can you worship a foreign god?"

[J]   He said to him, "I have received this tradition from my grandfather's house. 'It is better to sell yourself into service of a foreign god than to go begging for sustenance.'"

[K]   [David] said to him, "God forbid. He [your grandfather] never said such a thing! [You have corrupted the tradition and erred.] Rather he said, 'It is better to sell yourself into service that is foreign to you ['*bwdh šhy' zrh lk* and not '*bwdh zrh,*] than to go begging.'"

[L]   Since David saw how much [Jonathan] loved money, what did he do? He made him his treasurer.

[M]   In this regard [the verse says], "And Shebuel the son of Gershom, son of Moses, was chief officer in charge of the treasuries" (1 Chron. 26:24). [Jonathan was called] Shebuel because he returned [*šb*] to serve God ['*l*] with all his heart and with all his might. "He was the chief officer in charge of the treasuries," that is, David appointed him [Jonathan] to be his treasurer.

[N]   They raised an objection to R. Samuel bar Nahman, "Lo, it is written, '[Jonathan] and his sons were priests to the tribe of the Danites until the day of the captivity of the Land' (Judg. 18:30). [How can you say that David appointed him treasurer?]"

[O]   He said to them, "When David died, Solomon succeeded him and replaced his officers. And [Jonathan] went back to his old corrupt ways [and served as a priest of idolatry for the Danites].

[P]   In this regard [the verse says, 'Now there dwelt an old prophet in Bethel' (1 Kings 13:11). They say that [idolater in Jereboam's kingdom] was he, [Jonathan the Danite]."

[XII.A]   One who sees the sun in its full cycle, [once in twenty-eight years] or the moon in its full cycle, or the clear firmament recites the blessing, "Blessed [art Thou, O Lord, our God, King of the Universe,] who made creation." (Cf. T. 6:6.)

[B]   Said R. Huna, "This refers only [to one who sees the clear firmament] during the rainy season and only after three [consecutive rainy] days." In this regard [the verse says,] "And now men cannot look on the light [when it is bright in the skies, when the wind has passed and cleared them. Out of the north comes golden splendor; God is clothed with terrible majesty]" (Job 37:21–22).

[C]   One who sees the new moon recites, "Blessed [art Thou, O Lord, our God, King of the Universe,] who renews the months." For how long [during the first phase of the moon may one recite this blessing]?

[D]   R. Jacob bar Aha in the name of R. Yose, "During the first quarter."

[E]   E. Aha and R. Hanina in the name of R. Yose, "Until the crescent fills. [Until the half moon appears]."

[F]   The rabbis from Caesarea said, "Until fourteen days pass."

[G]   Said R. Yose b. R. Bun, "Very well. [E and F say the same thing.] The crescent does not fill up until fourteen days pass. So for the first fourteen days [one who sees the moon] must recite the blessing."

[XIII.A]   In the Prayer [of the Additional Service for the new moon] R. Yose bar Nehorai said, "[You conclude the middle blessing:] 'Who sanctifies Israel and renews the months.'"

[B]   R. Hiyya bar Ashi said, "[You conclude it:] 'Who sanctifies Israel and the new moons.'"

[C]   Samuel said, "One must recite [on the new moon the paragraph recited on the festivals:] 'O Lord our God, bestow upon us the blessing of thy holy festivals, etc.'."

[D]   Rab said, "One must mention the season [as on the festival: 'Thou hast given us in love, O Lord our God, appointed times for gladness, festivals and seasons for joy this day of the new moon, etc.']."

[E]   Taught R. Hoshaiah, "And let them be for signs and for seasons and for days and for years" (Gen. 1:14). [This verse is brought to support A and C, that one recites a blessing when one sees the sun in its cycle ("years") and the new moon ("seasons")—P.M.]

[XIV.A]   One who passes between graves [in a cemetery], what does he recite? "Blessed [art Thou, O Lord, our God, King of the Universe,] who resurrects the dead." (Cf. T. 6:6.)

[B]   R. Hiyya in the name of R. Yohanan [says he recites], "Blessed [art Thou, O Lord, our God, King of the Universe,] who is true to his word to resurrect the dead."

[C]   R. Hiyya in the name of R. Yohanan [says he recites], "He who knows your numbers, He shall awaken you, He shall remove the dust from your eyes. Blessed [art Thou, O Lord, our God, King of the Universe,] who resurrects the dead."

[D]   R. Eliezer in the name of R. Hanina [says he recites], "He who created you with justice, and sustained you with justice, and removed you [from the world] with justice, and will resurrect you with justice; He who knows your numbers, He shall remove the dust from your eyes. Blessed [art Thou, O Lord, our God, King of the Universe,] who resurrects the dead.''

[E]   This is the case [that one recites this blessing only if he passes among the graves of] the Israelite dead. But concerning [one who passes among the graves of] the gentile dead, he says, ''Your mother shall be utterly shamed, and she who bore you shall be disgraced. Lo, she shall be the last of the nations, a wilderness dry and desert'' (Jer. 50:12).

[XV.A]   **One who sees a rainbow in the sky recites, ''Blessed [art Thou, O Lord, our God, King of the Universe,] who remembers the covenant''** [T. 6:5]. R. Hiyya in the name of R. Yohanan, ''Blessed [art Thou, O Lord, our God, King of the Universe,] who is true in his covenant and who remembers his covenant.''

[B]   R. Hezekiah in the name of R. Jeremiah, ''All the days of the life of R. Simeon b. Yohai, not one rainbow was seen in the sky.'' [His merit alone sustained the generation and there was no need for the rainbow as a reminder to God that he would not again bring a destructive flood to the world.]

[XVI.A]   R. Hezekiah in the name of R. Jeremiah, ''If R. Simeon b. Yohai would say, 'Valley, valley. Fill up with gold coins!' It filled up.'' [So great was his power.]

[B]   R. Hezekiah in the name of R. Jeremiah, ''So R. Simeon b. Yohai would say, 'I saw [in a vision] the inhabitants of the world-to-come [heaven] and they will be few! But even if there be just three, my son and I will be among them. And if there be [just] two, my son and I will be those two!'''

[C]   R. Hezekiah in the name of R. Jeremiah, ''So R. Simeon b. Yohai would say, 'Let [the merit of] Abraham come before God [on behalf of all those who lived] from his time to mine. Let my merit come before God [for those who shall live] from my time until the end of all generations. And if [my merit] will not suffice, then combine the merit of Ahiyah the Shilonite [cf. 1 Kings 11:15] with mine, and we shall come before God [on behalf of] the entire nation.'''

[XVII.A]   Why did they see fit to juxtapose [in Mishnah 9:2D–E the rule regarding the blessing one recites for] good tidings and [the rule regarding the blessing one recites] for the rains?

[B]   R. Berekhiah in the name of R. Levi, ''On account of [the juxtaposition of these matters in the verse], 'Like cold water to a

thirsty soul [i.e., like rain], so is good news from a far country'"
(Prov. 25:25).

[C]   How much rain must fall before one is required to recite a
blessing?

[D]   R. Hiyya in the name of R. Yohanan, "At the beginning [of the
season, to require a blessing, enough must fall] so that there is a
flow [of some water to irrigate the ground]. And at the end [of
the season, enough must fall] to completely soak the surface [of
the ground]."

[E]   R. Yannai in the name of R. Ishmael in the name of R. Simeon
b. Laqish, "At the beginning [of the season, enough rain must
fall] so that there is flow; at the end [of the season] enough [rain
must fall]—enough to dissolve the wine-barrel-sealing clay."

[F]   Do you need [the rain to actually] dissolve the clay seal? Rather
[it means enough must fall so that the mud on the ground looks]
like clay that was dissolved [for sealing].

[G]   R. Yose in the name of R. Judah, and R. Yonah in the name of
Samuel, "At the beginning [of the season enough must fall] so
that there is a flow; and at the end [of the season] even a small
amount."

[H]   R. Yosah in the name of R. Zeira, "[All these measures] were
given [to specify the amount of rainfall needed to permit people]
to suspend a fast [that was declared on account of a drought]."

[I]   R. Hezekiah and R. Nahum [Tanhum] and R. Ada and R. Bimi
[R. Ada bar Abimi] were sitting.

[J]   Said R. Tanhum to R. Ada bar Abimi, "Is it not reasonable [that
these amounts specify the minimum rainfall needed before one
may recite] a blessing?"

[K]   He [Ada] said to him, "Yes."

[L]   Said R. Hezekiah to R. Ada bar Abimi, "Is it not reasonable
[that these amounts specify the minimum rainfall needed before
one may] suspend a fast [decreed on account of a drought]?"

[M]   He [Ada] said to him, "Yes."

[N]   [Hezekiah] said to him, "Why did you say yes to him [Tanhum]?"

[O]   He [Ada] said to him, "I answered him [Tanhum] in accord with
my master's view."

[P]   Said R. Mana to R. Hezekiah, "And who is your master?"

[Q]   He said to him, "R. Zeira."

[R]   He said to him, "We have said: R. Yose in the name of R. Zeira, '[The measures specify the minimum rainfall] to suspend a fast.' [How then did you agree with Tanhum that these measures also refer to the minimum rainfall before one must recite a blessing?]" [No answer is given.]

[XVIII.A]   R. Judah bar Ezekiel said, "My father used to recite this blessing over rainfall: 'May your name, our king, be magnified, and sanctified, and blessed, and glorified for each and every drop of rain that you cause to fall for our sake. For you separate each droplet by itself [as it says], 'For he draws up the drops of water, [he distills his mist in the rain]'" (Job 36:27).

[B]   [Draws up, *ygr'*, means that he separates each drop] as it says [in the usage], "And a deduction shall be made [*wngr'*] from your valuation" (Lev. 27:18). [A small amount shall be separated from it.]

[C]   Said R. Yudan, "Moreover, [Ezekiel's prayer suggests that he caused the raindrops to fall by measures [according to the needs of each field]. As it says, 'He meted out the waters by measure'" (Job 28:25).

[D]   R. Yose bar Jacob went to visit R. Yudan of Migdal. When he got there, rain began to fall. And he heard his voice saying [in prayers], "Thousands and ten of thousands of times must we give thanks to Your name, our king, for each and every drop of rain which You cause to fall on our behalf. For You render favor for those who need it."

[E]   He [Yose] said to him [Yudan], "Where did you get [this prayer]?"

[F]   He said to him, "This is the blessing R. Simon recited over rainfall."

[XIX.A]   [Returning to the earlier teaching XVII.C:] And how much rainfall will create "a flow [to soak into the ground to irrigate it]?"

[B]   "Enough [must fall] to fill a vessel three handbreadths deep," the words of R. Meir.

[C]   R. Judah says, "At the beginning of the season [the first two weeks of Heshvan], if one handbreadth [falls in the first rainfall of the season, it will saturate the ground]. In the second [part of the season, the third week of Heshvan], if two handbreadths [fall in the first rainfall of the season, it will saturate the ground because the ground is harder]. In the third [part of the season, the third week of Heshvan and the first week of Kislev], if three handbreadths [fall in the first rainfall of the season, it will saturate the ground because the ground is even harder by that time]."

[D]   It was taught: R. Simeon b. Eleazar says, "For each handbreadth of rain which falls from above, the earth gives forth from below two handbreadths.

[E]   "What is the basis [in Scripture for this statement]? 'Deep calls to deep at the thunder of thy cataracts'" (Ps. 42:7).

[F]   And R. Levi said, "The waters up above are masculine, and the waters down below are feminine."

[G]   What is the basis [in Scripture for this statement]? "[Shower, O heavens from above, and let the skies rain down righteousness;] let the earth open" (Isa. 45:8)—like a woman who opens to a man; "That they may bring forth salvation" (ibid.)—this refers to procreation; "And sprout forth righteousness"—this refers to the rainfall; "I the Lord have created it" (ibid.)—for this puropse I created it, to set in order and populate the world.

[H]   R. Aha taught it in the name of R. Simeon b. Gamaliel, "Why is it called a flow [which soaks in], rbyʻh? Because it makes the earth fertile [rwbʻh]." [The same word refers both to irrigation and sexual relations.]

[I]   R. Haninah bar Yaqa in the name of R. Judah, "The roots of wheat stalks go down three [var.: fifty] cubits into the ground. The roots of young fig trees penetrate even through rock-hard ground."

[J]   It was taught: R. Ishmael b. Eleazar says, "The ground only absorbs enough to saturate the [soil's] uppermost layer."

[K]   If that is so, how will the [deep] roots of the carob or of the sycamore [ever find moisture]?

[L]   Said R. Haninah, "Once every thirty days waters rise up from the deep to water them."

[M]   And what is the basis [in Scripture for this statement]? "I, the Lord, am its keeper; every moment [lrgʻym, at intervals] I water it" (Isa. 27:3).

[**XX.**A]   Said R. Zeira, "If one sees prices decline, or that produce is abundant, or that the river provides enough to irrigate the province, he recites, 'Blessed [art Thou, O Lord, our God, King of the Universe,] who is good and does good.'

[B]   "If they told someone his father died, he recites, 'Blessed [art Thou, O Lord, our God, King of the Universe,] the true judge.'"

[C]   If someone's father died and [later] he inherited his estate, he [also] recites, "Blessed [art Thou, O Lord, our God, King of the Universe,] who is good and does good.'"

Unit **I** adds to Mishnah an appropriate brief comment on the fear of the destructive power of earth tremors. Unit **II** cites the material regarding the comet to elaborate on the dangers of meteors, and justify the practice of reciting a blessing when seeing one.

Unit **III** goes further into the subject of earthquakes. Unit **IV** is not relevant to the present subject matter, but is included here because it is a second question asked by Elijah of Nehorai, following materials attributed to him in unit **III**.

Unit **V** returns to comment upon the rule of Mishnah regarding reciting a blessing over lightning and thunder. The unit cites as support a Tosefta passage. Unit **VI** reflects further on the ramifications of the law of Mishnah. Units **VII** and **VIII** deal with the blessing over and further traditions concerning the winds.

Unit **IX** comments directly on Mishnah's rule regarding one who views the sea. Unit **X** extends the concept of the previous to a new law. It asks what blessings one who visits Jerusalem frequently must recite. Unit **XI** is irrelevant to the present context, included here because of its attribution to Simeon Qamatraya.

At unit **XII** the Talmud cites Tosefta regarding blessings one recites upon seeing the sun or moon at certain times, and comments upon it. Unit **XIII** continues on the related subject of the blessings one recites in the liturgy for the new moon.

Unit **XIV** refers to the law of Tosefta, regarding the blessing one recites in a cemetery. Unit **XV** cites Tosefta concerning the blessing to recite upon seeing a rainbow. It then adds a related teaching in the name of Hezekiah about the powers of Simeon bar Yohai. At unit **XVI** the Talmud adds three traditions, unrelated to our context in content, but inserted here by shared attribution. All are about Simeon and are attributed to Hezekiah.

Units **XVII–XIX** explain and expand upon Mishnah's rule that one recites a blessing over rainfall. Unit **XX** concludes with a brief discussion of some aspects of reciting blessings for good tidings.

9:3

[A]   *One who built a new house, or bought new clothes says, "Blessed [art Thou, O Lord, our God, King of the Universe, who kept us alive, and sustained us, and] brought us to this occasion."*

[B]   *One recites a blessing over evil, as he would recite over good. And one recites a blessing over good, as he would recite over evil.*

[C]   *And one who cries out over a past occurrence, lo, this is a vain prayer.*

[D]   *How so? One whose wife was pregnant and he recited, "May it be thy will that she bear a male child," lo, this is a vain prayer.*

[E]   *One who was coming down the road, and he heard cries in the city and recited, "May it be thy will that these [cries] do not come from my house," lo, this is a vain prayer.*

[I.A]   Said R. Hiyya bar Ba, "[This rule that he recites a blessing applies] not only to new clothes, but also to worn clothes, if they are new for him."

[B]   R. Jacob bar Zabdi in the name of R. Hiyya bar Abba said, "If one buys [new clothes], he says, 'Blessed [art Thou, O Lord, our God, King of the Universe,] who kept us alive, and sustained us, and brought us to this occasion.'

[C]   "If they are given to him he says, 'Blessed [art Thou, O Lord, our God, King of the Universe,] who is good and does good.'"

[D]   R. Ba, the father of R. Ba Mari, in the name of R. Aha, "If one buys them he says, 'Blessed [art Thou, O Lord, our God, King of the Universe, who kept us alive and sustained us, and] brought us to this occasion.'

[E]   "If they were given to him he says, 'Blessed [art Thou, O Lord, our God, King of the Universe,] who is good and does good.'

[F]   "When one puts on clothing, he says, 'Blessed [art Thou, O Lord, our God, King of the Universe,] who clothes the naked.'"

[II.A]   [One recites a blessing over the performance of all the commandments.]

[B]   One who makes for himself a sukkah recites, "Blessed [art Thou, O Lord, our God, King of the Universe,] who sanctified us with his commandments and commanded us to make a sukkah" [T. 6:9].

[C]   [One who makes a sukkah] for others [recites, "Blessed art Thou, O Lord, our God, King of the Universe,] to make for Him a sukkah for his sake."

[D]   When he enters to dwell in it he recites, "Blessed [art Thou, O Lord, our God, King of the Universe,] who sanctified us with his commandments and commanded us to dwell in a sukkah."

[E]   Once he recites the blessing for [the commandment to dwell in] it on the first night of the festival, he need not recite it again [for the remainder of the festival].

[F]   Likewise, one who makes for himself a lulab recites, "Blessed [art Thou, O Lord, our God, King of the Universe,] who sanctified us with his commandments and commanded us to make a lulab."

[G]   [One who makes a lulab] for another [recites, "Blessed art Thou, O Lord, our God, King of the Universe,] to make a lulab for his sake."

[H]   When he takes hold of it [to fulfill the commandment] he recites, Blessed [art Thou, O Lord, our God, King of the Universe, who commanded us] to take hold of the lulab," and "Blessed [art Thou, O Lord, our God, King of the Universe,] who has kept us alive, [and sustained us, and brought us to] this occasion." And he must recite the blessings each time he takes hold of it.

[I]   One who makes for himself a mezuzah recites, "Blessed [art Thou, O Lord, our God, King of the Universe, who sanctified us with his commandments and commanded us] to make a mezuzah."

[J]   [One who makes a mezuzah] for another [recites, "Blessed art Thou, O Lord, our God, King of the Universe, who sanctified us with his commandments and commanded us] to make a mezuzah for his sake."

[K]   When he sets it [in the door post] he recites, "Blessed [art Thou, O Lord, our God, King of the Universe,] who sanctified us with his commandments and commanded us regarding the commandments of the mezuzah."

[L]   **One who makes for himself tefillin [recites, "Blessed art Thou, O Lord, our God, King of the Universe, who sanctified us with his commandments and commanded us to make tefillin."]**

[M]   **One who makes for others tefillin [recites, "Blessed art Thou, O Lord, our God, King of the Universe, who sanctified us with his commandments and commanded us to make tefillin for his sake."]**

[N]   **When he puts them on he recites, "Blessed [art Thou, O Lord, our God, King of the Universe,] concerning the commandment of the tefillin."**

[O]   **One who makes fringes [in a garment] for himself [recites, "Blessed art Thou, O Lord, our God, King of the Universe, who sanctified us with his commandments and commanded us to make fringes."]**

[P]   **[One who makes fringes] for others [recites, "Blessed art Thou, O Lord, our God, King of the Universe, who sanctified us with his commandments and commanded us to make fringes for his sake."]**

[Q]   **When he puts them on, [he recites, "Blessed art Thou, O Lord, our God, King of the Universe, who sanctified us with his commandments and commanded us concerning the commandment of fringes."]**

[R]   **One who separates heave-offerings and tithes recites, "Blessed [art Thou, O Lord, our God, King of the Universe] who sanctified us with his commandments and commanded us to separate heave-offering and tithes."**

[S]   **[One who separates these] for others recites, "Blessed [art Thou, O Lord, our God, King of the Universe,] to separate heave-offering and tithes for his sake."**

[T]   **He who slaughters must recite, "Blessed [art Thou, O Lord, our God, King of the Universe, who sanctified us with his commandments and] commanded us regarding slaughtering."**

[U]   **He who covers the blood recites, "Blessed [art Thou, O Lord,** our God, King of the Universe, who sanctified us with his commandments and commanded us] concerning the covering of the blood."

[V] He who circumcises must recite, "Blessed [art Thou, O Lord, our God, King of the Universe, who sanctified us with his commandments] and commanded us regarding circumcision."

[W] The child's father recites, "Blessed [art Thou, O Lord, our God, King of the Universe, who sanctified us with his commandments] and commanded us to bring him into the covenant of Abraham our forefather."

[X] Those [guests] who are standing [at the ceremony] must recite, "Just as you have brought him into the covenant, so shall you bring him to Torah, and marriage [and good deeds]."

[Y] The one who recites the blessing [that follows the ceremony] must recite this blessing, "Blessed [art Thou, O Lord, our God, King of the Universe,] who sanctified [Isaac] the beloved in the womb and placed the mark of His statute in his flesh, and [placed] as a seal on his offspring the sign of the sacred covenant. So on the merits of this, living God, our support, our rock, you commanded us [to circumcise our sons] so we may save our beloved kindred from destruction. Blessed art Thou, O Lord, who establishes the covenant." [The version of this passage in T. 6:9–13 has several additions and omissions and a slightly different order. Some commentaries identify Abraham as the "beloved."]

[III.A] When does one recite the blessing over [the performance of] the commandments?

[B] R. Yohanan says, "Prior to performing them."

[C] R. Huna says, "At the same time one performs them."

[D] R. Huna follows Samuel's view.

[E] For R. Yose b. Bun said in the name of Samuel, "All of the commandments require that one recite a blessing at the time one performs them, with the exception of the sounding of the shofar [on the New Year's day], and of immersing oneself [in a ritual bath]."

[F] And some say [to exclude also from those acts for which one recites a blessing before performing them, the act of] consummating a marriage. [In these cases you recite the blessing after the action because there is the possibility in the case of shofar and consummating the marriage that one may not be able to complete the proper action. And in the case of immersing in a bath, in some instances, one is not permitted to recite a blessing beforehand because he is unclean.]

[G]   Said R. Yonah, "There are other [commandments for which one may recite the blessing after performing the action. For example, you may recite the blessings over] the tefillin of the arm [after putting it on, anytime] before you remove it. And [you must recite the blessing over] the head tefillin before you set it in place [on your head].

[H]   "But if you recited the blessing [over the head tefillin] after you put it on, lo, it is on already [and it is too late to recite the blessing.]" [It is too late to recite two separate blessings over the tefillin because one must follow this sequence. First one puts on the arm tefillin, then one recites the blessing for the head tefillin before putting it on. Later one may recite the blessing over the arm tefillin, before removing it. But one may not put on the arm tefillin, then put on the head tefillin and subsequently recite the blessing over the head tefillin. P.M. explains that in that case the single blessing will apply willy nilly to both the arm and head tefillin, and one will forfeit the opportunity to recite two separate blessings.]

[I]   When does one recite the blessing for slaughtering [an animal]? R. Yohanan says, "Before one slaughters [the animal]." Yose b. Nehorai says, "After one slaughters it." Why [after slaughtering it]? Lest the slaughtering be invalid [and the blessing be in vain.]

[J]   [If this is a concern], he should wait to recite the blessing until he examines the animal's neck passages [to see if the windpipe and esophagus were severed properly and until he also examines the animal's entrails for defects which might render it prohibited for consumption.]

[K]   [This is not necessary for we have a principle:] The presumption is that the entrails will be found fit.

[L]   It was taught [in this regard:] If one slaughtered [an animal] and wolves dragged its entrails away [before he could examine them, we rule that the animal] is fit for consumption. Should we not suspect perhaps that [the intestines] were [previously] punctured [and the animal was unfit for consumption]?

[M]   R. Ba in the name of sages there [in Babylonia], "The presumption is that the entrails will be found fit." [See P.M. and Luncz on textual variants here.]

[VI.A]   Piska: *And one who cries out over a past occurrence, lo, this is a vain prayer.*

[B]   *How so? One whose wife was pregnant and he recited, "May it be thy will that she bear a male child," lo, this is a vain prayer* [M. 9:3C–D]. The House of Yannai say, "Our Mishnah refers to a situation where the woman is sitting in the labor chair. But before that time one may pray [for a male child]."

[C]   Said R. Judah b. Pazzi, "Even if she is sitting in the labor chair, the sex of the fetus can be changed [by God], in accord with the verse, 'Behold, like the clay in the potter's hand, so are you in my hand, O house of Israel'" (Jer. 18:6).

[D]   Rabbi [said] in the name of the House of Yannai, "Originally [as a fetus], Dinah was a male. After Rachel prayed, she was changed into a female. In this regard it says, 'Afterwards she bore a daughter, and called her name Dinah' (Gen. 30:21). After Rachel prayed, Dinah was changed into a female."

[E]   And R. Judah b. Pazzi said in the name of the House of R. Yannai, "Our mother Rachel was one of the earliest prophetesses. She said, 'Another shall descend from me.'

[F]   "In this regard it is written, 'She called his name Joseph, saying, 'May the Lord add to me another son'" (Gen. 30:24). She did not say, 'other sons.' Rather she said, 'Let another one be descended from me." [She knew that Jacob would have one more son and she prayed that it would be through her. At that moment, Leah's fetus changed into a female.—P.M.]

[V.A]   What may one who was coming home off the road say [if he hears cries in the city, M. 9:3E]? "I am sure that they do not come from my house [showing his faith in God]."

[B]   Hillel the Elder says, "[He should recite this verse,] 'He is not afraid of evil tidings'" (Ps. 112:7).

Unit **I** expands upon Mishnah's rule regarding the recitation of a blessing over new clothes. Unit **II** cites the lengthy Tosefta passage about blessings one must recite over the performance of the commandments, a subject not raised here by Mishnah. Unit **III** takes up a new issue, related to the passage in Tosefta, concerning when one does recite the blessings over the performance of the actions associated with the commandments.

Units **IV** and **V** elaborate on what Mishnah calls a vain prayer.

9:4

[A] *One who enters a town recites two prayers, one on his entry, and one on his exit.*

[B] *Ben Azzai says, "[He recites] four [prayers], two on his entry, and two on his exit.*

[C] *"He gives thanks for the past and cries out for the future [both upon his arrival and his departure]."*

[I.A] **One who enters a town recites two prayers, one on his entry and one on his exit.**

[B] **What does he say when he enters? "May it be thy will, Lord my God, God of my fathers, that you bring me into this town in peace."**

[C] **What does he say when he exits? "I give thanks to thee, Lord my God, that you brought me into this town in peace. So may it be thy will that you bring me forth from this town in peace."**

[D] **Ben Azzai says, "[He recites] four [blessings], two on his entry and two on his exit."**

[E] **He says, "May it be thy will, Lord my God, God of my fathers, that you bring me into this town in peace."**

[F] **Once he has entered, he says, "I give thanks to thee, Lord my God, God of my fathers, that you brought me in in peace. So may it be thy will that you bring me forth in peace."**

[G] **When he is exiting, he says, "May it be thy will, Lord my God, that you bring me forth in peace."**

[H] **Once he has exited, he says, "I give thanks to thee, Lord my God, God of my fathers, that you brought me forth in peace. So may it be thy will to bring me to my house in peace." Or, "[That you bring me] to such and such a place in peace" [T. 6:16].**

[I] **[These laws apply] in regard to [one who travels through] an** area of gentile settlement. But [one who travels through] an area of Jewish settlement need not recite the blessings.

[J]   But if it is known as a place where executions occur, even if it is an area of Jewish settlement, one must recite the blessings.

[II.A]   One who enters an outhouse recites two blessings, one when he enters, one when he leaves.

[B]   When he enters what does he say? "May you be honored, most honorable ministering angels. These are our ways. Make the way clear for us. Blessed is the most honored God." And when he leaves what does he say? "Blessed [art Thou, O Lord, our God, King of the Universe,] who formed man in his wisdom. . . ."

[C]   **One who enters a bathhouse recites two prayers, one when he enters, one when he leaves** [T. 6:17].

[D]   What does he say when he enters? "May it be thy will, Lord my God, that you protect me from the flames of the fire, and from injury by the steam, and from the collapse of the building. And may nothing occur to endanger my life. But if something happens, may my death atone for all of my sins. And save me from this and similar dangers in times to come."

[E]   And what does he say when he leaves? "I give thanks to you, Lord my God, for you saved me from the fire."

[F]   Said R. Abahu, "All this refers only to a bathhouse that is heated by a furnace [i.e., artificially]. But when one uses a bathhouse that is not [artificially] heated by a furnace, he says only, "[Protect me from] injury by the steam."

[G]   R. Hilkiah and R. Simon in the name of R. Joshua b. Levi, "When reciting the prayers for [protection in] the bathhouse, one does not have to stand up."

Unit **I** cites an appropriate Tosefta passage, and comments upon it. Unit **II** expands further on the subject of reciting blessings on entry and exit from places of danger.

9:5

[A]   *A person is obligated to recite a blessing over bad fortune, just as he recites a blessing over good fortune.*

[B]   *As it says, "And you shall love the Lord your God with all your heart, and with all your soul, and with all your might"* (Deut. 6:5).

[C]   *"With all your heart"—with your two desires, with your desire for good, and with your desire for evil.*

[D]   *"With all your soul"—even if He takes your soul.*

[E]   *"With all your might"—with all your wealth.*

[F]   *Another interpretation: "With all your might [m'dk]"—for every measure [mydh] which He metes out for you [mwdd lk], thank Him [mwdh lw] greatly [m'd m'd]. [This interpretation is based on a play on words.]*

[G]   *A person should not act frivolously opposite the Eastern Gate [of the Temple] for it faces the Chamber of the Holy of Holies.*

[H]   *One shall not enter the Temple mount with his walking stick, or with his overshoes, or with his money bag, or with dust on his feet.*

[I]   *And one should not use [the Temple mount] for a shortcut.*

[J]   *And spitting [while on the Temple mount is forbidden, based on an inference] from a qal wahomer [an argument a minori ad majus].*

[K]   *[At one time] they used to say "forever" at the conclusion of all blessings recited in the Temple.*

[L]   *After the heretics tried to corrupt [the tradition] by saying, "[Based on what you say,] there is only one world [and no after-life in the world to come]," they ordained that one should say "forever and ever."*

[M]   *And they ordained that a person should greet his associate with God's name.*

[N]   *As it says, "And behold Boaz came from Bethlehem and he said to the reapers, 'The Lord be with you!' And they answered, 'The Lord bless you'"* (Ruth 2:4).

[O]   *And [as further support for this practice] it says, "[The angel greeted Gideon asying,] 'The Lord be with you mighty man of valor'"* (Judg. 6:12).

[P]   *And it says, "[Hearken to your father for he gave birth to you and] do not despise your mother when she is old"* (Prov. 23:22).

[Q]   *And it says, "It is time for the Lord to act, for thy law has been broken" (Ps. 119:126).*

[R]   *[In K's margin: R. Nathan says, "Thy law has been broken. It is time 'to act' for the Lord."]*

[I.A]   R. Berekhiah in the name of R. Levi, "[One must recite a blessing over misfortune] on account of the verse, 'But Thou, O Lord, art on high forever' (Ps. 92:8). Whatever you [O Lord] do is justified.

[B]   "It is the way of the world that when a human king sits and grants a pardon, all praise him. But when he invokes the death penalty, all murmur against him. [They ask] why he has gotten carried away in his judgments. But this is not [how people respond to judgments] of the Holy One, blessed be He. Rather [whatever his judgment, they always say,] 'But Thou, O Lord, art on high forever.' Whatever you [O Lord] do is justified."

[C]   R. Huna in the name of R. Aha, "'A Psalm of David. I will sing of loving-kindness and justice; to thee, O Lord, I will sing' (Ps. 101:1). David said to the Holy One, blessed be He, 'If you act toward me out of loving-kindness, I will sing, and if you act toward me out of justice, I will sing. Either way, to thee O Lord, I will sing.'"

[D]   Said R. Tanhuma b. Judah, "'In God, whose word I praise, in the Lord, whose word I praise' (Ps. 56:10). For both [God's] attribute of justice, and the [Lord's] attribute of mercy, I praise."

[E]   And sages say, "'I will lift up the cup of salvation and call on the name of the Lord' (Ps. 116:13). 'I suffered distress and anguish. Then I called on the name of the Lord' (Ps. 116:3–4). For both [salvation and distress] he 'called on the name of the Lord.'"

[F]   Said R. Yudan b. Pilah, "Thus Job said, 'The Lord gave, and the Lord has taken away; blessed be the name of the Lord' (Job 1:21). Just as he gave with mercy, so he took with mercy. Moreover, when he gave, he consulted with no one. But when he took, he consulted with his court."

[G]   [This accords with the following tradition:] Said R. Eleazar, "Anywhere it says [in Scripture], 'And the Lord,' [it means] he acted together with his court.

[H]   "The primary source [in Scripture] of this general principle [is the following:] ['And Micaiah said, . . . I saw the Lord sitting on this throne, and all the host of heaven standing beside him on his right hand and on his left; and the Lord said, 'Who will entice Ahab?' . . . 'Now therefore behold, the Lord has put a lying spirit in the mouth of all these your prophets;] the Lord has spoken evil concerning you'" (1 Kings 22:19–20; 23).

[II.A]   Let love motivate your actions and let fear motivate your actions. [How so?] Let love motivate your actions. And if you begin to despise [the commandments or Torah], recall that you love [God]. And one who loves [God] cannot despise [His commandments].

[B]   Let fear [also] motivate your actions. And if you begin to rebel [against God's commandments or Torah], recall that you fear him. And one who fears does not rebel.

[C]   There are seven kinds of pietists: The showy [pietist], the haughty [pietist], the bookkeeper [pietist], the parsimonious [pietist], the repaying [pietist], the fearing [pietist], the loving [pietist].

[D]   The showy [pietist] carries his good deeds on his shoulder [to show them off].

[E]   The haughty [pietist] says, "Wait for me. I am [busy using my time] to fulfill the commandments! [I have no time for you.]"

[F]   The bookkeeper [pietist] pays off each debt [i.e., sin] by performing a commandment [good deed].

[G]   The parsimonious [pietist] says, "From the little I have, what can I set aside for performing commandments?"

[H]   The repaying [pietist] says, "Tell me what sin I have committed and I will perform a commandment to offset it." [These five types are negative, pompous, ostentatious models.]

[I]   The fearing [pietist emulates] Job. The loving [pietist emulates] Abraham. And none is more beloved of God than the loving [pietist who emulates] Abraham.

[J]   Abraham, our forefather, even transformed the evil desire [within him] into good. As it is written, "And Thou didst find his heart (*lbbw*—a plural form—suggesting more than one form of desire) faithful before thee" (Neh. 9:8). [In spite of all his 'heart's desires' he was faithful.]

[K]   Said R. Aha, "He made a deal [with his evil desire so that he could control it. As it says,] 'And didst make with him the covenant, . . .' (ibid.).

[L]   "But David could not withstand [the power of his evil desire] and he had to destroy it.

[M]   "What is the basis [in Scripture for this statement]? 'My heart [*lby*—the evil desire] is stricken within me'" (Ps. 109:22).

[III.A]   R. Aqiba was being tortured [lit.: being judged] by the evil Tinneius Rufus. When [he was close to death,] the time to recite the *Shemaʿ* approached. He began to recite the *Shemaʿ* and he smiled.

[B]   He [Tinneius] said to him, "Elder, either you are a sorcerer [who does not feel pain] or you mock the torture [that I inflict upon you]."

[C]   He [Aqiba] said to him, "Woe unto you. I am neither a sorcerer, nor a mocker. But [I now was thinking,] all my life when I recited this verse, I was troubled and wondered when I would be able to fulfill all three aspects [of this verse]: 'And you shall love the Lord your God with all your heart, and with all your soul, and with all your might' (Deut. 6:5). I have loved Him with all my heart. And I have loved him with all my wealth. But I did not know how I would [fulfill the verse and] love him with all my soul.

[D]   "And now the time has come [for me to love him] with all my soul, and the time has come to recite the *Shemaʿ*. It is now clear to me [how I shall serve Him with all my soul]. For this reason I now am reciting and smiling." And just as he said this, his soul passed from him.

[E]   Nehemiah Emsoni served R. Aqiba for twenty-two years [as his disciple]. And [Aqiba] taught him [what one could include in the interpretation of a verse based on the presence of the particles in the Torah] *'t* and *gm* [and what one could exclude in the interpretation of a verse based on each particle] *'k* and *rq*.

[F]   He said to him, "What about that which is written, 'You shall fear [*'t*] the Lord your God'" (Deut. 6:13)?

[G]   He said to him, "[The presence in the verse of the particle *'t* teaches: You shall fear] Him and His Torah."

[IV.A]   Piska. *A person should not act frivolously* (M. 9:5). It was

taught: [One who is North of the Temple Mount] when he passes
water, he should face North. When he moves his bowels, lo, he
should face South.

[B]   Said R. Yose b. R. Bun, "In this regard it was taught: 'From
Mount Scopus or closer [to the Temple one must follow this
practice.]'"

[C]   R. Aqiba says, "[One must follow this practice] in any place.
And especially in a place where there is no wall [separating the
person and the Temple Mount]."

[D]   It was taught: One who moves his bowels should not face east-
west but should face in another direction.

[E]   R. Judah says, "[This practice only applied] during the time the
Temple was standing."

[F]   R. Yose says, "From Mount Scopus or closer [one must follow
this practice]."

[G]   R. Aqiba says, "In any place and especially in a place where
there is no wall [separating the person and the Temple Mount]."

[H]   Said R. Aqiba, "I followed R. Joshua to observe his habits."

[I]   They said to him, "What did you see?"

[J]   He said to them, "I saw him sitting with his side facing west. He
did not uncover himself until he sat down. He did not sit down
until he had rubbed the place [he sat to clean it]. And he did not
wipe with his right hand, but with his left."

[K]   So Simeon b. Azzai used to say, "I followed R. Aqiba to observe
his habits." They said to him, "What did you see?" [Etc., as in J.]

[V.A]   It was taught: *One should not enter the Temple mount [with his
walking stick] or with his overshoes, [or with his money bag] or
with dust on his feet* [M. 9 : 5].

[B]   **Or with his money tied in his purse [lit.: garment], or with his
money bag tied about him.**

[C]   **What is the basis [in Scripture for this statement]? 'Guard
your steps when you go to the house of God'** (Qoh. 5 : 1 RSV).

[D]   **R. Yose b. R. Judah says, Lo, it says, "He went up to the
entrance of the king's gate, for no one might enter the king's
gate clothed with sackcloth"** (Esther 4 : 2) [T. 6 : 19]. He said,

"If this is how one must act before the gate of such spittle, how much moreso must one [dress properly when one comes] before the gate of God."

[E]   *One should not use [the Temple Mount] for a shortcut. And spitting [there is forbidden, based on an inference] from* qal wahomer [M. 9:5] [as follows:] **If out of respect alone wearing a shoe is forbidden by the Torah, spitting which is a disgrace is surely forbidden** [T. 6:19].

[VI.A]   It was taught: They did not respond 'Amen' [after a blessing was recited] in the Temple. What did they respond? "Blessed be the name of his glorious kingdom for everlasting."

[B]   **Whence that they did not respond 'Amen' in the Temple? We derive it from the verse, "[Then the Levites] said, 'Stand up and bless the Lord your God from everlasting to everlasting. Blessed be thy glorious name which is exalted above all blessing and praise'"** (Neh. 9:5).

[C]   **Whence that one must so respond to every blessing? We derive it from "exalted above all blessing"** (ibid.) [T. 6:22].

[VII.A]   Said R. Joshua of the South, "In three instances a decree was issued by an earthly court and the heavenly court confirmed it.

[B]   "And they are (1) [the decree concerning] the ban on using the property of Jericho [that it either go the treasury of the Lord, or be destroyed, cf. Joshua 6:18–19]; (2) [the decree concerning the obligation to read on Purim] the scroll of Esther; (3) [the decree to] greet one's fellow with God's name."

[C]   The ban on using the property of Jericho [was confirmed by God and the heavenly court, as the verse says,] "Israel has sinned" (Joshua 9:11). [They took from the property that God had forbade them.] Was it not Joshua who issued the decree? The verse teaches that the heavenly court confirmed their decree.

[D]   The [obligation to read] the scroll of Esther [was confirmed by God and the heavenly court as it says,] "The Jews ordained and they accepted" (Esther 9:27). Rab said, "'Accepted' means the heavenly court confirmed [the obligation to celebrate Purim and read the scroll of Esther]."

[E]   [The practice of] greeting one's fellow with God's name [was confirmed by the heavenly court as it says,] "And behold Boaz came from Bethlehem [and he said to the reapers, 'The Lord be with you!' And they answered, 'The Lord bless you'"] (Ruth 2:4).

[F]   But whence that the heavenly court confirmed [the propriety of this practice]? We derive this from another verse, "And the angel of the Lord appeared to him [Gideon] and said to him, 'The Lord is with you, you mighty man of valor'" (Judg. 6:12).

[G]   R. Abun in the name of R. Joshua b. Levi, "[The practice] of tithing [during the period of the second Temple] also [was decreed by man and confirmed by God in the heavenly court]. As it says, 'Bring the full tithes [into the storehouse, that there may be good in my house; and thereby put me to the test, says the Lord of hosts, if I will not open the windows of heaven for you and pour down for you an overflowing blessing]'" (Mal. 3:10).

[H]   What does, "An overflowing blessing ['d bly dy]" mean? R. Yose bar Simeon bar Ba in the name of R. Yohanan, "It is something about which one can never say, 'We had enough [dyy] of this blessing.'"

[I]   R. Berekhiah and R. Helbo and R. Abba bar Ilai in the name of Rab, "[It means you shall receive so many blessings] that your lips will tire from saying [in thanksgiving], 'Enough blessing for us! Enough blessing for us!'"

[VIII.A]   *"Do not despise your mother when she is old"* (Prov. 23:22) [M. 9:5P]. Said R. Yose bar Bun, "If the words of the Torah seem old when you say them, do not despise them." What is the basis [in Scripture for this statement]? "Do not despise your mother when she is old."

[B]   Said R. Zeira, "If your motherland [lit: 'wmh, nation] becomes weak, arise and fortify it, as Elkanah did when he led Israel to the pilgrimage festivals. In this regard it says, 'Now this man [Elkanah] used to go up year by year from his city to worship and sacrifice to the Lord of hosts at Shiloh' (1 Sam. 1:3). [And he encouraged others to join with him, cf. S.H.]"

[C]   *"It is the time for the Lord to act, for thy law has been broken"* (Ps. 119:126). R. Nathan transposed the verse. *"Thy law has been broken, it is the time for the Lord to act"* [M. 9:5].

[D]   R. Hilkiah in the name of R. Simon, "One who only studies Torah occasionally ['tym], lo, it is as if he destroys the covenant."

[E]   What is the basis for this? [He reads and interprets the verse as follows:] "They break thy law, who only on occasion ['t] act for the Lord."

[F]   It was taught: R. Simeon b. Yohai says, "If you see that people have abandoned the Torah, stand right up and fortify it and you shall receive reward on behalf of all of them [who return to the Torah]."

[G]   What is the basis [in Scripture for this statement]? [He reads the verse:] "If they have abandoned thy law, it is time to act for the Lord."

[IX.A]   **Hillel the Elder used to say, "You should scatter at the time of gathering. And you should gather in at the time of scattering."**

[B]   **And so Hillel used to say, "When you see that the Torah is beloved to all Israel and all rejoice in it, then you must spread it about. And if this is not the case, then you must gather it in"** [T. 6 : 24].

[C]   Said R. Eleazar, "Just as an infant must nurse all through the day, so every person in Israel must toil in the study of Torah all through the day."

[D]   R. Yonah in the name of R. Yose b. Gezerah, "All discussions are bad. But discussions concerning the Torah are good. All fictions [var.: silences] are good. But fictions concerning [the study of the] Torah are bad." [So Jastrow, s.v. kdyb'.]

[E]   Said R. Simeon b. Laqish, "In the Scroll of the Pious they found the following written: 'If you forsake me for one day, I shall forsake you for two.'

[F]   "[This may be explained through a parable:] Two persons set out on the road, one from Tiberias and one from Sepphoris. They meet at one place of lodging. Then they take leave of one another [and go in different directions]. After each has travelled one mile, they find themselves two miles apart. [So it is if God and Israel go off in different directions.]"

[G]   [Another parable:] Concerning a woman who awaits a certain man. As long as he intends to marry her, she sits and waits for him. But if he directs his intentions elsewhere, she may go and marry another. [So it is if Israel turns its attention from God.]

[X.A]   It was taught: **R. Meir used to say, "There is no person is**

Israel who does not perform one hundred commandments each day [and recite blessings for them].

[B]   "One recites the *Shema'* and recites blessings before and after it. And one eats his bread and recites blessings before and after. And one recites the Prayer of Eighteen Blessings three times. And one performs all the other commandments and recites blessings for them."

[C]   And so R. Meir used to say, "There is no person in Israel who is not surrounded by commandments.

[D]   "[Every person wears] tefillin on his head, tefillin on his arm, and has a mezuzah on his door post, the mark of circumcision in his flesh, and four fringes on his garment around him."

[E]   So did David say, "Seven times a day I praise thee for thy righteous ordinances" (Ps. 119:164). And so he says, "The angel of the Lord encamps around those who fear him and delivers them" (Ps. 34:7).

[F]   When he [David] entered the bathhouse and realized that he was naked, he said, 'Woe is me for I am stripped of the commandments.' But when he saw the mark of circumcision in his flesh he praised the Lord [in his Psalm] saying, "To the choirmaster according to the *sheminith*" (Ps. 12:1) [The eighth, *sheminith*, is an allusion to circumcision on the eighth day] [T. 6:24–25].

[G]   Said R. Eleazar in the name of R. Haninah, "Disciples of the sages foster peace in the world. What is the basis [in Scripture for this statement]? 'All your sons shall be taught by the Lord, and great shall be the prosperity of your sons'" (Isa. 54:13).

Unit **I** suggests possible scriptural bases for the rule that one recite a blessing over misfortune. Unit **II** expands upon Mishnah's references to the love of God with both of one's inclinations [M. 9:5C–D], and appends some relevant independent material. Unit **III** adds additional materials to amplify M. 9:5D.

Unit **IV** explains what M. means when it refers to frivolous behavior. Unit **V** provides further exegesis of M., based mainly on citations out of Tosefta.

Unit **VI** continues to cite T. to systematically explain M. In the lengthy section at unit **VII,** the Talmud provides a basis for the practice of greeting one's friend in the name of God. Unit **VIII** adds to M. Units **IX** and **X** cite Tosefta passages about the value of the study of Torah and the performance of the commandments and add to them, closing the tractate on a hopeful note.

Abbreviations, Bibliography, and Glossary

A.Z.: Abodah Zarah

alt.: alternative reading

ALW: A. Lukyn-Williams, *Tractate Berakoth: Mishna and Tosefta.* New York: 1921.

b.: Talmud Babli; ben

B.M.: Baba Mesia

Ber.: Berakhot

Bik.: Bikkurim

Bokser: Baruch Bokser, "Annotated Bibliographical Guide to the Study of the Palestinian Talmud," in *Principat (ANRW II. 19.2),* ed. Wolfgang Hesse. Berlin and New York: 1979.

Chron.: Chronicles

Dan.: Daniel

Danby: Herbert Danby, *The Mishnah: Translated from the Hebrew with Introduction and Brief Explanatory Notes.* London: 1933.

Deut.: Deuteronomy

Drosh.: A. Droshkewicz, ed. *Novellae and Explanations of Elijah Ben Solomon (GRA) on Tractate Berakhot.* Reprint, Jerusalem: 1973.

dylm': formal introduction to a tale

E.P.: *editio princeps.* Daniel Bomberg, *The Palestinian Talmud.* Venice: 1523–24.

Ed.: Eduyot

Elbogen: Ismar Elbogen, *The Historical Development of Jewish Prayer.* Revised Hebrew Version by J. Heinemann. Jerusalem: 1972.

Eleazar: Tzvee Zahavy, *The Traditions of Eleazar ben Azariah.* Missoula: 1977.

Erub.: Erubin

Exod.: Exodus

Ezek.: Ezekiel

Gen.: Genesis

Geniza: *Yerushalmi Fragments from the Geniza. I.* L. Ginzberg, ed. New York: 1909. Reprint Jerusalem: 1969.

Ginzberg: L. Ginzberg, *A Commentary on the Palestinian Talmud.* New York: 1941. Reprint New York: 1971.

Git.: Gittin

Goren: S. Goren, *HaYerushalmi HaMeforash*. Jerusalem: 1961.

GRA: Rabbi Elijah b. Solomon Zalman of Vilna, 1720–97, emendations.

Hallel: portion of the liturgy consisting of Psalms 113–18

Heinemann: Joseph Heinemann, *Prayer in the Talmud: Forms and Patterns*. English version by R. S. Sarason. Berlin: 1977.

Hershler: M. Hershler, ed. *Ginze Rishonim*. Berakhot. Jerusalem: 1967.

Hertz: Joseph H. Hertz, *The Authorized Daily Prayer Book*. New York: 1974.

Horowitz: Charles Horowitz, *Der Jerusalemer Talmud in deutscher Ubersetzung. Band I Berakhoth*. Tubingen: 1975.

Idelson: A. Z. Idelson, *Jewish Liturgy and Its Development*. New York: 1932.

Isa.: Isaiah

Jastrow: Marcus Jastrow: *A Dictionary of the Targumim, the Talmud Babli and Yerushalmi and Midrashic Literature*. New York: 1950.

Jer.: Jeremiah

Judg.: Judges

Katsh: Abraham Katsh, "Tractate Berakhot from the Genizah." Hebrew. In *Sefer Shazar*, Jerusalem: 1973.

Kel.: Kelim

KFP: Tzvee Zahavy, "*Kavvanah* for Prayer in the Mishnah and the Talmud." In *New Perspectives on Ancient Judaism*. J. Neusner, ed., ch. 3. Lanham, MD: 1987.

L: Leiden manuscript of Yerushalmi Berakhot; *The Palestinian Talmud. Leiden MS. Cod. Scal. 3. A Facsimile of the Original Manuscript*. 4 vols. Jerusalem: 1970.

L.S.: E. Lohse, and G. Schlichting, eds., *Die Tosefta. Text, Ubersetzung und Erklarung. Seder Zeraim*. Heft 1–3. Kohlhammer: 1956–1958.

Lam.: Lamentations

Lev.: Leviticus

Lieberman, TK: Saul Lieberman, *Tosefta Ki-fshutah: A Comprehensive Commentary on the Tosefta*, pt. I. New York: 1955.

Lieberman, TZ: Saul Lieberman, *The Tosefta: Zeraim*. New York: 1955.

Luncz: A. M. Luncz, *Talmud Hierosolymitanum*. Jerusalem: 1907.

M.: Mishnah

M.H.: Mareh Hapenim Commentary, M. Margoliot

m'sh: formal introduction to a tale

Mal.: Malachi

Meg.: Megillah

Mezuzah/ot: amulets affixed to doorposts

Miq.: Miqvaot

MLBP: Tzvee Zahavy, *The Mishnaic Law of Blessings and Prayers: Tractate Berakhot*. Brown Judaic Studies, 88. Atlanta: 1987.

MS: manuscript

NAEJP: Tzvee Zahavy, "A New Approach to Early Jewish Prayer." In *History of Judaism: the Next Ten Years*. B. Bokser, ed. Brown Judaic Studies 21. Chico, CA: 1980.

Nasi: prince, officer

Neh.: Nehemiah

Neusner, Invitation: Jacob Neusner, *Invitation to the Talmud.* New York: 1973.

Neusner, B. Ber.: Jacob Neusner, *The Talmud of Babylonia. An American Translation. I: Tractate Berakhot.* Brown Judaic Studies, 78. Chico, CA: 1984.

Neusner, Introduction: Jacob Neusner, *The Talmud of the Land of Israel. Vol. 35, Introduction: Taxonomy.* Chicago: 1983.

Neusner, Society: Jacob Neusner, *Judaism in Society: The Evidence of the Yerushalmi.* Chicago: 1983.

Num.: Numbers

P.M.: Pene Moshe Commentary, M. Margoliot

Pes.: Pesahim

Piska: formal term making reference to Mishnah

Prayer: The liturgy of eighteen blessings

Prov.: Proverbs

Ps.: Psalms

Qid.: Qiddushin

Qoh.: Qohelet, Ecclesiastes

R.: Rabbi

R.H.: Rosh Hashanah

R: *Palestinian Talmud Codex Vatican 133.* Jerusalem. Reprint Jerusalem: 1971.

RSV: Revised Standard Version

S.H.: Sefer Haredim commentary, E. Azikri. In Zhitomir, ed., of Y., 1860.

S.Y.: *Sde Yehoshua,* commentary and edition of Y. Benvenisti.

Constantinople: 1662. Reprint Jerusalem: 1972.

S.: Sirilio edition of Yerushalmi Berakhot, *Yerushalmi Zera'im (British Museum MS 403–5).*

Sacks, Tos.: Nissan Sacks, ed., *Tosafot Rabennu Yehudah Sirleon. Berakhot.* Vol. I. Jerusalem: 1969.

Sacks: Nissan Sacks, *The Mishnah with Variant Readings. Order Zera'im (I).* Jerusalem: 1972.

Sam.: Samuel

San.: Sanhedrin

Schwab: M. Schwab, *Le Talmud de Jerusalem.* Reprint Paris: 1960. *The Talmud of Jerusalem,* 1886. Reprint New York: 1969.

SEJP: Tzvee Zahavy, *Studies in Early Jewish Prayer.* Forthcoming.

Shema': daily liturgy of Deut. 6:4–9, 11:13–21, and Num. 15:37–41.

SSR: Tzvee Zahavy, "Sources for the Seasonal Ritual in the Third through Fifth Centuries." *Proceedings of the Ninth World Congress of Jewish Studies.* Jerusalem: 1986.

T., Tos.: Tosefta

Tamar: Y. Tamar, *Ale Tamar.* Givataim: 1979.

Tefillin: phylacteries

Ter.: Terumot

Toh.: Tohorot

Tos.: Tosefta

TTB: Tzvee Zahavy, "Tosefta Tractate Berakhot." In *The Tosefta Translated from the Hebrew. First Division. Zera'im.* J. Neusner, ed. New York: 1986.

var.: variant reading

Y.: Yerushalmi, Talmud of the Land of Israel, the Palestinian Talmud

Yad.: Yadayim

Zab.: Zabim

Zab: male unclean in accord with the rules of Lev. 15

Zabah: female unclean in accord with the rules of Lev. 15

Zeb.: Zebahim

Zech.: Zechariah

zimmun: invitation to recite the blessings after the meal

ZT: M. S. Zuckermandel, *Tosephta: Based on the Erfurt and Vienna Codices.* Reprint, Jerusalem: 1970.

Transliterations

א	=	ʾ	ל	=	l
ב	=	b	מ, ם	=	m
ג	=	g	נ, ן	=	n
ד	=	d	ס	=	ś
ה	=	h	ע	=	ʿ
ו	=	w	פ, ף	=	p
ז	=	z	צ, ץ	=	ṣ
ח	=	ḥ	ק	=	q
ט	=	ṭ	ר	=	r
י	=	y	שׁ	=	š
כ, ך	=	k	שׂ	=	s

ת = t

Index of Biblical and Talmudic References

357

General Index

BM
506
.B6
Z33
1989

BM
506
.B6
Z33

1989

(99)
58.00